WeekendProjects

McArthur & Company
Toronto

Weekend Projects

50 Favourite Decorating Projects from House & Home Magazine

Edited by COBI LADNER Foreword by LYNDA REEVES

This book is dedicated to:
Our loyal readers and viewers who inspire us with their ideas and proud snapshots of completed projects. And our hard-working editors who never complain when they get paint on their clothes.

This Canadian edition published in 2002 by
McArthur & Company
322 King St. West, Suite 402
Toronto, Ontario
M5V 1J2

Editor: Cobi Ladner
Design: Hambly & Woolley Inc.
Cover photo: Luis Albuquerque

National Library of Canada Cataloguing in Publication Data

Main entry under title:
Weekend Projects: 50 favourite decorating projects from Canadian house & home

Projects selected from Canadian house and home.
ISBN 1-55278-289-1

1. Workshops. I. Ladner, Cobi II. Title: Canadian house and home.

NK2115.B47 2002 684'.08 C2002-900456-X

The publisher would like to acknowledge the financial support of the Government of Canada through the Book Publishing Industry Development Program (BPIDP) and the Canada Council for our publishing activities. The publisher further wishes to acknowledge the financial support of the Ontario Arts Council for our publishing program.

Printed in Canada by Transcontinental Printing Inc.

Contents

Foreword

The Joy of Making

I remember a time, not so long ago, when I had no choice but to make most of the things that I craved for my rooms. Usually I had seen them in magazines but not in the stores, or I just could not afford to buy them. As much as I enjoyed refinishing furniture, needlepointing pillow covers, sewing slipcovers and window coverings, making lamps, and turning flea-market finds into wonderful furniture, I looked forward to the day when I would be able to buy more and make less.

Eventually, that day came, and I stopped making things and instead spent my time searching and shopping. I went the other way, and I filled my rooms with things that were more expensive and obviously not homemade. But as my rooms evolved, I grew bored. I missed the thrill of making things. I missed the satisfaction of finding the perfect fabric at a bargain price, combining it with a remnant of trim that was really meant for something else, and creating an exquisite pillow, one that was admired by everyone who sat on the sofa. Along the way, I noticed that the best rooms always seemed to include elements that were original and witty, that can't easily be bought. Most of all, I missed the joy that comes from making it yourself.

So I'm back at it. Today it's the small things that I have time for. I needlepoint on airplanes and holidays, I cover photo albums with fabric, and I paint wicker furniture and make pillows. They're small things, but immensely satisfying. My days are frantically busy and I'm often asked what'll I do when — eventually — I stop, or slow down. The answer comes easily: a summer off and the chance to make some of these inspiring projects would be a dream come true!

There are so many wonderful ideas in this book that I know you'll find some to inspire you. At *House & Home* magazine and on *House & Home* TV, decorating projects have always been the most challenging and ultimately satisfying thing that we offer our readers and our viewers. Our projects are original interpretations of the things that we want most for our own homes. Our editors search the stores and the design books for a look or a treatment that's new and refreshing. They study them carefully, and then they find a way to make them, as simply and stylishly as possible. The results often astonish me. I hope they delight you.

Lynda Reeves

Lynda Reeves
Publisher and Founder, *Canadian House & Home* Magazine

Introduction

The Life of an Armoire

It was the fall of 1992. I was in the job of my dreams, as the decorating editor of *Canadian House & Home* Magazine, and working on the "Weekend Workshop" story for the upcoming February issue. The hottest piece of furniture on the market then was the Armoire. Even the name sounded sophisticated. I desperately wanted one for my own home.

I thought that if I wanted one that badly and was unable to afford what was available in the stores, there must be others in the same boat. We came up with an easy building plan for a basic wooden box, deep enough to house a standard television set (24 inches in those days!) and with a choice of three door styles — one fabric and chicken wire, one punched tin, and one made with garden lattice.

I loved them so much that, after the story was done, I asked if I could buy all three myself! When the truck with the armoires pulled into my tiny driveway, I realized what I had done — as did my husband, Bob. Our house was just over a thousand square feet, and each of the armoires was the size of a very large refrigerator. Two went up the stairs — just. One went in the TV room, one in the guest room. The third stayed downstairs in the living room. The house felt about three times smaller. But I had my armoires.

When we moved a few years later, the armoires were a bit of a sticky point with Bob — and the friends who were helping us move. They couldn't believe we got them in, let alone thought we could get them out. Our new house was two thousand square feet. I sold one armoire to my painter. We still used one for the TV, but its punched-tin doors were replaced, as the sharp edges and the new baby didn't mix. And the white lattice one worked beautifully in the nursery.

For our third move, a few years later, we hired professionals. The new house was over three thousand square feet. We had no formal dining furniture or built-ins, so the white lattice armoire went in the dining room to hold china and linens. It was repainted, appropriately, in a colour called Eating Room Red and is doing the job quite nicely. Alas, the only suitable spot for the second one was the basement, and the low ceiling height wouldn't allow it to stand up. In the end, I caved in and sold it too. So now, ten years later, with three times the space and one-third the armoires, I think I finally have the ratio right.

One day I will probably look for a lovely antique cabinet to replace my red monster, but that doesn't feel pressing. Though the doors now hang a little crookedly, it's doing the job, and whenever I see it, it reminds me of the old days and my determination.

Since that February 1993 issue, we have published 80 "Weekend Workshop" stories. The magazine has changed a lot over the years, but our love for DIY projects hasn't. I always know we have a real winner on our hands when a knock comes at my door, and an editor asks if she can take home the latest creation.

Cobi Ladner

Cobi Ladner
Editor, *Canadian House & Home* Magazine

Craft

01

IT'S THE SMALL ITEM WITH THE INDIVIDUAL TOUCH THAT GIVES A ROOM ITS SOUL

Project

Wreathed in Glory

EIGHT NEW WAYS TO HANG HOLIDAY CHEER.

Editor's note:
Think outside the traditional "holiday" box: hang a grouping of mini wreaths, or create one that shines year-round. For more control and less mess when assembling, spray adhesive into a plastic container and then apply it with a brush.

Difficulty level:
Easy

Projects:
Simple boxwood twist
Mohair wreath
Two-colour fig wreath
Contemporary berry wreath
Picture frame wreaths
Bird-themed wreaths

Don't have a whole weekend to spend on holiday craft projects? We've put together a selection of do-it-yourself wreaths, each of which you can make quite simply and quickly at home — and still feel like you've embraced the crafting spirit that so often overcomes us during the holiday season. All of the wreaths presented here are created by embellishing pre-made wreath forms. Most of the projects are inexpensive; only a few use more luxurious materials.

SIMPLE BOXWOOD TWIST

Even the smallest wreath adds to the festivity. Dress up a place setting with a simple boxwood twist — we sized ours to perfectly frame the embroidered monogram on our vintage linen napkin. Shape a leftover sprig of boxwood into a mini-wreath and secure it with florist's wire. Adorn it with sumptuous crushed-velvet ribbon and miniature tree ornaments. Alternatively, use these tiny wreaths to make placecards: frame circles of paper labelled with dinner guests' names.

PHOTOGRAPHY BY YVONNE DUIVENVOORDEN

MOHAIR WREATH

This soft and fuzzy mohair wreath is a wonderful holiday adornment for a child's bookshelf or the foot of a bed. It's made with a 5"-diameter foam wreath form and a ball of mohair yarn. Unravel half the ball of mohair, cut it and rewind the unwound half into a second ball. This will allow you to double-up the yarn and create a fuzzier wreath. Holding two strands together, wrap them around the form, making sure the wound threads are pressed tightly together on the form to hide the foam beneath. Knot yarn when you get back to the starting point, leaving at least 12" of yarn on each side of the knot. Using the remaining mohair, wind up two tiny balls of yarn and tie these to the dangling 12" lengths of yarn.

Project 01: Wreaths

MATERIALS & TOOLS

- Ribbon
- Ornaments
- Boxwood
- Reindeer moss
- Artificial fruit
- Artificial quail eggs
- Large greenery wreath form
- Lichen wreath
- Partridge
- Vintage linen napkin

TWO-COLOUR FIG WREATH

The sensual shape and subtly vibrant jewel-toned colouring of the two-colour fig have made it a new favourite fruit in the design world and the perfect replacement for the oft-used red pomegranate in holiday decorating. To make this two-colour fig wreath, "eyeball" the placements of artificial figs on a foam wreath form, and wire and hot-glue them into place. Fill in the uncovered parts of the form with reindeer moss (if it doesn't stay in place on its own, hot-glue to secure). Finish the wreath with a full, layered bow; ours is made of purple satin ribbon with a top layer of green organza, which mimics the two-toned colouring of the figs.

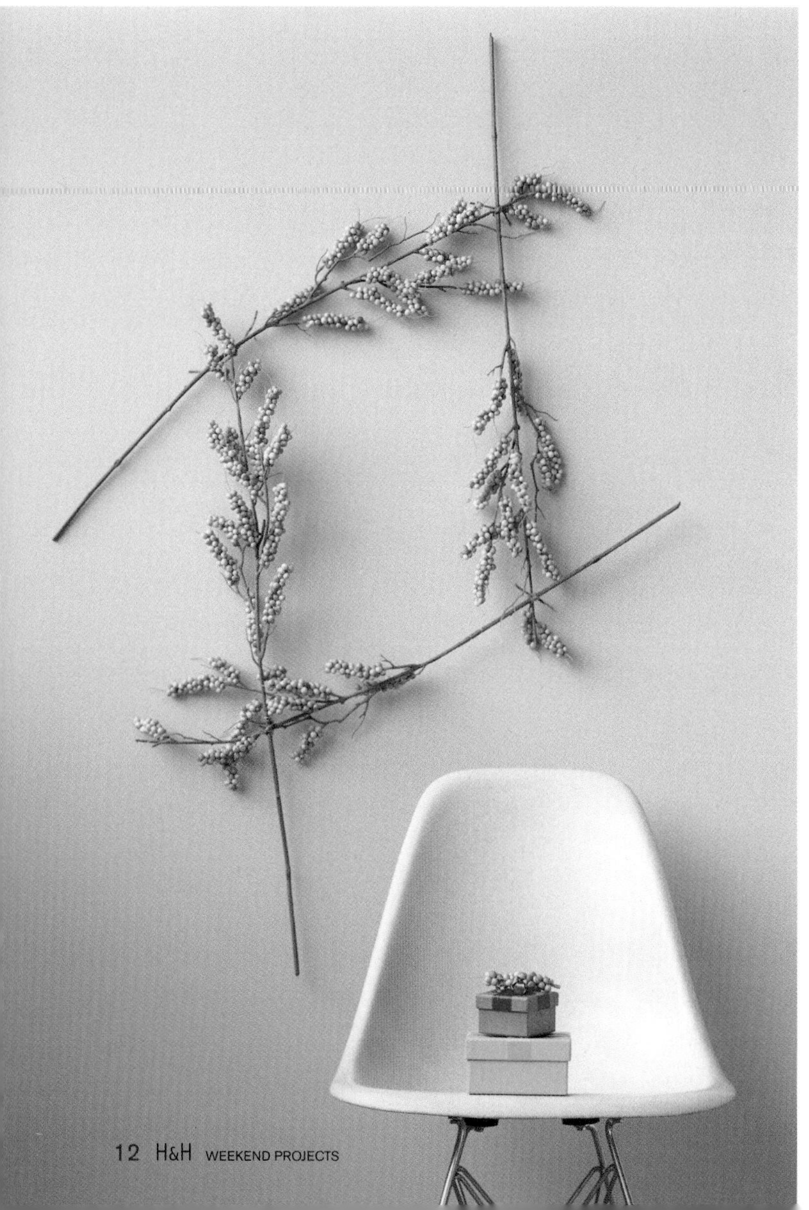

CONTEMPORARY BERRY WREATH

Keeping it simple is a modernist's ideal, but that shouldn't mean a holiday wreath is impossible — just keep it uncomplicated. Here four artificial "twigs" of holiday berries (available at upscale craft stores) are fastened together using twine and hung (on two nails placed at different heights) slightly askew for a contemporary take on a traditional berry wreath.

PICTURE FRAME WREATHS

These gilt-edged picture frame wreaths use inexpensive flea-market-find frames as bases for simple boxwood wreaths. To make, cut 12" lengths of florist's wire, fold in half and hot-glue folded ends to back of picture frame: one at each corner and one at the middle of each long side. Cut a good number of 3" to 4" lengths of boxwood. Fasten these in a long row by wiring their bases together with florist's wire. Make two rows equal to the height of the frame, and two rows equal to the width. Fasten these within the interior of the frame (shown above right) as if they were a picture, or attach the boxwood lengths around the exterior edges of the frame (far left). (Though we used fresh, you could use artificial boxwood; this would allow your wreath to be used in future years.)

BIRD-THEMED WREATHS

Linked by colour and theme, these three bird-themed wreaths look suitably festive hung in a row on a robin's egg-blue wall. And they're easy to make with just a few materials.

Partridge Wreath

To make the ribbon-upholstered partridge wreath, wrap 3"-wide satin ribbon around a small standard foam wreath form and tie it in a topknot. Affix a pretty artificial partridge (available at craft stores).

Feather Wreath

The sumptuous feather wreath is made with an inexpensive feather boa. Bend a wire coat hanger into a circle (ours is large, but a small feather wreath would also look lovely). Wrap the wire in masking tape or bias tape (this will act as the base onto which to sew the boa). Using large slipstitches and thread that matches the boa, sew the "spine" of the boa to the hanger. Cut the boa so that it only overlaps slightly at the top. If needed, trim any feathers that stick out oddly so that the wreath looks like a precise circle. Tie a pretty ribbon in a topknot to disguise the spot where the ends of the boa meet.

Quail-Egg Wreath

A lichen-covered wreath is the base for our quail-egg wreath. Hot-glue faux quail eggs around the form one at a time, being careful that their placement and angle are as uniform as possible.

Project

Cameo Roles

TURN HUMBLE FURNISHINGS INTO ELEGANT PIECES WITH ROMANTIC RELIEF DESIGNS.

Editor's note:
Subtle background colours are what make these pieces so beautiful; anything too dark or bright will contrast with the appliqués too much. Try this technique on any nondescript furnishings or cabinetry.

Difficulty level:
Average

Projects:
Mirror
Picture frames
Bed frame
Washstand
Storage box & journals
Bookmarks

There are few things so pretty as a china-cabinet display of Wedgwood's classic Jasperware or a row of framed cameo-inspired silhouettes hanging in a bedroom. Their look is romantic, evocative of eras gone by, and somehow treads a careful line between ornate and subtle. With that in mind, we set to creating a collection of elegant bedroom furnishings and accessories — projects big and small — that take their stylistic cues from raised detailing: cameos (medallions with a profile cut in raised relief), silhouettes (pictures consisting of an outline, such as a person's profile, filled in with solid colour) and anaglyphs (decorations carved in low relief). To create the relief designs, we've used easy-to-find materials, such as cameo buttons, wooden appliqués and moulding, and popular Anaglypta wallpaper and borders.

We gave a standard dressing mirror a trumeau-style treatment that recalls fine Wedgwood Jasperware. The elegant mirror is suited as much to a living or dining room as a bedroom. We backed it with a sheet of medium-density fibreboard (MDF) that's painted an elegant taupe colour, and embellished it with white-painted mouldings, trims and appliqués.

PHOTOGRAPHY BY VIRGINIA MACDONALD

Project 02: Decorative appliqués

MIRROR

MATERIALS & TOOLS

1	piece 3/4"-thick MDF cut to 3' x 7'
1L	latex primer
1L	paint (for body of mirror)
	4' paint-ready crown moulding
	4' paint-ready baseboard trim
	Handsaw
	Mitre box
	3/4" finishing nails
	1" x 1" scrap wood (to support crown moulding)
	Wood glue
	Countersink
	Wood filler
	Fine-grit sandpaper
1L	white paint for trim
	20" x 60" bevelled-edge mirror
	1 tube clear silicone adhesive
	Simple 1/2"-wide wood trim
	Wood-composite appliqués

Step 1. Prepare MDF, cut mouldings

Prime MDF using a latex primer and allow to dry. Paint MDF with coloured paint (we used Sico's Sandcastle 4149-42). Allow to dry. To cut the crown moulding to size, at the left end cut a 45° mitre across the front face of the crown moulding starting at the top of the moulding and moving down and towards the right to the bottom of the moulding. Then along the bottom edge of the moulding measure to the right the width of the MDF piece (ours was 3' wide). Cut another 45° mitre from that spot on the bottom edge of the moulding upwards and to the right across the front face of the moulding. You will need two other small pieces of moulding to wrap around the side of the mirror. Cut these with 45° mitres on one side and a flat edge on the other. To cut the baseboard moulding to size, cut 45° mitres across the depth of the moulding so that the narrower face of the moulding is 3' wide. Cut edge pieces of moulding, with 45° mitres across their depths on only one side each. Prime all crown and baseboard pieces. Before you apply the crown moulding, first glue and nail a 3'-long piece of scrap wood (we used 1" x 1") about an inch below the top of the MDF — it should be positioned to hold the crown moulding out at a 45° angle.

Step 2. Attach and paint mouldings

Glue and nail the crown moulding in place using countersunk finishing nails. Glue and nail side pieces of crown moulding in place. Glue and nail baseboard moulding, and the small side pieces, flush against the MDF using countersunk finishing nails. Fill all nail holes with wood filler and sand smooth to prepare for painting. Paint crown and baseboard mouldings with trim paint (we used Sico's Light Sugar 4150-11).

Step 3. Attach mirror to MDF

With the MDF lying face up, centre mirror at an equal distance from the sides of the MDF (ours is 8" from each side), 8" from the bottom of the baseboard trim, and 16" from the top of the crown moulding, to leave space for appliqué at the top. Mark with a pencil where the mirror will be attached. Apply a bead of silicone adhesive around the inside of this rectangle, and apply a large "X" of adhesive on the centre of the mirror back. Affix the mirror into place. Place heavy stacks of books on mirror, and allow to dry at least 12 hours.

Step 4. Cut, paint and attach trim

Use a handsaw and mitre box to cut four pieces of 1/2"-wide wood trim to 60" (to make the sides of the rectangles that flank the mirror). Give all ends a 45° mitre. Cut four pieces of the same trim to 6" (to make tops and bottoms of rectangles). Cut two 34"-long pieces of the same trim and two pieces to 8" to make the rectangle that sits above mirror. Prime and paint this trim and five wood-composite appliqués using a small sponge brush and your trim colour paint (white). Again, with mirror lying flat, use wood glue to attach trim to MDF, nail in place with finishing nails (countersink, fill holes with wood filler, sand and touch up with trim paint). Measure to make sure each wood composite appliqué is in place and centred, and affix to MDF using wood glue and countersunk nails as above.

Use leftover pieces of Anaglypta wallpaper and border to dress up small items, like these simple picture frames. We covered one frame with the Anaglypta, and used the paper as matting within the other frame. To reiterate the relief-pattern theme, we used the frames to show off antique wood and metal appliqués.

PICTURE FRAMES

The frame used for this project must be wide enough to show the pattern of the wallpaper. If you are making a second frame with embossed-wallpaper matting, use an identical frame for a matched set.

MATERIALS & TOOLS

- Plain wood frames
- Embossed wallpaper or border (we used Anaglypta)
- Spray adhesive
- Paint and sponge brushes

Frame

Measure your frame. Cut one strip of wallpaper border for each of the frame's four sides. "Mitre" the ends of each strip to 45° so that the corners will match up perfectly. Glue to frame using spray adhesive, and allow to dry. Paint the frame (and the wallpaper) with a sponge brush, and allow to dry. Apply a second coat of paint if needed.

GLOSSARY

Anaglypta/anaglyph: Work in low relief; a brand name for a thick, embossed wallpaper.

Cameo: 1. A decoration carved in relief; usually the raised design and background are contrasting colours. 2. A medallion with a raised-relief profile.

Embossed: Carved or moulded in relief.

Relief: 1. The projection of forms from a level background. 2. A work of art featuring such projection.

Project 02: Decorative appliqués

BED FRAME

We painted our bed chocolate brown, but any dark colour that contrasts with cream-coloured appliqués would suit this project.

MATERIALS & TOOLS

- Simple metal bed frame
- Melamine paint (for frame)
- Latex paint (for trim)
- Sponge brushes
- Fine-grit sandpaper
- Wood-composite appliqués
- Clear silicone adhesive

Step 1. Paint bed frame

Disassemble bed frame, and clean it if necessary. Using a sponge brush, give the frame two coats of melamine paint (this will give it a very durable finish), allowing it to dry completely between coats.

Step 2. Paint and apply trims

Paint wood-composite appliqués with latex paint (we used Sico's Light Sugar 4150-11). Sand gently between coats. Mark the placement of the appliqués, and affix to head and footboard using clear silicone adhesive. Allow to dry overnight. Reassemble bed.

Even the plainest furnishings find romantic expression when painted and adorned with relief detailing. We refinished this simple metal bed by painting it chocolate brown and adhering creamy white reliefs and rosettes — wood appliqués from a building-supply store — to the headboard and footboard. What was once suited to a '40s boarding school dorm now seems like it would be more at home in a Parisian poet's studio.

We turned a plain metal bed and garage-sale washstand into romantic boudoir pieces by treating them with fresh paint, wallpaper with a raised pattern and wood appliqués. Hung like a painting, a tin ceiling panel, distressed to show its relief pattern, makes an artful complement.

We refurbished this washstand — now a much-refined version of its former self — with an embossed wallpaper border. We finished the drawer-front and door panels with Anaglypta border (painted creamy white) and painted the other surfaces a soft taupe. For a shot of colour, the interior is painted soft pink. (We used Sico's Cashmere paint on a number of these projects; whether brushed or rolled, it gave the surfaces a wonderfully soft, smooth finish.)

WASHSTAND

We used a wallpaper border to cover this piece since the width of the border was just right, but you could also use standard-sized wallpaper for larger pieces of furniture.

MATERIALS & TOOLS

- Washstand or side table with drawers
- Fine-grit sandpaper
- Base paint (for washstand)
- Trim paint (to cover wallpaper)
- Accent paint (for inside furniture)
- Paintbrush
- Embossed wallpaper (we used Anaglypta)
- Spray adhesive

Step 1. Prepare washstand

Remove all hardware, and remove drawers and doors from washstand. Sand and paint each piece. We chose taupe (Sico's Sandcastle 4149-42), and painted the inside of the washstand pink (Sico's Rich Rose 4139-31). Let dry and apply second coat if needed.

Step 2. Attach wallpaper

Measure wallpaper pieces to fit door panels, drawer fronts and side panels of washstand. Make sure you evenly centre the pattern of the wallpaper onto each surface. Using spray adhesive, glue the wallpaper pieces to the washstand and allow to dry at least four hours.

Step 3. Paint wallpaper

Using a sponge brush, paint wallpaper with trim paint (we used Sico's Light Sugar 4150-11). Let dry. Reattach doors and replace all hinges and hardware.

STORAGE BOX & JOURNALS

MATERIALS & TOOLS

- Storage box and journal
- Spray adhesive
- Embossed wallpaper (we used Anaglypta)
- Self-adhesive construction paper (for journals)
- Paint and sponge brushes

Storage Box

Paint the base of your box if desired (we painted ours taupe). Wrap top of storage box with wallpaper much like wrapping a present, and attach it with spray adhesive. Paint wallpaper using a sponge brush.

Journals

Cut pieces of embossed wallpaper and self-adhesive construction paper to size to cover the front and back of your journal in a configuration that suits you (we alternated papers between covers and spines). Paint the wallpaper with white paint. Attach to the journal with spray adhesive.

BOOKMARKS

MATERIALS & TOOLS

- Assorted wide ribbons
- Needle and thread
- Cameo buttons

Cut wide ribbon to 12" lengths. With a needle and thread, sew cameo button to ribbon, about 2" from one end

We incorporated the cameo and anaglyptic looks into three simple craft projects. Diaries and a photo storage box are covered with remnants of Anaglypta wallpaper and self-adhesive construction paper in pretty pink and rich brown. Strips of decorative ribbon are adorned with antique-style cameo buttons (from button or sewing-supply stores) to make pretty bookmarks.

Project

Works of Heart

EIGHT UNIQUE HANDCRAFTED GIFTS TO PLEASE EVERYONE ON YOUR LIST.

Editor's note:
Personalized, handmade gifts are well-received at any time of year. Consider one of these next time you're in the market for a special anniversary, shower, or even wedding present.

Difficulty level:
Easy

Projects:
Stationery kit
Tealight holders
Champagne flutes
Notebook
Framed letters
Gift tags
Monogram wreath
Hand towels

"I made it myself!" These words, uttered as a gift is placed in your hands, can send shivers down the spine of even the most open-minded, as visions of doily-and-popsicle-stick trivets dance in your head. But take heart. The eclectic collection of crafts we feature here are beautiful to look at and easy to make, and there's one guaranteed to please even the most discerning recipient, young or old, male or female. They range from the unusual, like tealight holders and framed letters, to useful: a notebook, stationery and embroidered hand towels. The etched champagne flutes are just plain indulgent. Readily available materials and simple assembly mean you can craft several in an afternoon. And afterwards, you can rest easy in the knowledge that when you proudly say "I made it myself," the enchantment you see is genuine.

Opposite: These bejewelled tealight holders add colour and sparkle to the holiday table. They're easily made by wrapping bead-studded wire around simple glass tealight holders.

Right: Put together a do-it-yourself stationery kit for noted correspondents. Buy blank embossed note cards with envelopes, an ink pad and stamp of the recipient's initial, sealing wax and a wax stamp of the same initial. To get the stationery started, stamp a few cards and place a seal on a number of envelopes, then package the whole collection in a gift box trimmed with a band of coloured paper.

PHOTOGRAPHY BY DONNA GRIFFITH

Project 03: Personalized gifts

TEALIGHT HOLDERS

MATERIALS & TOOLS

- Clear glass tealight holders
- Wire (fine-gauge and medium-gauge)
- Colourful beads
- Tealights

Step 1. Measure and cut medium-gauge wire long enough to run from inside the lip of the glass tealight holder, up over the rim, down one side, under the bottom, up the other side and over the lip back into the holder (see Diagram). Cut a second piece to the same length.

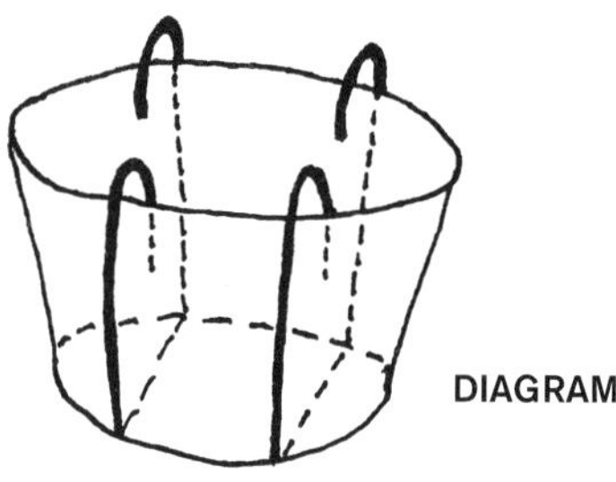

Step 2. Thread wire with beads and twist and "knot" where needed to hold beads in place and fit around holder vertically. Make sure that no beads run underneath the holder.

Step 3. Measure and cut fine-gauge wire to run around the holder horizontally, thread with beads and twist and wrap to secure to the vertical wires.

Step 4. Place tealights inside.

CHAMPAGNE FLUTES

MATERIALS & TOOLS

- Plain champagne flutes
- Selection of fonts (from a computer or a font book, available at art-supply stores)
- Tracing paper
- Transfer paper (available at art-supply stores)
- Small paintbrush
- Glass paint (available at art-supply stores)

Step 1. From a book of fonts or a printout of computerized fonts, select the letter(s) you'd like to transfer onto the glass.

Step 2. Trace the letter with tracing paper. Cut a small square that runs around the letter from the tracing paper and tape that onto transfer paper. Tape the transfer paper onto the glass (so that the letter is level horizontally and in the spot you wish it to appear on the glass). With a pencil, retrace the shape of the letter — this will trace the letter onto the glass. Remove the stencil and transfer paper.

Step 3. With a small paintbrush, paint white glass paint within the marked lines. This will take a very steady hand, so make sure you're in a good work spot and the glass is resting securely. If needed, apply a second coat of paint.

Step 4. Repeat for all the glasses you wish to monogram. We used a couple's initials, and decorated one glass with an ampersand.

Step 5. As per the paint's instructions, bake the glass to set the paint.

NOTEBOOK

MATERIALS & TOOLS

- Notebook
- Fabric
- Needle and thread
- Ribbon

Step 1. Lay the notebook open on the wrong side of the fabric. Trace the book, and then draw lines 1/2" outside of each of those lines (this will be a seam allowance). Allow an extra 3 to 4" on each end for flaps, much like a dust jacket shape. Cut out this shape.

Step 2. Embroider a simple script initial on what will be the front of the cover (we placed ours in the bottom right-hand corner).

Step 3. Hem the edges of the flaps. With the cover inside out, stitch the flaps to the cover with a 1/2" seam allowance, and continue that stitch around the book to also hem the edges of the cover where there are no flaps. Turn right side out and insert book.

Step 4. Stitch or glue coordinating ribbon to the inside of the flap edges.

FRAMED LETTERS

MATERIALS & TOOLS

- Small bare-wood picture frames
- Spray paint
- Sandpaper
- Selection of fonts (from a computer or a font book, available at art-supply stores)

Step 1. Disassemble each frame by carefully removing the backing and glass from each one. Spray-paint the wooden frames black. Let dry completely. Lightly sand the frames to give them a smooth finish.

Step 2. Select a font from a book or from a printout of computerized fonts. Using a photocopier, shrink or enlarge the letters you choose to fit inside the picture frames.

Step 3. To translate the letters to a reverse colour scheme (i.e., a white letter on a black background, as we did), either scan the letters into a computer system, translate and print out, or have a photocopy shop do it for you.

Step 4. Trim the printouts to fit the frames, and insert into the frames. Reassemble the frames, but before closing each one, make sure letter is straight.

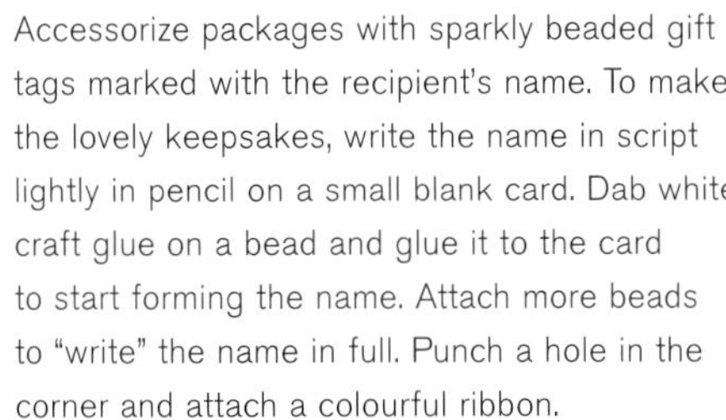

Accessorize packages with sparkly beaded gift tags marked with the recipient's name. To make the lovely keepsakes, write the name in script lightly in pencil on a small blank card. Dab white craft glue on a bead and glue it to the card to start forming the name. Attach more beads to "write" the name in full. Punch a hole in the corner and attach a colourful ribbon.

Put a personal spin on holiday decorating with a monogrammed ivy "wreath." If you're giving it as a hostess gift, present it the day before the party so it can be mounted somewhere special ahead of time. To make the wreath, twist 16-gauge wire into an elegant script letter. Wrap the letter with long clippings of English ivy (we purchased ours from a florist). If needed, fasten the ivy in place with snippets of thin florist's wire or clear fishing line.

Embroidered with a single initial, these crisp linen hand towels make a thoughtful hostess gift (or a housewarming or wedding gift at any time of year). Coordinate the towel colour with the recipient's bath or powder room. Buy a simple single-letter embroidery pattern at a craft shop, and follow the directions on the packaging. Drop the towels by the day before the party.

04 Project

Praising Cane

THIS CLASSIC NATURAL MATERIAL SHOWS ITS VERSATILITY IN THREE DIY PROJECTS WITH A DISTINCTLY MODERN EDGE.

Editor's note:
Give these pieces an aged look by applying a coat of brown stain to the cane. Since cane can be unwieldy, start with a simpler project – like the frames – to get a feel for handling it.

Difficulty level:
Average

Projects:
Bulletin board
Shutters
Picture frames

Made by weaving together strands of the durable bark from the rattan palm, caning has traditionally been used in casual tropical decor, classic British Colonial furniture and country antiques. But here we've created three projects with a modern temperament: pieces that are short-order recipes for adding subtle texture and colour to living spaces. Framed in white or pale colours, cane has a sunny, but modern, country freshness, as in our privacy shutters. For two of our projects — the bulletin board and picture frames — we modified existing pieces by facing them with sheets or cutouts of cane. The privacy shutters and desk accessories are almost completely composed of caning, or "webbing." Leftovers from the larger sheets of caning can be used to make or decorate smaller items, such as the pencil cups, baskets and blank notebooks. And, of course, we bet you'll be so inspired, you'll want to create your own projects using our techniques.

Like a large, spare work of modern art, this oversized bulletin board brings a swath of subtle colour and texture to the home office. The sheet caning (here we used fine open webbing) was glued to a large piece of corkboard, then trimmed with moulding subtly painted in the same colour as the wall.

PHOTOGRAPHY BY DONNA GRIFFITH

Aboutcaning...

Pre-woven sheets of caning, or "webbing," are sold by the foot in varying widths (our sheets were 2' wide).

The caning is available in a variety of patterns and sizes, from modern cane webs to traditional open webs. We used different types for each project, but unified the look of the projects by leaving all the caning its original blond colour. Much like unfinished wood, webbing can be painted (with either latex or oil-based paints) or stained if you desire a different look.

The how-to is a snap. In some projects, the cane is simply cut to fit and glued or set in place. In others, it is sprayed with water to enhance its flexibility, and then air-dried to regain its tautness.

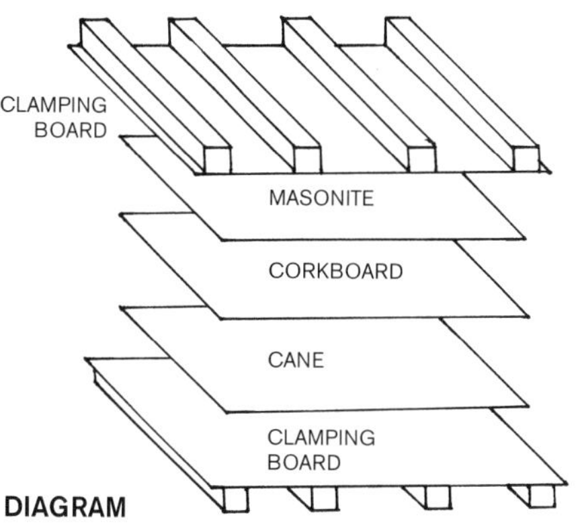

We found our pre-woven cane at W.H. Kilby and Co. (Toronto, 416-656-1065), which will mail-order across Canada.

BULLETIN BOARD

Our finished bulletin board is 2' x 5', but this project can be adapted to fit any size. Plain, unframed corkboard is available in various sizes at most office-supply stores, or art and craft-supply stores.

MATERIALS & TOOLS

18'	2" x 2" pine
2	3' x 6' sheets melamine
24	1 1/2" finishing nails
	Spray bottle
	2' x 5' sheet pre-woven cane (we used fine open cane web)
4	clamps
	2' x 5' Masonite board
	White glue, roller, paint tray
	2' x 5' sheet plain corkboard
	1" x 1" outside corner trim
	Measuring tape
	Handsaw
	Paint
	100-grit sandpaper
	Mitre box

Step 1. Make clamping boards
Create clamping boards by nailing four 24"-long pieces of 2" x 2" onto each melamine sheet, at equal intervals (see Diagram).

Step 2. Moisten cane
Spray cane with water on both sides. Let sit 15 minutes. Get clamps and glue ready.

Step 3. Glue cane
Lay Masonite on work surface with the smooth side up. Lay sheet of cane over top, right side down. Pour glue into paint tray.

Project 04: Caning

Use roller to apply a thin coat of glue to the wrong side of cane.

Step 4. Construct board
Transfer cane sheet onto flat side of clamping board, glued side up. Place corkboard on top of it, cork side down. Roll a coat of glue onto smooth side of Masonite, and flip over on top of corkboard so glued side of Masonite is on back side of corkboard. Place second clamping board over top of Masonite layer (see Diagram 1). Clamp and let dry 6 hours.

Step 5. Cut trim
Using a handsaw, cut trim to fit edges of finished board, with about 2" extra on each piece. Our finished board was 2' x 5', so we cut 2 pieces of trim to 2'-2", and 2 pieces of trim to 5'-2". Sand and paint trim.

Step 6. Apply trim
Clean up edges of finished board with sandpaper. Using a mitre box and handsaw, mitre ends of trim to fit finished board. Glue and clamp in place. Allow to dry overnight.

SHUTTERS

These shutters are made from four panels, each panel consisting of caning stretched within two wood frames. Our window area covered was 42 1/4" by 48 5/8". Adjust all measurements to fit your own window size.

MATERIALS & TOOLS

16	5' long 1/2" x 2 1/2" pine or poplar (8 of these will be cut lengthwise)
	Handsaw
	White wood glue
64	3/4" finishing nails
	Hammer
	100-grit sandpaper
	Paint, paintbrush
	15' pre-woven cane (we used #73 modern cane web)
	Spray bottle
	Staple gun
8	3" bifold door hinges (with screws)
	Drill
	Screwdriver

Step 1. Measure opening

Measure the area you would like to cover. Subtract 1/4" from the height measurement, and subtract 5/8" from the width across. This will allow space for hinges. Our four panels measured 42" x 12" each.

Step 2. Cut wood

Have the lumber dealer cut eight pieces of the wood from 2 1/2" wide to 1 7/8" wide. Keep the leftover, "off-cut," wood for Step 5. Use a handsaw to cut eight pieces of the 2 1/2"-wide wood to 7" lengths, and eight pieces to 42" lengths. These pieces are for the face layer of the frames. Next, cut eight pieces of the 1 7/8"-wide wood to 12" lengths, and eight pieces to 38 1/4" lengths. These are for the back layer of the frames.

Step 3. Make frame panels

Start with the face layer (made of 2 1/2" pieces). Arrange pieces on a table with the 7" top and bottom pieces between the 42" side pieces. Create four panels in this fashion. Next, arrange back layer (made of 1 7/8" pieces) on top of the face pieces, with 38 1/4" side pieces between 12" top and bottom pieces.

Step 4. Secure panels

Be sure that both face and back layers are fitting flush around the outer edges. Lift off one back piece at a time, spread a thick bead of glue along face piece, and replace back piece. Repeat with all panels. Hammer four evenly spaced 3/4" finishing nails along each side piece, and two along each top piece. Allow glue to dry for one hour. There should now be four panels made up of a double layer of frames.

Step 5. Cut and place cane inserts

Sand and paint each panel to match your window frame. Cut pre-woven cane into four sheets, each 1/2" larger all around than the face opening of the panel. Mist both sides of cane pieces with water and let sit for 20 minutes. Staple into place within each panel from the back side. Use leftover, or "off-cut," wood to make 16 1/2" x 1/2" cubes of wood. Place a cube in each inner corner on back of panels. Nail into place with 3/4" finishing nails. Cane will stretch to a tight fit as it dries.

Step 6. Hinge and hang shutters

Measure and mark with a pencil where hinges will be on panels (ours were 3" from top corner and 3" from bottom corner). Screw hinges into place on shutters. Measure and mark with a pencil where hinges will be on window frame, allowing 1/8" swing space from windowsill to bottom of shutters. Drill holes in window frame and hang shutters.

PICTURE FRAMES

We used cane mats to dress up plain ready-made black picture frames (ours were Ikea's Ribba and Reslig frames in various sizes and shapes) and black-and-white photographs. For cane, we used superfine open cane web and #73 modern cane web. Different frame styles, cane webs and artwork will give unique results, so experiment before committing to a certain look. Cane left over from other projects can be used for these mats. Do not wet the cane for this project.

MATERIALS & TOOLS

- Ready-made picture frames
- Pre-woven cane
- Heavy white card
- Pencil
- Prints and photos

Step 1. Select canes and designs

Decide on configuration of paper and cane mats. Use card paper only if you would like layers of both white and cane matting. Cane can be either in front of, or behind, the paper layer. To make cane or white card paper fit the frame, disassemble the frame and lay glass on top of wrong side of cane or card paper. With a pencil, trace around the perimeter of the glass to mark cane and/or paper to this size. Use a ruler and your prints or photographs to determine where inner squares of mats will be cut, and mark with a pencil.

Step 2. Cut mats

Using sharp scissors, cut paper and cane to size, according to your designs. Cut cane carefully to prevent fraying along the edges. To cut the inner rectangle or square from each mat, simply use scissors to carefully poke a hole in the centre of the mat, and cut outward from this hole. Be sure that inner edges are straight, as they will be visible when finished.

Step 3. Assemble frames

Reassemble frames, layering cane and paper mats according to your design. Before closing the frame, turn it over to be sure the configuration pleases you. Adjust if necessary, then close the frame.

Project

Beauty Treatment

THREE SIMPLE PROJECTS BRING PRETTY BOHEMIAN CHARM TO A BATHROOM.

Editor's note:
Be sure to plan out your painted motif to work with the placement of other items – mirror, sconces, vanity – so they hang together as a vignette; pull your motif from the fabrics in your bathroom.

Difficulty level:
Average

Projects:
Hanging bathroom organizer
Paint treatment
Jewelry pincushion

In fashion, the minimalist moment has passed. Austere clothing has been replaced by ornate dresses in embroidered silks, and sequins, ribbons and beads adorn everything from baguette handbags to the cuffs of tried-and-true blue jeans. For home DIYers, introducing this feminine, Bohemian-inspired look is best carried out in a private space — a boudoir or bathroom, where just a touch of ornamentation will have maximum impact. We kept it simple by using a patterned fabric as the inspiration for our three projects. We selected a twig-and-berry motif from an intricate embroidered-look silk, and recreated the simplified pattern on the wall with colourful paint, and on a hand towel, lampshades and a shot-silk bathroom organizer with beads. For an even simpler accent, we made a jewelry pincushion adorned with just a single strand of beaded ribbon.

With a bit of paint and a bit of fabric we added feminine flair to this plain bathroom. Our three project designs are based on the patterned fabric used to trim the hand towel.

PHOTOGRAPHY BY DONNA GRIFFITH

Project 05: Bath embellishments

Inspired by a vintage French embroidered lingerie bag, this bathroom organizer, perfect for toiletries, face cloths and dainties, is treated to pretty beaded detail on each pocket. The beading is kept simple so it doesn't overwhelm the bag.

HANGING BATHROOM ORGANIZER

MATERIALS & TOOLS

- Kraft paper
- Scissors
- 1 yd. washable silk blend
- 1 yd. medium-weight press-on interfacing
- Tailor's chalk
- Tape measure
- 2 packages bias tape
- 1 package straight pins

Step 1. Cut body pieces

On kraft paper, trace main body for the bag; it should be 10" w. x 30" l. Use the edge of a saucer or a teacup to round both corners at one end of rectangle to create the rounded top of the bag. Using this as a pattern, cut two pieces of silk and 1 piece of interfacing. Trim interfacing by 1/2" all around edges and press to wrong side of one piece of silk.

Step 2. Cut pocket pieces

Cut three pieces of silk measuring 6" w. x 12" l. Cut three pieces of interfacing measuring 6" x 6". Fold each piece of silk in half widthwise, press folded edge, unfold, and press interfacing to one half. Refold silk in half at edge of interfacing. Using a saucer or a teacup and tailor's chalk, round the bottom of each piece to create three U-shaped pocket pieces. Trim with scissors.

Step 3. Assemble and apply pockets

Using tape measure, follow exterior pocket edge all around, excluding top edge, to get total length of U-shape (it should be approximately 12"). Add 2" to this measurement. Cut three strips of silk to measure 1 1/2" w. x the final measurement (ours was 14"). Fold 1" down at both ends of each strip and topstitch. Line up wrong side of one strip with wrong side of one U-shaped pocket front, sandwich between bias tape, pin and sew together. Repeat for each pocket. With tailor's chalk, mark position of pockets on the front of the lingerie bag. At raw edge of each pocket side wall, fold back 1/4" and press; pin to marked position on front of main body piece and topstitch in place.

Step 4. Sew main body together

With wrong sides of main body facing, and starting at bottom corner of bag, pin bias tape to raw edges of main body and topstitch in place. For neat bottom corners, unfold bias tape, turn in raw edges, refold bias tape, press and sew in place. Make a loop of bias tape and handstitch to top of bag.

Step 5. Beading

Trace out a design from within a patterned fabric using tailor's chalk. Bead with matching colours.

PAINT TREATMENT

MATERIALS & TOOLS

- Acrylic-based craft paints (we used Delta Cerami Coat Candy Bar Brown, Bittersweet Orange, Tangerine and Bright Yellow; to get the proper shade of green, we used Delta Cerami Coat in Light Jade and Village Green mixed equally with Hauser Medium Green folk art paint)
- Art brush with narrow bristles (we used Windsor & Newton Monarch round #4)
- Tracing paper
- HB pencil
- 4B pencil

To break up the expanse of bathroom wall, a colourful pattern was painted below the bottom corners of the mirror. The twig-and-berry motif was taken from the intricate embroidered-look silk that is used to frame the hand towel (see page 29). The design and its palette are similar to the beadwork that decorates the other pieces.

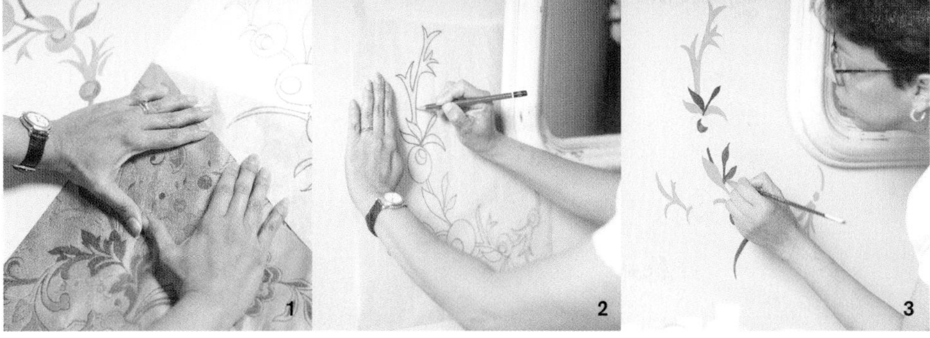

Step 1. Choose pattern

Choose a motif from a patterned fabric. It should complement the decor of the area where you wish to apply it. We chose a twig-and-berry motif to wrap around the bottom of our mirror. Photocopy and enlarge the motif to the desired size.

Step 2. Make pattern

Using tracing paper and HB pencil, trace image. On underside of paper, use heavier 4B pencil to retrace image. Create a sample-board painted to match your wall colour. Test out pattern and colours on sample-board (see Photo 1).

Step 3. Trace image onto wall

Tape tracing paper to wall with HB pencil side out, and retrace image. The 4B pencil facing the wall will transfer onto the wall (see Photo 2). If you are repeating the image as we have done, do a second traced image on paper but use your heavy pencil on the right side. Reverse the image and repeat tracing.

Step 4. Paint image

Paint motif one colour at a time with a wet brush to create a slight watercolour effect (see Photo 3). Allow to dry completely.

JEWELRY PINCUSHION

MATERIALS & TOOLS

- 1/4 yd. each of two coordinating fabrics (we used striped and dotted silks)
- 1 small package polyester pillow stuffing
- 3/4 yd. beaded ribbon

Step 1. Measure and cut silk

Measure a square 1" larger all around than size of pincushion you are making. Add 1/2" seam allowance to all sides. Cut out one square of each fabric to this measurement. We made a 6" x 6" cushion, so we cut two squares measuring 7 1/2" x 7 1/2" each.

Step 2. Sew and stuff cushion

With right sides facing, sew squares together leaving 4" gap on one edge. Fill cushion with stuffing until it is plump. Handstitch the gap closed.

Step 3. Finish with ribbon

Begin by tucking ribbon between stitches at one corner of the cushion. With diagonal spiral motion — think of the stripes on a candy cane — handstitch ribbon to cushion at seams. Tuck end of ribbon in at starting point.

A jewelry pincushion, made from coordinating pin-dot and striped silks, is trimmed with beaded ribbon. Propped on a chair or dressing table, this little gem keeps jewelry handy and tangle-free.

Project

Good Things in Small Packages

EASY-TO-MAKE WRAPS AND PARCELS FOR GIFT-GIVING.

Editor's note:
These aren't just easy to make – some are virtually ready made, using widely available gift bags, cookie sleeves, even plastic baggies.

Difficulty level:
Easy

Projects:
Cardboard takeout containers
Sheer fabric envelopes
Corrugated cardboard envelopes
Corrugated plastic box

Ogling beautiful packages and imagining what lies within is half the pleasure of any gift, as those who delicately untape their presents and set aside the pretty wrapping will attest. A chic parcel, crafty box or personalized envelope can elevate gift-giving to an event. To help you make your own unique packaging, we teamed up with graphic designer Kathryn Klar, who designs exquisite custom invitations, cards, notepaper and packaging through her Toronto-based company Tulip Press. Our wraps are easy to make using paper, plastic and cardboard. Sheer, clear and textured materials embellished with delightful tags and ties, and filled with treats in candy colours, make the ordinary extraordinary. And it's all reusable for seasons to come — a true cause for celebration.

Ordinary cardboard boxes are transformed when artfully wrapped in vibrantly coloured Japanese paper. We covered the box tops and bases in contrasting colours and screwed on a metal filing cabinet label in lieu of a name tag. (Line underside of box lid with paper to cover tips of screws.) After the holidays, the boxes can be used to store photos.

Today's chicest stores parcel their wares in smooth vellum bags; purchase them in bulk at bag-supply outlets that sell to the public. Translucent bags filled with cleverly wrapped packages will tempt the eye.

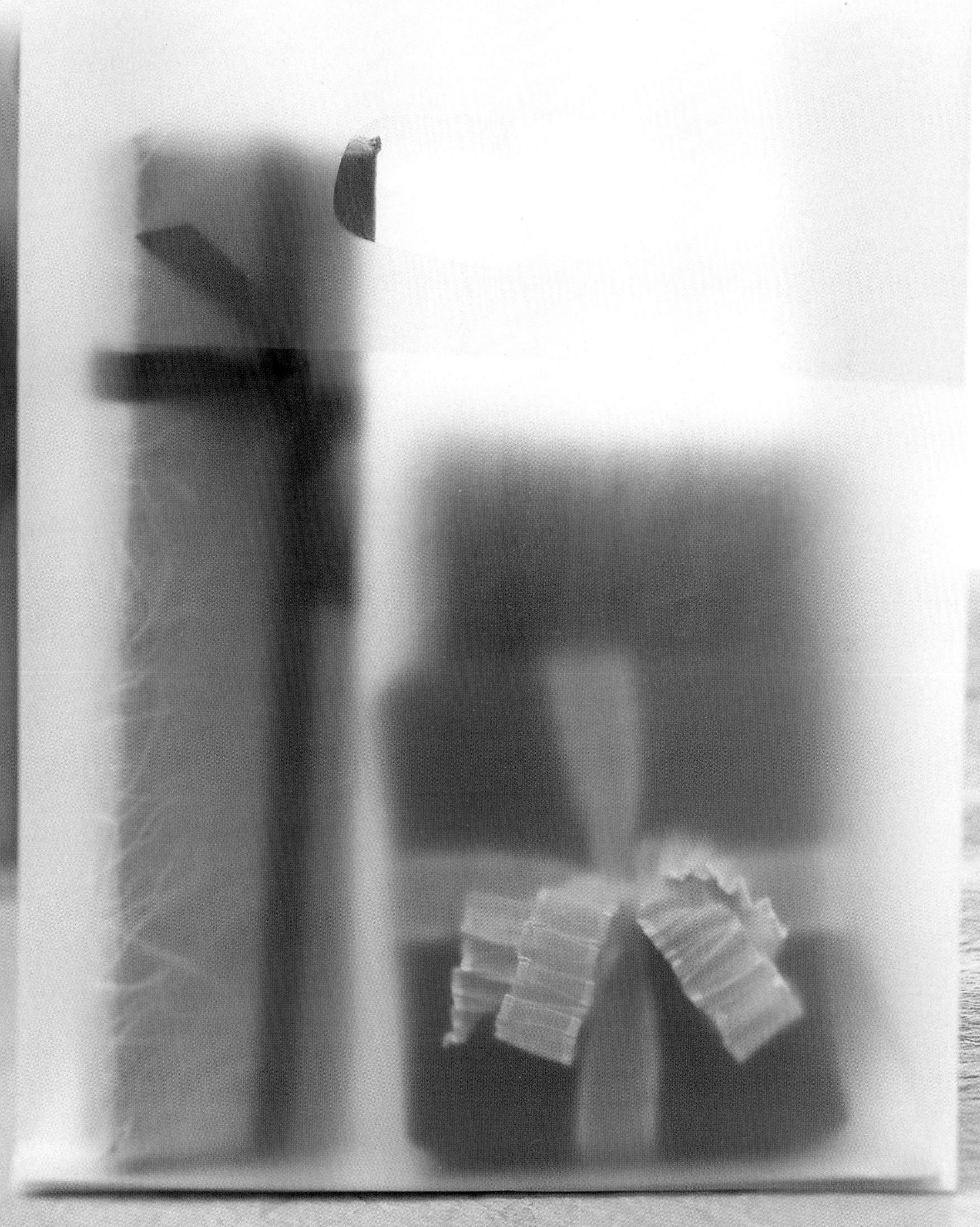

PHOTOGRAPHY BY VIRGINIA MACDONALD

Project 06: Gift wrap ideas

Cardboard takeout containers are a thrill to receive – even if they aren't full of chop suey! Using a template, we made our containers from crisp white corrugated cardboard and stuffed them with plenty of shredded paper and brightly coloured ribbon. A pretty plastic hair accessory does double-duty as a name tag clip.

CARDBOARD TAKEOUT CONTAINERS

The template on page 36 has been reduced in size. To get your template to the proper size, blow this one up 200 per cent on a photocopier. Cut along the outer edge.

MATERIALS & TOOLS

- 1 large sheet of corrugated cardboard
- Scissors
- Utility knife or sharp pen
- Ruler
- Hot-glue gun

Step 1. Cut cardboard

Lay cardboard face down on a protected work surface. Lay template on the backside of the cardboard and trace around the edge. Cut out cardboard to template shape. Make an incision along the solid slit in the bottom left tab. Refer back to our template for colour guides, or transfer colours onto the wrong side of your cardboard with coloured pencils.

Step 2. Create folding guides

Lay template on the backside of your cardboard cutout. With a utility knife or sharp pen, score along dotted lines, making sure not to slice off pieces of your template. Use a ruler or straight-edge to guide scoring. The scoring should make impressions in the cardboard.

Step 3. Fold cardboard

Fold along each pink line, right sides together. Fold along each green line, right sides together. Glue together area inside each pink and green pair. Repeat directions for blue and purple lines. You should have an open box with a flap protruding from each corner.

Step 4. Tuck in flaps

Pair together two flaps on either side of one box-top tab (not the male or female tab). Pair together remaining two flaps on either side of the opposite box-top tab (not the male or female tab). Glue each pair of flaps to the side of the box that they flank. Stuff box with shredded paper or tissue, and decorate to your liking.

Enclose tiny trinkets in sheer fabric envelopes; the colour and shape of your gift will be tantalizingly obscured. Put the envelopes to use after the holidays to store delicate treasures like silk scarves or lingerie.

SHEER FABRIC ENVELOPES

These directions are for a 6" by 8" envelope; alter your measurements for the size of envelope you desire. All seam allowances are 1/4".

MATERIALS & TOOLS

- Kraft paper (at least 20" long and 10" wide)
- Sharp sewing scissors
- 1 yd. of sheer fabric
- A braided loop or two pieces decorative ribbon
- 1 button

Step 1. Create templates

Lay a piece of kraft paper on a flat surface. Draw an 8 1/2" by 19 1/4" rectangle onto the kraft paper and cut out with scissors. From the top left corner of the rectangle, measure in along the top line 4 1/4" and make a mark. The mark should be at the centre of your top edge. From the top left corner of the rectangle, measure down 6 1/4" and make a mark. Repeat for the right side. Draw a line from the top centre mark to each of the side marks. Cut along each line, creating a triangular flap. On another piece of kraft paper, trace this flap. At each end of the 8 1/2" bottom line of this flap, measure down 1". Draw a horizontal line between the ends of each 1" line. Cut out the shape. This will be your facing template.

(continued on page 36)

Don't keep holiday gifts a secret when the contents themselves are colourful and fun. Zipper-top freezer bags make quick and easy peek-through packaging for soaps, candy or crayons. Customize bags with adhesive letters from an art-supply store (place the bag over lined paper to apply letters in a straight line). Use the recipient's name or a quirky saying that plays off what's inside the bag.

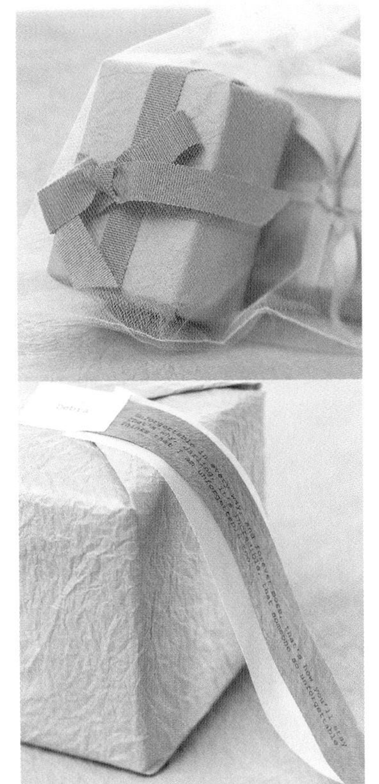

Above: A cloud-like drawstring tote made of sheer tulle enfolds pleasingly wrapped packages. Simply fold a length of tulle in half; sew along the fold and up each side, leaving the top open. Fill with gifts and gather at the top, tying with decorative ribbon.

Left: Announce your gift with a lyrical streamer tag. Snip lengths of coordinating wrapping paper into long streamers (we used textural handmade Japanese paper). Type a poem, line from a favourite song or meaningful saying onto the streamer. Attach the streamer to the top of the parcel with a plain white sticker tag.

Tiny tins and tubes labelled and filled with indulgent treats make unique stocking stuffers, and can be reused to hold jewelry or coins. We marked names and quirky greetings on plastic tubes and watchmaker's cases, purchased at a hardware store, with adhesive letters. (Use masking tape as a baseline to line up letters.)

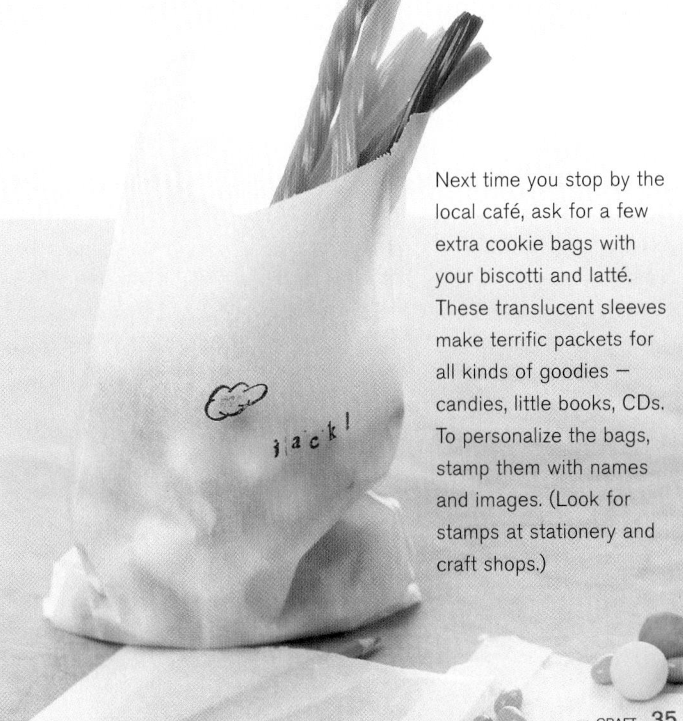

Next time you stop by the local café, ask for a few extra cookie bags with your biscotti and latté. These translucent sleeves make terrific packets for all kinds of goodies — candies, little books, CDs. To personalize the bags, stamp them with names and images. (Look for stamps at stationery and craft shops.)

Instead of the traditional greeting card, give gift certificates or money in corrugated cardboard envelopes. We embellished ours with pretty button closures and soft ribbon ties. Tubes made from the same cardboard are ideal for packaging small keepsakes – like a bottle of perfume, pair of cufflinks or strand of pearls.

Step 2. Cut fabric

Trace your two template pieces onto your sheer fabric and cut out with scissors.

Step 3. Sew fabric

Place your facing piece right side down on a surface. Fold the bottom edge up 1/4" and topstitch in place. Repeat for the bottom edge of your main piece of fabric. Place your main fabric right side up on your work surface. From the bottom hem on your main piece of fabric, measure 6" up each side and fold up horizontally at that point. Right sides together, sew along each 6" side. Place facing piece right side down on top of the corresponding flap piece on the main panel. Right sides together, sew up one diagonal edge, pausing at the point where it meets the other diagonal edge. At the point, insert the ends of your braided loop, or the end of your piece of ribbon, so that the looped end is in between the two pieces of fabric. Continue sewing, pivoting at the point and continuing along the other diagonal edge, leaving the horizontal bottom edge open. Sewing tip: If you are sewing with organza fabric, be sure to set the tensions on your sewing machine appropriately, and make sure you are using a silk needle, so the fabric will not jam in your machine. Try sewing the fabric between two layers of tissue paper; this will help if you encounter problems. The tissue paper will tear off easily after you sew each seam.

Step 4. Press envelope

Turn envelope right side out and press carefully. Make sure the point of the flap is pressed out correctly. Stitch bottom edge of facing to the body of the envelope. Press flap into position over body of envelope. Sew corresponding button or end of ribbon onto the outside of the body of the envelope where it meets the point of the flap. Slip loop over button, or tie pieces of ribbon together.

CORRUGATED CARDBOARD ENVELOPES

Our template (next page) was reduced to fit on the page. To get your template to the standard size, blow it up 200 per cent on a photocopier. Cut along the outer edge.

MATERIALS & TOOLS

1 large sheet of corrugated cardboard
Scissors
Utility knife or sharp pen
Hot-glue gun

Step 1. Cut cardboard

Lay corrugated cardboard face down on a protected work surface. Lay template onto the backside of the cardboard and trace around the edge. Cut out cardboard to template shape. Transfer letters on template to same positions on backside of cardboard.

Step 2. Create folding guides

Lay template back onto the backside of your cardboard cutout. With a utility knife or sharp pen, score along dotted lines, making sure not to slice off pieces of your template. The scoring should make impressions in the cardboard.

Step 3. Fold box

Lay cardboard cutout right side down on a work surface. Fold up the tab, wrong sides together. With a hot-glue gun, dab a few dots of glue along the right side of the tab. Fold up side B so that the wrong sides of section A and B are facing. Press down side B to glue-covered side of tab. Fold in flaps C and D. Insert gift into tube box. Fold in flap E and F to close. Decorate with ribbon or a card as desired.

CORRUGATED PLASTIC BOX

Our template was reduced to fit on the page. To get your template to the proper size, blow it up 400 per cent on a photocopier. Cut along the outer edge.

MATERIALS & TOOLS

1 large sheet corrugated plastic
Scissors
Utility knife
Drill and 1/8" drill bit
4 pieces 4" ribbon
1 piece 8" ribbon

Step 1. Cut plastic

Lay corrugated plastic face down on a protected work surface. Lay template onto the backside of the plastic and trace around the edge. Cut out plastic along all solid lines. Drill through hole markings.

Corrugated plastic boxes make sheer but sturdy cases that have contemporary flair. Pierce the box sides, thread with ribbon and knot to hold box together. Cap it off with a flat box top with a ribbon handle.

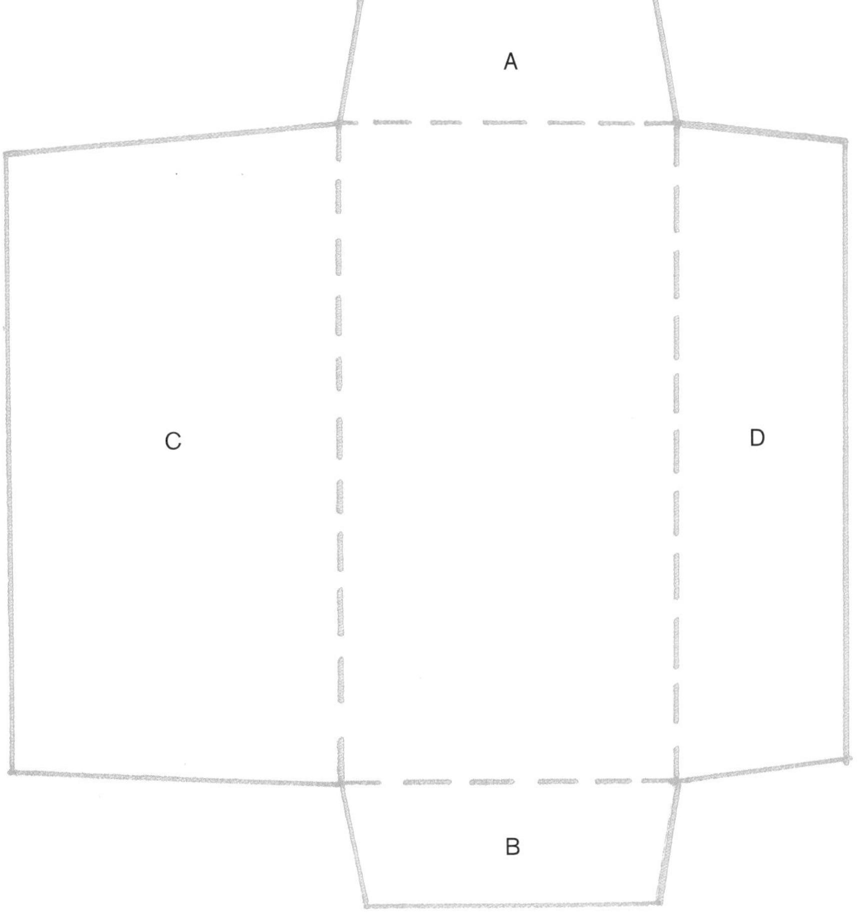

Step 2. Create folding guides

Lay template onto the backside of your plastic cutout. With a utility knife, score along dotted lines, making sure not to slice off pieces of your template. The scoring should make impressions in the plastic.

Step 3. Fold box

Place plastic cutout right side down on a work surface. Fold up all four sides of your box. One side will be higher than the others — this will be the back of your box. Thread 4" lengths of ribbon through the holes at each corner where two sides meet. Knot each length of ribbon to hold sides closed.

Step 4. Make top

Knot ends of 8" ribbon together to form a loop. Push loop up through hole in the centre of the box top and knot again so ribbon doesn't slide back out. The box top should rest against the tallest side of the box.

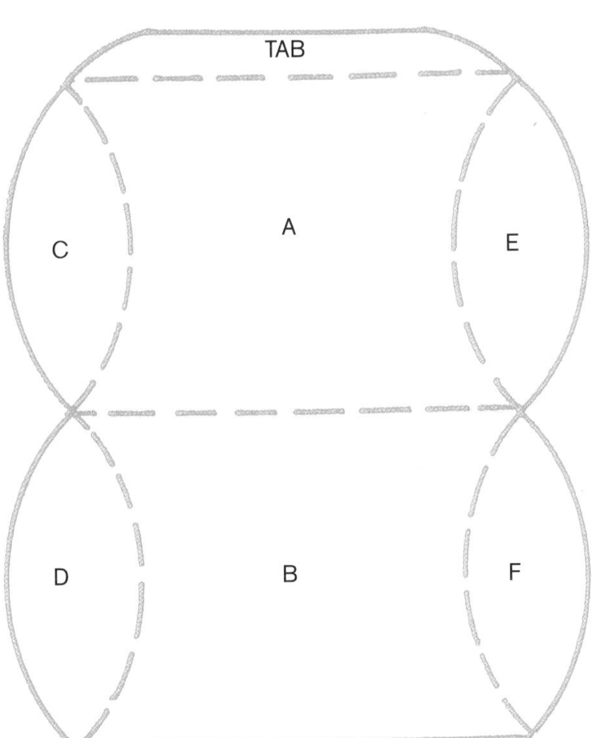

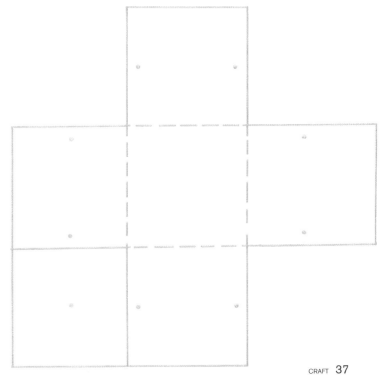

Project

Tortoiseshell Buttons

TURN EVERYDAY OBJECTS INTO CLASSIC HOME ACCESSORIES.

Editor's note:
Beads would make an interesting alternative to buttons for these projects. Whichever you choose, just remember: the impact is in the repetition. Don't mix too many different colours or sizes.

Difficulty level:
Easy

Projects:
Cushion cover
Cigar box
Buttons as art
Ribbon bookmarks
Guest towels and laundry bag
Lantern and lampshade
Magnets

Smooth, shiny, and radiating a rich amber lustre, the classic tortoiseshell button (faux only, please!) dresses up just about anything it adorns. Not just for clothing, tortoiseshell can be used to transform everyday objects into exquisite accessories or handsome keepsakes. Against white, its neutral colour creates a crisp, summery look. With a needle, thread and a handful of buttons, cotton tea towels become elegant guest towels. With a hot-glue gun, turn oversized buttons into magnets; fasten neat rows of buttons onto cigar boxes and candle shades; or affix them to standard-issue price tags for clever gift labels. Select a project and button up on a summer afternoon.

A simple white linen cushion turns chic when studded with glossy tortoiseshell buttons. The cover is made of two oversized dinner napkins stitched together and decorated in a geometric pattern.

PHOTOGRAPHY ... OB FIOCCA

A few of our favourite things: a wooden cigar box covered with shiny buttons; grosgrain ribbon bookmarks (include them along with a gift book); and buttons as "art," mounted on ivory-coloured suede and framed for display.

Project 07: Ideas using buttons

CUSHION COVER

MATERIALS & TOOLS

- 2 plain white cotton or linen napkins, 22" square
- 5 gross tortoiseshell buttons
- Brown thread and needle
- Cushion form

Sold almost everywhere, and easy to work with, large white dinner napkins are ideal for this project. We used flanged, European-sized, 22"-square dinner napkins. The seam serves as a guideline for sewing the first row of buttons and for sewing the napkins together. Begin by designing and sketching your pattern on paper. A geometric pattern is easier to sew than one involving curves. Use one size and style of button to enhance the effect. Our pattern consists of a border of two rows of buttons (sewn parallel to the inner stitch line of the flange), but depending on the size of the buttons, you may opt for more or fewer rows. Bring pattern into centre of cushion to create a focal point. Sew buttons onto the first napkin (to become the front of the cushion). For quick sewing, avoid knotting the thread after stitching each button. Instead, run thread on the wrong side of the napkin from button to button, knotting every 5 or 6 buttons. Note: Sew buttons at least 1/2" inside the seam to ensure that the foot of the needle can get by them when stitching cushion together. Once complete, sew the front to the second napkin (the back of the cushion), wrong sides together, stitching along the edge of the flange. Leave a space large enough through which to stuff cushion form. Stitch closed by hand, or stitch on metal or Velcro closures.

CIGAR BOX

MATERIALS & TOOLS

- Cigar or craft box
- Tortoiseshell buttons
- Hot-glue gun and glue sticks

Choose your favourite cigar box or buy one at a cigar shop for this project. A wooden cigar box, if available, is ideal, though cardboard craft boxes are also suitable. Use buttons of one style and size, and glue them as close together as possible — we staggered the buttons for the best coverage. Try covering the entire box, or, if you prefer, cover only the top, leaving the sides exposed.

BUTTONS AS ART

MATERIALS & TOOLS

- Varying sizes of new or antique tortoiseshell buttons (we also used antique mother-of-pearl buttons, collected from flea markets, for variety)
- Frame
- Piece of cardboard to fit in frame
- Piece of quilt batting same size as cardboard
- A car chamois, 1/2" larger all around than cardboard and batting
- Needle and thread
- Masking tape

Lay quilt batting on top of cardboard. Lay chamois on top of both; pull taut, fold edges securely over cardboard and attach to back with masking tape. Lay buttons on chamois and, when you're happy with the arrangement, mark position of buttons lightly with a pencil. Attach buttons tightly, so that chamois puffs up around them, knotting thread and pulling through from back to front. Insert in frame. If you wish, photocopy an attractive insignia, as we did, and glue to top and bottom of mat for a finishing touch.

RIBBON BOOKMARKS

MATERIALS & TOOLS

- Grosgrain, velvet or satin ribbon
- Tortoiseshell buttons
- Needle and thread
- Pinking shears or diagonal scissors

Sew the prettiest buttons you can find onto lengths of ribbon to make unique bookmarks. A single spectacular button, or three buttons of gradating sizes sewn in a row, works especially well. Trim edge of ribbon with pinking shears or diagonal scissors, or hem to prevent fraying.

Paired with satin or gingham ribbon, buttons turn plain cotton tea towels into elegant hand towels. A laundry bag is personalized with a button monogram.

Polished tortoiseshell buttons dress up plain candle shades and add character to hurricane lanterns when threaded on thin wire; at night, the buttons glow as the candles flicker.

Wheretobuybuttons

- Look in shops where sewing notions are sold.
- If your city has a "fashion district" where fabric stores are clustered, shop there for large quantities of unusual buttons.
- Check the Yellow Pages for wholesale button companies that are open to the public – some sell in a "gross," a quantity of 140. At about $10, it's less expensive than buying by the handful.
- For a project that requires many buttons, buy less-expensive buttons in bulk; buy special buttons for smaller projects.

GUEST TOWELS & LAUNDRY BAG

MATERIALS & TOOLS

- Plain white tea towels
- Tortoiseshell buttons
- Ribbon
- Brown or white thread and needle
- White laundry bag

Guest Towels

Handwash tea towel to preshrink, then fold and press into "guest towel" shape. Sew a length of ribbon across the width of the tea towel, approximately 2" from the bottom edge. Next, lay an assortment of buttons across the ribbon and, when satisfied with your design, sew them on. Use a variety of styles or, if you prefer a cleaner look, use only one style of button. Note: Hand wash only.

Laundry Bag

Lay buttons on bag to form desired initials, or sketch your initials first with pencil or tailor's chalk; any marks will be covered by the buttons. Tip: Arrange buttons in the top third of the bag, where the fabric surface is smooth and flat, just below the gathered drawstring area. If you position the initials in the centre of the bag they will lose their impact and float in the large, empty space. Sew on buttons using method described for cushion cover. Note: Hand wash only.

LANTERN & LAMPSHADE

MATERIALS & TOOLS

- Tortoiseshell buttons
- Tortoiseshell beads
- Brass wire
- Small candlestick or chandelier shades
- Hot-glue gun and glue sticks

Decorative Wire

Clear tortoiseshell buttons and beads work best for this project because they allow the glow and flicker of candlelight to pass through them. Using wire snips, cut a piece of brass wire approximately 18" to 20" long. Thread it through the buttonholes, spacing buttons approximately 2" apart as you go — the wire's stiffness will keep buttons in place. Use buttons and beads of different shapes and sizes, for an imaginative, ornamental look. Create several lengths of decorative wire and wind around a glass hurricane lantern.

Candlestick or Chandelier Shade

With a hot-glue gun, attach buttons to fabric or cardboard shades. You may wish to sketch a design on paper before glueing down buttons, especially on cardboard, which will tear if buttons are removed. Our shade uses small buttons on the top edge and larger buttons on the bottom to give it weight.

MAGNETS

MATERIALS & TOOLS

- Large tortoiseshell buttons
- Hot-glue gun and glue sticks
- Magnets

Reserve your favourite or vintage buttons for this project, and use the largest buttons you have. Small, plain magnets are available at most home supply and hardware stores. With a hot-glue gun, attach magnets to the backs of your buttons.

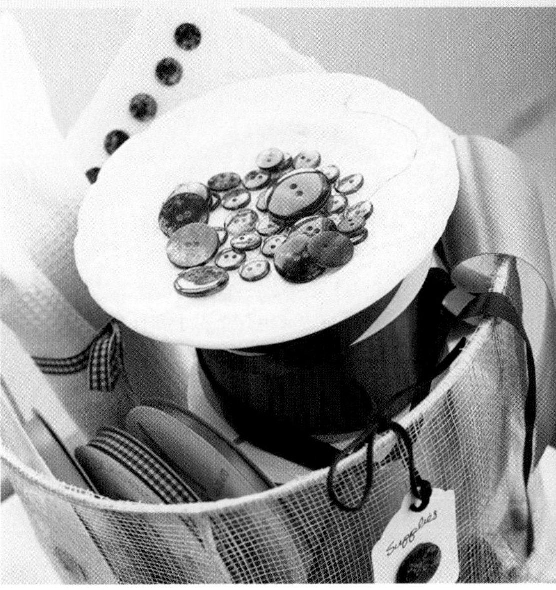

With a hot-glue gun, fasten tiny magnets to your favourite buttons for a fridge with magnetic personality.

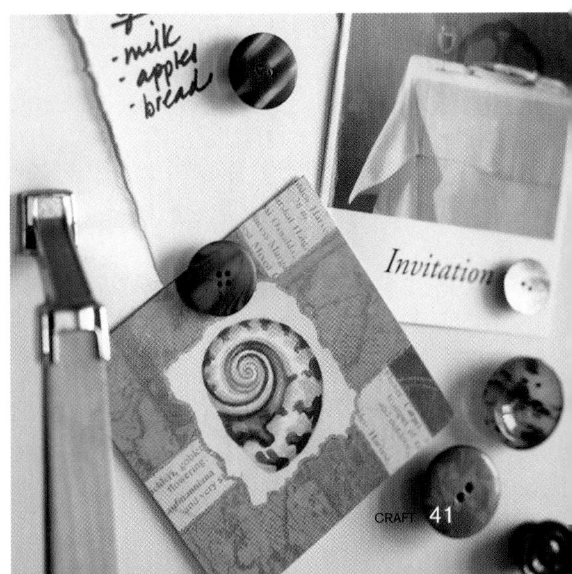

Project 08

Words & Music

USE SHEET MUSIC TO TRANSFORM FURNITURE INTO ONE-OF-A-KIND PIECES.

Editor's note:
Though it was crafted several years ago, this sheet-music-sheathed dresser still looks current – testimony to the timeless appeal of black-and-white graphics.

Difficulty level:
Easy

Inspired by the ordered artistry of the motifs of song, we offer a stylish alternative to the paint treatments and découpage designs that have become so popular. Our talented artist has used musical notation to turn a dresser into a personalized piece. Simply unearth that sonata you played in school or call upon the muses to spur your own creative talents.

SHEET MUSIC CHEST OF DRAWERS

This découpage project by Toronto decorative artist Janis Zroback is a wonderful way to refurbish an old piece of furniture or transform a new one. We used an old chest of drawers because the shape and size of the piece provided ample space to showcase the graphic and detailed nature of sheet music. Photocopies work just as well as originals and your local library or conservatory of music should have lots of interesting scores to choose from.

MATERIALS & TOOLS

- Sheet music or photocopies of sheet music
- Weldbond glue
- Small paintbrush
- TSP (trisodium phosphate)
- Good-quality primer paint
- Ivory latex paint, eggshell sheen (we used Benjamin Moore 919)
- Low-lustre latex varnish (we used Benjamin Moore One Hour Latex Varnish)
- Sponge brushes
- Burnt Umber artist's oil paint
- Paint thinner
- Black acrylic paint
- Sandpaper

Step 1. Prepare the piece of furniture

If your piece of furniture is old, wash it thoroughly with TSP until clean. Fill any holes with filler, then sand if necessary. Depending on the condition of the piece, brush on one or two coats of primer. Once dried completely, brush on two or three finish coats of a soft ivory-coloured latex paint, like Benjamin Moore 919. Sand lightly between coats of paint. Tip: If you are using old sheet music, look for a paint that approximates the aged yellow colour of old paper.

Step 2. Plan your design

Assemble several sheets of music and lay them out on the piece of furniture you have chosen. Our chest of drawers was completely covered with the sheet music: sheets were trimmed to fit the top, sides and drawer fronts of the chest, leaving only the legs and edges bare. Depending on the size of the furniture piece and the effect you want to create, you may want to use less paper and leave more painted surface visible. Note the different details on the music sheets — some may be more interesting than others and you may want to reserve them for a focal position, glueing them on an angle so that they stand out.

Step 3. Paste the paper

Mix Weldbond glue with an equal amount of water and brush it on a small section of the first surface you intend to decoupage. (Top, sides and front of the furniture should be decoupaged separately; otherwise the glue will dry out.) Carefully place sheet music on the wet glue, laying it down page by page. As you go, smooth each sheet from the centre out, using firm pressure with a sponge or cloth to prevent bubbles from forming. Cover one area at a time and allow the entire piece to dry overnight.

Step 4. Varnish and antique the piece of furniture

Brush on one coat of varnish and allow it to dry. Then make up an antiquing glaze as follows: squeeze out 1" of Burnt Umber artist's oil paint and thin it with paint thinner to the consistency of a watery glaze. Apply the glaze over the painted areas of the furniture (i.e., those not covered with paper) in small sections, brushing on and then wiping off lightly with a clean cloth. The glaze will adhere to the recessed areas of the wood — indentations, carving and reveals. Allow to dry overnight. Apply at least three more coats of varnish over the entire piece, allowing each to dry completely between applications. If you are decoupaging a chest of drawers, try painting the drawer pulls black and finishing them with three coats of varnish.

PHOTOGRAPHY BY MICHAEL MAHOVLICH

Sewing

02 COLOUR, PATTERN, TEXTURE: FABRIC CAN TRANSFORM A ROOM

SHEER BLISS IT'S IN THE BAG **WINTER WEAR** FLOOR PLAY **WINDOW DRESSING** SUMMER DRESS **UNDER COVER** TAILORED BEDROOM

Project

SheerBliss

FIVE SMART SEWING PROJECTS GIVE TODAY'S NEW SHEER FABRICS STAR STATUS.

Editor's note:
Make sewing slippery sheer fabrics easier by placing tissue paper between the layers of fabric before stitching. Then pull the tissue out, making sure you don't leave any stray bits in the stitches.

Difficulty level:
Average

Projects:
Euro sham cover
Sheer pillowcase
Bolster pillow
Sheer duvet cover
Roman blind

Long a favourite cover-up for windows, sheer fabrics — along with their style counterparts, frosted glass and translucent plastic — have recently been showing surprising mettle, proving themselves newly flexible, highly fashionable and just as clearly at home in a modern room as they've been in traditional spaces. Here, these gauzy organdies and linens bring a contemporary edge to pretty floral bed linens, yet soften the look of a clean-lined bath. Our sewing projects make use of today's popular coloured sheers, as well as basic whites. For a crisp finish in a floral-themed bedroom, stitch up our duvet and pillow covers. For the bath, make our two-toned semi-sheer Roman blind, and, as a final flourish, use the diaphanous remnants as trim for accessories or toiletries that can be left prettily on display.

This bedroom gets its fresh edge from bedding slipcovers in cool sheers. We fitted the pretty floral-covered duvet into an envelope of sheer white fabric tied closed with simple tabs. We made a white semi-sheer cover to go over a pink waffle-weave sham on the standard pillow and a floral cover for the bolster pillow with sheer white ends. Finally, we added a shot of bright colour with a hot pink slipcover for the Euro sham.

PHOTOGRAPHY BY ALAN KAPLANAS

EURO SHAM COVER

Our sham was 26” x 26” with a 3” flange, but adjust your measurements as necessary if using a different size of pillow.

MATERIALS & TOOLS

3 yds. sheer fabric
Scissors
Needle and thread
Iron

Step 1. Cut fabric and fold square

Cut a piece of sheer fabric to 33” x 72”. Give both 33” ends a 1” hem. Bring the two hemmed ends together, right sides together, and overlap them by 3” on what will be the back of the pillowcase. This will create a 33” square.

Step 2. Sew fabric into square

Sew along the top and bottom of this square, using a 1/2” seam allowance. Turn right side out and press. You should have a 33” square with an overlap at the back.

Step 3. Create flange

Sew 3” in all along the outside edge to create a 3” flange. Insert pillow form.

SHEER PILLOWCASE

Our finished pillowcase was 20” x 28” to fit a standard pillow, but adjust measurements as necessary for a different size.

MATERIALS & TOOLS

1 yd. 65"-wide sheer fabric
Scissors
Needle and thread
Iron

Step 1. Cut and hem sides

Cut two pieces of sheer fabric to the size of the pillow, plus 4 3/4” longer and 1 1/2” wider, to accommodate seam allowance and hems. Hem one end of both pieces (separately): fold over 2”, then 2” again, and stitch.

Step 2. Sew pillowcase

Place the two pieces together, right sides out, and stitch around three sides, 1/4” from edge, leaving hemmed ends open. Turn inside out (right sides together). Sew around three sides again, 1/2” in from edge, to encase the original 1/4” seam allowance. Press, and turn right sides out.

Step 3. Make ties

Create desired number of ties (we used three pairs of 1” x 10” ties), by cutting strips of fabric to 2 1/2” x 12”. Fold strips lengthwise into 1”-wide strips, with raw edges tucked in. Press and stitch closed. Fold both ends over 1/2”, then 1/2” again, press, and stitch. Sew ties evenly spaced along open end of pillowcase with a corresponding tie on opposite side of opening.

BOLSTER PILLOW

MATERIALS & TOOLS

1 yd. solid fabric
1 yd. sheer fabric
Kraft paper
2 yds. ribbon
Scissors
Needle and thread
Safety pin
Iron

Step 1. Measure bolster form

Measure the length and diameter of the bolster pillow you are covering. Add the length to the diameter, and add 2” to this number (measurement A). Measure around the bolster pillow and add one inch (measurement B). On kraft paper, create a rectangle using measurements A and B.

Step 2. Cut fabrics

Divide the length of the rectangle into three equal sections. The middle section will be the solid fabric panel in the centre of the pillow, and the outer sections will be the two sheer panels. Cut two sheer panels, adding 1/2” for seam allowance all around. Cut solid fabric panel, adding 1” for seam allowance all around.

Step 3. Sew fabrics together

Sew three panels together with solid panel in centre, with 1/2” seam allowance at each seam. You should have one rectangle made up of a solid fabric panel with two sheer panels on each end. For a decorative touch, topstitch ribbon over both seams. Give the sheer ends of the tube a 1” hem.

Step 4. Finish bolster cover

With right sides together, fold rectangle in half lengthwise, matching seams. Sew to create a tube shape with 1/2” seam allowance. Turn right side out. Use a safety pin to thread a ribbon through hem channels on ends of sheer pieces. Using a safety pin, thread a ribbon through each hem channel. Insert bolster pillow form, gently pull ribbon tight, and tie in a bow.

SHEER DUVET COVER

Our finished duvet cover was 62” x 85” to fit a single duvet, but adjust measurements as necessary for a different size.

MATERIALS & TOOLS

6 yds. 65"-wide sheer fabric
Scissors
Needle and thread
Iron

Step 1. Cut and hem sides

Cut two pieces of sheer fabric to the size of your duvet, plus 4 3/4” longer and 1 1/2” wider, to accommodate seam allowance and hems. Hem one end of both pieces (separately): fold over 2”, then 2” again, and stitch.

Step 2. Sew duvet cover

Place the two pieces together, right sides out, and stitch around three sides 1/4” from edge, leaving hemmed ends open. Turn inside out (right sides together). Sew around the three sides again, 1/2” in from edge, to encase the original 1/4” allowance. Turn right sides out.

Sheer fabrics and pretty embellishments soften the tailored lines of the linens and accessories in this bathroom. We put a twist on a traditional roman blind: to let in lots of light, the tops of these window coverings are made of sheer white fabric, and for privacy, the bottoms are a gauzy tan linen.

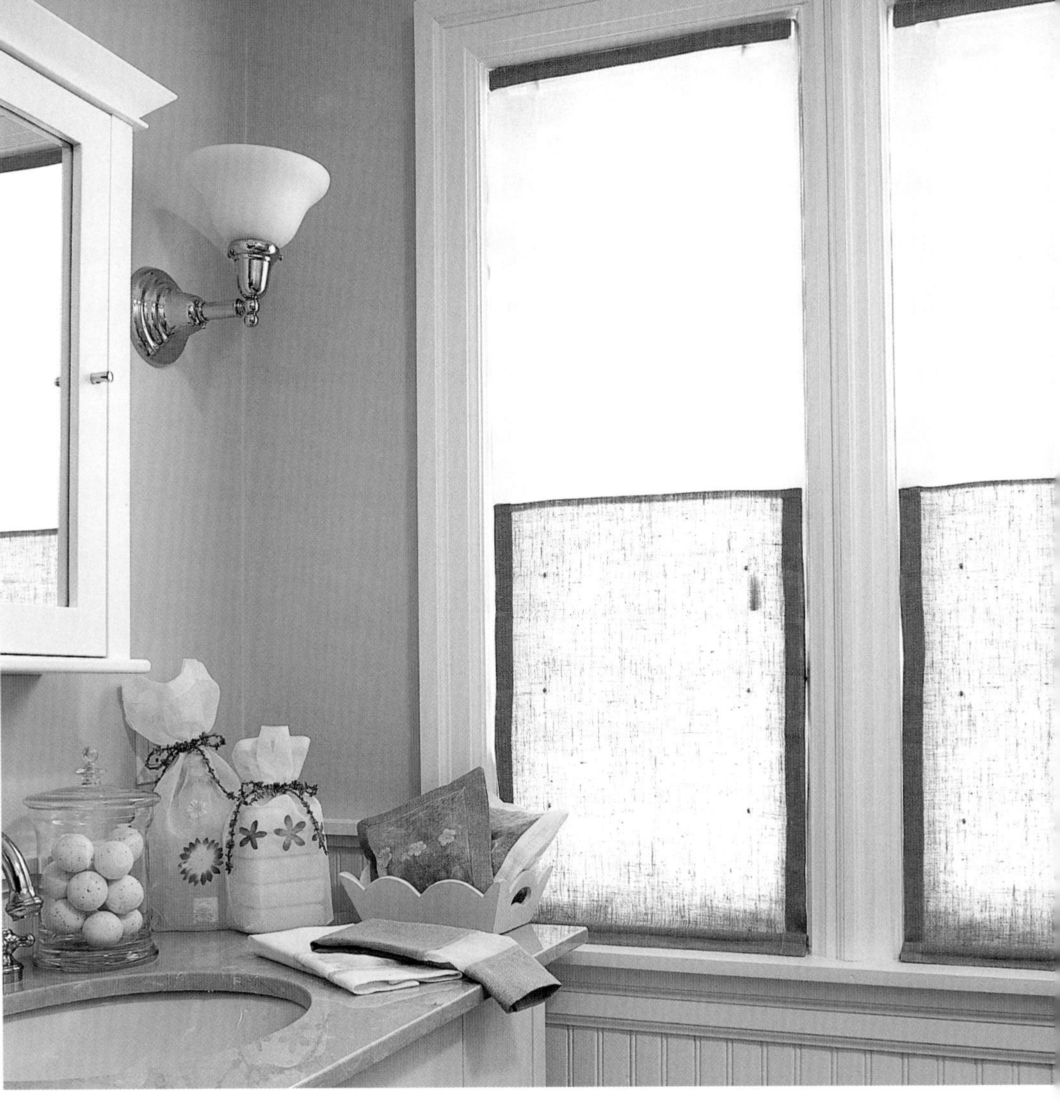

Step 3. Make ties
Create desired number of ties (we used seven pairs of 1" x 10" ties), by cutting strips of fabric to 2 1/2" x 12". Tuck in raw edges and fold strips lengthwise into 1"-wide strips. Press and stitch closed. Fold both ends over 1/2", then 1/2" again, press, and stitch. Sew ties, evenly spaced, along open end of duvet cover with a corresponding tie on opposite side.

ROMAN BLIND

Roman blind kits, consisting of plastic rings, tape, nylon string and hanging hardware are available at most drapery or fabric stores.

MATERIALS & TOOLS
- 1 1/2 yds. white silk organza
- 1 1/2 yds. linen
- Roman blind kit (at sewing-supply stores)
- Velcro
- 1/2"-diam. dowelling cut to width of blind
- 1/2" x 1/2" pine cut to width of blind
- Eye screws
- Scissors
- Needle and thread
- Iron
- Staple gun
- Drill
- 1" screws

Step 1. Determine measurements
Measure your window to determine the finished size of your blind. (Ours was 17" w. x 46" h. inside the window frame.) The division between the sheer fabric and the solid fabric should fall over the centre mullion of the window. Before cutting fabrics, add 1 1/2" to the length, and 4" to the width of the top sheer piece, and 12" to the length and 4" to the width of the solid fabric for seam and hem allowances.

Step 2. Sew fabrics together
Sew the sheer fabric to the solid fabric with a 1/2" seam allowance, and press the seam down against the solid fabric so it will not be visible through the sheer. Add a 2" strip of the solid fabric along the top of the sheer panel, to help stabilize the Velcro (to be sewn along the top later). Press the seam allowance for this strip upwards against the solid fabric.

Step 3. Sew edges and hems
Press the sides under 1", then 1" again, and hem. Press bottom under 2", then 2" again, and hem. Stitch across the bottom hem, 1" up from the bottom, to create a channel for the dowelling, which will keep the blind hanging straight. Again, so it doesn't show through the sheer fabric, press the top edge over 1/2". Place hook side of a 1/2"-wide strip of Velcro across the width of the top of the blind, and stitch in place (set aside other half of Velcro for later use). Insert dowelling into channel, and stitch channel ends closed.

Step 4. Attach rings
Follow instructions from blind kit for attaching the rings to the blind. Start from the bottom, and position rows of rings about 2" in from sides of blind.

Step 5. Hang blind
Wrap 1/2" x 1/2" strip of pine with leftover solid fabric and attach fabric to pine with a staple gun. Pre-drill holes in window frame where you will be hanging the blind. Screw covered wood strip into window frame. Staple the other half of the Velcro onto front of covered strip. Determine the point where the top of each vertical row of rings will meet the wood strip. Insert eye screws into bottom of wood strip at this point, so that they hang down and line up with each row of rings. String blind with nylon cord from blind kit, according to package instructions, starting from the bottom. Run cord through eye screws and across top, leaving enough cord to fall about halfway down length of blind when closed. Hang blind by pressing Velcro strips together.

Project

It's in the Bag

THREE EASY SEWING PROJECTS UPDATE THE '70S CLASSIC BEANBAG CHAIR AS FUNKY MOBILE SEATING FOR THE KIDS.

Editor's note:
Break with convention: forgo that new rec room or playroom sofa and use beanbag chairs as your furniture instead. Durable and affordable, they're big enough for adults and just the right level for pint-sized loungers.

Difficulty level:
Average

Projects:
Pocket beanbag
Drum–shaped beanbag
Small cube stool

Decorating with kids in mind has come of age. Today, there's no need to close the door of a separate rumpus room to hide the mishmash of small-sized pieces. Children's furnishings are now as smart-looking as their adult equivalents, and are just as likely to inhabit the family room as dad's favourite chair. For these projects, we've updated the classic '70s-style beanbag to create stylish – but distinctly fun – seating kids can use all through the house. Each bag is covered with soft, freshly coloured denim. We treated a cone-shaped beanbag to a blue jean pocket, a hiding spot for books or stuffed toys. We covered a drum-shaped bag in five colours for a lively new look, and turned the trendy cube into a beanbag stool that can be dragged into place by its handle. Our bags are double-seamed for durability and slipcovered so laundering is a snap.

Left: A drum-shaped beanbag becomes a favourite spot for reading.

Right: These cube stools with handles pull into place as seating at a small table. By stuffing them almost full we made them solid instead of floppy like other beanbag seats.

All of our beanbags consist of an inner muslin form filled with beanbag stuffing, securely sewn together to ensure no stuffing will escape, and an outer cover. All of our covers can be laundered. They are made of denim, but cotton duck and other sturdy fabrics would also be suitable. All seams are double- or triple-stitched to withstand rough-and-tumble treatment from kids. Prewash all cotton cover fabric to allow shrinkage before sewing. All beanbag chairs can be made with new beanbag fill purchased from an upholstery supply store, or with fill from an old beanbag chair. Our slipcovers can also be made to transform old beanbag chairs of the same shape.

POCKET BEANBAG

Our two pocket beanbags are made in different sizes. The smaller bag has a 27"-diameter bottom and is intended for toddlers. The larger bag has a 30"-diameter bottom and is for children aged three to five. These directions are for one small beanbag, with the size changes for the larger beanbag given in brackets.

MATERIALS & TOOLS

- 2 yds. muslin
- Scissors
- Large compass
- Pencil
- Kraft paper
- Tape measure or long string
- Wide-mouthed funnel or funnel made of stiff paper
- Beanbag fill
- 2 yds. (2 1/2 yds.) denim
- 24"- (28"-) long heavy zipper or duvet zipper cut to size
- Triple-stitch attachment*

* Or follow French seam or flat fell seam directions.

Step 1. Make paper patterns

On kraft paper, use compass to draw one circle measuring 28" (31") in diameter for bottom of beanbag. Cut two pattern pieces from kraft paper to this size. Determine circumference of circle. Divide this number by five, and use tape measure or string to mark five evenly spaced points around circumference of circle. Now use a ruler to draw a straight line from each of the five edge marks to the centre of the circle. This will give you five equal pie-shaped

PHOTOGRAPHY BY DONNA GRIFFITH

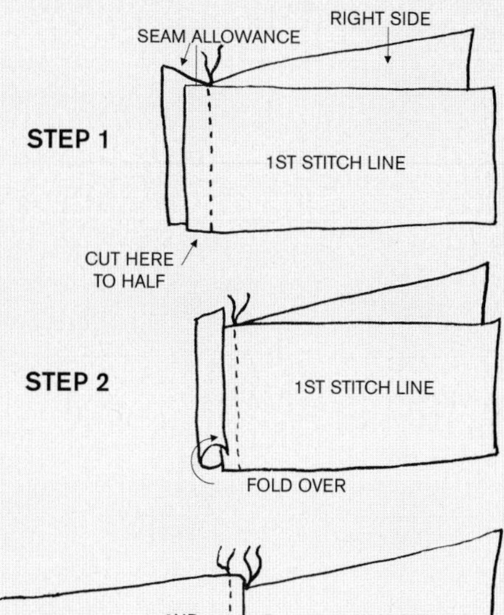

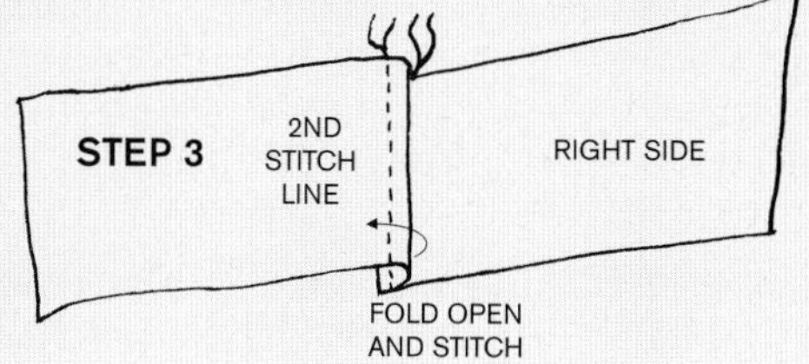

Tosewspecialseams

French Seam

Sew the seam with wrong sides together, turn the fabric so that right sides are facing to enclose seam and sew again. Press enclosed seam to one side so that it isn't bulky.

Flat Fell Seam

With right sides together, sew seam, leaving 1/2" seam allowance. Trim back one raw edge of allowance to half (see Step 1). Fold other half of allowance over trimmed edge to enclose seam (see Step 2), fold open, and sew (see Step 3).

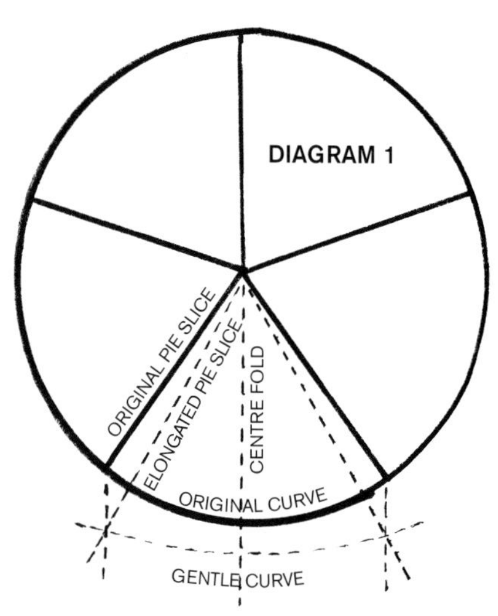

Project 10: Beanbag chairs

pieces. Cut one pie-shaped piece from kraft paper to use as a pattern. Fold in half length-wise. This will create a centre line. Unfold. Place this single-pie-slice pattern on kraft paper and trace again. Mark the centre points at top and bottom, and draw a line up through both marks. At points where side lines meet curved line, draw 1"-long lines to the centre line, and then redraw your bottom curve to meet both points, making the new curve gentler than original (see Diagram 1). Now redraw your sides from bottom to top middle point. This will create an elongated pie-shape. To make pocket pattern, draw a rectangle measuring 8" (10") wide by 9" (11") long (see Diagram 2). Add 2" to top of pocket. Draw a line directly down centre measuring 1" beyond bottom of pocket. Draw a line from this centre point to the bottom of each side line to create jean pocket shape.

Step 2. Make muslin form

From muslin, cut out five pie-shaped pieces and one bottom circle piece. With right sides facing, pin pie-shaped pieces of fabric together. Align carefully to ensure all five meet at one point. Sew together, leaving a 1/2" seam allowance. Attach bottom piece, leaving a 4" gap. Use a wide-mouthed funnel or paper funnel to insert fill. Handstitch the gap closed, going back over the stitches two to three times to ensure a secure seam.

Step 3. Make cover

Cut out five pie-shaped pieces, two half-circle pieces for bottom, and one pocket piece from denim, leaving a 1" seam allowance. Sew pocket detail onto one pie-shaped piece before making cover. To do this, turn top 2" down and press to create flap within pocket. Turn edge 1/2" under all around pocket (except top), press and baste. Centre pocket within pie-shaped piece, pin in place, and topstitch right at edge of pocket. To create topstitch detail, sew pocket in place with a second line of stitching 1/4" inside first line of stitching. With right sides facing and using a 1/2" seam allowance, sew all five pie-shaped pieces together. Press both sides of each seam down in same clockwise direction all around top. Create topstitch detail by sewing a second line of stitching 1/2" from seam, on same side of each seam. Insert zipper across circular bottom. With right sides together, sew along straight edge of two bottom half-circle pieces to make one large circle. Press seams open. With zipper head facing down, lay zipper along seam, baste in place and sew all around zipper. Release stitched seam to expose zipper. The length of the zipper needs to be equal to the diameter of the circle in order to fit the form inside the slipcover. Sew top to bottom. Insert muslin form. Close zipper.

DRUM-SHAPED BEANBAG

MATERIALS & TOOLS

- Kraft paper
- Pencil
- Scissors
- Large compass
- Tape measure
- Long piece of string
- Ruler
- 4 yds. muslin
- Wide-mouthed funnel or funnel made of stiff paper
- Beanbag fill
- 2 yds. main colour denim*
- 3/4 yd. each of 4 other colours denim
- Cotton thread
- 33" zipper (duvet zipper recommended)
- 2" covered-button-making kit
- Triple-stitch attachment**

* This will make bottom as well as one piece of pie shape for top and rectangle for side.
** Or follow French seam or flat fell seam directions.

Step 1. Make muslin form

Cut two circles of muslin measuring 34" in diameter. Use a compass and pencil to first make two 33"-diameter pattern pieces from kraft paper, cutting muslin pieces an extra inch all around for seam allowance. Use a tape measure or string to measure around the circumference of the circle, and cut one long strip of fabric to this length (approximately 10'-5") and 15" wide to form the side piece of the beanbag. With a 1/2" seam allowance and with right sides facing, sew top and bottom pieces to side strip leaving 14" gap for inserting fill. Turn right-side-out. Using a wide-mouthed funnel, or a funnel made from a piece of stiff paper, pour fill into form. Handstitch the gap closed, going back over the stitches two to three times to ensure a secure seam.

Step 2. Cut beanbag bottom

Fold one of the kraft-paper patterns in half, and cut two half-circle pieces for beanbag bottom from denim, with 1" added to all edges for seam allowance. The two halves will be zippered together in Step 5.

Step 3. Make pie-shaped pieces

Using the other 33"-diameter kraft-paper pattern and long piece of string, determine circumference of circle (should be approximately 10'-5"). Divide this number by five (should be approximately 25"). Use tape measure or string to mark points every 25" around circumference of circle. Now use a ruler to draw a straight line from each of the five edge marks to the centre of the circle. This will give you five equal pie-shaped pieces. Cut one pie-shaped piece from kraft paper to use as a pattern. Cut one pie-shaped piece from each of the five fabric colours with an extra 1" all around edges for seam allowance.

Step 4. Make side pieces

Lay tape measure or string along curve of pie-shaped piece. Cut one piece of each colour of fabric measuring this number in length (should be approximately 25" for each piece) and 15" wide.

Step 5. Sew bottom and attach zipper

With right sides together, sew along straight edge of two bottom half-circle pieces to make one large circle. Press seams open and insert zipper as in Pocket Beanbag, Step 3.

DIAGRAM 2

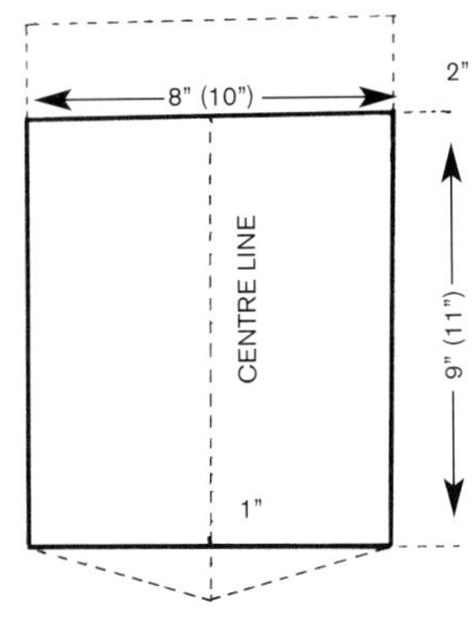

Step 6. Sew together top pieces

With right sides facing, pin pie-shaped pieces of fabric together. Align carefully to ensure all five meet at one point. Sew five pieces together leaving 1/2" seam allowance. Using leftover fabric, make covered button according to kit instructions. Sew securely into place where all five colours meet at centre of beanbag top. This is a fun decorative detail, and also hides your work in the spot where getting the five points to meet can be tricky.

Step 7. Sew together remaining pieces

Sew all side pieces together, following the colour scheme on the beanbag top (ours was red, yellow, orange, green, blue). Pin side pieces to top with right sides facing, taking care to align the seams and colours. Sew top to sides and sides to bottom. Turn right-side-out and insert muslin form through zipper in bottom. Close zipper.

SMALL CUBE STOOL

MATERIALS & TOOLS

- Scissors
- 1 yd. muslin, dressmaker's cotton or scrap material to make forms
- Cotton thread
- Wide-mouth funnel or funnel made of stiff paper
- Beanbag fill
- Heavy upholstery thread for hand-stitched closing
- 1 yd. denim
- Triple-stitch attachment*

* Or reinforce all seams following French seam or flat fell seam directions.

These measure 12" h. x 14" d. x 14" w., and have a handle on one side so kids can easily drag them into place.

Step 1. Make muslin form

Cut four pieces of muslin measuring 13" x 15" for sides and two pieces measuring 15" x 15" each for top and bottom (the extra 1" all around edges will accommodate a 1/2" seam allowance). With right sides facing, sew all four sides together along the 13" sides. Attach top and bottom leaving a 4" opening at bottom for inserting fill. Beanbag fill pours like water; use a wide-mouthed funnel or make a funnel from a piece of stiff paper to neatly direct fill into form. The more fill you use, the firmer the beanbag will be. For stools, fill forms at least 3/4 full or more, depending on how firm you want them. Using heavy upholstery thread, handstitch 4" opening closed, sewing over the seam two to three times to ensure that it is secure and that no beanbag fill will escape.

Step 2. Make cover

Cut four pieces of denim cover fabric measuring 13" x 15" for sides, and two pieces measuring 15" x 15" each for top and bottom. Cut one piece measuring 6" w. x 7" l. for handle. Fold handle piece in half lengthwise with right sides together, and sew along raw edges, leaving a 1/2" seam allowance. Turn right-side-out. Press with seam running down centre of piece to form handle. Sew side and top pieces together as in Step 1. Pin handle to the top edge of the centre of one side piece, on right side with raw edges aligned. Sew top to side pieces as above but with handle ends sandwiched between one side and top.

Step 3. Insert muslin form

Insert the filled muslin form into the cover. Handstitch the bottom piece to the side piece to close the beanbag. A zipper could be used, but would interfere with the lines of the cube. The cover can be removed with a stitch-ripper, and then stitched up again to seal the cube after it has been washed and dried.

Project 11

Winter Wear

EASY-SEW WOOL MELTON ACCESSORIES WITH DETAILS STRAIGHT FROM THE FASHION RUNWAYS.

Editor's note:
Introducing soft elements into modern interiors can be a challenge, but felt (or lookalike melton) is a natural for the job. It's fuss-free, with no patterns or frills, and durable to boot.

Difficulty level:
Average

Projects:
Patchwork rug
Appliqué floor pillow
Journal cover-up
File folder cover-up

Felt has grown up. You may remember it from kindergarten cut-and-paste. Today it's the hottest textile around, inspiring designers to dizzying heights of adult play, evidenced by the scads of felt-covered rugs, ottomans, lampshades and even floppy decorative bowls in high-end accessory shops. But good felt is expensive (up to $100 per yard) and can be hard to find, so we've come up with four projects that achieve the look on a budget, substituting wool melton ($15 to $20 per yard) for felt. Melton looks similar to felt, has the durability of wool and is easy to sew. With details straight from the runways, these are simple, stylish projects — a patchwork rug, a floor cushion, and file folder and journal covers — that take the craft out of feltwork.

Our four projects, using easy-sew wool melton and fashion-forward techniques, are both modern and nostalgic. Choose subtle colours that work well together, like our taupe, sage green, pale grey and charcoal grey meltons, and keep details clean by using a single repeated appliqué motif or colour of thread.

Left: Made with wool melton left over from the other two projects, the simple file folder and journal cover-ups apply a variety of sewing techniques – appliqué, zigzag stitching and exposed seams.

PHOTOGRAPHY BY VIRGINIA MACDONALD

Project 11: Wool melton accessories

Blanketstitch

A blanket stitch is typically used over a straight raw edge or a folded edge in order to make it look neater. Here, we used a blanket stitch to seam pieces of fabric together. With right sides of fabric facing and pre-punched holes lined up, fasten the working thread at one end and work stitches through holes at right angles to the edge. Take the stitch through the holes, looping the yarn behind the needle before pulling it through to form a loop on the edge of the fabric.

PATCHWORK RUG

This reversible patchwork rug can be made with top and bottom each in a single colour, or with a multicolour patchwork on both sides as shown here. We made a 6’ x 6’ rug, but any size could be made using this simple technique, including a long runner.

MATERIALS & TOOLS

- Scissors
- 10 1/2 yds. wool melton*
- Spray-on fabric adhesive
- Set square
- Tailor’s chalk
- Hammer and nail
- 2 50-g balls yarn
- Darning needle

* If you are making a two-colour carpet, allow 5 1/4 yds. each colour, or any configuration of colours that adds up to 10 1/2 yds.

Step 1. Cut melton and make double-sided squares
Cut 18 squares of melton, each 26” x 26”. Use spray-on fabric adhesive to glue two pieces of melton together. For ease of glueing, line up two squares wrong sides together. Pull back one-half of top square, spray the half-exposed underside of top piece and the half-exposed top side of bottom piece. Allow to dry until tacky (see directions on can for exact timing). Press together and repeat on other half. Repeat process until you have nine double-sided squares of melton. Using a set square, mark pieces to 24” x 24” with tailor’s chalk. Cut to 24” x 24” squares.

Step 2. Make stitching holes
At one corner of a square, use tailor’s chalk to make one mark 1/4” in from the top and side. This marks the position of your first stitching hole. Mark remainder of holes at 1/2” intervals all around the square. Repeat on all remaining squares. Using a hammer and nail, punch a hole at each mark on all nine squares.

Step 3. Lay out squares
If you are making a multicolour carpet, lay out all squares on the floor and play with placement until you are happy with the configuration of colours.

Step 4. Sew squares together
Take two squares and place right sides together, matching pre-punched holes on one side. With yarn and darning needle, sew together using a loose blanket stitch (see box above), then open the two squares to a flat position. Repeat with three more sets of two squares. Sew all four pairs together then fit in the final square, to make three rows of three squares.

Step 5. Finish edges
Finish edges with a blanket stitch.

APPLIQUÉ FLOOR PILLOW

MATERIALS & TOOLS

- 1 1/2 yds. wool melton (for five squares of patchwork, pillow back, main background colour; we used taupe)
- 1/2 yd. wool melton in another colour (for four squares of patchwork; we used grey)
- 1/2 yd. third colour melton (appliqué leaf colour; we used green)
- Scissors
- Kraft paper for leaf motif template
- Tailor’s chalk
- Sewing machine
- Straight pins
- Spray-on fabric adhesive
- Heavy nylon thread and appropriate needle (as per thread packaging)
- 1 30” zipper
- 36” x 36” pillow form

Step 1. Cut melton
Cut one 37” x 37” square from first colour melton. Cut five 13” x 13” squares from the same fabric. Cut four 13” x 13” squares from second fabric.

Step 2. Make leaf motif templates
Draw leaf motif on kraft paper and cut out. Cut nine 10” x 10” squares of third colour melton. Using tailor’s chalk, trace leaf template shape onto melton. Using sewing machine, create stay-stitch line by sewing on chalk line. Cut leaf from fabric just outside stay-stitch line. Repeat for all squares.

Step 3. Appliqué leaves to squares
Lay nine squares in patchwork pattern on floor and put leaves in place. Spray-glue leaves to squares, then pin each leaf in place. With tailor’s chalk, draw stem and veins on leaves. With standard zigzag stitch, stitch each leaf around the edge, and on stem and vein marks. Using a standard sewing machine set on regular zigzag stitch, the heavy nylon thread will create an exaggerated stitch look.

Step 4. Sew squares together
With right sides facing, and with 1/2” seam allowance, sew patches together in pairs as in patchwork rug instructions. Open up each pair of squares and zigzag along top seam to create a decorative detail.

Step 5. Sew zipper into pillow back
Zipper is sewn 3” from bottom edge of pillow so it doesn’t interfere with zigzag stitching around edges. Place zipper with head facing down on wrong side of pillow back, centred and 3” from bottom edge of melton. Pin in place and sew all around. Using sharp scissors, cut fabric to expose zipper. This creates a zipper opening with an unfinished edge.

Step 6. Sew pillow sides together
With right sides facing and 1/2” seam allowance all around, sew pillow top and bottom together. Trim seam allowances and turn right side out. Repeat zigzag detail stitch all around edge seam. Place pillow form inside.

JOURNAL COVER-UP

MATERIALS & TOOLS

Fabric, paper and spray adhesive left over from other projects could be used for this project.
Journal, preferably hardcover
Scissors
1/4 yd. wool melton in each of two colours (1/2 yd. total)
Heavy nylon thread
Sewing machine and appropriate needle
Tailor's chalk
Kraft paper to make leaf motif
Spray-on fabric adhesive

Step 1. Determine size of cover-up pieces

Open journal, measure front, back and spine, and add measurements together. Add another 3/4" all around. Cut out this size of rectangle (or square) from two colours of melton. Using 1/2" seam allowance, sew pieces together. For extra detail, add a leaf appliqué to main fabric following instructions for appliqué from floor pillow before sewing pieces together.

Step 2. Cut cover to insert journal

Decide main cover colour and border colour. With border colour facing up, measure in three inches from side edges, and trace a line with tailor's chalk. Cut a slash along this line, starting just inside the stitching line at top, and stopping just short of the stitching line at the bottom. Be careful not to cut through the other piece of melton. Repeat on other side of journal cover. This creates the opening where the cardboard journal cover will slide into the melton cover.

Step 3. Make border

Trim main fabric to just outside of stitch line. Leave second fabric original size, to form border (see photo above).

Step 4. Sew zigzag detail

Open journal cover flat and sew one straight zigzag line down exact centre, where journal spine will sit. Insert journal into cover.

FILE FOLDER COVER-UP

MATERIALS & TOOLS

Fabric, paper and spray adhesive left over from other projects could be used for this project.
Cardboard file folder
Tailor's chalk
Kraft paper
Scissors
1/4 yd. wool melton in each of two colours (1/2 yd. total)
Leftover scrap in third colour (for sides and leaf catches)
Heavy nylon thread
Sewing machine and appropriate needle
Spray-on fabric adhesive
12" twill tape or cord

Step 1. Make templates

Measure front, bottom, back and flap of cardboard file folder. Add 1/2" all around for seam allowance, and draw and cut out a rectangle to these measurements on kraft paper to make main pattern template. Shape top and bottom of pattern to match file folder shape exactly, but with 1/2" extra still added around all edges. Draw another pattern template the same measurements and shape as upper half of file folder front that is covered when flap is closed (see photo, page 54), plus 1/2" extra around all edges. (Template should be approximately one-quarter size of front of file folder, with shaping at top.) On another piece of kraft paper, trace and cut out shape of flap alone, adding 1/2" all around, making rounded edges the exact shape as on the main pattern template. (This is to make a pocket on the underside of the fabric flap that the file folder flap will slide into.) Measure sides of folder and add 1/2" all around to measurements. Trace onto kraft paper and cut out.

Step 2. Cut melton

Fold the main pattern template in half lengthwise and cut it down the centre. Cut two pieces of melton, each a different colour, using these half-pattern templates. Fold the upper-half template in half and cut down the centre. Cut two pieces of melton to correspond to these pieces, in the opposite colours of the main front pieces. Cut one piece of melton (either colour) using the flap pocket pattern template. Cut two pieces for sides from third colour melton.

Step 3. Sew main pieces together

With right sides together, sew two main piece fabric halves to create one large piece. Open seams and sew standard zigzag stitch along seam on right side. With right sides together, sew two upper-half pieces, open seam and zigzag along seam on right side. Lay upper-half patchwork piece on top of main piece with right side facing out. Sew along top and sides using regular stitch. Sew along bottom using zigzag stitch, securing piece firmly. With wrong sides together, sew flap piece to main piece using 1/2" seam allowance.

Step 4. Attach side pieces

Wrap fabric around cardboard file folder exactly as it will sit when finished. Mark where side pieces will sit. Sew side pieces in place.

Step 5. Trim extra fabric

Trim all around file folder to 1/4" from outside of seam lines.

Step 6. Make leaf catches

Using spray-on fabric adhesive, glue two leftover pieces of melton together. Draw two leaves with veins on fabric using tailor's chalk. Sew along vein lines and around leaves with small zigzag stitch. Cut leaf edge, trimming close to, but just outside zigzag stitch. Sew leaf catches to file folder by hand. Use twill tape as a tie.

Project 12

Floor Play

CASUAL YET SOPHISTICATED, THESE COLOURFUL FLOOR CUSHIONS ARE EASY TO SEW.

Editor's note:
Tailored but cosy, these cushions are great for softening the hard lines of a modern room. Covered with denim or colourful twill, they would also make fun and durable seating for kids' rooms or playrooms.

Difficulty level:
Average

Projects:
Channelled roll cushion
Cube cushion
Slab cushion

Pull up a cushion and get down to earth — floor seating is back in vogue! Right in step with pared-down "East meets West" style, floor cushions are simple, chic furnishings — an updated version of the memorable beanbag chair. The styles shown here — roll, cube and slab — represent advanced, intermediate and easy levels of sewing respectively. The cushions are filled with Dacron-wrapped foam, and we've included instructions on how to make these forms yourself. Lush fabrics, like silk and velvet in hot pink and orange, give these basic shapes an unexpected jolt of sophistication; use durable fabrics like fleece or denim for family room versions, or retro ultrasuede for a look that's funky, fashionable and fun.

A chanelled floor mat is ideal for lounging in front of the fireplace. The cushion is rolled at one end to create a headrest – in fact, the whole mat can be easily rolled up for storage. Toronto interior designer Brian Gluckstein shows this cushion style in many of his interiors; we took inspiration from Gluckstein for our own version.

PHOTOGRAPHY BY VIRGINIA MACDONALD

Check the Yellow Pages for upholstery and fabric supply stores that sell foam and Dacron to the public. Four-inch-thick foam is sold in full- or half-size slabs (a full-size slab is 88" long), but for a small fee some suppliers will cut the foam to a desired size. If you purchase a large slab of foam, you can easily cut it yourself using a knife-blade saw. Dacron is sold by the bag in fabric supply stores; it is often referred to as quilting batting. We used "sheet Dacron" for these projects.

CHANNELLED ROLL CUSHION

Due to the size of this cushion, you might want to ask a friend to help out. Use a heavy-duty sewing machine needle as the roll is quite thick.

Finished size: 12' l. x 30" w.

MATERIALS & TOOLS

4	yds. 1/2"-thick x 30"-wide foam
4	bags Dacron
	Spray adhesive (we used Super 77 by 3M)
8 1/2	yds. silk fabric

Step 1. Make form

The form for this cushion roll is made from 1/2"-thick x 30"-wide foam sandwiched between two layers of Dacron. Using scissors or a small electric knife (such as a carving knife), cut a 12'-long piece of foam. Using a spray adhesive, sold at art-supply and hardware stores, sandwich the layer of foam between two layers of Dacron. For the best results when using spray adhesive, spray in a sweeping motion, covering both facing surfaces evenly.

Step 2. Cut and sew fabric

Cut two pieces of fabric to 12 1/4' x 33". Sew fabric, right sides together, leaving an opening at one end to insert the form. Turn fabric casing right side out. Insert form carefully and smooth it out, making sure form is lying flat inside cover. Sew up open end.

Step 3. Mark channels

Because pushing a thick foam form through a home sewing machine can be quite difficult, sew channels close together. For example, space channels 2" apart rather than 4" (though we spaced our channels 4" apart). The closer together the channels, the easier they are to sew, as closer seams will compress the foam. On one side of the cushion, starting from the top end, use a tape measure and tailor's chalk to make marks, evenly spaced, along the length of the fabric, to indicate the location of each channel. Make the same marks on the other side of the cushion, starting, again, from the top end. Once you have marked the spacing of the channels on both sides of the cushion, use tailor's chalk to draw lines across the width of the cushion, joining each pair of marks together.

Step 4. Sew channels

Sew along each line to the centre of your pillow. As you sew towards the centre, make sure the foam form does not shift within the cover (enlist a helper to support the roll as you run it through the sewing machine). Compress the form as you feed it under the presser foot — it will become more and more of a challenge as you make your way towards the centre of the cushion. Also, make sure the tension on the presser foot is very light to allow for the thickness of the pillow to be quilted, and that your sewing machine is big enough to handle the amount of material passing under the arm. When you reach the centre of the cushion, start at the other side and work your way toward the centre again to complete the quilting. Repeat along the length of the roll.

Square cube cushions are this year's must-have multipurpose furnishing: use them as seating, for ottomans or footstools, or lined up in a row to create a coffee table. The medium-density foam form gives these cushions the stability and firmness to support a cup of coffee as well as the strength to support your weight.

CUBE CUSHION

Finished size: 20" l. x 20" w. x 16" h.

MATERIALS & TOOLS

1	full slab 4"-thick medium-density foam
1	bag Dacron
	Spray adhesive (we used Super 77 by 3M)
2 1/2"	yds. velvet fabric

Step 1. Make form

This form was constructed from four 4"-thick foam pieces, bonded together using spray glue. Using a knife-blade saw, cut four pieces of foam to 20" x 20". Layer the pieces one on top of the other to create a cube. Mist facing sides of each piece with spray adhesive, sold at art-supply and hardware stores. For the best results when using spray adhesive, spray in a sweeping motion, covering both facing surfaces evenly. Wrap the entire form in sheet Dacron, cutting and form-fitting it, then glueing it down well with the spray adhesive.

Brightly coloured silk cushions pull up nicely to a low coffee table for a casual dinner with friends. The cushions are 30"-square slabs – big enough to sit on comfortably, but not overwhelming in a small space. The cushion covers are made entirely from two, rather than several, separate pieces of fabric, a style of cover known as a "false box," and a technique that can be applied to other sewing projects.

Step 2. Cut fabric

The cushion cover is made of six fabric panels — four side panels and top and bottom panels. For the side panels, cut four pieces of fabric to 17 1/2" x 21 1/2". For the top and bottom panels, cut two pieces of fabric to

DIAGRAM 1

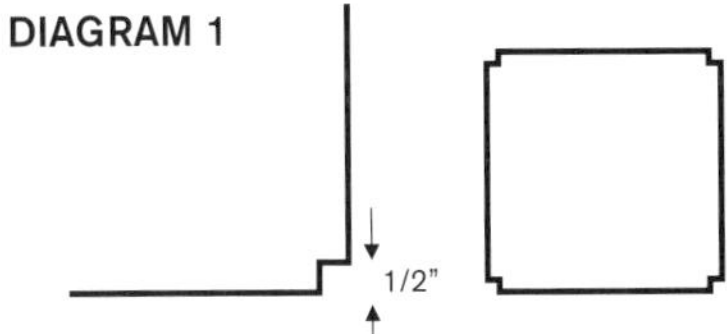

21 1/2" x 21 1/2". By notching the corners you will avoid pivoting sharply at each corner when sewing the cover. To notch the corners on all six panels, measure out from each corner 1/2" on either side and make a mark. Cut inward from each point until the cuts meet to make a 1/2" notch (see Diagram 1).

Step 3. Sew cushion cover

Sew each of the four side panels to the next, 17 1/2" end to 17 1/2" end, right sides together, to form a row. Sew the far left edge of the first panel to the far right edge of the last panel, right sides together, to form a tube consisting of four sides, right sides facing inward. Sew the top panel to the top edge of all four sides, right sides together, making sure the needle of the sewing machine is resting directly in the point of the notch at each panel corner. Sew one edge of the bottom panel to one bottom edge of one side, right sides together, leaving the other three sides open in order to insert the form. Turn cube cover right side out. Carefully insert form into cover, smoothing out any twisted seams. Slipstitch the three remaining edges of the bottom piece to the bottom edges of the remaining three sides. If possible, have a friend compress the foam as you slipstitch, so the edges will be tight.

SLAB CUSHION

Finished size: 30" w. x 30" l. x 4" h.

MATERIALS & TOOLS

1/2	slab 4"-thick foam
1	bag Dacron
	Spray adhesive (we used Super 77 by 3M)
2	yds. silk fabric
	30" zipper

Step 1. Make form

The interior form is made from 30"-wide, 4"-thick medium-density foam. Using a knife-blade saw, cut the foam to a 30" length to make a 30" square. Cut Dacron to fit the foam. Lightly mist both the foam and Dacron with spray adhesive, sold at art-supply and hardware stores, and join them together. For the best results when using spray adhesive, spray in a sweeping motion, covering both facing surfaces evenly.

Step 2. Cut fabric

Cut two squares of fabric to 35 1/2" x 35 1/2".

Step 3. Sew fabric

Place squares of fabric right sides together and stitch down one side with large basting stitches, leaving a 1/2" seam allowance. Press the seam flat. Centre a 30" zipper, face down, on the seam. Stitch the zipper down, reinforcing well at both ends. Remove basting stitches to expose zipper. With right sides together, stitch the remaining three sides together.

Step 4. Make "false box"

Pull apart the two pieces of fabric with your hands so that the corners jut out. Choose one corner and lay it flat so that the seams line up, one on top of the other. Pin through the seam. From the tip of the corner, measure downward, along the lined-up seams, 2 1/4" and make a mark. Draw a 4 1/2" line perpendicular to the seam at that point. Stitch across the seam along the line you just made, making sure you backstitch well at the beginning and the end (see Diagram 2). Snip off the corner, about 1/2" above the new seam. Repeat on all four corners and turn right side out.

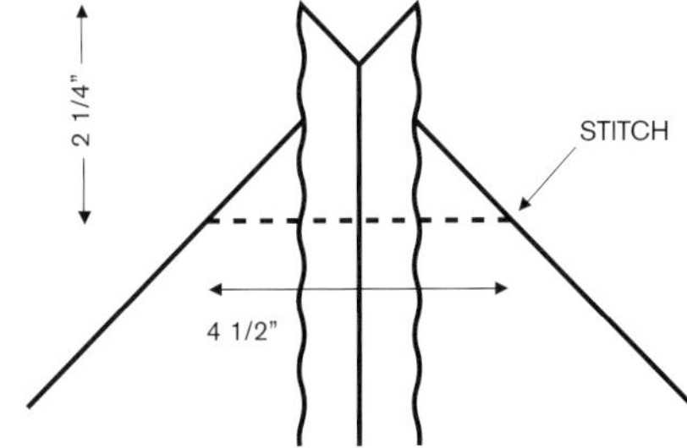

DIAGRAM 2

Step 5. Insert cushion form

Insert the form through the zipper, compressing the form as you go, until it is completely inside the cover. Smooth out the foam, then smooth out the seams so they are all travelling in one direction. If the corners appear "hollow," fill them out with extra pieces of Dacron. Zip up the cushion, compressing the foam. Make sure the zipper does not catch on the Dacron.

Project 13

Window Dressing

THREE BREEZY SUMMER CURTAINS YOU CAN SEW.

Editor's note:
Fresh and fun, these are curtains you'll pull out year after year as respite from winter's neutrals. The screen is a simple and inexpensive alternative to installing frosted glass to disguise an unappealing view.

Difficulty level:
Average

Projects:
Pop-in window panel
Sheer striped panel
Patchwork panels

Like cottage furniture draped in refreshing white cotton slipcovers, or porch rockers spruced up with a glossy coat of colour, windows deserve a summer makeover. Our lightweight treatments offer barely-there coverage and a splash of colour in three styles. Two are simple sewing projects: a gauze sheer in alternating colours and silk patchwork panels. The first is a unique pop-in window panel fashioned like an artist's canvas that's stretched over a frame. All styles are unlined, allowing light to filter through; clip-on curtain rings are the only hardware. This year, give windows a rest from their winter wardrobe and treat them to a new summer dress.

Inspired by the construction of an artist's canvas, this window panel is almost an architectural element in itself. A linen screen, accented with a coloured border, is stretched over a frame of medium density fibreboard. Measured to fit inside the moulding and rest on the sill, the panel pops in and out with ease. Use it to camouflage an unsightly window or unpleasant view, or for a room where you want privacy without forfeiting natural light.

PHOTOGRAPHY BY VIRGINIA MACDONALD

POP-IN WINDOW PANEL

MATERIALS & TOOLS

- 3/4" medium density fibreboard (MDF) or pine
- 3/4" nails
- Wood glue
- Mitre box
- Handsaw or mitre saw
- Hammer
- Sandpaper
- Paint
- Paintbrush
- 1 1/2 yds. of cotton gauze (for main cloth panel)
- 1 1/2 yds. of cotton gauze (for screen border)

Frame

We used 3/4" MDF for our window frame because it is exceptionally smooth and easy to paint. The MDF should be cut as wide as your widest window mullion, so only glass is seen through the fabric screen. Our frame was 26 1/2" wide.

Step 1. Measure the inside width of the window frame to determine the width of your panel. Decide how high you want your panel to be and measure from the windowsill up to this desired height. We made a panel that rises from the windowsill up to the horizontal cross piece, three-quarters the height of the window. Note: If you're using a thin fabric (like cotton gauze, as we did), deduct 1/8" from each of your original frame measurements, as the fabric will add girth to the frame once it is stretched over it. If you're using a thick fabric, deduct 1/4" from each of your measurements.

Step 2. With a mitre saw, or a handsaw and mitre box, cut two side pieces and a top and bottom piece. Mitre the ends of each piece so that each end is angled 45°.

Step 3. Apply dabs of wood glue to the ends of each piece and, using 3/4" nails, nail the four pieces together.

Step 4. Lightly sand the edges of the frame until they're smooth, and paint the frame in a colour similar to the colour of your border fabric.

Border

The border is sewn directly onto a cotton gauze "screen," then stretched over the frame and fastened to the back using a staple gun. The mitred corners of the border will line up with the mitred corners of the frame.
The border will lie just inside the frame.

Step 1. Measure the outside width of the frame. Our frame measured 39" x 26 1/2". Draw a line on drafting paper representing that measurement. Label the ends of the line A and B. Measure the inside width of the frame and determine the depth you want your border to be (our depth measured 5"), then draw another horizontal line, at that width, parallel to the first, at that depth. (Add 2" of excess fabric all around the outer edges of the border to be sure you'll have enough fabric to staple the border to the back of the frame.) From points A and B, draw 45° diagonal lines from the outer width of the frame in to the inner width. See Diagram. Add a 1/4" seam allowance to all edges. Cut two pieces of fabric to these measurements.

Step 2. Repeat the measuring technique described in Step 1 for the length of the border and cut out two pieces of fabric to these measurements.

Step 3. Stitch together one width-long border piece and length-long border piece with right sides together using a 1/4" seam allowance and stopping 1/4" short of the inner edge. Repeat for the other three corners. Press open seam allowances of mitred corners. Turn inner edge in 1/4" and press.

Main Gauze Panel

Step 1. Cut out a main gauze panel that is the size of the wood frame plus 2" on all sides. Lay the gauze border right side up on top of the right side of the main gauze panel and pin into place. Topstitch along the inner edge of the border.

Step 2. Place bordered fabric panel over the frame; make sure that the mitred corners of the fabric are directly over the mitred corners of the frame.

Step 3. Pull the fabric around the edges to the back of the frame, using even tension. Staple the fabric onto the backside of the frame. Pleat corners and trim away excess fabric.

Step 4. Place screen into window frame.

DIAGRAM

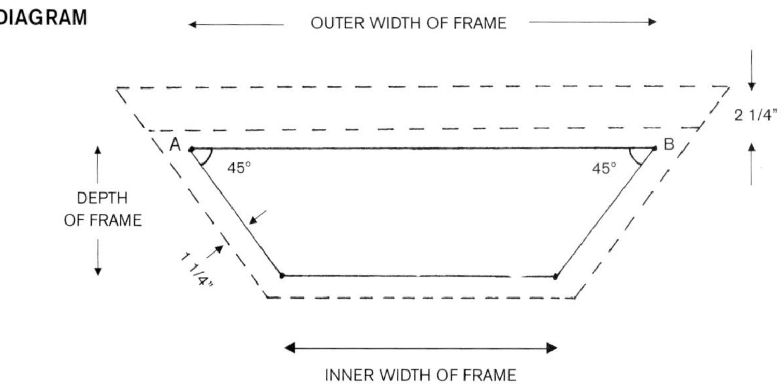

Left: A drapery panel of gauze stripes filters light exquisitely, so it need not be tied back; let it fall instead in soft folds to the floor.

Right: As sunlight filters through, the patchwork panels create a stained-glass effect. Each square of raw silk, in five delicate shades, measures 18" x 18".

SHEER STRIPED PANEL

MATERIALS & TOOLS

Fabric: approx. 3 yds. of gauze per colour; two colours recommended (this measurement will depend on the size of the window you're covering)
Clip-on curtain rings
Curtain rod

Step 1. To determine the finished width of the panel, multiply the width of the window by 2 and add 4" (2" per side) for side hems. Divide by 5 to get the width of each fabric strip. The finished length is the distance from rod to floor plus 6" (2" for the top hem, 4" for the bottom hem). Our finished width was 86"; the finished length was 92". We used five strips — three strips of lavender and two strips of yellow — and cut each strip of colour 18" w. x 98" l.

Step 2. Using pinking shears, cut out panels of coloured gauze.

Step 3. Sew together with a 1/2" seam allowance, alternating each colour. If you have a serger, finish the raw edges, leaving a 1/4" seam allowance. Otherwise, finish raw edges with a zigzag stitch.

Step 4. Hem the top and sides by turning the edges 1" twice. Hem the bottom by turning the edges 2" twice.

Step 5. Press all seams and edges on low heat. Hang panel from curtain rod using clip-on curtain rings.

PATCHWORK PANELS

MATERIALS & TOOLS

Fabric: approx. 2 yds. of silk per colour; five colours recommended (this measure will depend on the size of the window you're covering)
Clip-on curtain rings
Curtain rod

Step 1. To determine the finished width of each panel, multiply the overall width of the window by 1 1/2 and divide by 2. To calculate the width of each individual silk square, divide this number by 3. For the length, measure the distance from your hanging point to the floor, plus 6" (2" for the top hem, 4" for the bottom hem). To calculate the length of each silk square, divide this number by 5. In our project, each panel was 54" wide and 92" long. These measurements allowed for 20" squares, which included a 1/2" seam allowance. Therefore, each panel had three squares in width and five squares in length.

Step 2. Using pinking shears, cut out squares of silk. Determine the order of colours that will create the random patchwork effect. Label each square with masking tape to record their order.

Step 3. Sew together the three squares that form the first row, leaving a 1/2" seam allowance between squares. Press seam allowances open. Repeat for the other rows and press seam allowances open. Repeat for second panel. Sew together rows to make each panel, pressing seam allowances open.

Step 4. Finish top and side edges of each panel using a 1" seam allowance, turned twice. Finish the bottom edge of each panel using a 2" seam allowance, turned twice. The hemmed edges will create squares slightly smaller around the perimeter of the panel than in the centre. Press all seams and edges on low heat.

Step 5. Hang panels from rod using clip-on rings. The effect will be that of a colourful patchwork quilt.

Project 14

Summer Dress

TRANSFORM BASIC GARDEN FURNITURE WITH SIX EASY-SEW IDEAS.

Editor's note:
For a more current, natural palette, slipcover the armchairs with white cotton duck, trim the tablecloth with brown burlap and sew bistro and bench cushions out of brown-and-white ticking or awning-stripe fabric.

Difficulty level:
Average

Projects:
- Bistro chair cushion and cap
- Slipcovers
- Tablecloth
- Ground cushion
- Bench seat cushion
- Terrycloth cushions

It's time to pull out the patio furniture again. For those of us whose decorating budget doesn't stretch quite as far as the back porch, that might mean unearthing a jumble of mismatched or tired-looking tables and chairs. But don't despair — we've created six easy sewing projects that bring colour, comfort and a coordinated look to plain outdoor furnishings. For the standard resin armchair, we've designed a full-length slipcover; for classic folding bistro chairs, a jaunty back cap and seat pad. Our garden bench gets a softly shaped, weather-resistant cushion made from Sunbrella, a fabric designed for outdoor use that we've also used for an oversized ground cushion. Finishing touches include colourful throw cushions made from inexpensive terrycloth and a cotton tablecloth embellished with a border of bright fabric paint. Summer living should be easy and casual but not without style, and these projects fit the bill.

A hodgepodge of mismatched furnishings take cover to make a lively grouping.

PHOTOGRAPHY BY CURTIS TRENT

Note: Before beginning any of these projects, wash and dry your fabric to prevent shrinkage when washing finished pieces.

Project 14: Garden furniture cover-ups

BISTRO CHAIR CUSHION AND CAP

MATERIALS & TOOLS

1 yd. 54"-wide fabric
14" zipper
1 pillow form approx. 18" x 18"

Step 1. Measure and cut back cap
As folding bistro chairs vary in size, we have not included exact dimensions. However, 1 yard of fabric should be enough to cover most models. The back cap is intended to cover just the wooden slats of the back.

Measure width and height of chair back. Add 1 1/2" to width for seam allowances and 1 1/2" to height for hems. Fold fabric in half and mark these measurements onto it. (The fold line will become the top edge of back cap.) Cut out without unfolding.

Step 2. Sew back cap
Unfold cutout fabric and refold it, right sides together. Sew side seams with a 3/4" seam allowance. Press seams to one side. Turn bottom edges up 3/4", press, turn up another 3/4" and stitch. Press.

Step 3. Measure and cut seat cushion
Measure width and depth of seat. Add 4" to width and 4" to depth (so the cushion cover will accommodate a thick pillow form) plus an extra 1 1/2" to each measurement for seam allowances. Mark the fabric and cut two panels to these measurements. Set aside.

Step 4. Make ties
You will need four ties per cushion. For each tie, cut a strip of fabric 18" long and 2" wide. Fold each strip in half along its length, wrong sides together. Press. Open fabric out and press raw edges in so they meet at the fold line you have just created. At one end of each tie, turn in raw edge about 1/4", then fold tie in half lengthwise. Press. Stitch across width of tie at folded end, pivot, then stitch along length, staying as close to the edges as possible. (You don't need to stitch down the raw edge of the other end as it will be inserted into the seam of the cushion cover.)

Step 5. Insert ties and make zipper opening
Place one panel of cushion fabric on a flat surface, right side up. Lay one pair of ties (one tie directly on top of the other) over it, about 1 1/2" in from one side, with the raw edges of the ties flush with what will be the "back" edge of the cushion. Lay another pair of ties 1 1/2" in from the other side. Lay the second panel of cushion fabric on top of all this, right side down (i.e., so the right sides of the two panels are facing) and pin. Along the "back" edge, make a mark about 2" in from the side. Stitch from the side until you reach the 2" mark, then pivot and backtrack a few stitches, so the ties are sewn between the two fabric panels. See Diagram 1. Repeat at other side. Open out the panels so you have one large rectangular piece and, with wrong sides still up, press seams open.

Step 6. Insert zipper
Lay the zipper right side down along opening and, using a zipper foot, stitch along length of zipper, as close to the teeth as possible. At end, pivot and repeat down other side. Turn fabric right side up and press fabric over zipper so fabric edges meet over the zipper teeth. With fabric still right side up, use a regular sewing machine foot to topstitch 1/4" away from zipper teeth, all around zipper opening. This will keep the teeth of the zipper hidden when the zipper is closed. See Diagram 2.

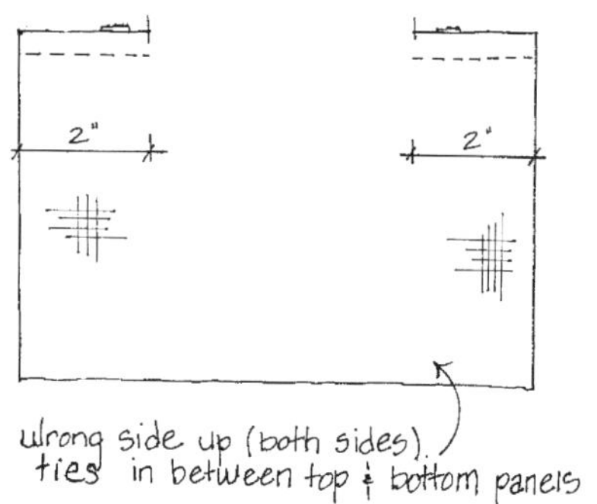

DIAGRAM 1

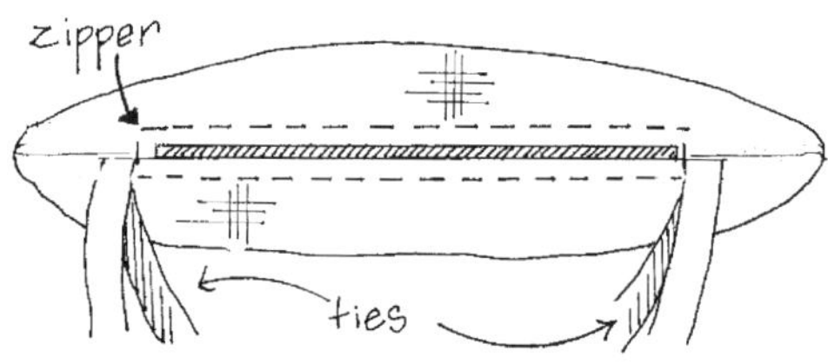

DIAGRAM 2

Step 7. Finish cushion
Now that the zippered edge is complete, fold so right sides are together. Stitch along one side using a 3/4" seam allowance, pivot and stitch the "front" edge, pivot again and stitch the second side. Unzip zipper, turn the cover the right way out, and with a blunt instrument (e.g., the end of a knitting needle), gently push corners out.

SLIPCOVERS

This is a loose-fitting slipcover that is easy to install and remove and doesn't have any ties or zippers. The slipcover is made from seven separate panels: back, front, seat, outside arms and inside arms. To prevent costly mistakes, inexpensive fabric lining is used to make a template of the slipcover panels before cutting them from the decorative fabric.

MATERIALS & TOOLS

4 yds. decorative fabric per chair
4 yds. fabric lining
Masking tape
Tailor's chalk

DIAGRAM 3

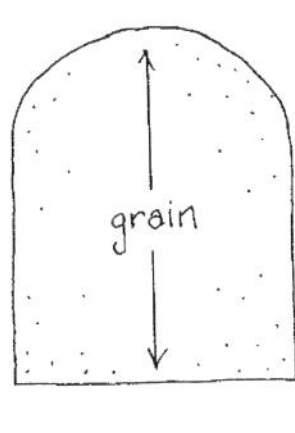

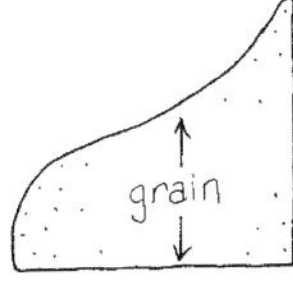

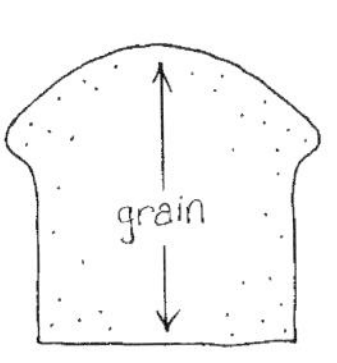

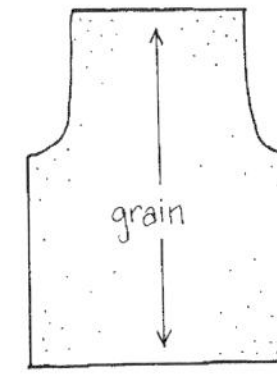

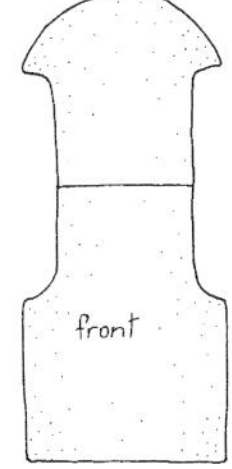

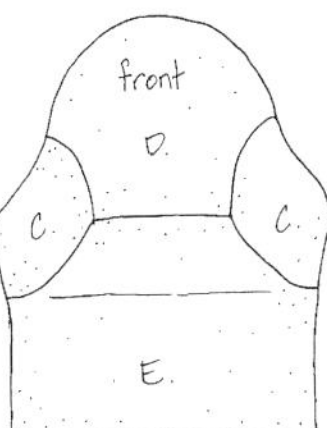

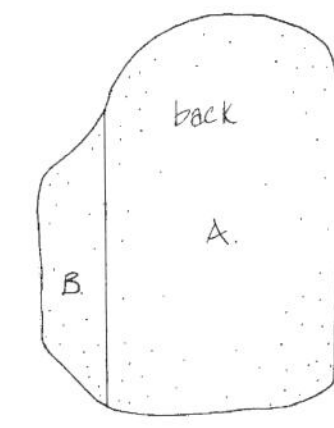

Step 1. "Dissect" chair

Using masking tape, tape a "meridian" line down the centre of the chair back and the centre of the chair front. Also place pieces of tape at the point where the arms join the back of the chair, and a piece across the back of the seat where it joins the chair back.

Step 2. Make back panel template

From fabric lining, cut out a generous piece, at least 6" longer and wider than the back of the chair. Draw a pencil line down the centre of this piece to indicate the grain of the fabric (this will help you keep the fabric straight when you're fitting it to the top of the chair). Next, drape the piece of fabric over the back of the chair so that the line you have drawn matches up with the masking tape line on the chair (excess fabric will overlap over the front of the chair and puddle on the floor at the back). To hold the lining in place, tape it to the chair in a few places.

Using tailor's chalk, trace the shape of the chair back onto the lining fabric, following the curve; stop when you reach the tape marks where the chair arms join the back. Also mark a hemline at the bottom of the lining, at the point where it just grazes the floor. Remove the lining from the chair and lay it on a flat surface.

At the point where the curve of the back ends and the arms begin, draw a chalk line straight down until you meet the marked hemline. Add 3/4" to sides and top for seam allowance, plus 4" to bottom for hem. Cut panel out of the lining. This is your back panel. See Diagram 3A.

Step 3. Make outside arm panel template

To make the outside arm panel template, repeat the draping process from Step 2 on one arm, using the grain line to keep the fabric straight and tape marks on the arm to indicate where to begin drawing the chalk outline. Trace curve of the arm down to hemline. (You only need to do this once; you can use the same template twice when cutting out your decorative fabric, since the outside arm pieces are mirror images.) Remove lining from chair, lay flat and add 3/4" to sides and top for seam allowance, plus 4" to bottom for hem. Cut out panel. See Diagram 3B.

Step 4. Make inside back and inside arm panel templates

Repeat the draping process from Step 2, using the meridian tape line on the inside of the chair back to keep the lining straight. Draw the curve of the chair back onto the lining, stopping where it meets the seat. Lay lining flat on floor, add 3/4" to all sides and cut out. See Diagram 3C. For inside arm, drape fabric over arm and trace the curve of the arm from the point where it meets the chair back to the point where it meets the seat. (You only need to do this once; you can use the same template twice when cutting out decorative fabric, since inside arm pieces are mirror images.) Remove from the chair and lay flat. Add 3/4" to all sides and cut out. See Diagram 3D.

Step 5. Make seat and chair front templates

The seat and front of the slipcover are made from one piece of fabric. Repeat the draping process from Step 2, using the meridian tape line on the chair seat to keep the lining straight, draping the fabric over the seat and down over the front of the chair. Trace the shape, remove fabric and lay it flat. Add 3/4" to sides and top for seam allowance and 4" to bottom for hem. Cut out. See Diagram 3E.

Step 6. Cut decorative fabric

Lay the template panels over the decorative fabric and cut out all seven pieces.

Step 7. Sew slipcovers

Sew the slipcovers in two large sections, first the back and then the front. Make the back by sewing the outside back panel (A) to one outside side panel (B) with right sides together. Repeat for the other outside side panel. Press seams towards centre back. Make the front of the slipcover by sewing the inside back panel (D) to the seat panel (E). Press seams upwards. Then sew each of the inside arms (C) to the seat/back panel. Lastly, sew the back panel to the front panel. See Diagrams. Finish the slipcover by turning up a 2" hem, pressing, then turning up another 2". Press and sew.

TABLECLOTH

Finished size: 52" x 52".

Our tablecloth measured 52" x 52", with a 2 1/2" border, which we painted a vibrant red. Before cutting and sewing, wash and dry fabric: whenever you use fabric paint, fabric should always be prewashed.

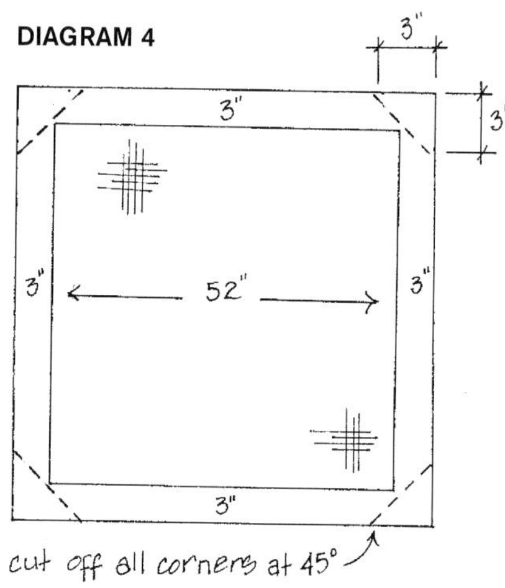

MATERIALS & TOOLS

- 2 yds. 60"-wide white cotton fabric
- Kraft paper
- Fabric paint (we used Pebeo)
- Small brush
- Iron

Step 1. Cut fabric

Cut a square of fabric 58" x 58".

Step 2. Mitre corners

Measure 3" in from outside edges of fabric square and, using tailor's chalk, mark a square that measures 52" x 52" on the fabric. At each corner, draw a line that cuts across this 3" "border," touching the corner of the inner rectangle to create a triangle with 45° angles at the corners. See Diagram 4. Cut the corners off along the diagonal lines, so you are left with an octagon. With fabric right side up, fold one diagonal edge of the octagon so the "points" of the octagon meet, and pin. Stitch the folded fabric closed, using a 1/2" seam allowance. See Diagrams 4 to 6. Repeat for other three corners. When all corners are stitched, turn

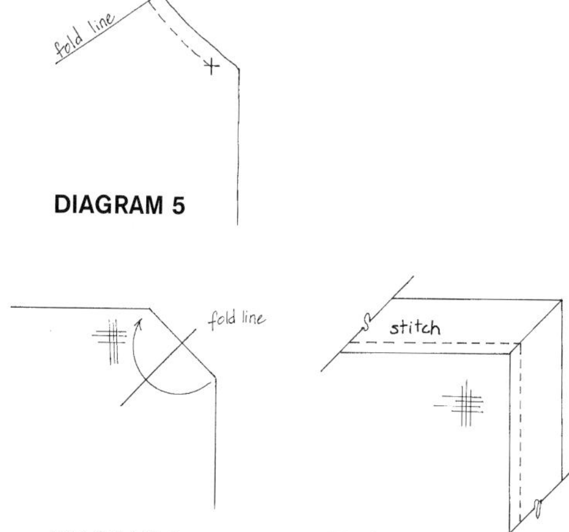

them inside out and turn fabric square wrong side up. You should have a border on the back of the tablecloth that measures about 3".

Step 3. Stitch down border

Fold raw edge of border under 1/2" and pin. Topstitch 1/4" from inner edge of border. See Diagram 7. Press.

Step 4. Decorate edges

On a large surface, lay out a protective covering of kraft paper. Lay the cloth on top of it, right side up. Begin "filling in" the border with paint, using the edge of the cloth and the line of topstitching as your guides. Start at one corner and work your way around all four sides, using paint sparingly to avoid a thick, uneven layer. Leave paint to dry completely (at least 24 hours). Lay a cloth over the painted border and "set" paint with an iron on medium heat, or follow instructions on paint container.

Project 14:
Garden furniture cover-ups

GROUND CUSHION

Finished size: 30" x 30"

MATERIALS & TOOLS

- 2 yds. outdoor acrylic or Sunbrella fabric, 48" wide
- 1/2 yd. contrasting outdoor acrylic or Sunbrella fabric, for piping
- 4 yds. 1/4" cotton piping cord
- 1 24" zipper
- 30" x 30" foam cushion form

Step 1. Measure and cut cushion panels

Cut two pieces of fabric measuring 31 1/2" x 31 1/2" (30" plus 3/4" seam allowances).

Step 2. Make piping

Make 6 yards of "bias" from the contrasting fabric. With the fabric flat in front of you, fold one corner of the fabric across the grain to meet the lengthwise grain. Mark this fold with a pencil. Open up the fabric with the pencil line on top and, using a ruler, mark off lines parallel to the fold line and 2" apart.

Cut along these lines to make strips. Place two strips right sides together and stitch. Repeat until you have a 6-yard strip of bias. Press seams open and trim. See Diagrams 8 and 9.

To cover the piping cord, fold the bias strip over the cord, right side out. Keep cord at the centre with raw edges of bias strip meeting. Stitch near but not through the cord. The seam will be hidden when the piping is stitched onto the cushion cover.

Step 3. Attach piping to fabric panel

On one fabric panel, with right side facing up, pin piping around the perimeter of the fabric so that raw edges of piping are flush with raw edges of fabric (i.e., so raw edges of piping face outward, not towards the centre of the cushion panel). Clip seam allowance of piping at corners to allow it to turn corners without bunching. Stitch piping down, making stitches as close as possible to the piping cord.

DIAGRAM 8

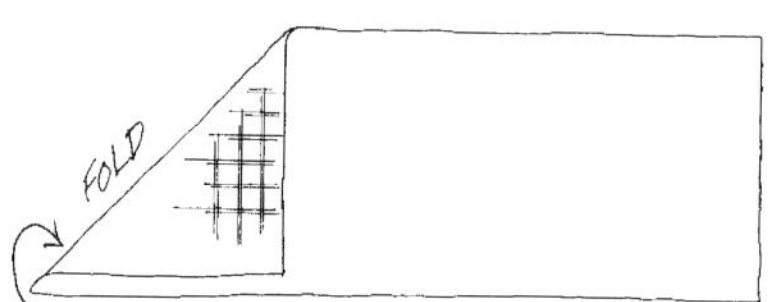

DIAGRAM 9

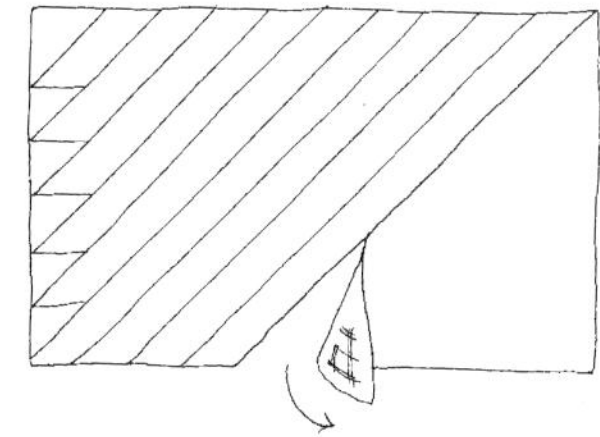

DIAGRAM 10

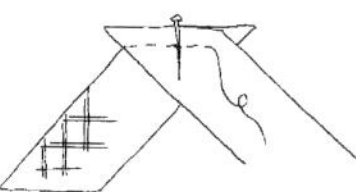

DIAGRAM 11

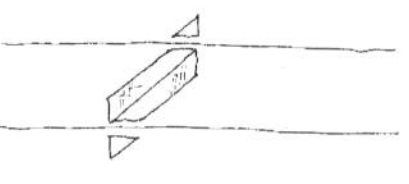

Step 4. Sew panels together
Place second panel on top of panel with piping, right sides together. Choose the edge on which you want to have the zipper. On this edge, make a mark 2" in from each side. Beginning at one of these 2" marks, stitch around the cushion cover, stopping when you reach the 2" mark at the other side. You will be left with an opening large enough to accommodate the zipper. Press.

Step 5. Insert zipper and finish cushion
Lay the zipper face down over the opening and pin. Using a zipper foot attachment, stitch along the length of the zipper, first along the edge of the panel with the piping sewn to it, then along the edge of the other panel. Unzip the zipper, and turn the cushion right side out. Zip up and use a regular sewing machine foot to topstitch through decorative fabric 1/4" away from zipper teeth, all around zipper opening. This will keep the teeth of the zipper hidden when the zipper is closed. Insert cushion form.

BENCH SEAT CUSHION

This cushion features "Turkish" corners — soft pleats at each corner that give the cushion a casual appearance.

Note: Since fabric is usually only sold in 48" or 54" widths, you will have to seam together pieces to make a cushion long enough to fit most benches. If you don't want seams, you can use a solid fabric sideways — this is called "railroading." This method won't work with stripes, however, unless you want them running horizontally along the length of the bench.

Finished size: 60" x 16" x 3"

MATERIALS & TOOLS
4 1/2 yds. Sunbrella fabric, 48" wide
1/2 yd. contrasting Sunbrella fabric, for piping
6 yds. 1/4" piping cord
Tailor's chalk
48" zipper
60" x 16" x 3" foam or feather pillow form

Step 1. Make cushion panels
For the top centre panel of the cushion, cut a piece of fabric large enough to cover the depth of the bench, plus half the thickness of the cushion form on each side, plus 3/4" on each side for seam allowance. (Since we were working with 48"-wide fabric, our bench was 16" deep, and our foam was 3" thick, we cut a panel 16" + 1 1/2" + 1 1/2" + 3/4" + 3/4" = 22" deep x 48" wide.) Cut another piece of fabric the same size and then cut it in half. With right sides together, stitch the small panels to either end of the large (centre) panel, matching the pattern so that it repeats properly. Trim away an equal amount of excess fabric from either end of this new large panel, so that it measures 60" wide (or the width of your bench) plus 2" at either end for pleats. Repeat above procedure to make the bottom panel of cushion. See Diagram 12.

Step 2. Make Turkish pleats
Lay out top and bottom panels, right sides up. Measure 2" in from both sides of each corner and mark with chalk. With right sides together, fold one corner, bringing chalk marks together to form a pleat. See Diagram 13. Spread corner flat and pin to hold the pleat. Stay stitch. Repeat for all corners on top and bottom panels.

Step 3. Make piping and attach to top panel
From the 1/2 yard of contrasting fabric, make piping. See Ground Cushion, Step 2 for directions. Stitch it to the top panel of the cushion. See Ground Cushion, Step 3.

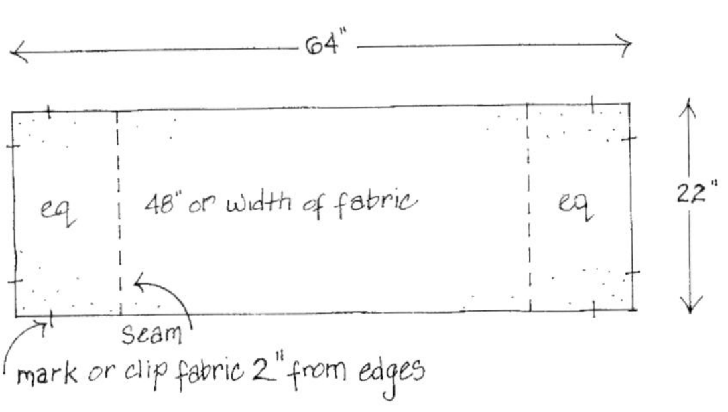

DIAGRAM 12

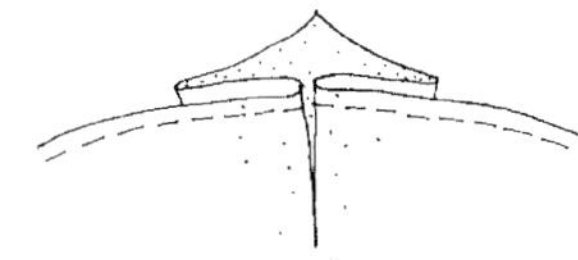

DIAGRAM 13

Step 4. Insert zipper and finish cushion
See Ground Cushion, Steps 4 and 5, stitching in 6" from corners instead of 2". Insert cushion form.

TERRYCLOTH CUSHIONS

For a great selection of colours, use bath towels; each towel will make one cushion. Prewash towels to ensure minimum shrinkage when cushion covers are washed. Buy pillow forms 1" larger than finished size of cushion.

Finished size: 16" x 16"

MATERIALS & TOOLS (for two cushions)
2 bath towels
2 12" zippers
2 17" pillow forms

Step 1. Cut fabric
Cut out two squares, 17 1/2" x 17 1/2", from each towel. Trim 1/2" from around corners to prevent "dog-eared" corners on finished cushion.

Step 2. Insert zipper and finish cushion
See Ground Cushion, Steps 4 and 5, ignoring references to piping. Insert cushion form.

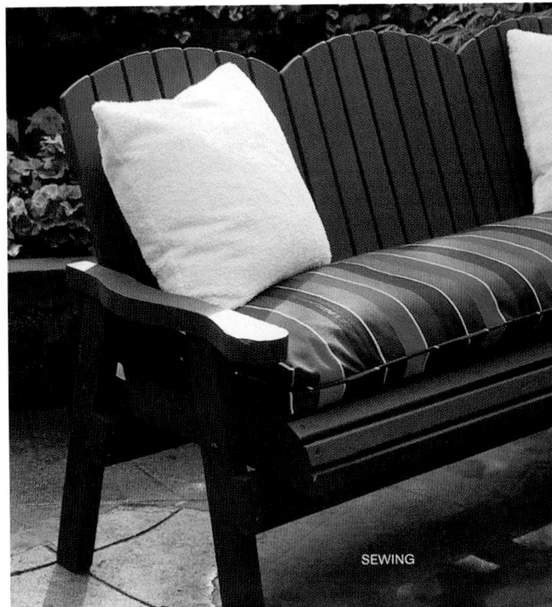

Project

UnderCover

STEP-BY-STEP INSTRUCTIONS FOR MAKING FOUR WARM AND BEAUTIFUL THROWS.

Editor's note:
Our directions for this must-have home accessory can be tailored to suit any decor. Take inspiration from a colourful patchwork quilt (all the rage) or make lightweight throws to counter summer air conditioning.

Difficulty level:
Average

Projects:
Reversible coating fabric throw
Menswear throw
Velvet damask throw
Polar fleece throw

In defiance of winter's bone-chilling winds, we present the ultimate antidote to cold weather: soft and luxurious throws that are equally at home over the back of a sofa or draped across your knees. We've used unconventional but widely available fabrics, like warm wool coating fabric and tweedy suiting cloth, to create throws you won't find in any store. Our directions will teach you how to self-border reversible fabric, sew patchwork panels with flanged borders, detail with woollen stitchery and embellish with a variety of trims. Take inspiration from our unusual fabric combinations and gorgeous colour schemes, and then get sewing — you'll soon be curled up beneath the cover of a comforting throw.

Upper left: Reversible wool coating fabric is a natural for throws: not only is it soft and warm, but also when the edges are turned over and topstitched, a contrasting border is created. Fluffy pompoms spaced every few inches dot the field.

Upper right: Classic menswear suiting fabrics and a paisley pattern come together in this tailored patchwork design. Plain camel-coloured wool fabric is used for the underside and for a wide border that surrounds the patchwork panel.

Lower right: Soft velvet damask and sumptuous gold satin are sewn together and embellished with gold fringe to create an elegant sofa throw.

Lower left: This cosy throw, made from easy-care polar fleece, is perfect in a child's room or a casual, contemporary interior. The four edges are folded in and mitred at the corners to create a border, then detailed with high-contrast cross-stitching.

PHOTOGRAPHY BY MARK MAINGUY

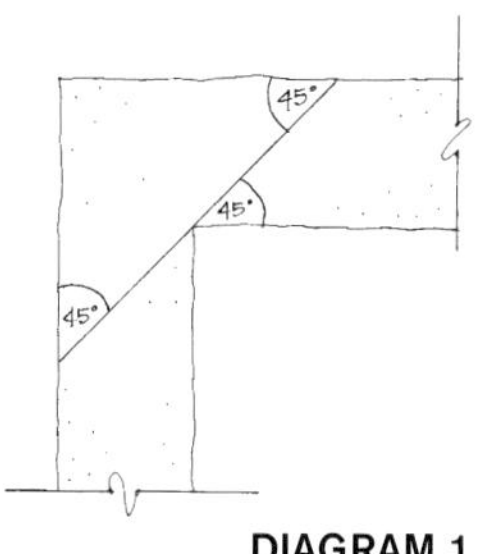

DIAGRAM 1

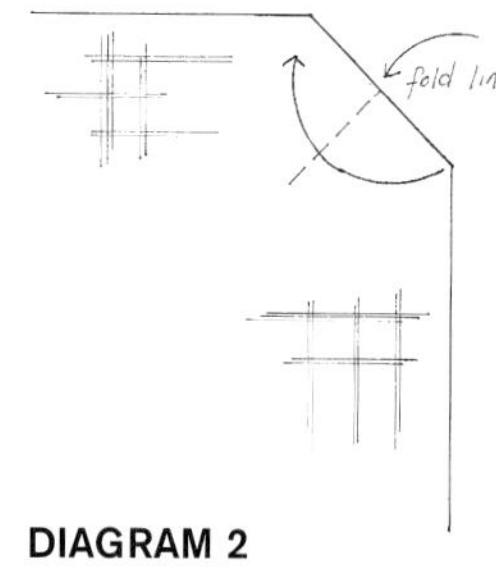

DIAGRAM 2

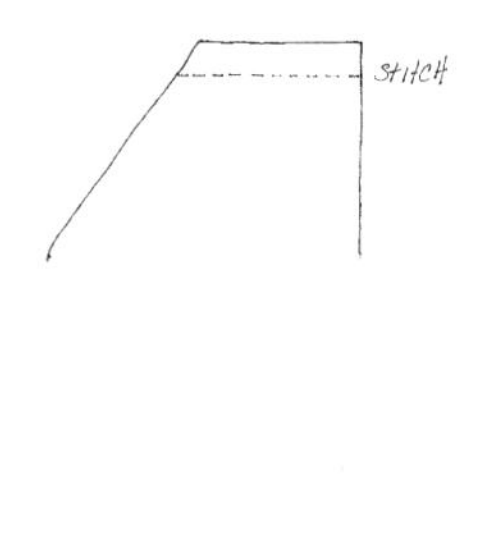

DIAGRAM 3

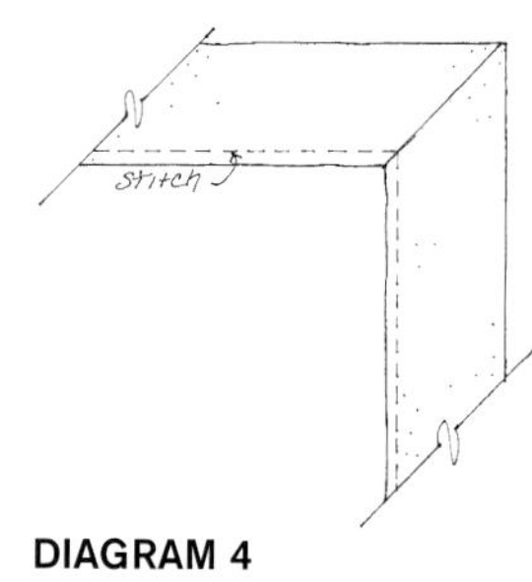

DIAGRAM 4

REVERSIBLE COATING FABRIC THROW

Finished size: 54" x 66"

MATERIALS & TOOLS

- 2 yds. two-colour reversible wool coating fabric
- Thread to match
- 50 pompoms, about 1" diam.
- Sharp scissors
- Measuring tape
- Tailor's chalk
- Long straight edge
- 45° square

Step 1. Cut the fabric

Measure and mark a rectangle that is 59" x 71". Measure 2 1/2" in from outside edges and, using tailor's chalk, mark another rectangle inside the first one that is 54" x 66".

Step 2. Mark points for pompoms

With fabric still laid flat, mark a point near one corner of the inner rectangle, 3" in from the top and side. Measure and mark points 12" apart to form a grid. In the centre of each 12" x 12" square in the grid, mark another point.

Step 3. Mitre corners

At each corner, draw a line that cuts across the "border," touching the corner of the inner rectangle to create a triangle with 45° angles at the corners (see Diagram 1). Cut the corners off along the diagonal lines, so you are left with an octagon. Turn fabric wrong side up. Fold one diagonal edge of the octagon so the "points" of the octagon meet, and pin (see Diagram 2). Stitch the folded fabric closed, using a 1/2" seam allowance (see Diagram 3). Repeat for other three corners. When all corners are stitched, turn them inside out and turn the fabric right side up. You should have a border that measures about 2 1/2".

Step 4. Stitch down border

Fold raw edge of border under 1/2" and pin. Topstitch 1/4" from inner edge of border (see Diagram 4).

Step 5. Sew on pompoms

At all marked points sew on a pompom, being sure to sew through the thick centre and to pull thread to secure tightly. Knot on back of throw.

MENSWEAR THROW

Finished size: 40" x 50"

MATERIALS & TOOLS

- 1/2 yd. each of four different types of fabric
- 3 yds. of camel-coloured wool fabric 54" wide
- Thread
- Sharp scissors
- Measuring tape
- Tailor's chalk
- Long straight edge
- Thick paper for template

Step 1. Cut template

Measure and cut an 11" square from the paper.

Step 2. Cut patchwork fabrics

Using the square template, mark and cut 20 squares from the four fabrics. You can vary the number of squares you cut of each fabric so that your final look is more random.

Step 3. Sew patchwork

Lay your squares out — four across and five down — in different arrangements until you arrive at one you find pleasing. Stitch together four rows of five squares (lay two squares right sides together and stitch down one side, using a 1/2" seam allowance). Press all seams flat. Sew the four lengths together, aligning raw edges carefully, using a 1/2" seam allowance.

Step 4. Cut backing

Unlike the other throws with borders, the border and backing on this throw are made from separate pieces of fabric. For the backing, mark and cut a 41" x 51" piece from the camel fabric.

Step 5. Attach backing to patchwork

With right sides together, align backing rectangle with patchwork rectangle and pin. With a 1/2" seam allowance, stitch three of the four sides together, leaving one 41"-wide side unstitched. Press seams to one side and turn the "pillowcase" shape you've created right side out. Turn raw edges of unstitched side under 1/2", press, pin and topstitch to close.

Step 6. Cut border pieces

On the remaining camel fabric, mark four 13"-wide pieces, two 51"-long and two 41"-long, to be used for the border. Create "points" on the border pieces by marking at the centre of each short side, and 6 1/2" in from the end of each long side. Join these marks to create an "arrowhead" shape (see Diagram 5). Cut pieces out.

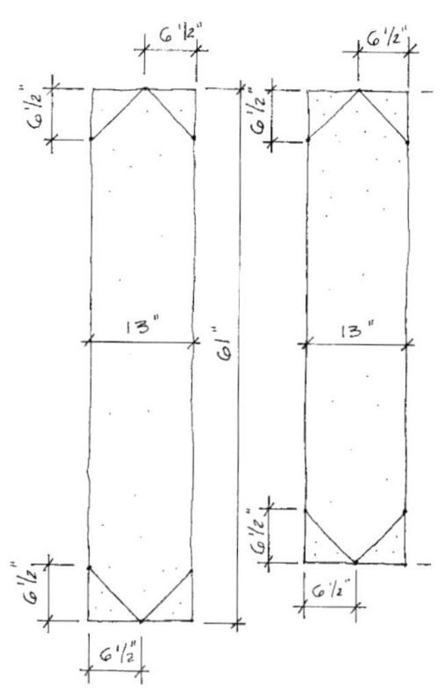

DIAGRAM 5

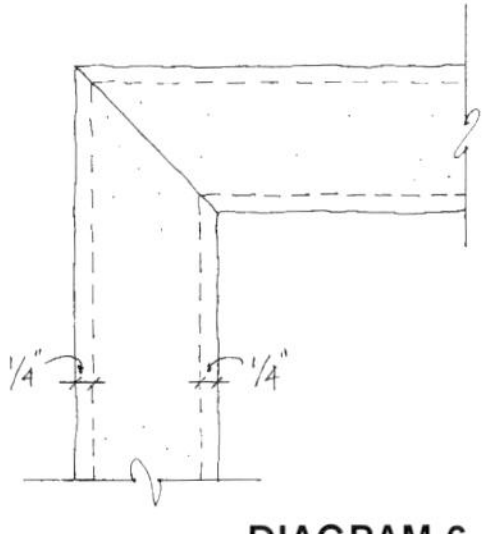

DIAGRAM 6

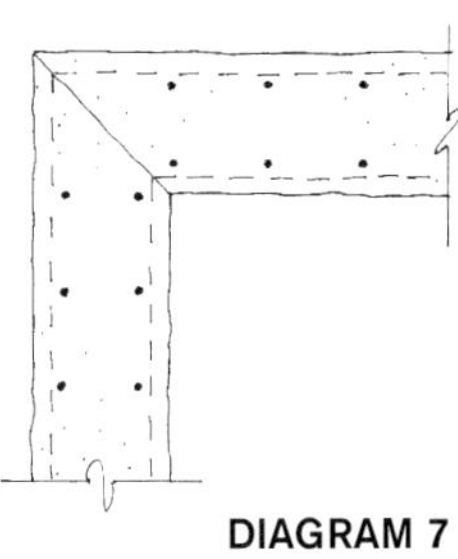

DIAGRAM 7

Step 7. Attach border

Turn the patchwork section over so the backing faces up. With right sides together, lay each of the four border lengths along their corresponding edge (i.e., the edge that's the same length) on the backing, with their raw edges aligned with the finished edges of the throw. Pin, and sew with a 1/2" seam allowance.

Step 8. Mitre corners

At each corner, align the angled edges of the "arrowhead" points and pin. Sew, the corners together using a 1/2" seam allowance. Cut away excess fabric and press seams open. Each corner is now mitred.

Step 9. Sew border down

Turn mitred corners out and place throw flat, patchwork side facing up. Turn the raw edges of the border under 1/2", and pin the fabric so it frames the patchwork. Use a slipstitch to invisibly secure border front to patchwork. (Another option is to topstitch border to patchwork, but be careful to line up topstitching with seam where you attached the border to the back.) Press.

VELVET DAMASK THROW

Finished size: 50" x 54"

MATERIALS & TOOLS

1 1/2 yds. velvet damask
1 1/2 yds. satin
3 yds. 3"-long fringe
Thread
Sharp scissors
Measuring tape
Tailor's chalk
Long straight edge

Step 1. Cut the fabric

Measure and mark a rectangle 51" x 55" on both the velvet damask and the satin. Cut out fabric rectangles.

Step 2. Sew two pieces together

With right sides of fabric facing, align edges, pin and, with a 1/2" seam allowance, stitch three of the four sides together, leaving one 51"-wide side unstitched. Press seams to one side and turn the "pillowcase" shape you've created right side out. Turn raw edges of unstitched side under 1/2", press, pin and topstitch to close, as close to the edge of the fabric as possible.

Step 3. Attach fringe

Cut the fringe in half. Pin one-half to each of the two 50"-wide ends. Turn unfinished ends of fringe under to hide. Topstitch a seam around the edges of the decorative border on the fringe.

POLAR FLEECE THROW

Finished size: 50" x 62"

MATERIALS & TOOLS

2 yds. polar fleece
1 ball thick yarn in contrasting colour
Darning needle
Polyester thread to match polar fleece
Sharp scissors
Measuring tape
Tailor's chalk
Long straight edge
45° square

Step 1. Measure and cut the fabric

Since polar fleece has quite a "memory" or stretch, you should stabilize it before marking and cutting by pinning it to a carpet or area rug. Using a straight edge and tailor's chalk, measure and mark a rectangle 57" wide x 69" long. Next, measure in 3 1/2" from all sides and mark a smaller rectangle inside the first one, 50" wide x 62" long. Cut out along lines of larger rectangle.

Step 2. Mitre corners

At each corner, draw a line that cuts across the "border," touching the corner of the inner rectangle to create a triangle with 45° angles at the corners (see Diagram 6). Cut the corners off along the diagonal lines, so you are left with an octagon. Turn fabric wrong side up, but don't pin to rug yet. Fold one diagonal edge of the octagon so the "points" of the octagon meet, and pin (see Diagram 6). Stitch the folded fabric closed, using a 1/2" seam allowance (see Diagram 7). Repeat for other three corners. When all corners are stitched, turn them inside out and turn the fabric right side up. This creates the border.

Step 3. Stitch down border

Pin fabric to rug again. Fold the raw edge of the border under 1/2", pin in place and baste. Topstitch all the way around the border 1/4" from outer and inner edges (see Diagram 7).

Step 4. Add cross-stitch

Thread a darning needle with about two arm's lengths of yarn (enough to sew a number of stitches but not so much that your yarn gets knotted and tangled) and knot one end. Use chalk to mark two rows of dots at equal distances along the border (see Diagram 7). Stitch one length of yarn through one top dot, one lower dot, one top dot, as if you were lacing shoes. When your piece of yarn runs out, knot it on the back of the throw. Run a second length of yarn, repeating the above pattern, but starting with a lower dot, so you have Xs on both sides of the fabric.

Project 16

Tailored Bedroom

SEVEN EASY-SEW PROJECTS.

Editor's note:
When mixing patterns (like stripes with florals or checks), keep the look current by sticking to monochromatic or two-colour schemes.

Difficulty level:
Average

Projects:
Bed hanging
Box-pleated bedskirt
Flanged pillow shams (2)
Pillowcases (2)
Flanged duvet cover
Chair slipcover
Patchwork chair cushion

Here, we've created an ensemble of tailored linens. Using favourite ticking and floral fabrics from Waverly, we've outfitted the bedroom from top to bottom — from the skirt and flanged duvet on the bed, to the chair slipcover, pillow shams and bed hanging. Artful details of ribbon, buttons and pleats give each treatment a professional finish and pull together this crisp and coordinated room.

When sewing with patterned fabrics, you will require extra fabric for matching patterns (usually between 1/2 yard and 1 yard). If unsure how to calculate for repeats, take your project measurements to your fabric store; they will tell you how much extra you require.

BED HANGING

Note: Throughout these directions, we refer to a "double hem." This is a hem which is folded over twice before stitching.

MATERIALS & TOOLS

5 yds. 54"-wide fabric (extra fabric required for matching print)
5 yds. 1"-wide grosgrain ribbon
Decorative rod (we used a 3/4" bamboo pole)
1" screw-in eye hooks

Step 1. Cut two panels of fabric, 90" x 54". Cut nine lengths of ribbon 20" long.

Step 2. With right sides together, sew the two fabric panels together along 90" side using a 5/8" seam allowance. Trim to 1/4" and press to one side. Overcast or zigzag raw edge.

Step 3. Turn and press to the back a double 1" hem on both 90" sides and across the bottom. Stitch 1/8" from folded edge. Turn, press and stitch a double 1 1/2" hem at top edge.

Step 4. On wrong side, mark with pins for nine pleats. Along top edge, place one pin at centre seam and one in 3" from each side. Mark for three more pleats, evenly spaced between centre pin and 3" marks on each half of panel. One pleat at a time, using the pin as a fold line marker, fold fabric forward on both sides of pin so right sides of fabric are facing. Mark for stitching of pleat 2" to left of fold.

Step 5. At 2" mark, stitch from top down 1 1/2" through all layers. Open up pleat and bring back fold line in alignment with stitching line. Pin to secure, then press. Repeat for all pleats.

Step 6. Fold ribbon in half and insert folded edge inside top opening of each pleat, allowing about 1" of ribbon to feed in. Pin to secure.

Step 7. Topstitch across top edge of panel, 1/4" from top and through all layers of fabric and ribbon. Tie curtain onto rod with double knots in the ribbon.

Step 8. Mount the rod to the wall with screw-in eye hooks, evenly spaced at either end of the pole and in the middle.

PHOTOGRAPHY BY TED YARWOOD

BOX-PLEATED BEDSKIRT

MATERIALS & TOOLS

3 yds. 54"-wide fabric (extra fabric required for matching print)
1 queen-sized flat sheet

Step 1. Cut sheet to width and length of bed, adding 2" to width and 4" to length.

Step 2. Cut a curve at both bottom corners, relating it to shape of bed corners. Turn, press and stitch a double 1 1/2" hem at top edge of sheet.

Step 3. Mark centre-point on bottom edge and on each of curved corners. Measure drop from top of boxspring to floor. Add 3" to this length. Cut six widths of skirt fabric to this measurement.

Step 4. Join two widths together, selvage edge to selvage edge, with right sides together. Stitch 5/8" from edge, trim to 1/4" and zigzag to finish. Press seam flat and turn, press and stitch a double 1" hem at bottom edge. Turn, press and stitch double 1" hems at sides as well. Repeat twice with remaining four widths of fabric.

Step 5. Fold sides of one panel towards back, each approximately 8", and form a double 8" inverted box pleat centered on middle seam line. This will be the end panel.

Step 6. Align ends of end panel with mid-curve marks on sheet. Place right sides together and adjust fullness of pleats to allow fabrics to lie flat. Stitch 1" from raw edge.

Step 7. Take one of remaining panels, fold a double 5" inverted box pleat at centre seam and a single 5" fold at one end. This will be the right panel of skirt. Repeat for left panel.

Step 8. Pin right sides together to sheet, aligning unpleated end with top of sheet and bottom pleat with mid-curve mark. Adjust fullness of pleats if required. Stitch as before. Trim seams to 1/4" and overcast. Press seams towards sheet and press pleats flat.

FLANGED PILLOW SHAMS (2)

MATERIALS & TOOLS

1 1/2 yds. textured fabric
1 1/2 yds. drapery lining (or solid coordinating fabric)
Quilt batting

Step 1. Cut one piece of textured fabric 36" wide and 28" long. From drapery lining, cut two pieces 23" wide and 28" long.

Step 2. Lining sections: Turn, press and stitch a double 1" hem on 28" right-hand side of one piece and on left-hand side of the other.

Step 3. With right sides together, place one piece of lining against textured fabric, aligning unhemmed side, top and bottom, and pin. Align second piece of lining at other side of textured fabric. The lining pieces will overlap at the centre.

Step 4. Stitch through all layers around entire outer edge of sham, 5/8" from raw edge. Trim seams to 1/4" and clip corners diagonally to reduce the bulk. Overcast or zigzag seams to finish. Flip right side out and press.

Step 5. Mark a second stitching line 3" in from outer edge on all sides. Cut strips of quilt batting 3" wide to fit along each edge of sham and insert inside sham, working up to outer edges. Topstitch through all layers along the 3" line. Repeat for second sham.

PILLOWCASES (2)

MATERIALS & TOOLS

1 1/2 yds. damask fabric
1/2 yd. striped fabric
2 1/2 yds. grosgrain ribbon
Glue stick

Step 1. From damask, cut two pieces 27" x 43". From stripe, cut two pieces 43" x 10", with the 10" line parallel with the stripe.

Step 2. With right sides together, sew one damask piece to the stripe along the 43" side with a 5/8" seam allowance. Trim the seam to 1/4" and overcast. Press towards the stripe layer.

Step 3. Working on the right side, apply the ribbon with the glue stick, centring it over the seam line, and topstitch along both edges of the ribbon.

Step 4. Fold the fabric in half, right sides together, aligning the two ends and the ribbon-covered seam. Stitch down the end seam and across the bottom. Trim the seam and overcast.

Step 5. With the sham still inside out, fold the raw edge of the stripe to the wrong side by 1". Fold towards wrong side again, bringing the 1" folded edge down to the seam attaching stripe to damask. Press flat and handstitch. Turn right side out and press flat.

Step 6. Repeat steps 2 to 5 for second pillowcase.

FLANGED DUVET COVER

MATERIALS & TOOLS

(for queen-sized: 88" wide x 90" long)

5 yds. 54"-wide main fabric (extra fabric required for matching print)
5 yds. 54"-wide contrast fabric
8 1" buttons

Step 1. From main and contrast fabrics, cut two 54" widths 95" long. Divide one width of each fabric in half to give you two 27" x 95" pieces. Also cut one 4" x 88" strip of main fabric and one 3" x 88" strip of contrast fabric.

Step 2. Right sides together, attach one half-panel main fabric to each side of the 54" panel. Trim the seams to 1/4" and overcast. Press. Trim this complete panel to 96" by removing equal amounts off each side of the panel (approximately 5 1/2"). Repeat for the contrasting fabric.

Step 3. Turn under 1" and press on long edge of 3" x 88" contrast fabric strip and both short edges. With right sides together, centre unpressed edge along top edge of contrast fabric panel. Stitch 5/8" from edge through both layers. Trim edges of main panel down to stitching line at both sides of fabric strip to neaten.

Step 4. Fold and press strip toward back. Pin to secure and stitch in place along the three folded edges.

Step 5. Centre main fabric strip right sides together on main fabric panel and stitch to within 1" from each end of the fabric strip. Trim the main panel edges to the stitching line and press all layers away from the main panel. Turn and press the other long edge of the fabric strip under 1".

Step 6. Fold in half, right sides together, aligning pressed edge with the stitching line. Sew the two side seams. Trim seams and turn right side out.

Step 7. Press and pin the folded edge in place at stitching line. Machine stitch through all layers. Mark and stitch eight evenly spaced points for buttonholes. Mark for button placement at corresponding point on other strip and sew on buttons.

Step 8. With right sides together, align the main fabric top with contrast layer. Pin and stitch on both sides and bottom, and at top edge up to the button panel.

Step 9. Clip the corners and trim the seams. Turn right side out and press. Topstitch through both layers and along both sides and bottom, 3" from the folded edge to create flange.

CHAIR SLIPCOVER

MATERIALS & TOOLS

3 yds. fabric (approx.)
6 1/2 yds. grosgrain ribbon

Step 1. Beginning with chair back, measure from back of seat up to top of chair and back down to floor. Cut one length of fabric to this measurement plus 1". To determine width of this panel, check chair width at several points to find widest measurement and add 1".

Step 2. Turn, press and stitch a double 1/4" hem on all four sides of this panel. Place panel over chair back. Mark for placement of three ribbon ties on each side — one at seat level, and two more evenly spaced on chair back. Mark corresponding points on panel back. Cut twelve 18" lengths of ribbon and pin to each point. Stitch to secure.

Step 3. For seat cover, measure from floor up to the front of seat and to chair back. Add 1" to this length. Cut this panel to 6" wider than widest part of chair covered by this section (i.e., seat and front legs).

Step 4. Turn, press and stitch a double 1/4" hem at top and bottom (short sides) of panel and drape over chair. Pin to secure or hold in place with tape. Mark this panel to exact contour or angle of seat. Add 1/2" to each side and cut this new shape.

Step 5. For side panels, measure from seat top to floor at both side front and side back of chair, and along seat from front to back, along side edge. Add 1/2" to all these measurements and cut one panel for each side. With each panel, turn, press and stitch a double 1/4" hem at bottom and both sides.

Step 6. With right sides together, pin side panel to side edge of seat/front panel. Stitch 1/2" from edge. Trim seams and press towards seat panel. Overcast edges. Repeat for other side panel. Turn, press and stitch a double 1/4" hem on all remaining edges of front panel.

Step 7. Cut two 4" lengths of ribbon. Fold each in half and pin. Sew one at either corner of skirt panel top. Place skirt over seat and hang back panel in place. Insert bottom ribbon on each side through ribbon loops at back of skirt and tie ribbons into bows.

PATCHWORK CHAIR CUSHION

MATERIALS & TOOLS

Fabric remnants
Grosgrain ribbon
Cushion form (20" x 10") or fibrefill
Glue stick

Step 1. Cut a 10" x 10" square from striped fabric and one each 8" x 10" rectangle from brocade and print fabrics. Using 1" seams, sew pieces, right sides together, to form a 10" x 20" rectangle.

Step 2. Trim the seams to 1/4" and overcast. Press to one side. Cut two 10" pieces of ribbon. Glue ribbon over right sides of each seam to attach and stitch along both edges of ribbon.

Step 3. Cut one layer of stripe for the back, 10" x 20". Place right sides facing over patchwork section and pin. Stitch on all four sides leaving a 10" opening in middle of one long side.

Step 4. Clip corners and trim seams. Overcast and flip right side out. Press and insert cushion form. Handstitch opening closed.

Paint

03

A QUICK AND EASY MAKEOVER IS AT HAND IN EVERY CAN OF PAINT

GET ON BOARD COLOUR BLOCKING

Project 17

Get on Board

FIVE BLACKBOARD PAINT PROJECTS THAT BRING BISTRO CHARM TO THE DINING ROOM AND KITCHEN.

Editor's note:
Easy to execute, these projects are also easy on the wallet. When it's time to change the writing on the wall (or the door), invest in a proper blackboard eraser for the cleanest backdrop.

Difficulty level:
Easy

Projects:
Dining table
Framed blackboard wall
Framed placecards
Alphabetized CD chest
Painted door

With a hint of school-day nostalgia and a dash of sidewalk café charm, blackboards are as appealing as they are practical. Here, we've devised five playful ways to put easy-to-use blackboard paint to work at home in the kitchen and dining room. In our punchy, bistro-style dining room, a black-painted door announces the night's menu, chalk-labelled placecards show guests where to sit, CDs are neatly filed in an alphabetized chest of drawers, and even the dining table itself is a giant chalkboard. If you want to get your feet wet before diving into the blackboard look, paint a swath of black in a corner of the kitchen, frame it with crisp white moulding and let the board take over from messy notes and lists, or use it for an extra-large calendar. You'll find that everyone in the family, and even guests, will want to get in on the fun, filling the boards with notes or inspiring messages. But the best part is, this look is truly easy to achieve (see our "Blackboard basics" on the next page). You won't have to stay late after school to get an A+ on these projects!

PHOTOGRAPHY BY JOANNE TSAKOS

Project 17:
Blackboard paint projects

DINING TABLE

When you purchase the 4' x 8' piece of MDF, if possible, have the store cut it to size for you. We chose to make our table 38" x 72", and had the MDF cut to this size. For a table base, we used Sture trestles from Ikea.

MATERIALS & TOOLS

1	4' x 8' piece 5/8"-thick MDF
3	8'-long pieces corner moulding
3	8'-long pieces half-round moulding
	Hammer
	Measuring tape
	Mitre box and saw
	Clamps
	Wood glue
	Hammer
	Sandpaper
1L	primer
1L	blackboard paint
2	trestles

Step 1. Apply blackboard paint
Sand, prime and paint the MDF according to the instructions in "Blackboard basics."

Step 2. Attach corner moulding
The tabletop's moulding border serves as a ledge for chalk (see Diagram for the cross-section). Mitre the corner moulding to the dimensions of the MDF board. We used two 38"-long (inside edges) pieces, and two 72"-long (inside edges) pieces with a 45° mitre at each end. Apply wood glue to the back of the first piece of corner moulding and attach it to the edge of the MDF so that the top of the vertical side of the moulding is flush with the top of the MDF (see Diagram). Using 1" finishing nails, nail the moulding to the MDF. Continue to install the corner moulding along the edge of the MDF using this process.

Step 3. Attach half-round moulding
The half-round moulding forms a lip at the outside edges of the corner mouldings. Measure the outside length of the corner moulding pieces. Mitre the half-round moulding into four pieces to fit onto the

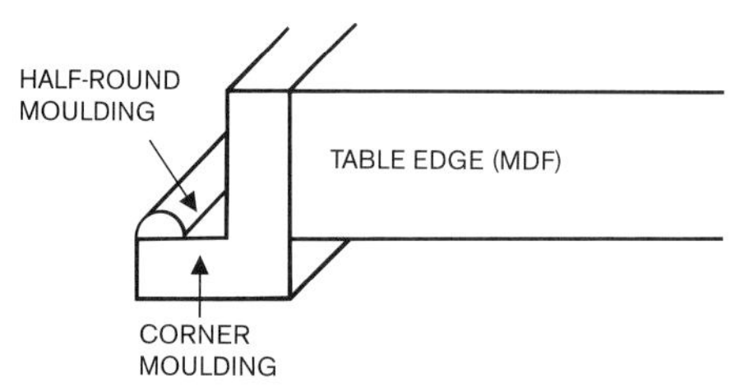

DIAGRAM

corner moulding. Attach a piece of half-round moulding to the horizontal lip of the corner moulding so that the outside edge of the half-round moulding is flush with the outside edge of the corner moulding (see Diagram). Attach the half-round moulding with wood glue only (use clamps to hold the moulding in place while the glue dries).

Step 4. Assemble table
Set up two trestles in the dining area and place the completed tabletop on the trestles.

FRAMED BLACKBOARD WALL

Decide how much of the wall you want to cover with blackboard. In this case, contributing design editor Suzanne Dimma painted the top half of the wall above the existing wainscotting — a 4' h. x 5' w. space. She made the frame from four pieces of 1" x 4" moulding. You can purchase this moulding at a building-supply store.

MATERIALS & TOOLS

4	pieces 5'-long 1" x 4" moulding
	Handsaw
	Low-tack masking tape
	Sandpaper and cloth
1L	primer
1L	blackboard paint
	Paint (for frame)
	Wood glue
	1 1/2" screws

Step 1. Measure and cut moulding
If possible, have the store mitre the four pieces of moulding to length as per the dimensions of your desired blackboard surface. If you cannot, cut it yourself with a handsaw, making sure that the ends have exact 45° angles.

Step 2. Prepare and paint wall
Tape off the surface to be painted. Place the tape on the wall 1" in from where the outer edge of the frame will lie. On Suzanne's wall, the bottom of the frame lies 1/2" above the top of the wainscotting. Prime and paint the wall according to the instructions in "Blackboard basics."

Step 3. Paint moulding
Paint the moulding pieces (and let dry) before attaching them to the wall. Suzanne used the paint colour of the room's trim and wainscotting for a clean, contemporary look.

Step 4. Attach frame to wall
Once the blackboard and moulding paints are completely dry, apply glue to the moulding and attach it to the wall using 1 1/2" screws.

FRAMED PLACECARDS

Inexpensive wood picture frames are widely available at decor and craft stores. Ours measured 4" x 6". A 1/8"-thick sheet of Masonite (also known as "hardboard") can be purchased in sheet form at building-supply stores. At the store, get this sheet cut into 12 pieces, each measuring 5 7/8" x 3 7/8".

MATERIALS & TOOLS

12	4" x 6" picture frames
1	sheet Masonite
1L	primer (for hardboard)
1L	blackboard paint (for hardboard)
1L	latex primer (for frame)
1L	latex paint (for frame)

Step 1. Prepare frames
Remove the glass inserts and cardboard backings from each frame.

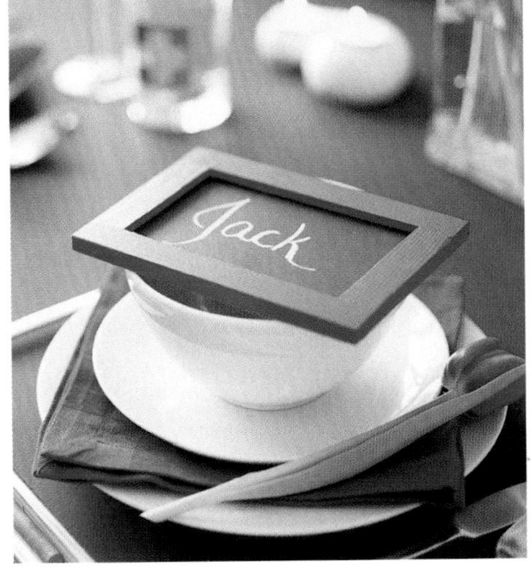

Step 2. Apply blackboard paint
Sand, prime and paint the Masonite according to the instructions in "Blackboard basics."

Step 3. Paint picture frames
Paint the picture frames to finish the look. We painted some of our picture frames with Benjamin Moore 1314, a bright red. We left others unfinished so that we could alternate them with the painted versions at place settings. Once all paint is dry, reassemble frames (with Masonite in place of glass).

ALPHABETIZED CD CHEST

Any box with multiple drawers will work for this project. Our miniature wooden chest of drawers came unfinished. In keeping with our bistro theme, we painted it a cheery red.

MATERIALS & TOOLS

	Storage box
	Sandpaper and cloth
1L	primer (for drawer fronts)
1L	blackboard paint (for drawer fronts)
1L	latex primer (for chest frame)
1L	latex paint (for chest frame)

Step 1. Apply paint
Remove the drawers from the chest, and lightly sand each drawer front. Wipe clean with a damp cloth to remove any dust. Paint drawer fronts according to instructions in "Blackboard basics." Prime and paint the outside of the chest frame in a contrasting colour, and allow to dry. Insert the drawers into the chest and label the drawer fronts with chalk as desired.

PAINTED DOOR

We painted the inner panel of our door, which created a "frame" for the blackboard section.

MATERIALS & TOOLS

	Low-tack masking tape
	Sandpaper
1L	blackboard paint
1L	primer

Step 1. Prepare door
Use masking tape to mark off the section of the door you would like to paint.

Step 2. Apply paint
Sand, prime and paint the section according to the instructions in "Blackboard basics."

Blackboard**basics**

Using blackboard paint is a snap. You'll have to invest a little time, but the actual technique is quite simple. The keys to success are to apply several coats (two to three), let each dry thoroughly, and allow the final coat to cure for several days before writing on the surface.

To prepare the surfaces, lightly sand the area with 120- or 140-grit sandpaper (this will allow the paint to adhere best to the surface). Wipe the surface with a damp cloth to clean away all dust.

- Using low-tack masking tape, carefully tape off the area you will be painting.
- Apply a coat of primer (use Benjamin Moore's Fresh Start 023 primer on already-finished surfaces and BM Alkyd Enamel Underbody 217 on raw wood). Let dry overnight.
- Apply a coat of blackboard paint (we used Moore's Blackboard Coating 287, an interior flat alkyd). Let dry overnight.
- Apply a second coat of blackboard paint. Let dry thoroughly. If needed, apply a third coat. To let the final coat dry thoroughly, wait at least three days (and ideally seven) before writing on the blackboard surface.

Project

Colour Blocking

A FRESH NEW PAINT TECHNIQUE THAT'S AS EASY AS DRAWING A STRAIGHT LINE.

Editor's note:
Unlike fancy faux finishes, these fresh treatments have staying power. Accuracy is key here, so if you've got uneven floors and ceilings, skip the grid and opt instead for the panel or ceiling projects.

Difficulty level:
Average

Projects:
Patchwork pattern
Wall panels
Dropped ceiling/frieze

With watchwords like clean-lined and geometric, this new paint effect is anything but fussy. Our three projects use paint colour to add structure to featureless rooms: paint subtle "panels" on a wall, visually lift a ceiling with a contrasting hue, or highlight a wall or small space with a striking patchwork of complementary pale tones. A tone-on-tone palette is necessary to keep the look understated, so we've used a combination of clear, cool pastels. While the faux finishes of years past can have timeless appeal, colour blocking is a fresher, subtler look for the pared-down modern home. And you don't need to be an artist to get dramatic results. Careful preparation — precise measuring and taping — guarantees success.

This patchwork of fresh colour is a modern alternative to traditional finishes like stencilling, sponging or ragging. Use it to enliven a child's room or a small powder room, or create a "feature wall" in a larger room. Choose colours that are sympathetic – of equal tone and value – so that no one colour jumps out of the pattern. Design your own palette, or take inspiration from a fabric as we did. An ice cream-coloured silk (used on the accent pillows) was the perfect starting point; we chose five shades of paint to match.

PHOTOGRAPHY BY TED YARWOOD

Project 18: Colour-blocked walls

PATCHWORK PATTERN

This patchwork of coloured squares can be used to enliven a child's bedroom or bathroom, or to create a single feature wall in a larger room. If you paint just one feature wall, the other walls in the room should be painted one of the five colours in the patchwork. This project is best suited to even walls; if a wall is crooked, the squares will be out of alignment. We suggest using sponge brushes, as opposed to bristle brushes, for this project, as sponge brushes do not leave brush strokes.

MATERIALS & TOOLS

- Stepladder
- Sandpaper and filler (as needed)
- Primer
- Heavy cardboard
- Chalk or chalk pencil
- Spirit level
- Paper and pencil
- Painter's tape
- Sponge brush or small roller
- Five colours of latex paint

Step 1. Prep and prime walls

Lightly sand wall surface and fill any holes with filler. Sand filled areas and prime walls.

Step 2. Mark grid on wall

With a tape measure, measure the height and width of the wall from the top of the baseboard to the ceiling. Based on these measurements, determine an appropriate square size. To get a perfect grid of squares, your square size should be able to divide into both the height measurement and the width measurement. Our squares measured 15" by 15". Cut a square from heavy cardboard. This will act as a template for your painted squares. Starting in a corner of the room at the baseboard, press the template against the wall and, with chalk, make small marks at all four corners of the template. Continue to work along the baseboard in this manner, marking the four corners of the template onto the wall as you go (see Photo 1). Continue marking additional rows until you hit the ceiling. With a spirit level and chalk, draw lines on the wall to join up the corner marks (see Photo 2). You will have made a pattern of perfect squares.

Step 3. Mark squares

Before you begin painting the squares, make a diagram of the wall grid and indicate what colour each square will be painted. This will ensure that you do not repeat colours. We used five different colours: pink, yellow, green, lilac and blue. (If you use fewer colours, you'll end up with more repetition.) Referring to your diagram, mark each square with a letter indicating the colour it is to be painted. You will be working with all five colours at once.

Step 4. Tape off squares

Using painter's tape, carefully tape off every second square (see Photo 3). These will be painted first. Make sure the tape adheres securely to the wall to prevent paint seepage.

Step 5. Paint every second square

Using a sponge brush or small roller, paint each square with two coats of paint in the colours you have marked. Remove tape promptly after painting square, and let paint dry overnight.

Step 6. Paint remaining squares

The following day, tape off and paint the remaining squares (see Photo 4).

WALL PANELS

The size of the panels will vary depending on the height and width of your walls. Our panels measure 53" high by 22" wide, and start approximately 15" above the baseboard. The two lilac tones were taken from the same paint chip. Paint companies generally provide chips that show colours gradated from light to dark, so it should be easy to choose colours that will work with each other for this layered effect. Use the lighter colour as the base colour and the darker shade (the next shade down on the paint chip) as the panel colour. For this project we used a sponge brush, as opposed to bristle; sponge brushes don't leave brush strokes.

MATERIALS & TOOLS

- Stepladder
- Sandpaper and filler (as needed)
- Primer
- Lighter-coloured latex paint for base coat
- Darker-coloured latex paint for panels
- Tape measure
- Chalk or chalk pencil
- Spirit level
- Painter's tape
- Sponge brush or small roller
- Paint tray

Step 1. Prep and prime wall

Lightly sand wall surface and fill any holes with filler. Sand filled areas and prime walls. Once primer is dry, apply base coat (i.e., the lighter colour) to wall.

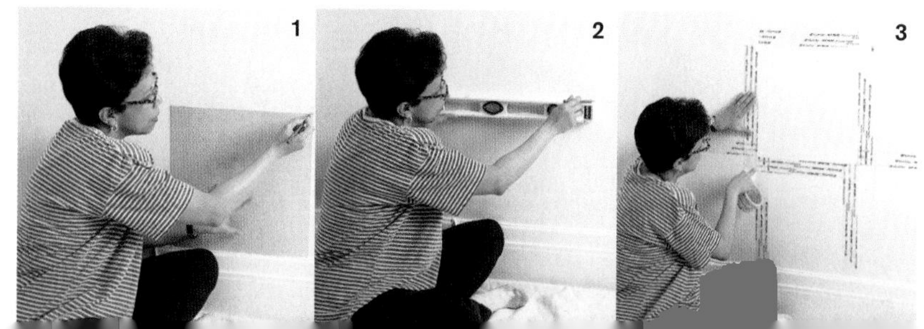

Step 2. Measure and mark panels

Measure the height and width of your wall. The amount of wall space will determine the number and size of panels that will look best. Our panels are spaced 11" apart, and they start 15" above the baseboard. When determining the size of your panels, consider the items (mirrors, paintings, photographs) you will be hanging within the panels. Our clocks measured 16" in diameter, and we chose to leave 3" on either side.

Starting from either end of the room, measure out for the first panel. Using a tape measure and chalk, make marks to indicate the panel edges. With chalk and a spirit level to ensure accuracy, join the marks together to create the outline of a rectangular panel.

Next, measure and mark the space in between the panels (we measured an 11" space), and join the marks using a spirit level to ensure accuracy (see Photo 5). (We had already painted one panel when we measured to the next, as pictured, but we suggest measuring out all panels and then painting.) Measure and mark the next panel. Continue measuring and marking the panels in this way.

Step 3. Tape panels

Using painter's tape, carefully tape off the marked panel areas (see Photo 6). Make sure the tape adheres securely to the wall to prevent paint seepage.

Step 4. Paint panels

With a sponge brush or roller, apply two coats of paint to each panel, allowing paint to dry thoroughly between coats (see Photo 7). You can use the brush to cut around the edges of the panel, then fill in the centre using the roller, or use a brush alone as we did. Remove the tape promptly after the second coat has been applied.

DROPPED CEILING/FRIEZE

MATERIALS & TOOLS

- Stepladder
- Sandpaper and filler (as needed)
- Primer
- Paintbrush
- Roller and paint tray
- Darker coloured latex paint for ceiling and frieze
- Lighter coloured latex paint for walls
- Tape measure
- Chalk or chalk pencil
- Spirit level
- Painter's tape

Step 1. Prep and prime walls

Lightly sand wall surface and fill any holes with filler. Sand filled areas and prime walls.

Step 2. Paint ceiling

With a brush, "cut in" the ceiling colour (i.e., the darker colour) around the edges of the room where the ceiling meets the wall, and paint the ceiling using a roller. Ceilings are always painted before walls so that if there are drips or splatters, the fresh wall colour will cover these. Let the ceiling dry completely.

Step 3. Paint walls

With a brush, "cut in" the walls at the ceiling and baseboard around the room and paint them with the lighter wall colour using a roller. Let dry completely and repeat with a second coat.

Step 4. Measure frieze

The frieze is the "dropped" part of the ceiling. With a measuring tape, measure and mark the frieze band approximately 24" down from the ceiling. The appropriate height of this band really depends on the size of the room, ceiling height and door moulding height — a matter of eyeballing your room rather than an exact science. Ours is exactly 27" down from the ceiling. Mark the drop measurement every few feet with small chalk marks. Use a spirit level to join up the marks and draw a straight chalk line around the room.

Step 5. Tape frieze

Tape off the frieze, making sure the tape adheres securely to the wall to prevent seepage. If your walls are uneven or crooked, as can be the case in older homes, adjust the tape accordingly: step back, eyeball the taped line and move the tape up or down so that the taped area is as straight as possible.

Step 6. Paint frieze

With a brush for cutting in the edges and a roller, paint the frieze the same colour as the ceiling. Apply two coats if necessary, removing tape promptly after the second coat has been applied. Paint with caution at this stage, as you do not want to drip the frieze colour onto the freshly painted walls.

Step 7. Paint baseboard

Consider painting baseboard in same colour as ceiling; use an oil-based gloss in the same colour as the ceiling. If you do not have a baseboard, "fake" one by measuring 10" to 12" from the floor up, marking the measurements with chalk, joining the marks to make a straight line, taping and painting as you did with the frieze.

4

5

6

7

Garden

04

STYLE COMES TO THE BACKYARD IN TIME FOR THE LAZY DAYS OF SUMMER

SUN SHOWERS MIRROR, MIRROR **HANGIN' OUT** BUILD A CEDAR POTTING BENCH **BACKYARD CLASSIC**

Project

SunShowers

LATHER UP AND COOL DOWN IN THIS FUN AND FUNCTIONAL OUTDOOR SHOWER.

Editor's note:
Easy to transport – or dismantle come winter – this shower is a boon for cottagers and pet owners. Try making it from cedar and let it weather to a soft, natural grey.

Difficulty level:
Difficult

Admit it. On a sweltering summer day, it's sometimes awfully tempting to don a bathing suit and let loose with the kids under the sprinkler. But for those of us too modest to frolic on the front lawn, there's a more sedate — albeit equally refreshing — solution: an easy-to-build outdoor shower that lets you indulge in a little spa-like luxury in the privacy of your own backyard. Outdoor showers are all the rage these days and, with its elegant lattice panels and oversized "rainhead," this one makes an attractive addition to any garden. But the design is practical too. A floor of resin deck tiles that just drop into place and copper piping that hooks up to the garden hose mean it can be moved around to catch the summer sun, or quickly dismantled come autumn. There's also a tap set low on one of the panels that makes short work of cleaning muddy boots and little sandy feet. (Yes, the children can use this too — the novelty of it all might even have them lining up for a scrubdown.) Once you've built the main structure, paint the lattice to complement the exterior of your house, then have some fun dressing it up with hooks and towel bars, a soap dish, even a small mirror. Keep in mind that this isn't a warm shower. Depending on the weather, you'll find that the alfresco bathing experience ranges from invigorating to downright bracing. But don't let that throw cold water on your plans for summer fun — just hop in and enjoy.

PHOTOGRAPHY BY VIRGINIA MACDONALD

Project 19: Outdoor shower

This shower features an oversized chrome "rainhead" and grey-stained lattice on three sides to give bathers a measure of privacy. Joined with screws, the three panels can be dismantled for winter storage. Hooks, a soap dish (not visible) and towel bar are practical additions.

A tap makes cleaning muddy feet a snap. The shower floor is made from resin deck panels that are simply set on the ground. Although a special drain isn't necessary, it's a good idea to dig a few inches into the soil, then lay gravel before installing the panels.

While at the building-supply store, fit all the plumbing pieces together before purchasing to make sure each one connects properly with the next.

MATERIALS & TOOLS

Floor:

- 4 — 2' x 2' pressure-treated decking squares

Plumbing parts:

- 6' — 1/2"-diam. copper pipe
- 3/4" hose adapter
- 2 — 1/2" tee fittings
- 1 — sink faucet in threaded chrome
- 1 — 1/2" straight stop valve in chrome
- 2 — 1/2" 90° copper elbows
- 1 — 15-cm chrome arm
- 1 — 8" shower head in chrome

Additional items:

- 20 — 3" wood screws
- 1 — chrome towel bar
- 1 — chrome soapdish
- 1 or 2 — chrome hooks
- Garden hose
- 1 — gallon outdoor wood stain
- Handsaw
- Chisel and mallet
- Drill
- Wood filler
- Hammer
- Paintbrush
- Hacksaw
- Soldering kit

Lumber for back panel:

- 2 — pieces 2" x 2" pressure-treated lumber cut to 81 1/2"
- 2 — pieces 2" x 2" pressure-treated lumber cut to 35"
- 1 — piece 4' x 8' privacy lattice (cut to 36 1/2" x 80")

Lumber for side panels:

- 4 — pieces 2" x 2" pressure-treated lumber cut to 70"
- 6 — pieces 2" x 2" pressure-treated lumber cut to 23"
- 1 — piece 4' x 8' privacy lattice (cut to 2 pieces 24 1/5" x 47 1/2")

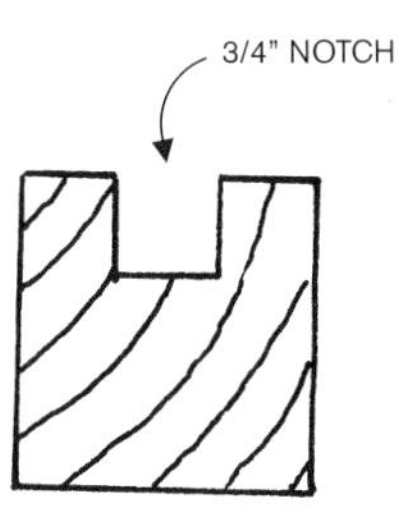

DIAGRAM 1

Step 1. Build back wall

To adapt the frame to hold the latticework, cut a 3/4" x 3/4" groove down the centre of each 2" x 2" piece (see Diagram 1) using a handsaw, chisel and mallet, or use a table saw if you have one. To assemble the back wall, insert the lattice into the grooves in the four 2" x 2" frame pieces (see Diagram 2). Pre-drill holes, and screw back frame together using 3" wood screws.

Step 2. Build side walls

Again, cut a 3/4" x 3/4" groove down the centre of the 2" x 2" frame pieces to fit the lattice into the frame (see Diagram 1). Assemble side panels (see Diagram 3), then pre-drill holes and fasten frame pieces together with 3" wood screws.

Step 3. Assemble and stain shower

To attach the side and back walls together, pre-drill and use 3" wood screws. Fit the four decking squares together to make the floor. The four pieces of decking we bought were too large for our shower, so we measured them and cut them into a configuration that fit within our frame. The decking simply drops in place on the ground and does not need to be attached to shower at all. Fill any screw holes with wood filler. Use exterior stain to stain shower structure and floor pieces. Let dry completely. Apply a second coat of stain if necessary. Allow to dry overnight.

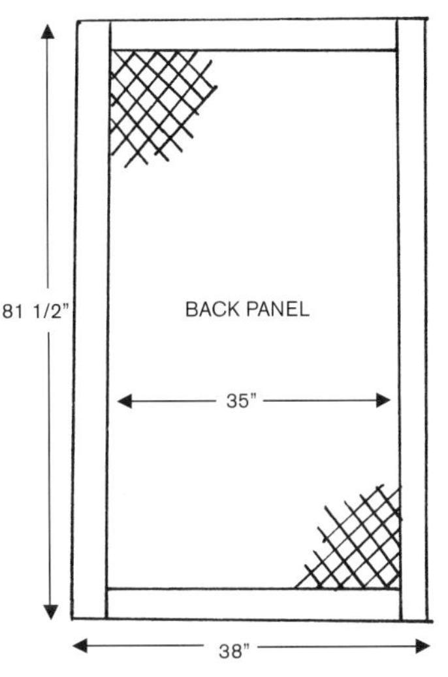

DIAGRAM 2

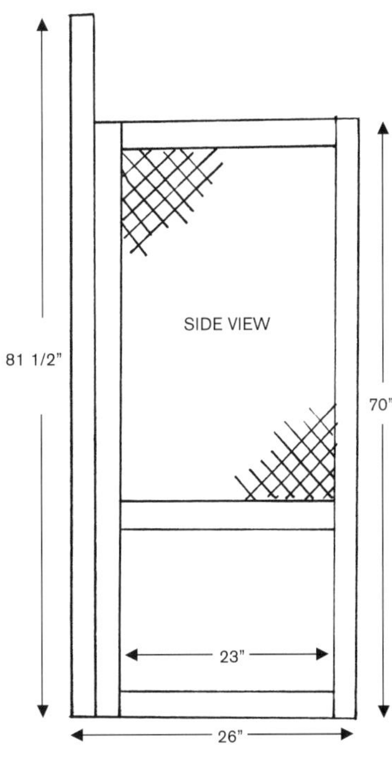

DIAGRAM 3

Step 4. Connect plumbing

Decide the heights at which you'd like to place your showerhead, shut-off valve and foot tap. Mark locations, and pre-drill a 3/4" hole through the lattice at each of these three heights. The plumbing is attached through the back wall. Do a "dry run" and connect all of the pieces before soldering them in place. Use a hacksaw to cut the copper pipe to fit the configuration you'd like. Use a soldering kit to attach all the plumbing parts together in place up the back wall of the shower (see Diagram 4).

Step 5. Attach accessories

Decide where you'd like to hang a soap dish, towel bar, hooks, etc. Pre-drill all holes at marked locations and attach to the lattice using hardware included in packaging of above items. Attach garden hose to adapter and enjoy!

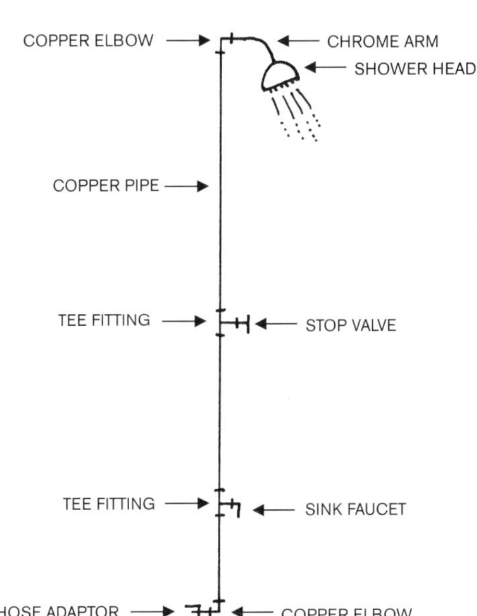

DIAGRAM 4

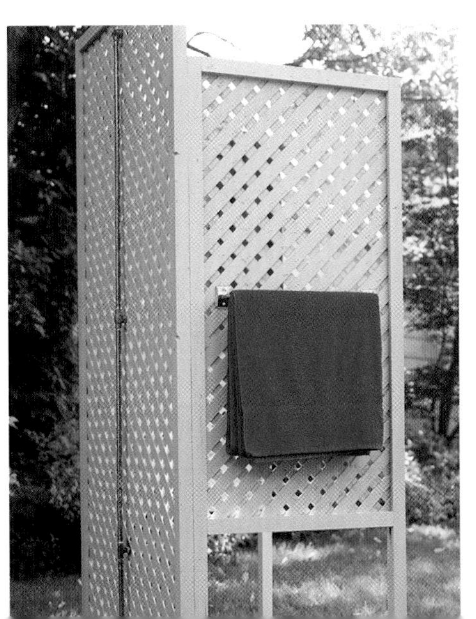

Copper piping attached to the garden hose delivers water to the tap and showerhead. The lattice enclosure is easy to build, but if you want an even simpler and less expensive alternative, just attach the showerhead to an outside wall of your house.

Project

Mirror, Mirror

PUT MIRRORS TO WORK IN THE GARDEN EXPANDING SPACE AND REFLECTING GLORIOUS GREENERY.

Editor's note:
Consider these projects for small, shady gardens where even a single mirrored piece will add light. You'll also create the illusion of space and trick the eye into seeing more pretty vistas.

Difficulty level:
Difficult

Projects:
Mirrored arbour bench
Barrel table
Heating grate mirrors

Come summertime, the Canadian outdoors turns lush and green and welcoming. It's where we suddenly long to spend all of our free time. But those of us who live in the city forgo ready access to the countryside. So we've come up with projects that, like the cool waters of the lakes and rivers in the wild, use reflection to help visually extend the landscape — here our gardens — and maximize our enjoyment of nature. In addition to creating the illusion of depth, mirrors can be used to bounce sunlight into dark corners of the yard or patio. Inspired by the lattice-framed mirrors we spotted in Toronto interior designer Sloan Mauran's garden, our mirrors-in-the-garden projects include a latticed arbour with a built-in bench, a side table that uses mirror as a pretty reflective tabletop and mirrored wall hangings that turn rustic metal heating grates into ornate frames. American author-naturalist Henry David Thoreau wrote of his beloved Walden Pond, "Walden is a perfect forest mirror, set round with stones .... Nothing so fair, so pure, and at the same time so large, as a lake, perchance, lies on the surface of the earth." We hope these projects will offer equally pleasing reflections of your favourite garden landscape.

We designed our cedar-trellised arbour with built-in bench to act as a pretty focal point in the yard and also, if needed, conceal unsightly garden tools or storage areas. The mirror reflects the garden in front of it, making the plantings appear to continue behind. Built of ready-made trellising and 2" x 4" cedar, the arbour is a free-standing unit that can be moved around the yard or even taken to a new house.

PHOTOGRAPHY BY DONNA GRIFFITH

MIRRORED ARBOUR BENCH

We used an arbour kit from Revy Home & Garden as the starting point for this project. The measurements given here are specific to that particular kit, so adjust your measurements accordingly if you select a different arbour kit.

MATERIALS & TOOLS

	Cedar arbour kit
2	pieces 2" x 4" x 44 1/2" cedar for bench front and back
2	pieces 2" x 4" x 25 1/4" cedar for bench sides
1	piece 2" x 4" x 22 1/4" cedar for centre brace
2	pieces 2" x 4" x 18" cedar back legs
2	pieces 2" x 4" x 18" cedar front legs with cut-out for 2' x 4'
2	pieces 2" x 4" x 14 1/2" cedar for front legs
5	pieces 1" x 6" x 47 1/2" cedar top
26	#8 2 1/4" decking screws
30	#8 1 1/4" decking screws
	5' x 8' cedar lattice (cut to size of arbour back)
	3-mm-thick mirror cut to size of arbour back
1	tube silicone adhesive
	Galvanized finishing nails
	Handsaw
	Drill
	Screwdriver
	Hammer

Step 1. Assemble arbour
Following the instructions that come with your kit, build the entire arbour.

Step 2. Build bench frame
Assemble the front, back and sides of bench using butt-joint construction (see Diagram). Pre-drill all holes and screw together using #8 2 1/4" decking screws. Install centre brace with 2 1/4" decking screws.

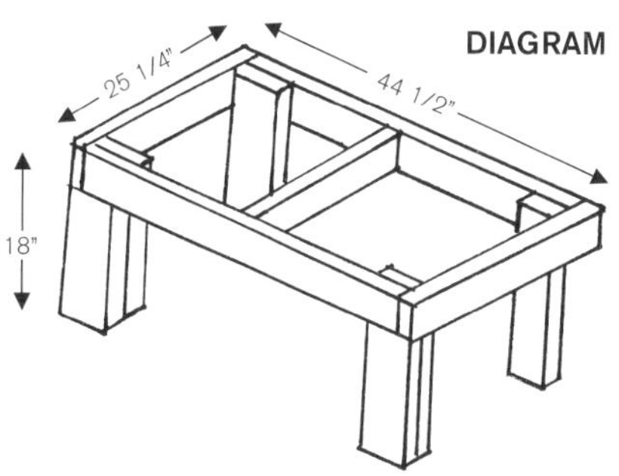

Step 3. Attach legs and top
Cut a corner from each of the two 18" front legs to accommodate the side pieces of the bench frame. Attach 18" back legs and 18" notched-out front legs using 2 1/4" decking screws. Attach 14 1/2" front legs to notched-out front legs using 2 1/4" decking screws. Starting with centre plank, attach five 1' x 6' cedar planks across the top of bench (leaving a 1/4" gap between each piece) using 1 1/4" decking screws screwed into centre brace and side pieces.

Step 4. Attach lattice and mirror
Have the mirror cut into two panels for ease of installation. Mirror should be cut 1/2" smaller than latticework all around to be sure it fits into arbour. Affix mirrors to latticework using silicone adhesive, applying adhesive to back of lattice (not to front of mirror). Press mirror(s) into place. Allow to dry overnight, lying flat with weights on top. Affix mirrored latticework to top and sides of arbour using galvanized finishing nails.

BARREL TABLE

MATERIALS & TOOLS

- Large banded wine or juice barrel
- 5-mm-thick mirror, cut to fit (ours was 12" diam.)
- Silicone adhesive for mirrors

Make a template out of kraft paper by tracing the circumference of the barrel top. Take template to a glass store to have a circle of mirror cut to size. We chose a sturdy 5-mm thickness for our mirror since it is being used as a table surface and needs to support the weight of the objects placed on it. Run a bead of silicone around the back of the mirror and press it firmly onto the top of the barrel. Weight down and allow to dry overnight.

Topped with a circle of mirror, a large banded wooden juice barrel looks to be full of rainwater. It's actually a durable side table for the yard or porch. This project uses sturdier 5mm-thick mirror (as opposed to the 3mm-thick type used in the other projects) because the mirror acts as the surface on which things will be set.

To bring a more formal indoor look outside, accessorize yards and terraces as you would your home. These antique floor grates have a romantic, weathered look that's well suited to the garden. We fitted them with 3mm-thick mirror backings and hung a group of three above a bench on the fence to create a focal point. They resemble peek holes into the next garden.

We were inspired by mirrored panelling that Toronto interior designer Sloan Mauran installed in her own backyard. Known for her sleek, urban traditional designs, Mauran brought the same level of style to her outdoor space. She had the mirror framed and fronted with grey-painted trellising, and attached it to the fence and the back wall of her garage to visually extend the space in her yard and give the whimsical illusion of windows to secret areas beyond the garden.

The mirrored panel installations in Sloan Mauran's backyard are constructed as individual framed units so that they can be moved to other areas or taken to a new house if needed.

HEATING GRATE MIRRORS

MATERIALS & TOOLS

- Variety of decorative iron heating grates
- 3-mm-thick mirror, cut to size (ours were 8" diam., 18" diam. and 12" x 16")
- Silicone adhesive for mirrors
- Drill with high-speed steel bit
- 2" decking screws

Vintage iron grates can often be found at flea markets or through a local architectural salvager. These mirror measurements are specific to the grates we used, so have mirror cut to fit the grates you find. Bring grates into a glass store and have a piece of mirror cut to fit the space behind it. Apply silicone on the underside of the grate and press grate carefully onto the mirror. Allow to dry overnight. Screw mirrored grates onto a fence using existing screw or nail holes, or use a high-speed steel bit to drill new holes in the grate.

Project

Hangin' Out

SPEND A WEEKEND MAKING ONE OF OUR STYLISH HAMMOCKS AND REAP THE REWARDS ALL SUMMER LONG.

Editor's note:
This inexpensive and very doable project makes an informal alternative to a chaise. To make drilling holes in the support bars of the country hammock easier, try substituting a length of 2-x-2 wood for the dowel.

Difficulty level:
Average

Projects:
City-slicker hammock
Country-style hammock

Made of strong, durable awning fabrics, our easy-sew hammocks bring relaxed summer comfort to any yard. The light-coloured fabric is designed to stand up to sun and rain, and the cosy hammocks are strung up with sturdy chains or nylon rope. (We used pale fabrics because dark colours get hotter in the sun.) For those who prefer a country look, our yellow-striped version is rigged up with white rope and wooden dowels. Add toss cushions made of scraps of gingham, toile and hankies and you've got a fresh, updated country-style hammock. If a more industrial look appeals, our multistripe hammock hung on chains will fit the bill. Pair it with comfy box-style ground cushions for extra seating, and a small city yard can seat even more summertime visitors. Both hammocks are designed to be tied between trees but can just as easily be affixed to hooks screwed into backyard fences or front porch walls. Let the lounging begin!

Our country-style hammock is inspired by traditional canvas hammocks of the past. To give it a new look, we paired the crisp yellow-and-white striped awning fabric with white nylon rope and wooden dowels, and accented it with graphic black-and-white pillows.

PHOTOGRAPHY BY DONNA GRIFFITH

For a more urban look, this hammock is rigged with metal chains. Crisp box-style cushions, also made with sturdy awning fabric, provide extra seating.

For our hammocks, we used light-coloured awning fabrics that will stay cool even on the hottest of summer days. We used 46"-wide awning fabric for both hammocks, which enabled us to hem just the ends of each hammock, as the edge of this fabric will not fray.

CITY-SLICKER HAMMOCK

This hammock is approximately 6 1/2' long, which requires the yardage listed below. If you would like to make yours longer, determine the length of hammock you desire, and add 6" to this length for hems at top and bottom. The strength-to-weight ratio of the chain should be high — we used size 2/0 chain to handle a load of 255 pounds. The length of extra chain needed will be determined by the distance between your trees.

MATERIALS & TOOLS

- 2 yds. striped awning fabric
- 1/4 yd. solid awning fabric (for ends)
- Synthetic topstitching thread (cotton thread can weaken in the sun)
- Canvas needle for sewing machine
- 14 1 1/4" stainless steel grommets
- 6 1/4" S-hooks (3 per end)
- 2 1/4" quick links
- 14' double-loop chain (4 pieces @ 30" each, 2 pieces @ 24" each)
- Extra double-loop chain
- Walking foot attachment for sewing machine (optional; since heavy awning fabrics cannot be pinned or basted easily, this attachment holds fabric in place)
- 2 pieces 40"-long, 1/4"-diam. steel rod

Step 1. Cut and attach end strips

Cut two strips of accent fabric to 4" w. x 47" l. (1" longer than width of hammock to give 1/2" hem at each end of strip). With raw edges together, wrong sides facing, sew a strip to each end of main hammock fabric. Flip fabric strip over, finger press along seam. Finger press the raw edge of strip 1/2" under. Finger press 1/2" hem inward at each side. Sew along two sides and one end of strip, leaving one side of pocket open to slip stabilizing rod into pocket.

Step 2. Place grommets and rod

Install seven evenly spaced grommets along each end strip. Allow enough space between grommets and bottom seam of pocket strip for rod to be slipped into place. Once rod is in place, sew hem on open end to encase rod in pocket. Repeat at other end.

Step 3. Rig up chain

With hammock on ground, attach S-hooks at outer and middle grommets (three at each end). At middle grommet, hook 24"-long chain onto S-hook and pull straight back towards quick link. Hook 30"-long chains to S-hooks at each end. Pull diagonally towards quick link. Repeat at other end. With extra chain, link one end into quick link, wrap around tree and secure again in the same quick link.

COUNTRY-STYLE HAMMOCK

This hammock is approximately 8' long, which requires 3 yards of fabric. If you would like to make yours shorter, determine length of hammock you desire, and add 12" to this length for hems at the top and bottom.

MATERIALS & TOOLS

- 3 yds. awning fabric
- Synthetic topstitching thread (cotton thread can weaken in the sun)
- Canvas needle for sewing machine
- Walking foot attachment for sewing machine (optional; since heavy awning fabrics cannot be pinned or basted easily, this attachment holds fabric in place)
- 28 3/4" stainless steel grommets
- 2 2"-diam. stainless steel O-rings
- 2 25' lengths of 1/4"-diam. twisted nylon rope
- 30' 1/2"-diam. twisted nylon rope
- 2 40"-long, 1"-diam. dowels
- Drill and drill bits
- Clamps (optional)
- Clothes iron (optional)

Step 1. Sew top and bottom hems

Measure 3" from each end of hammock fabric, and fold fabric back onto itself at these marks with wrong sides facing. Use your finger to crease another 3" at each end and fold under at these creases to create your hem (if needed, use lowest setting of clothes iron to create crisp crease, but direct heat can shrink awning fabric so we suggest finger pressing). Sew across width of fabric at both ends, creating a 3" hem. This larger hem stabilizes fabric for grommeting and makes for a stronger hammock.

Step 2. Add grommets

Measure in approximately 3 1/2" from each side, 1 1/2" from end, and mark with tailor's chalk for placement of outside grommets. Measure and mark for remaining grommets so they are equally spaced (approximately 3" apart, 14 at each end). We had our hammock professionally grommeted at a marine-supply store, but home-grommeting kits will also work.

Step 3. Drill dowel

We used two pieces of dowel as our stabilizing bars for this hammock (without these the hammock would fold up into itself when hung). Line up dowel with grommet line, and mark exact spots of grommets on dowel. Clamp dowel onto a work surface. Drill holes, beginning with a small drill bit, and work up to a drill bit that creates a hole large enough for the 1/2"-diam. nylon rope to pass through easily. After all holes are drilled, sand the dowel lightly to smooth out any rough spots.

Step 4. Thread rope onto hammock

Spread hammock out on the ground. Measure across the width of the hammock to determine the centre (should be 23" from each side). Place an O-ring, approximately 15" beyond this centre mark and pin it in place on surface so it won't shift. You will use one 25' length of 1/4"-diam. twisted nylon rope at each end of the hammock. Knot one end of nylon rope and pass length through first grommet from back of hammock to front. Knot again above grommet so it won't shift. Pass length through dowel hole, then diagonally up to and through O-ring. Continue process in reverse order to lace dowel in place. At 7th and 8th holes, tie another knot to prevent the dowel and hammock from touching (see photo, above). Continue until hammock is completely "laced." You should have 6" extra rope (at most). Trim after last knot is tied. Repeat this step at other end of hammock. Unpin O-rings.

Step 5. Adjust rope

Cut the 30' nylon rope in half. This will allow 15' of rope at each end of the hammock to tie around tree (adjust this length to suit the distance between your trees, and the length required to tie hammock at a comfortable height). Loop each length of rope through O-ring, and knot to secure.

Project

Build a Cedar Potting Bench

TRADITIONAL STYLING AND STURDY CONSTRUCTION MAKE THIS AN ESSENTIAL FOR THE BACKYARD OR GARDEN SHED.

Editor's note:
With its large work surface and ample storage space, this sturdy, good-looking unit would make a great craft table or workbench for the basement – just omit the basin hole.

Difficulty level:
Difficult

Even the most well-outfitted garden room, potting shed, garage or patio can become more functional with the addition of a practical, hand-hewn potting bench. Our bench offers plenty of storage space for tools, pots, seedling trays, pesticides and fertilizers, while its spacious, waist-level work surface provides a therapeutic alternative to backbreaking bending. The removable plastic tub is perfect for transporting potting mixture or peat moss; fill it with water and use it for rinsing pots or tools, or soaking seeds. Left in an outside location, the cedar — tempered by sun, rain and snow — will weather to a silvery grey. Used indoors, the wood will retain its warm hue. Straightforward in construction, this handsome bench can be built over a quiet summer weekend; its classic design looks terrific all year round.

With space for storage and an ample work surface with a removable plastic tub, this traditional cedar potting bench will whip garden supplies and chores into shape.

PHOTOGRAPHY BY TED YARWOOD

The potting bench measures 59 1/2" h. x 49 1/4" w. x 24" d. It can be used outdoors or inside. When using it outdoors or for more visual effect, finish it with a good-quality exterior preservative or stain. Pine can be substituted for cedar but must be stained or painted. The plastic sink-tub is optional. If you decide to omit it, simply use four 47 1/4" pieces of 5/4" x 6" cedar for the main surface, but install a beam underneath to support this surface.

MATERIALS & TOOLS

40 feet 2" x 4"cedar
50 feet 5/4" x 6" cedar
12 feet 2" x 8" cedar
12" x 14 3/4" plastic tub
Coated deck screws
Stain or clear preservative
Electric drill with screwdriver and drill bits
Adjustable square
Circular saw, handsaw or mitre saw
Jigsaw
Pencil, tape measure, hammer

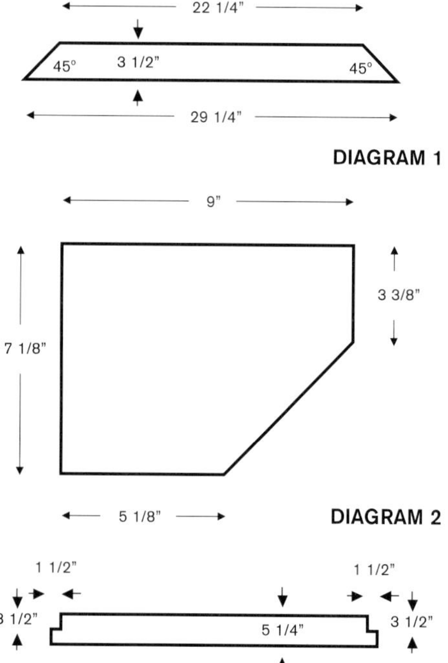

DIAGRAM 1

DIAGRAM 2

DIAGRAM 3

Step 1. Measure and cut cedar

Cut cedar pieces to the following measurements:

2 pieces 2" x 4" @ 56" (back legs)
2 pieces 2" x 4" @ 37" (front legs)
5 pieces 2" x 4" @ 22" (4 leg braces; 1 sink support brace)
2 pieces 5/4" x 6" @ 47 1/4" (main surface)
1 piece 5/4" x 6" @ 47 1/4" (backsplash)
4 pieces 5/4" x 6" @ 44 1/4" (bottom shelf)
2 pieces 2" x 4" @ 29 1/4" with a 45° mitre on both ends (back braces) (see Diagram 1)
1 piece 2" x 4" @ 15" (spacer bar)
2 pieces 5/4" x 6" @ 2 1/4" (main surface)
2 pieces 5/4" x 6" @ 30 1/4" (main surface)
2 pieces 5/4" x 6" @ approximately 23 1/8" (main surface side trim/apron – measure and cut these pieces once the bench is assembled to ensure a proper fit)
1 piece 5/4" x 6" @ 49 1/4" (main surface front trim/apron)
2 pieces 2" x 8" @ 47 1/4" (top shelf and shelf backing)
2 pieces 2" x 8" @ 9" (top shelf ends trimmed as per Diagram 2)

Step 2. Construct bench sides

Lay out two legs (a front and a back) in front of you so that the bottoms of the legs are facing you and the shorter (front) leg is on the right. Lay a leg brace on the legs with the bottom of the brace 11 1/2" up from the bottom of the legs. Use the square to ensure that the legs and the brace are at 90° to each other. Screw through the brace into the legs. Lay the upper brace on the legs so it is flush with the top of the front leg, and the bottom of the brace is 37" up from the bottom of the back leg. Screw through the brace into the legs. Lay out the second set of legs as you did the first but with the shorter leg on the left (see Photo 1). Attach the braces as you did on the first set.

Step 3. Attach bench top and back to legs

One 47 1/4" main surface piece must be trimmed to fit around the back legs. At both ends, measure and cut 3 1/2" into the width and 1 1/2" into the length (see Diagram 3).

Position the two bench sides so that the braces attaching the legs will be inside the legs. Attach the uncut 47 1/4" main surface piece to the top of the top braces at the front of the top braces, flush with the front of the front legs. This will be part of the main surface of the bench. The ends of the main surface piece should be flush with the outer edges of the legs. Screw the 47 1/4" piece with the corners cut out to the top of the top leg braces at the back of the bench. To create the backsplash for the main surface, attach the 47 1/4" backsplash piece to the back of the legs so that it is perpendicular to the main surface and rises 2" above the top of the main surface. Screw through the back of the backsplash into the back of the rear legs (see Photo 2). Use the square to ensure that the backsplash and the legs are at 90° to each other.

Step 4. Attach bottom shelf to bottom leg braces

Place one 44 1/4" bottom shelf piece flush with the back of the lower leg braces in between the two legs. Using two screws on each end, screw through the shelf board into the brace. Position and attach another bottom shelf board flush with the front of the lower leg braces. Repeat for the last two boards, spacing them evenly between the front and back boards with the ends even with the edges of the braces.

Step 5. Attach back braces

Position one mitred back brace so that one of its mitred ends rests on the bottom shelf (flush with the back of the back board) and the other fits tightly in the corner created by the insides of the upper leg brace and the main surface's backsplash (see Photo 3). Position the other back brace, resting it against the back of the bottom shelf and the other back corner created by the upper leg brace and the main surface's backsplash. The two back braces should sit tight up against each other on the bottom shelf. Affix each back brace with two screws through the bottom of the shelf into the bottom of the brace and one screw through the back of the backsplash and into the back brace.

Step 6. Finish main shelf

To support the left side of the sink-tub, a brace must be installed underneath the main surface. Attach the 22" sink support brace underneath the two boards that are already installed for the main surface and 13" from the inside edge of the top leg brace on the right side of the bench. Screw through the two top boards down into the support brace. (This support brace can be seen in Photo 4).

To support the 2 1/4" end pieces at the right-hand end of the main surface, place the 15" spacer bar in between the legs outside the leg brace and flush with the top of the legs and the top of the brace, and screw through the spacer bar into the leg brace. Leaving 1/4" between each board, attach the two 2 1/4" end pieces on the right side of the main surface (drill countersink holes in these small pieces beforehand so they won't split when you screw through them). These should be flush with the outside edges of the legs and the spacer bar. (There will be a 3/4" lip of the leg brace to support the sink-tub.)

On the other side of the sink hole attach the two final main surface pieces, screwing the left-hand ends to the left-hand leg brace and the right ends to the sink brace (see Photo 4). Space these pieces 1/4" apart and 1/4" from the already installed front and back main surface pieces. These final two pieces should also be flush with the outside edges of the legs (i.e., they will protrude 1 1/2" beyond the brace). On their right-hand ends they will leave a 3/4" lip of sink brace for the sink-tub to rest on. You now have a recessed edge for each end of the sink-tub. Trim the front and back boards of the top so that the tub will drop easily into the bench top. Place the tub upside down on the bench top, aligning the ends so that they would fit into the recessed ledges. Trace the front or back edges onto the two long boards of the top. With a jigsaw, trim the front and back boards of the top so that the tub will drop into the top and rest on the two ledges at its ends.

Step 7. Attach main surface trim/apron

Attach one piece of trim/apron to one end of the main surface, screwing through the trim/apron into the front and back legs in two places. The trim/apron piece should be flush with the top of the main surface and flush with the front of the front legs, but will protrude about 1" beyond the back legs (to be flush with the backsplash). Repeat for the trim/apron on the other end. Attach the front trim/apron piece to the main surface so that it is flush with the main surface top and with the outside edges of the side trim/apron on either end. Screw through the front trim/apron into the legs at two places at either end. Screw the front trim/apron to the sink support brace in two places as well.

Step 8. Attach top shelf

Screw the top shelf to the tops of the back legs so that the shelf is flush with the back and outside edges of the back legs. The top shelf backing is attached to the back of the shelf and legs, protruding above and descending below the top of the shelf. Screw the top shelf backing to the legs in two places at each end and screw through the backing into the top shelf in two places along the shelf. The part of the backing that descends below the shelf can be fitted with nails, hooks or thumbtacks to hold tools or tack up seed packets. Attach shelf sides flush with the top of the shelf back, screwing each to the top shelf in two places and to the top shelf backing in two places (see Photo 5).

Step 9. Stain the bench

We did not stain or treat our bench. An untreated cedar bench that is left outside will weather to a silvery grey colour, and will last many years. If you would like to finish your bench, stain it or treat it with a clear preservative (particularly if you have used pine). When stain is dry, place the plastic tub in the sink hole.

Project

Backyard Classic

BUILD AN ELEGANT TRELLISED GARDEN ARBOUR.

Editor's note:
Making this arbour is a two-person job – it's built to last, so once assembled, the sides and roof are heavy and fairly unwieldy. Installed, it's a stunning focal point that "leads" you through the garden.

Difficulty level:
Difficult

Here we tackle a classic backyard project: the garden arbour. Our elegant design features a peaked roof and trelliswork — perfect for climbing roses or vines. Painted a crisp white, it draws the eye into the garden and defines separate spaces within it. In a small yard an arbour commands attention as an entrance or exit, replacing the traditional gate. Standing more than seven feet tall when installed, this sturdy arbour is made of standard-sized pine, although pressure-treated wood or cedar can also be used.

Covered in climbing roses or left unadorned as a pure architectural form, a garden arbour creates visual interest and adds a note of romance to the landscape.

PHOTOGRAPHY BY ASHOK CHARLES

This arbour is constructed from two side sections made up of three 9' vertical posts, held together by horizontal crosspieces, diagonal trelliswork and a peaked roof.

MATERIALS & TOOLS

6 9' pieces of 2" x 4" pine
3 7' pieces of 2" x 4" pine
136' of 1" x 2" pine
6' of 1" x 4" pine
2" galvanized nails
2" coated wood screws
Wood preservative
Latex primer and paint, or wood stain
Tape measure
Adjustable square
Level
T-square
Handsaw or mitre saw
Mitre box
Hammer
Cordless or electric drill
Screwdriver or electric drill with screwdriver attachment
Stepladder
Shovel
Post hole digger

Step 1. Cut side posts

The six 9' pieces of 2" x 4" are your side posts. In order to fit neatly under the slope of the roof, the top ends of these posts must be angled. Measure and mark the posts at 8' 11". Using an adjustable square, start at the 8' 11" mark and draw an angled line across the wide face of one post at 15°. With a handsaw (or mitre saw set at 15°), cut off the top of the post along the angled line. Use this first post as a template to mark and cut the five remaining posts.

Step 2. Cut crosspieces and diagonal trellis pieces

Cut fourteen pieces of 1" x 2" pine @ 32" long for the horizontal crosspieces. Set aside. Now cut 24 angled pieces for the trelliswork. With an adjustable square, mark a 30° angled line across the 2" side of one end of a piece of 1" x 2". Cut along this line with a handsaw (or a mitre saw set at 30°). From the point or "toe," made by this cut, measure 18 3/8" along the wood and place a mark. This mark will be the "heel" of the other end of the trellis piece. With the adjustable square set at 30°, draw a line across the 1" x 2". It should be parallel to the angled cut at the other end. Cut. Use this piece as a template to mark and cut the remaining 23 pieces (see Photo 1).

Step 3. Assemble sides

Lay three of the side posts on their narrow edges on a flat surface with the top (angled) ends in the same direction and the long side of the angle facing down. Line up the angled ends, then measure and place a mark at 1" in from the heel of the angled ends, along the narrow edge of the posts. From this first mark, measure and place six more marks at 12 3/8" increments. With a T-square, draw a line across all three posts at each of the marks. These lines will be the top edge of each of the horizontal crosspieces. Spread the three posts approximately 15" apart. Place the first crosspiece at the top mark and, ensuring that it is square to one of the outer posts and that its end is flush with the outer face of the post, nail it to the post. Repeat this at the other outer post. You may need to shift the posts slightly to make the crosspieces sit flush. Measure the length of the crosspiece and place a mark exactly at its centre; this will be the location of the centre of the middle post. Align the centre mark of the crosspiece with the middle of the centre post and nail them together, making sure that you keep the post and crosspiece square. Repeat this for each of the crosspieces. You should now have one side made up of seven crosspieces and three posts. Repeat for the other side.

Step 4. Attach diagonal trellis pieces

Begin by placing the first pair of angled 1" x 2" trellis pieces at the top of the centre post, just below the top horizontal crosspiece, with the angled ends butted against each other and the opposite ends angling towards the outer face of the outside posts. Position these outer ends so that they are flush with the face of the posts and nail them down with 2" nails. Realign the ends that are butted together at the middle post and nail them to the middle post. Repeat this down the posts, alternating the direction of the diagonals (see Photo 2).

Step 5. Cut and assemble roof rafters

From the 7' pieces of 2" x 4" pine, cut six roof rafters @ 26 1/2" as follows: With your adjustable square, mark a 15° angle on the 4" side of one end of a piece of 2" x 4". Cut. From the "toe" of this angle, measure 26 1/2" along the edge and mark the location of the other angle. Measure and mark another 15° angle at this mark, parallel to the first angle, and cut. Use this rafter as a template to mark out and cut the remaining five rafters.

To help hold the rafters together, you will need three braces. Cut three 10" pieces of 1" x 2". Lay out a pair of rafters on a flat surface, with the angled ends butted together so that they form a V. Next, lay one of the 10" braces across the angled join where the rafters meet. Ensure that the brace does not project beyond the outer edges of the rafters. Screw them together, through each end of the brace into each of the rafters, staggering the screws so as not to split the brace. Repeat for the remaining two pairs of rafters.

Step 6. Cut roof trellis

Cut 12 pieces from the 1" x 2" pine @ 36" long. These pieces are 4" longer than the width of the roof so they will overhang the rafters on each side by 2". On each of the trellis pieces, measure and mark 2" in from either end, to indicate the location of the outer face of the rafters. Measure and mark the centre of each trellis piece to line up with the centre of the middle rafter.

Step 7. Assemble roof

Lay out the three rafter pairs. Hold the end of your tape measure at the point where two rafters meet and stretch the tape along the length of the outer edge of one of the rafters, placing marks at 5" increments. These marks are where the 1" x 2" trellis will be attached. Repeat for the five remaining rafters.
Stand the first rafter pair up. You will need some help for this step. This first rafter is the centre one. Take the first piece of 1" x 2" trellis and place it across the rafter, just below the point of the rafter, and centre the middle mark on the 1" x 2" on the middle of the rafter. Attach the 1" x 2" to the rafter with a 2" screw. With a square, check that the rafter and the 1" x 2" are at 90° to each other.

Stand up another rafter pair and fit it beneath one end of the 1" x 2". Align the rafter so that the 1" x 2" is just below the point of the rafter and so that the mark at 2" in from the end of the 1" x 2" is aligned with the outer face of this rafter. Screw the 1" x 2" to the rafter and ensure that the rafter and the 1" x 2" are at 90°. Repeat for the third rafter. Attach the remaining pieces of 1" x 2" at the marks down the length of the rafters. Make sure that the rafters and the roof trellis pieces are square, then attach the remaining 1" x 2" pieces to the other side of the rafters in the same manner (see Photo 3).

Step 8. Attach temporary braces

To attach the roof to the sides, it is necessary to stand the sides up. To keep them upright and in the correct position, you will need to temporarily hold them together with braces. Cut three pieces of 1" x 2" @ 42" long (the outside width of the finished arbour). Next, cut one piece of 1" x 2" @ 60" long, to serve as a diagonal brace that will keep the sides vertical or "plumb." Lay the two side sections of the arbour on their edges with the trellised sides facing out. Place one of the 1" x 2" braces across the 2" x 4" post at the location of the top crosspiece. Place the end of the brace flush with the outside of the crosspiece and screw through the brace into the post with a 2" screw. Repeat this procedure with another brace at the lowest crosspiece. Now attach the other ends of the braces to the other side section, again lining up the ends of the braces with the outer face of the crosspieces.

With a large square or a T-square, check that the angle between the post and the brace you have just attached is 90°, then screw the 60" brace diagonally to the two posts. Take the third 42" brace and start to screw 2" screws into it, about 2" in from each end. Set aside.

On level ground, carefully stand the arbour. Climb a stepladder with the third 42" brace and screw it into the other side of the arbour, aligned with the outside of the crosspiece, as close to the top of the arbour as you can. With a tape measure check the outside width of the arbour in various places and shift the structure around, if necessary, to make it square.

Step 9. Attach roof

To attach the roof rafters to the posts you will need to cut braces that will hold the roof to the sides. From the 1" x 4" pine, cut six pieces, approximately 9" long with a 30° angle cut on both ends. Carefully raise the roof over the top of the arbour and set it down on top of the posts. Each of the roof rafters should line up with one of the side posts. With your tape measure, check the amount that the roof extends beyond each side and adjust it so that the overhang is equal on both sides. At the intersection of each rafter and post, place one of the 1" x 4" braces. Line up the 30° angle at the end of the brace with the slope of the rafter and attach it with 2" screws to both the post and the rafter.

Step 10. Paint or stain arbour

Before installing, treat the bottom 30" of the posts, including the ends, with at least three coats of wood preservative. Let dry. Finish the rest of the arbour with latex primer and several coats of exterior latex paint or a water-resistant stain, allowing drying time between coats.

Step 11. Dig post holes and install arbour

Note: Before you dig the post holes, be sure that there are no buried pipes or cables. Call your hydro, gas, cable and telephone companies to confirm the location of their services.

Position the arbour in your desired location and mark on the ground the position of each of the posts. Dig six holes approximately 2'6" deep and 6" to 8" in diameter. Carefully lower the arbour posts into them. With the arbour set in place, use a level to check it for "plumb" (vertical) and "level" (horizontal). If you find that the arbour is tilting, lift up the low side or corner and push some dirt into the hole to raise it up. Once the arbour is level you can begin to "backfill" the holes using the earth you have dug out. Fill in with an 8" layer of earth. With a long stick or the handle of a shovel, pack down the layer of earth then add more until the holes are completely filled. Remove the support braces and touch up any spots that were missed with primer and paint, or stain.

Workshop

05

STEP BY STEP YOU'LL BUILD YOUR OWN SOLUTIONS FOR STYLISH LIVING

BRAND NEW LIFE FOUND STORAGE **CURRENT EXHIBITION** FABRIC SOFTENER **NUTS & BOLTS** SCREEN PLAY **BEHIND CLOSED DOORS** BUILDING CHARACTER **OPEN & SHUT** FLOOR SHOW **HEAD OF THE CLASS** BUILD A GARDEN SHED **REMAKING THE BED** VANITY FAIR **THE NEW SHEERS** FOUR INSPIRATIONAL MAKEOVERS **ALL IN A DAY'S WORK** MIRROR IMAGE **KITCHEN HANGUPS** CLOSET ASPIRATIONS **DISPLAY'S THE THING** SPACE SAVERS **BAMBOOZLED** EASY TO BUILD KITCHEN ISLAND **HALL ORGANIZER** EASY TO BUILD PLATE RACK **LIGHTEN UP**

Brand New Life

WE EMPLOYED THE THREE R'S — RESTORE, RESTYLE, RETHINK — TO TRANSFORM A CROP OF FLEA-MARKET FINDS.

Editor's note:
Finding an old piece with potential is important, but proper prep is the real key to success here. Take your time – cleaning, sanding, priming – and you'll reap the rewards with a better finished product.

Difficulty level:
Average

Projects:
Coffee table
Piano stool
Caned-back chair
Rushed-seat chair and stool
Sofa
Table with basket storage
Lamp
Film boxes

The way we see it, just because something cost a pittance doesn't mean we shouldn't invest time or money in fixing it up. Savvy fixer-uppers pay attention to the three R's of flea-marketing: restore, restyle and rethink. "Restoring" involves returning a piece, more or less, to its original glory — revitalizing it. "Restyling" means giving a piece new finishes or accents, and may even increase the worth of an item of lesser pedigree. "Rethinking" involves a complete conversion that changes a piece's function as well as its look. Here, we've decorated a living room solely with flea-market fix-ups — nine pieces that we restored, restyled or rethought. An Edwardian sofa, for example, was restored with wood stain and new upholstery. A painted metal lamp was simply restyled when plated in a more fashionable finish. And a large multipaned window was rethought by turning it into a hinged top for a coffee table with a display area underneath. The result is a room filled not with worn-out odds and ends but with finds that, given the time and attention they deserved, have been turned into stylish gems.

PHOTOGRAPHY BY LUIS ALBUQUERQUE

Repainting woodfurniture

Follow these basic steps when repainting your pieces:

- With a trisodium phosphate (TSP) solution and a clean rag, rub down the piece to remove any dirt, grease or residue. Let dry completely.
- Use a low-grit sandpaper (about 80 grit) to roughen the original finish of the wood so paint will adhere better.
- With low-tack masking tape, tape off any sections you don't want to paint. Prime the piece with a latex primer, and allow to dry overnight.
- Lightly sand piece using 120-grit sandpaper to smooth any remaining rough parts, and wipe away sanding dust with a slightly damp cloth.
- Apply one coat of latex paint to piece. Allow to dry thoroughly. Apply another coat if necessary. Remove tape while paint is still tacky.

COFFEE TABLE

To make a coffee table from this old window, we built a box with a beadboard bottom, mounted the box on turned wooden legs and hinged the window on top. Be sure the window you use is in good condition, with no broken or loose glass panes (replace or fix any that are in disrepair). The size of the table will depend on the size of the window you use; our 31" x 40" window was ample enough to become a coffee table. A smaller window could be made into a side table. Keep an open mind when you're out shopping (or garbage-picking!) for windows for this project.

MATERIALS & TOOLS

	Old wood-framed window in desired size
4	pieces 1" x 6" poplar (lengths will depend on window size)
	Wood glue
12	1 1/2" wood screws
4	turned legs
	1" x 1" poplar
	1 1/4" finishing nails
1	4' x 8' faux beadboard sheet
	Wood filler
	100-grit sandpaper
	1 quart latex primer
	1 quart latex paint
2	latches
1	large hinged toolbox handle
2	hinges
	Jigsaw
	Handsaw
	Drill with countersink bit
	Screwdriver
	Chisel
	Mallet
	Hammer
	Paintbrush

Step 1. Even out window edges

The outside edges of our window had to be evened out, so we measured them to equal distances and cut down the two wider sides with a jigsaw. The cut-down window size will determine the size of your table. After cutting, our window measured 31" x 40".

Step 2. Create base frame

Use four pieces of 1" x 6" poplar to create the base of the table. Create a frame the same size as your window, using a simple butt joint. Be sure ends of wood pieces butt together at 90° angles, and pre-drill two holes at each corner. Use wood glue and countersunk 1 1/2" wood screws to attach base pieces.

Step 3. Attach legs

To attach the legs so that they sit flush with the outside edge of the table, the top of the legs will need to be notched out on two sides to accommodate the frame. Measure and mark where the legs will need to be notched, and use a chisel and mallet to do this. Pre-drill holes through the sides of the table frame, and attach legs to frame using wood glue and countersunk 1 1/2" wood screws.

Step 4. Install beadboard bottom

The beadboard sheet acts as our table bottom. It needs to be supported by lengths of 1" x 1" wood that run around the bottom inside perimeter of the table base. Cut four pieces of 1" x 1" to fit around the bottom inside perimeter of the table base. Use wood glue and 1 1/4" finishing nails to attach these pieces in place. Cut beadboard sheet to fit inside the table base. When cut to size, drop it in from the top. Use wood glue and 1 1/4" finishing nails to attach beadboard to 1" x 1" pieces.

Step 5. Fill, sand and paint base

Use wood filler to fill all holes made by screw heads and nail holes on base. Sand entire unit using 100-grit sandpaper. Using latex primer, prime the table base. Allow to dry. Paint the table base in desired colour (we used Roman White P1836-4 by Para Paints).

Step 6. Attach window to table base

Sand any rough edges and scrape away any peeling paint from window frame and mullions. Follow refinishing steps from "Repainting wood furniture" (above left), using the same colour of paint as that used for the table base. Mark hinge locations with a pencil before pre-drilling holes for screws, then attach two latches and hinged handle to the edge of the window, and attach hinges to the window and table base.

PIANO STOOL

This stool had already been given a coat of primer, but we still followed the steps in "Repainting wood furniture" (above left). Since the previous owner had been sloppy with the primer, the cast-iron ball-and-claw feet needed to be cleaned. We used Varsol and a toothbrush to scrub the primer off the feet. Then we taped over the feet to protect them, and painted the rest of the stool.

CANED-BACK CHAIR

This chair's frame was repainted using the steps in "Repainting wood furniture." When a piece like this requires painting or staining as well as upholstering or caning, do the painting or staining first to avoid marking the new upholstery and/or caning. We had our chair professionally recaned and reupholstered. We took the chair to W.H. Kilby in Toronto for recaning, but this company also offers recaning kits for do-it-yourselfers. The seat was reupholstered by Plush n' Plump in Toronto, but could have been done at home by a do-it-yourselfer with basic upholstery skills.

RUSHED-SEAT CHAIR AND STOOL

This chair and footstool were not originally a set, but we faked it by treating them to the same black-painted finish and new rushing. Both were somewhat wobbly and in disrepair, so first we used wood glue and clamps to fix any broken parts. Once the glue was thoroughly dry, we repainted the pieces following the steps in "Repainting wood furniture." We used a matte black paint (Black P1912-5 by Para Paints). For the rushing, we contacted the Canadian National Institute for the Blind, who put us in contact with a craftsperson who rerushed the pieces. To find out about this service in your area, call the local C.N.I.B. office; visit www.cnib.ca for organization phone numbers across Canada. We chose a paper rushing, rather than the more standard natural sisal, for its softer feel.

SOFA

The sturdy frame of this sofa was in excellent condition but had been painted black at some point. Its original upholstery was deemed outdated and beyond repair. Once the old upholstery and horsehair stuffing were removed, the frame was treated to a "no dip" stripping and refinishing process. This method is much less harsh on old woods than traditional chemical dipping methods. We had our sofa stripped at No-Dip Furniture Stripping in Streetsville, Ont. Check the Yellow Pages in your city for a furniture stripper that offers this gentler method. Once stripped of its paint layers, our sofa frame turned out to have a burled-walnut veneer — definitely worth showing off. The antique dealer you purchase your piece from, or the stripping company should be able to assess whether your piece is worth stripping and refinishing. If it's not, simply repaint it. We stained the piece, as opposed to painting it, to ensure the elegant wood grain would show through. We used one coat of semi-transparent stain (Dark Walnut ST35 by Para Paints) mixed by the paint dealer at half-strength. After one coat of stain was brushed on, it was immediately rubbed with clean, dry cheesecloth while it was still wet to let the maximum amount of grain show through. The stain was allowed to dry overnight. The next day, we brushed on a coat of clear satin urethane to protect the wood and give it a subtle sheen. After letting this finish dry overnight, we took the sofa to be professionally reupholstered by Plush n' Plump in Toronto.

TABLE WITH BASKET STORAGE

We removed the decorative panel from the front of this table by laying the table on the floor face up and carefully cutting the panel away with a jigsaw. The freshly cut edges were sanded smooth, and the entire piece was repainted using the steps in "Repainting wood furniture."

LAMP

Replating is not a process that can be done at home. Our metal lamp was replated by Mayfair Plating in Toronto. To find a company that offers this sort of service in your city, look under "Plating" in the Yellow Pages. We had a satin nickel finish put on our lamp, but a variety of metallic finishes are available. Decide what is most suitable for the style or era of your piece.

FILM BOXES

To restyle our vintage film boxes, we removed the worn-out strapping and replaced it with pretty striped and grosgrain ribbon. Vintage postcards were cut to size to fit into the existing label slots.

Project

Found Storage

TAKE A SECOND LOOK AT YOUR WALLS: THEY MAY BE HIDING A SECRET STORAGE OPTION.

Editor's note:
If you have a special collection to display, arrange groupings before you begin this project and build cubbies to fit. Just be sure there's no wiring or pipes behind the drywall before you cut it.

Difficulty level:
Average

We're willing to bet on it: there's not a room in any house that wouldn't benefit from more storage space. But cramming more dressers, shelving or armoires into a room isn't always a suitable solution. In fact, a precious commodity lurks just behind those blank walls: found space. Here, we've built three recessed niches into a section of empty wall. The niches make great out-of-the-way spots to highlight favourite collections, or stash objects like books, toys or toiletries. They're made by cutting out drywall between wall studs, framing the holes with moulding, and painting them to coordinate with the room. (For a more modern and minimal look, leave the niches unframed — this will take a little more time and effort to drywall.) The niches can be built in a variety of configurations, either aligned vertically, as we did, or horizontally, perhaps along the ceiling line. All that's required is a room with basic stud-and-drywall construction — it's the standard in many homes — and a few simple tools and materials.

We carved a series of three recessed cubbies out of a standard stud-and-drywall wall, using basic tools, materials and methods. The recesses were framed with moulding and painted, and their insides were painted a darker shade than the walls to highlight collectibles.

PHOTOGRAPHY BY MICHAEL ALBERST

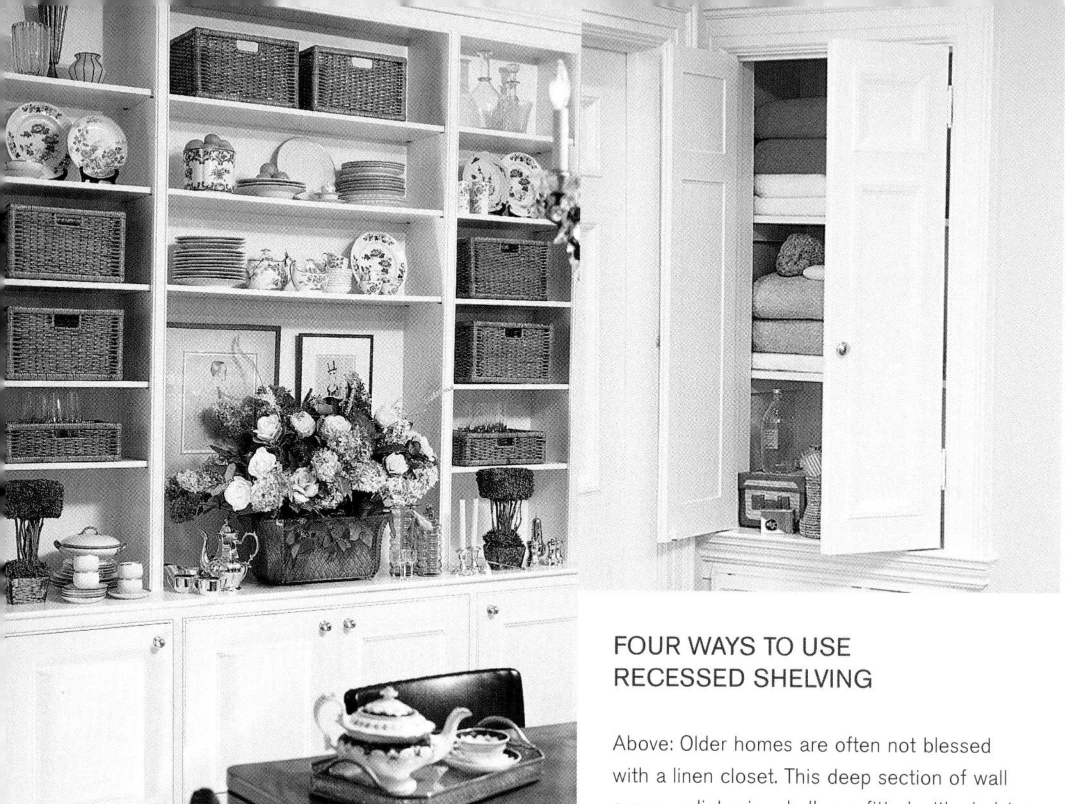

FOUR WAYS TO USE RECESSED SHELVING

Above: Older homes are often not blessed with a linen closet. This deep section of wall over a radiator in a hall was fitted with shelving and tailored panelled doors to store linens and cleaning supplies. For continuity, the closet has been trimmed in moulding to match the existing door frames.

Above left: A whole section of wall has been cut out to house a large shelving unit in this dining room. Cabinets built out at the base give the unit a furniture-like look and offer hidden storage, and open shelving above showcases china and silver.

Left: A desk and closet were carved out of this under-stair space in a kitchen. The chaos of the desk area is hidden in the drawers and cupboards. Pretty panelled doors, corner brackets and brass hardware make the unit elegant.

Below: A small, deep nook in a front hall is a perfect spot to drop keys and mail just inside the door, eliminating the need for a table in the tight space.

Project 25: Recessed storage

BUILT-IN WALL NICHES

We built our niches into an interior wall, but exterior walls can also be used for this project. If building into an exterior wall, you'll have to consider insulation: cut out any existing insulation and insert a thinner variety (such as Styrofoam) behind the niche. Stud configuration is usually slightly different on exterior walls, so the shape of niches on exterior walls may have to be adjusted.

MATERIALS & TOOLS

5' 1" x 4" lumber
1 1/4" drywall screws
20' 1/2" x 4" knot-free lumber
1 1/2" wood screws
4' x 8' 1/8"-thick Masonite (hardboard)
1" finishing nails
1 1/2" finishing nails
22' moulding
Stud finder
Pencil and measuring tape
Level
Carpenter's square
Electric drill
Flashlight
Drywall saw
Handsaw
Wood glue
Clamps
Screwdriver
Hammer
Mitre box
Countersink
Caulking gun and paintable latex caulk
Wood filler
100- and 120-grit sandpaper
Primer
Two colours paint
Paintbrush

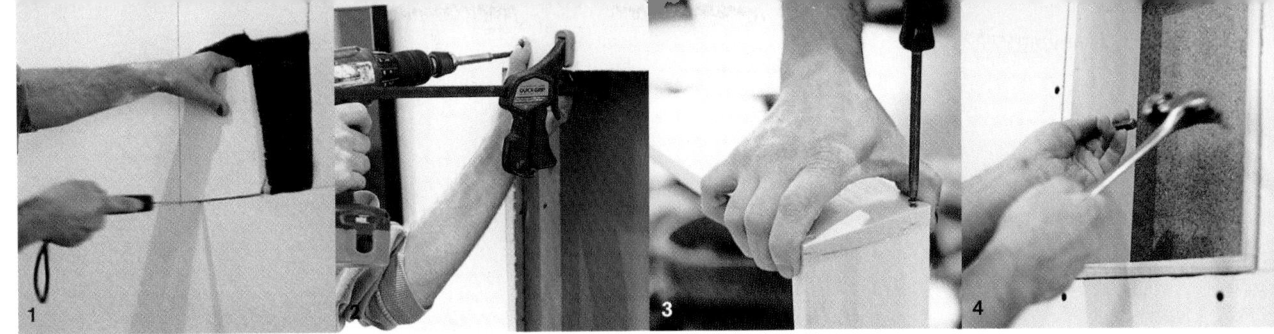

Step 1. Mark studs and niches
Using a stud finder, locate the studs within the wall space where you'd like to work. Mark stud locations on the wall with pencil. Based on where studs are positioned, decide where you'd like to build your recessed niches. The niches will have to be directly between two studs and should be wide enough to touch a stud on each side. In most houses, studs are 14" to 16" apart. Use a level, carpenter's square, measuring tape and pencil to mark out the desired size, shape and location of your niches. Our niches were 16" h. x 11" w. x 4" d.

Step 2. Cut openings
Drill a small "peep hole" (about 1" in diameter) into the centre of each marked niche shape. Shine a flashlight into each hole to check the niche area for wires and pipes. If nothing is in your way, use a drywall saw to cut out entire niche along marked lines (see Photo 1).

Step 3. Reinforce drywall
Reinforce the two sections of drywall between the three niches with pieces of 1" x 4" wood. Using a handsaw, cut four pieces of wood to the width of your niches. Apply wood glue along one 4" side of each piece. Clamp one length of wood in place along bottom edge of top niche, top and bottom edge of the middle niche, and top edge of bottom niche. Use countersunk 1 1/4" drywall screws to drill through drywall into wood (see Photo 2). Be sure to keep screws within an inch from the edge of the niche so that the moulding frame will cover them later.

Step 4. Build boxes
Using 1/2" x 4" knot-free lumber, wood glue and 1 1/2" wood screws, build three box frames to fit inside niches. Make each box 1/4" smaller all around than the size of your niches. Since this frame will be hidden by moulding and then painted, there is no need to mitre the corners (see Photo 3). Cut a piece of 1/8"-thick Masonite (hardboard) to fit the back of each frame. Run a bead of glue around back edges of frames, press Masonite into place on back of frame, and secure with 1" finishing nails. Wipe off any excess glue with a cloth. Repeat for all boxes.

Step 5. Install boxes in niches
Run a bead of wood glue inside niches, along studs on both sides and along reinforcement wood pieces. Insert box frames into niches, and hammer countersunk 1 1/2" finishing nails through boxes into sides and reinforcement wood pieces (see Photo 4).

Step 6. Cut and install moulding
At the four corners of each box frame, use a carpenter's square to mark lines on box edges, 1/8" in from outside edges of box (see Photo 5). This is where the moulding will be placed when it's installed. Use these marks to measure for the moulding. Cut moulding to size to fit around each niche. Use a handsaw and mitre box to create 45° angles at the end of each piece of moulding, with the short side of the moulding equal to the distance from one of the lines you've just marked to the next. Place four moulding pieces together on the floor to make sure they fit tightly together; adjust if needed. Run a small bead of wood glue onto moulding pieces one at a time. Fit moulding in place around niches, and secure to box edges with countersunk 1" finishing nails (see Photo 6).

Step 7. Caulk edges and fill holes
Run a thin bead of paintable latex caulking around the perimeter of the moulding where it meets the wall to fill in any gaps. While caulking is still wet, wipe off excess with your finger. Fill all nail holes with wood filler and allow to dry completely. Lightly sand all filled spots with 100-grit sandpaper.

Step 8. Prime and paint
Use latex primer to prime entire recessed niche and mouldings. We used Benjamin Moore Fresh Start primer. Allow to dry completely. Sand entire unit very lightly using 120-grit sandpaper. Wipe clean with a cloth. Paint mouldings using a trim colour (we used Benjamin Moore Cloud White CC-40). Allow to dry. Paint recessed niche a colour that is complementary to the rest of the room (we used Benjamin Moore Stuart Gold HC-10). Allow to dry completely (overnight is best) before placing objects in niches. You may need to repaint the wall around the niches to fix any blemishes caused by the construction.

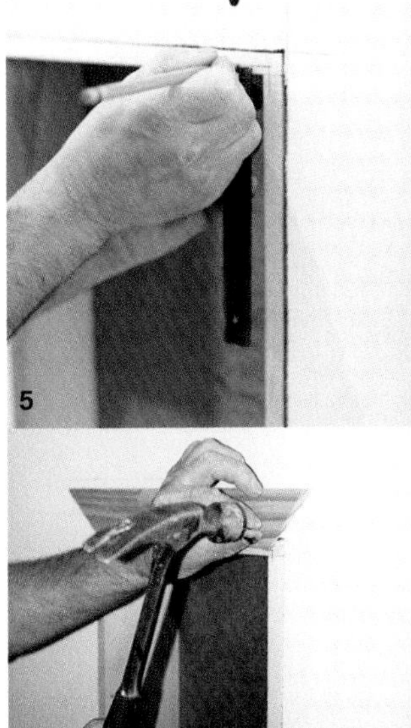

PHOTOGRAPHY BY MORGAN MICHENER

Project

Current Exhibition

THESE TWO HANGING SYSTEMS GIVE YOU GALLERY-STYLE PRESENTATION AT HOME.

Editor's note:
Artwork hung with this much care deserves a backdrop that really sets it off. If you can't decide on a wall colour, visit local galleries and take note of any particularly effective hues they use.

Difficulty level:
Easy

Projects:
Victorian spring clip system
Wire-hung picture gallery

Whether you are just completing renovations or looking to spice up an existing room, a well-displayed art installation can bring a crisp, professional gallery look to your home and provide a room with a unique decorative focus. We developed two hanging styles that are stylish, tailored and simple to install. You can pick up the materials at most home-supply stores when shopping for reno or gardening supplies. We put heavy-duty Victorian-style spring clips to work holding photographs in simple wooden "frames" you can make yourself. For a more industrial look, framed photographs were suspended by wire at various heights from a heavy-duty curtain rod mounted high up on the wall. Both systems are free of overt ornamentation, which gives the artwork centre stage. We complemented the industrial character of the systems by hanging graphic black-and-white photographs, but both systems would look lovely fitted with more colourful artwork. Similarly, the systems are suited to modern architecture, but could also be used in traditional settings to inject contemporary style. Both hanging styles are flexible: they can be extended horizontally or vertically to fit your wall space. The clipped frames would work hanging in a single row or running diagonally up a staircase wall to follow the angle of the stairs. Whichever system you choose, it will bring a clean, handsome look to family photos or favourite works of art.

We've put heavy-duty, cast-iron, Victorian-style spring clips (used to hold papers and files in a workshop) to work holding photographs set off by clipboard-style frames. It's a look that could work with almost any decorating style. The frames are made of rectangles of inexpensive fir-veneered plywood (any attractively grained soft wood will work here) stained a dark walnut colour, glass with buffed edges and antiqued upholstery tacks (in lieu of nails or screws). And the how-to is straightforward: cut and stain the wood, cut the glass (or have a glass retailer do it for you), fit the wood and glass together with upholstery tacks, attach clips, and hang.

PHOTOGRAPHY BY DONNA GRIFFITH

Project 26: Hanging systems

VICTORIAN SPRING CLIP SYSTEM

Our original photographs were 4" x 6", so we made our frames to fit those measurements. You may need to adjust the size of the plywood and glass to fit your photos/artwork if they are a different size.

MATERIALS & TOOLS

	4' x 6' sheet of 1/4"-thick fir-veneered plywood (or any soft wood with visible grain)
	Handsaw (if cutting wood yourself)
	Sandpaper
	Clean, soft cloth
	3"-wide foam paintbrush
	Dark walnut-coloured stain
4	8" x 12" pieces 1/8"-thick glass with buffed edges (cut to size by store)
8	bronze or burnished-metal upholstery tacks
4	large spring clips

Step 1. Prepare wood

We had our wood cut into 10" x 14" rectangles to suit 4" x 6" prints. This allows for a wide border all around the artwork. Sand edges of the boards until smooth, and wipe away dust with a soft cloth. Choose a side of the wood with the most attractive grain. Using foam brush, lightly cover surface with stain, working in smooth, broad strokes. Let this first thin coat of stain sink in, then apply a second coat. Allow to dry completely.

Step 2. Assemble frames

Cut your images to size if necessary. Centre an image on each board. Place glass over image. Insert upholstery tacks at the bottom edge of the glass on each print. Clamp glass in place with decorative spring clip at the top of the board.

Step 3. Hang frames

Hang on wall using a single nail and the small nail hole in the back of the clip.

This modern, industrial-style installation was inspired by displays in art and photography galleries. It is made of a heavy-duty curtain rod, picture-hanging wire and threading connectors (small metal blocks with two sets of holes for wire that are hammered closed to hold the wire in place). The artworks almost look as if they're floating, which distinctly softens the mechanical look. Extremely versatile, this system of hanging allows the photographs or paintings to be moved around on the rod or replaced altogether without having to drill new holes in the wall.

ANCHOR LOOPS
"DEAD" ENDS
THREADING CONNECTORS
BACK OF FRAME
WIRE
HANGING CLIPS
BACK OF FRAME

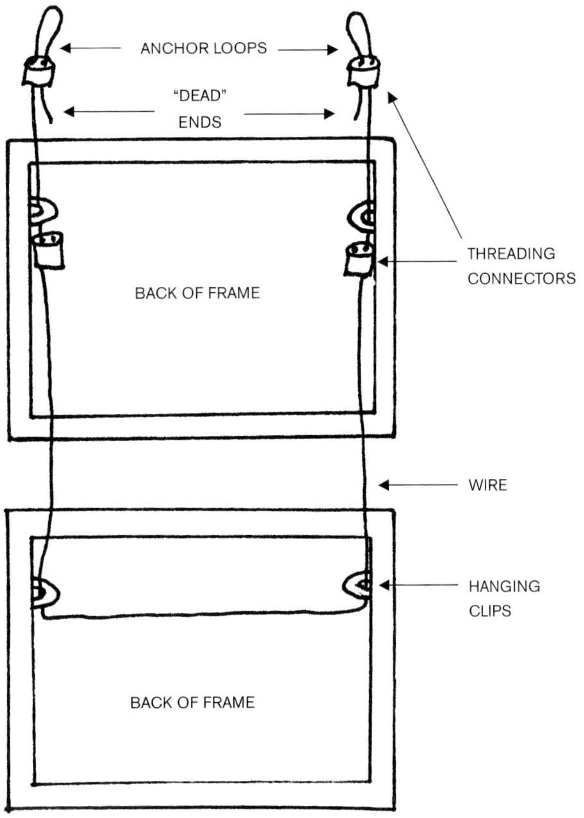

DIAGRAM

To hang one print over another, run one long piece of wire through the hanging clips on the back of frames. Clamp the threading connectors onto the wire to form both anchor loops, and to stop the top frame from sliding down the wire.

WIRE-HUNG PICTURE GALLERY

This system uses picture-hanging wire strung through threading connectors, which are small metal blocks with side-by-side holes in them. The connectors are hammered closed to hold the wire in place. They're available at hardware stores, usually in the same section as picture-hanging wire and hooks.

MATERIALS & TOOLS

- Drapery rod with brackets (1 bracket for every 4' of rod)
- Picture-hanging wire
- Threading connectors (1 pair per frame plus 1 per top loop)
- Pliers
- Hammer

Step 1. Decide on layout

On the floor, lay your framed artwork (with standard hanging clips already installed on frame backs) face down in the configuration you'd like to achieve on the wall. Place the rod above arrangement at the same distance from top of artwork as you'd like when it's hung on the wall. Keep in mind that you shouldn't hang more than two medium-sized framed pieces per single loop of wire. Also, when hanging two frames per loop, allow for at least 4" between frames.

Step 2. Prepare frames

Move the hanging clips at the back of each frame as close to the top as possible (this will help the artwork hang flat against the wall). The wire will thread through the holes in these clips.

Step 3. Start threading wire

To create the initial anchor loop that will hang over the rod, thread one end of wire up through one of the holes of the connector (leave a couple of inches loose at end) and then back down through the second hole in the connector, leaving a 2"-long loop to slide over the rod. With a pair of pliers placed around the metal connector, hammer down on the teeth of the pliers until the connector is pinched closed over the two wires, securing the wire loop in place. Snip the short end of the wire to a 1" tail. To make a clean cut, clamp the wire-cutting section of pliers down on the wire, and hammer down once on the handles of the pliers.

The "live" end of the wire is the continuous length of wire. The "dead" end is the short 1" tail end.

Step 4. Thread wire

To connect two pictures together, thread the live end of the wire down through the holes in the clips on one picture frame. Thread another connector along the live end of the wire, so that it stops just below the hole in the clip (see Diagram). Pinch this connector closed around the wire (one side of connector will be empty), so that when hanging, the frame will not drop beyond this height. Continue to thread the live end of the wire through the hole in the hanging hardware of the lower frame. You will work from top to bottom, across the back and then back up the other side of the pictures to the top again (see Diagram). Run the wire across the back of the lower frame and up through the hole in the clip at the other side. Thread a second connector onto the live wire. Pinch this connector just below the clip on the top frame. Thread the live wire through the clip, and create a second anchor loop. Snip off excess live wire with pliers, leaving a 1" tail. To hang a single print only: Create your initial anchor loop, as in Step 3. Thread the live end of the wire down through the hole in the clip. Run wire across the back of the frame over to clip on other side. Thread the wire up through this clip. Create a second anchor loop and cut off the excess wire.

Step 5. Hang system

Hang the curtain rod brackets (as per package instructions) on the wall at the appropriate height. There should be a bracket every 4' to properly support the weight of the rod and artwork. With frames lying on the floor in the proper configuration, thread loops onto the drapery rod one at a time while rod is still on the floor. With the help of another person, hang the curtain rod on its brackets. Adjust the frames along rod until they are evenly spaced out. You will have some room to play with the single-hung frames since the wire is a continuous loop that can be easily adjusted by sliding frame into desired position and adding more connectors.

Project 27

Fabric Softener

UPHOLSTERED WALLS ADD A TOUCH OF LUXE WITH A TAILORED MODERN EDGE.

Editor's note:
These projects are easy but work best with two pairs of hands. To keep costs down, use inexpensive fabrics, or upholster one really large panel in vintage fabric and hang it like a piece of art.

Difficulty level:
Average

Projects:
Channelled padded wall
Nine-square wall panelling

Today's best-looking walls are getting dressed for success in fabric-covered panels. This fashion-forward look is a rich, sophisticated alternative to wallpaper and evokes the mood of a sumptuous lounge or gentleman's reading room. Upholstering your walls is a relatively easy fix-up and is a wonderfully stylish way to cover up damaged or uneven walls. Try the project in a home office or den, or to create a feature wall in the bedroom. Here a typical rowhouse bedroom becomes a luxurious, almost boutique hotel-style retreat when a channelled upholstered wall is installed behind the bed. It's a pleasing modern look for an older house. And a small home office that lacks character suddenly seems like a perfect place to curl up with a good book when a single wall is treated to nine square panels covered in supple Ultrasuede. The basic materials and tools needed are inexpensive and readily available: particleboard for the backing, soft polyester foam to pad the board, fabric and a staple gun. Depending on your budget and your room's style, the fabric you choose can be luxurious or simple. Canvas, cotton twills and linens will be less expensive and look a little less formal. Damasks and faux leather or suede will be pricier, so you'll likely want to use them more sparingly, as we did with the smaller Ultrasuede squares on the library wall. Whatever your budget, look for a fabric that will inject some texture into the room's envelope, create a focal point and tie the space together.

We created a beautiful feature wall in a bedroom by treating the wall at the head of the bed to channelled upholstered panels in a creamy, subtly slubbed linen. Not only do the tall channels of upholstery fool the eye into seeing a taller, more open space, but the particleboard and batting provide some sound insulation from the adjoining row-house. To create this treatment, we covered tall particleboard panels with foam and fabric (stapled around the back of the panels), affixed the panels to the wall with Velcro and then added moulding in front of the panels.

PHOTOGRAPHY BY VIRGINIA MACDONALD

CHANNELLED PADDED WALL

The measurements given for this project are specific to the wall we treated. Be sure to measure your own wall carefully and adjust measurements accordingly.

MATERIALS & TOOLS

	Pencil and measuring tape
6	pieces 18" x 96" 1/2"-thick particleboard
6	pieces 18" x 96" 1"-thick soft polyester batting
6	pieces fabric cut to 24" x 102"
	Double-sided tape
	1/4" staples and staple gun
2	2"-wide, 9'-long Velcro strips
	Drill
9'	1" x 2" lumber

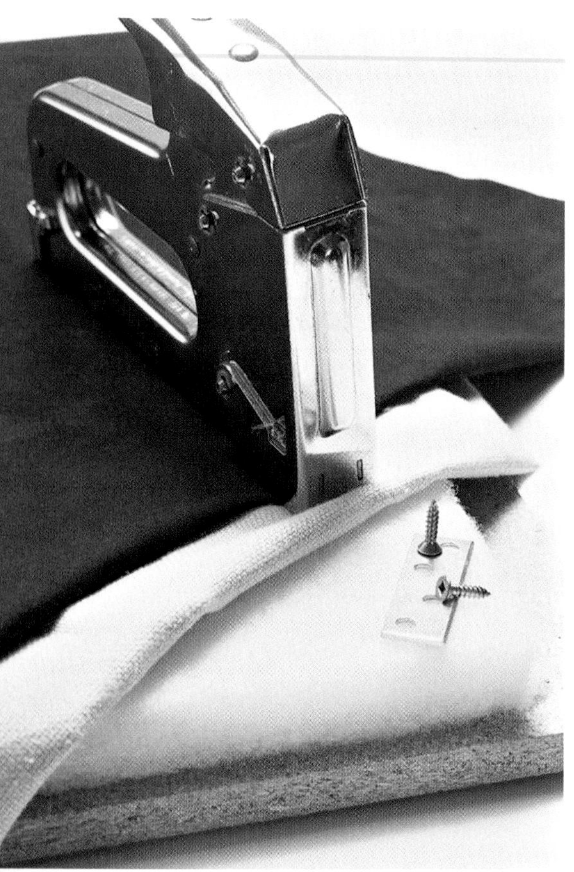

Step 1. Measure wall and cut panels

Remove any crown moulding from the wall you are treating, and set aside. Measure your wall and determine the size of panels you will upholster. Make sure you measure the wall carefully and divide the width of the wall into equal-sized pieces for cutting. Use a pencil to mark the panel locations on the wall. Our ceiling is 9' high, with a 7"-high baseboard moulding, and a 5"-high crown moulding. The wall is 9' wide, therefore we had six 8'-high and 18"-wide panels cut. Most lumber stores have a cutting service that can cut your particleboard to size.

Step 2. Cut batting and fabric

Cut six pieces of 1"-thick batting to the same size as the particleboard panels. Add 6" to the length and 6" to the width of this measurement, and cut six pieces of fabric to this larger size. Our fabric pieces were 24" x 102". This will allow the fabric to completely cover the panels and wrap around their backs.

Step 3. Cover panels

Apply strips of double-sided tape to particleboard panels. Lay batting onto panels. The tape will hold the batting in place as you attach the fabric. Lay fabric over top of batting layer. Wrap the extra 3" of fabric along each side around to the back of the panel. Using a staple gun and 1/4" staples, staple once in the middle of each side first, being sure to pull fabric taut before stapling. Continue to staple around back of panel until all fabric is attached.

Step 4. Attach panels to wall

Cut lengths of Velcro to the width of the panels. Use staples and a staple gun to attach Velcro strips across the top and bottom of each panel. Attach Velcro strips widthwise across top and bottom of wall (just above baseboard moulding at bottom) using staples and staple gun. Hang panels along wall, matching Velcro strips on each panel to corresponding strips on wall. The bottom of the panels should just touch the top of the baseboard moulding.

Step 5. Reattach crown moulding

We started with a fresh design and installed new crown mouldings, but you can reuse your original mouldings. To account for the thickness of the upholstered panels, screw a length of 1" x 2" lumber into the wall along the ceiling line. The mouldings are installed directly over top of this piece and affixed with longer screws to accommodate the thickness of the mouldings and added lumber. Drill and screw through panels into wall behind.

NINE-SQUARE WALL PANELLING

We made this decorative wall panel with nine 18" squares. Adjust your measurements if you'd like to create a different look or cover a larger or smaller area.

MATERIALS & TOOLS

- Pencil and measuring tape
- 9 pieces 18" x 18" 1/2"-thick particleboard
- 9 pieces 18" x 18" 1"-thick soft polyester batting
- 9 pieces fabric cut to 22" x 22"
- Double-sided tape
- 1/4" staples and staple gun
- 24 2"-linking braces
- 51 1/2" particleboard screws
- 3 heavy-duty picture hooks and hangers

Step 1. Measure and cut panels

Measure out and mark the location and configuration of the panels on your wall with a pencil. We made nine panels, each measuring 18" x 18". Most lumber stores can cut your particleboard to size.

Step 2. Cut batting and fabric to size

Cut nine pieces of batting to 18" x 18". Cut nine pieces of fabric to 22" x 22" (this will allow the fabric to completely cover the panels and wrap around their backs).

Step 3. Cover panels

Affix strips of double-sided tape to particleboard panels. Lay batting over panels. The tape will hold the batting in place as you attach the fabric. Lay fabric over the top of batting layer. Wrap the extra 2" of fabric around to the back of the panel. Using a staple gun and 1/4" staples, staple fabric to back of panel once in the middle of each side first, pulling fabric taut before stapling. Continue to staple around back of panel until all fabric is attached.

Step 4. Link panels together

Using three particleboard screws, attach one picture hanger to the centre of the back of three of your finished panels. With remaining 48 particleboard screws and 24 linking braces (two braces attaching each panel to the next), link all nine panels together, making sure that the three panels with hangers on the back form the top row.

Step 5. Hang unit on wall

On the wall where you've marked your panel configuration, mark the centre point of each of the top three panels (to line up with picture hangers affixed to panel backs). Install the three heavy-duty picture hooks into the wall at these three locations. hang the panels (the linked panels are quite heavy, so enlist the help of at least one other person).

We gave a home office the comfortably elegant feeling of a gentleman's library by upholstering and mounting nine 18" x 18" squares of particleboard. This type of wall installation is simpler to do than a full wall: the squares are covered in padding and fabric, fastened together and affixed to the wall with heavy-duty picture hooks. This wall treatment can be used almost anywhere and is an easy way to get the look without covering an entire wall. For a quirky '70s lounge look, extend this to cover a whole wall.

Project

Nuts&Bolts

CREATE A CHIC AND FLEXIBLE ENTERTAINMENT UNIT.

Editor's note:
Part of this unit's appeal is that it's a cinch to customize. For a fresh take in a playroom or family room, substitute paint-grade wood for oak, and paint each shelf a different colour.

Difficulty level:
Average

It's the sturdy metal elements — threaded steel rods and oversized nuts — that make this clever project so doable. Inspired by a media centre designed by readers Heather and Steve Cosman, our urban traditional unit is sized to accommodate magazines, books and collectibles. In addition to the stylish industrial aesthetic, the design has a strong practical appeal: shelf heights can be easily adjusted by threading the nuts higher or lower on the rods. You don't need a workshop full of tools for this project. Have the lumberyard cut your wood to size, then do some careful measuring and drilling of the shelves. You'll be rewarded with a unit that rivals much pricier store-bought storage systems.

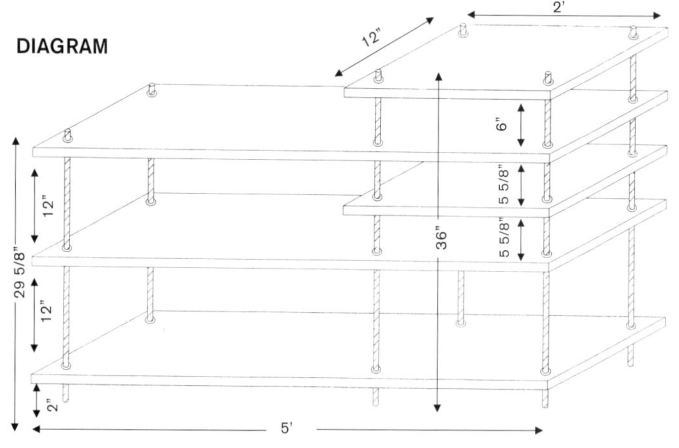

MATERIALS & TOOLS

- 3 6' l. x 12" d. wooden shelves
- 1 4' l. x 12" d. wooden shelf (cut in half)
- 6 5/8"-diam. x 3' l. threaded steel rods
- 52 steel nuts and washers (to fit rods)
- 6 non-slip steel nuts (for feet)
- Wood stain and varathane
- Jigsaw
- Tape measure and pencil
- Drill with 3/4" bit
- Electric sander or sandpaper
- Wrench
- Hacksaw

We created a low modern media-centre shelving unit of prefabricated solid oak shelves and threaded steel rods.

PHOTOGRAPH BY DONNA GRIFFITH

Step 1. Cut shelves to size

If possible, when you purchase the shelves, have the lumber store cut them to size for you. Cut the three 6'-long pieces to 5' each and the 4'-long piece into two 2'-long pieces. If the store won't do this, cut the shelves yourself with a jigsaw. It is important that the shelves are all the same length and width, as the size of the shelves later affects the location of the holes.

Step 2. Mark and drill holes

Use a pencil to mark the centre of each hole on every shelf by measuring 1 1/4" in from each end and side. Drill a hole in each shelf corner. As you drill each shelf, place it on top of the next shelf and remark hole locations to be sure that the next set of holes will line up exactly. Mark the middle set of holes in the 5'-long shelves once you have drilled the four holes in the 2'-long shelves. Place one 2'-long shelf on top of one of the longer shelves, and align the holes already drilled. Mark and drill the two centre holes on the long shelf.

Step 3. Apply finish

Sand the edges of the shelves that have been cut. If staining the shelves, apply the stain according to the manufacturer's directions. We stained our shelves a dark nut brown. Stain the underside of the shelves as well. Allow to dry. Apply a coat of varathane. Allow the first coat to dry thoroughly and sand lightly, then apply a second coat.

Step 4. Assemble media unit

When all the shelves are finished, start to assemble the media unit. Attach the six non-slip steel nuts to the bottom end of each rod. Holding rods vertically, thread a nut onto each rod to approximately 2" up from the non-slip nuts. Slide a washer down each rod to meet this nut, then insert the tops of the rods into the holes of one of the 5'-long shelves (see photo). Next, slide another washer down each rod to the top of the shelf and thread on another nut. The exact location of the shelves and nuts can be adjusted as you assemble the unit (see Diagram for the measurements). Continue by adding, in order, a nut, washer, shelf, washer, nut, until all pieces are attached.

Step 5. Adjust spacing and trim rods

Once you have assembled the unit, decide the height of the two threaded rods on the lower end of the unit. Leave enough of the rods to move the shelves up if you need to change their height slightly. Measure the position of each end of each shelf, then use a wrench to adjust and tighten the nuts as required. Use a hacksaw to cut down the two rods on the lower end to desired height.

Project

Screen Play

BUILD A GRACEFUL LATTICEWORK GARDEN TRELLIS.

Editor's note:
This project is fairly complicated but produces a very sturdy, elegant trellis. For an easier version, construct a frame that is not curved and nail pre-made lattice to the back, and then attach frame to a planter.

Difficulty level:
Difficult

Whether your garden consists of a few pots on a city balcony or a quarter-acre in the suburbs, it likely has a spot that would accommodate a classic trellis. Covered with climbing plants like ivy, clematis or morning glory, our latticework trellis can add lush colour to a treeless space, disguise an unattractive wall or fence, or act as a privacy screen on a deck. This handsome structure — built by George Meagher of The Trellis Works, a Toronto company that makes custom fences, latticework and planters — is a sturdier version of what's available at most nurseries and garden centres. If you've got a spare weekend, all you'll need to recreate this elegant design are basic woodworking tools, a few lengths of cedar and a little patience for precision measuring and cutting.

Painted a crisp white and topped with a pretty finial, this durable cedar trellis makes a charming focal point in any garden or outdoor living space. We attached ours to a plain brick wall and added a planter filled with boxwood to create interest while the climbing annuals are growing. The trellis could also be attached to a fence or wall behind a flower bed to support growing perennials.

PHOTOGRAPHY BY ANDREAS TRAUTTMANSDORFF

MATERIALS & TOOLS

4'	of 2" x 6" cedar (for curved top)
14'	of 2" x 2" cedar (for frame)
36'	of 5/16" x 1 1/2" cedar lath (for latticework)
	Decorative wood finial
	1" #6 wood screws
	1/2" nails
	1/2" brads and 3/4" brads
8	2" L-brackets
	Heavy cardboard
	Jigsaw
	Mitre box
	Screwdriver
	Hammer or nail press
	Waterproof wood glue
	Wood filler
	Sandpaper
	Set square
	Clamps
	Paint or stain (optional)

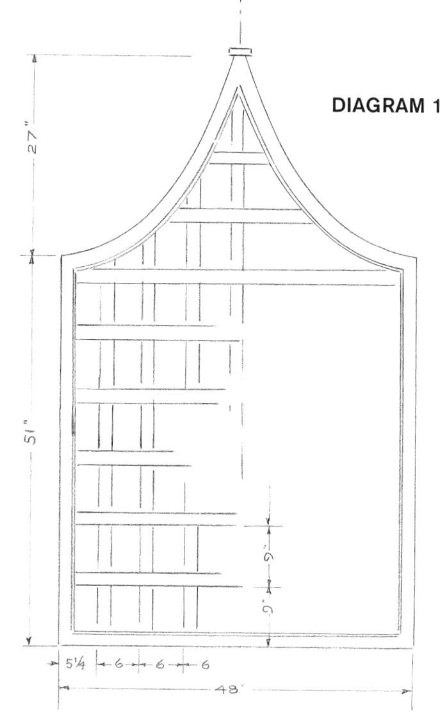
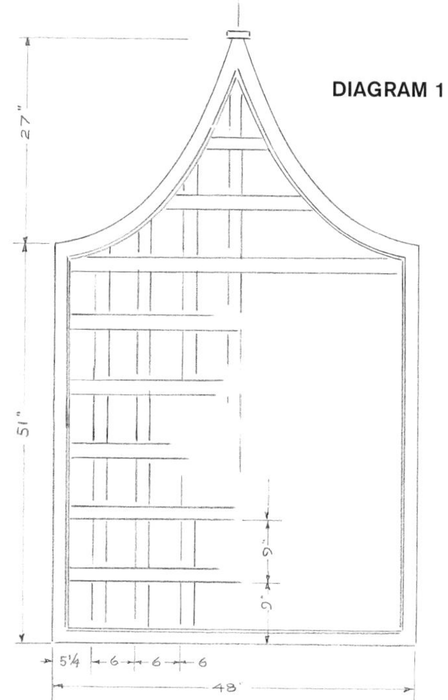

Step 1. Make template for trellis top

Enlarge Diagram 1 on a photocopier. Create a template for the curved trellis top by tracing this enlarged shape onto heavy cardboard. (You only need to make a template for one-half of the top since the second half is a mirror image.)

Step 2. Cut curved top pieces

To save wood, each side of the curved top is made of two pieces of cedar screwed together. Lay the template on a piece of 2" x 6" cedar as close to the edge as possible, and trace the outline of one half of it. Mark off the second half on the same piece of cedar, fitting it just above the first so that both can be cut from a 2' piece of cedar (see Photo 1). Repeat for second side of curved top. Cut out, using a jigsaw.

Step 3. Join curved top pieces

Apply waterproof wood glue to the ends of the two curved pieces, and screw them together with 1 1/2" #6 wood screws to create one side of the curved top (see Photo 2). Repeat for other side.

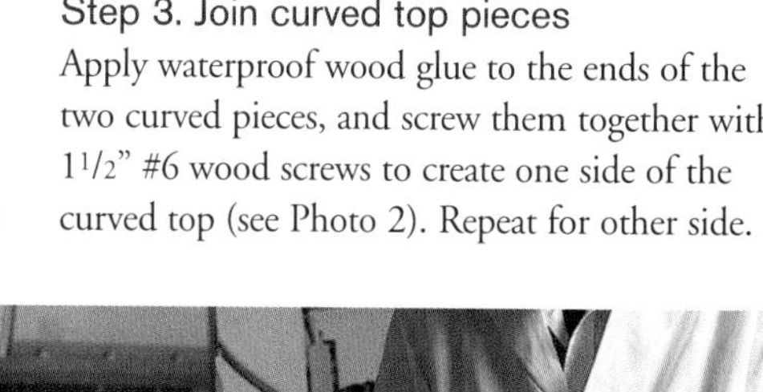

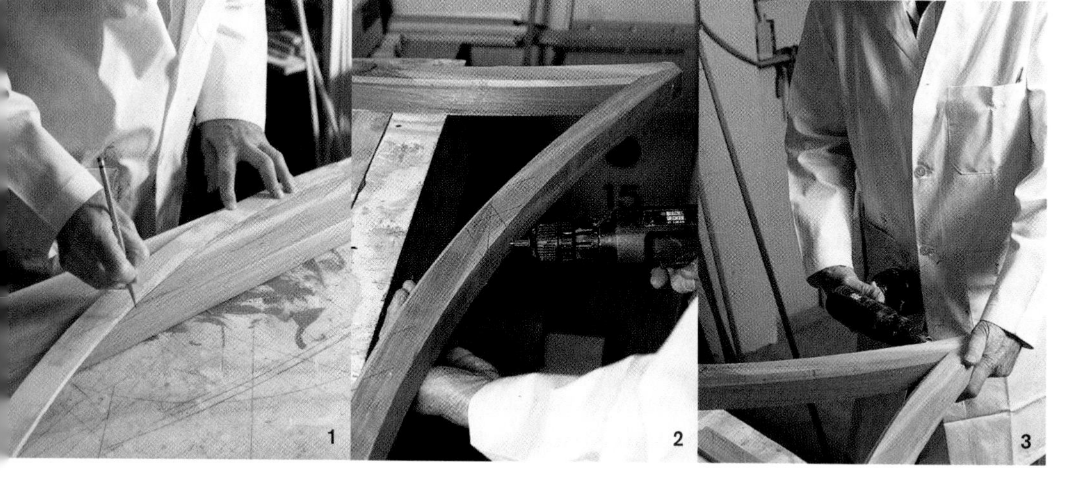

1 2 3

Step 4. Assemble top of trellis

To create the curved top of the trellis, lay the two curved sides on a flat surface, so their top ends meet. Apply waterproof wood glue and screw them together, using 1 1/2" #6 wood screws, screwing from the side (see Photo 3). If edges are not completely flush, fill with wood filler and sand.

Step 5. Cut side and bottom pieces

From 2" x 2" cedar, cut two pieces to 51" long (sides of trellis) and one piece to 48" long (bottom of trellis).

Step 6. Join sides to bottom

Mortise the corners where the side and bottom pieces will be joined. To do this, on one end of each side piece and both ends of the bottom piece, draw a line across the wood, 1 1/2" in from the end. Make another line on the end, at half the depth. Be sure to measure carefully. Using a mitre box, saw carefully through the wood at the 1 1/2" mark, stopping at the line that indicates half the depth. Then saw in from the end along the half-depth mark, so that you have cut away a square half the thickness of the wood. Lay the pieces together so that the cutout portions of the side pieces rest on the cutout portions of the bottom piece, making a neat joint. Attach with wood glue and screw together using 1" #6 screws (see Photo 4). Fill any cracks in the joints with wood filler. Let dry. Sand smooth.

Step 7. Join sides to top

Mortise the corners where the side pieces will join the curved top. To do this, lay the curved top on the ends of the side pieces. With a pencil, mark the angle of the top across the top of each side piece and another halfway down on the end, as in Step 6. On the curved pieces, make a mark 1 1/2" in from the end, and another halfway down on the ends. Cut, glue and screw together as in Step 6, and then fill and sand.

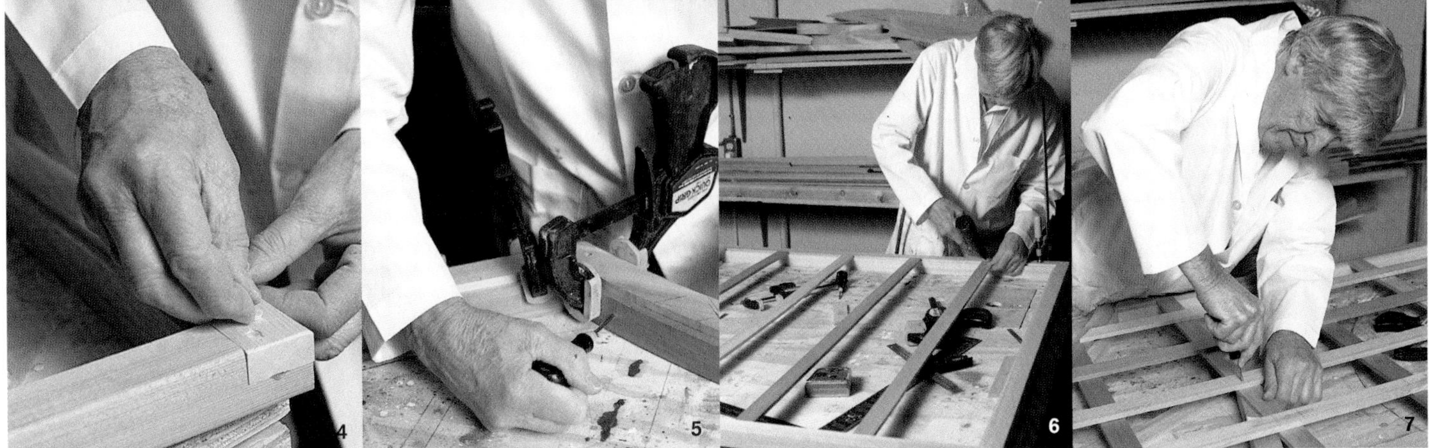

Step 8. Complete frame

Cut a piece of 5/16” x 1 1/2” lath to fit along the inside edge of the bottom of the frame. With the frame lying on a flat surface, glue, clamp and nail the lath to the frame so that it protrudes from one side of the frame (what will be the front) by about 1/4” and forms a “lip” or ledge on what will be the back of the frame, onto which the lath will be nailed to form the latticework (see Diagram 2). Cut 2 pieces of lath to fit along the inside edges of the curved top. To attach them, apply wood glue, then gently bend them along the curves, clamping to hold in place (see Photo 5). Nail on. Cut 2 pieces of lath to fit along the inside edges of the sides of the frame. Glue, clamp and nail in place. Allow to dry according to glue package directions.

Step 9. Check frame measurements

Before adding the crisscrossed lath, check that the frame is square by measuring each corner with a set square, and measuring diagonally from outside corner to outside corner. The two diagonal measurements should be equal. The frame will still have some flexibility at this point; if it isn’t square, shift it until it is square, then use clamps to secure it in place on your work surface if possible.

Step 10. Cut horizontal slats

For the horizontal slats, cut five pieces of lath to 45” long, one to 23” long and one to 11” long. Lay one 45” piece across the bottom of the frame and mark the locations of the vertical pieces that will cross it using the measurements in Diagram 1. Mark the lath locations across the bottom of the frame as well.

Step 11. Cut vertical slats

For the vertical slats, cut one piece of lath to 76”, two to 65 3/4”, two to 58 1/4” and two to 53 1/4”.

Step 12. Mark slat locations

Lay the 76” piece of lath along one side of the frame, and mark the locations of the horizontal pieces that will cross it using the measurements in Diagram 1; mark these measurements along the side of the frame as well. To mark the locations of the top two horizontal pieces that lie across the curved top, extend a T-square or a strip of lath from the 76” vertical piece to the curved top, and mark.

Step 13. Install horizontal pieces

Place one of the 45” horizontal pieces across the centre of the frame, and the four other 45” horizontal pieces on the frame as per the markings you made in Step 12. The horizontal pieces should fit neatly just inside the 2” x 2” cedar, resting on the lip created by the trim (see Photo 6) installed in Step 8. Apply a dab of wood glue to both surfaces where the lath sits on the lip, then nail on with 1/2” nails. Lay the 23” piece and the 11” piece at the appropriate markings and, with a pencil, mark on them the angle of the curved piece. Saw their ends off so they sit neatly inside the 2” x 2” cedar.

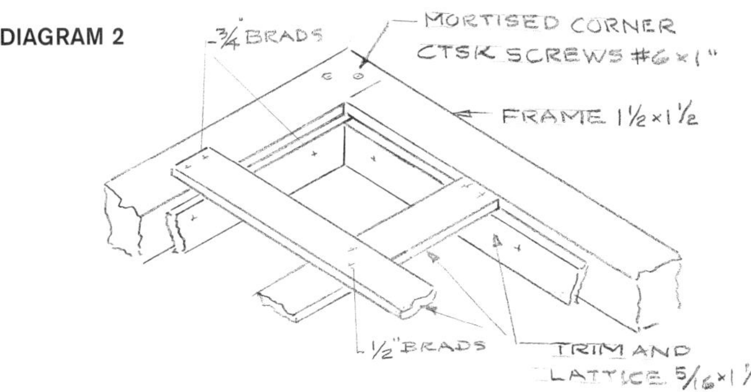

DIAGRAM 2

Step 14. Install vertical pieces

Lay the seven vertical lath pieces across the horizontal pieces, so they line up with the marks you made (on the centre piece and across the bottom of the frame) in Step 10. They should overlap the bottom of the frame by about 1/2”. With a pencil, mark on them the angle where they meet the curved top and saw their ends off so they don’t protrude beyond the edges of the curve.

Step 15. Reinforce lattice joints

Apply a dab of wood glue to the ends of all the vertical pieces and to each spot where vertical and horizontal pieces cross. Nail on the ends of all the vertical pieces using 3/4” brads. Nail together all the joints using 1/2” brads, starting at the centre and working outward. Slide a scrap of wood under each joint before you nail it, to avoid breaking the lath (see Photo 7). Note: George is using a nail press but a small hammer will work just as well.

Step 16. Attach finial

To apply the finial, from a scrap piece of lath, cut a small block slightly larger than the point at the top of the frame. Sand this piece smooth. Countersink a 1 1/2” wood screw into it. Glue and nail the block to the top of the frame so the point of the screw faces upward. Screw the finial onto the protruding screw.

Step 17. Sand and finish

Sand the trellis lightly. Paint or stain it, or leave natural. Left untreated, the cedar will weather to an attractive silvery-grey colour.

Step 18. Hang trellis

Attach the trellis to a wall or fence with eight 2” L-brackets (four on each side) screwed into the sides of the frame, evenly spaced.

Project 30

Behind Closed Doors

STYLE AND STORAGE IDEAS TO RE-OUTFIT THE CLOTHES CLOSET.

Editor's note:
Remember that if you don't have the time or budget to retrofit your closet hardware, a quick coat of paint and an organizational makeover will give fresh life to even the most cluttered cupboard.

Difficulty level:
Easy

Projects:
Wire shelving system
Wood and canvas storage system

Clothes closets are the catch-alls — even the black holes — of our homes. They're the keepers of our clothing and accessories, plus a few storage boxes, luggage, files, vacuum cleaners... you name it. As our wardrobes change and expand, old pieces of clothing get pushed into the closet's depths, and newer items scramble for space in the more accessible areas. Belts are strung up on nails; shoes are strewn on the floor. The disorder can be discouraging, but an overhaul may seem daunting, or just too expensive. Here, we've transformed two typical bedroom closets that were not living up to their potential. Both had abundant "dead space" (on door backs, along side walls, beneath hanging clothes) and a general lack of organization. We fitted each with a different storage system. Following is a rundown of our tips and measurements. Now you can set up a new system that will bring order, and perhaps even a little beauty, to your closet.

In this double-door closet, we pressed virtually every square inch into service by installing a wire shelving system. We started by ripping out the old shelving and repainting the space. We then installed the coated-wire closet system, which is mounted on tracks that are screwed to the closet walls. We raised the rod height from 67" to 70", created a variety of alternatives for hanging clothes (shorter clothes are stored in a new two-tiered section), and added matching wire drawers for folded clothing and racks for storing belts, shoes and scarves. We maintained the mirror on the inside of one door — it was already a smart use of space. Sturdy, colourful boxes keep other items (like hats, dress shoes and out-of-season clothes) tidy and dust-free. The new lower rod system also creates a small but handy shelf space at waist level.

BEFORE

PHOTOGRAPHY BY DONNA GRIFFITH

Project 30: Sorting the closet

DOUBLE-DOOR CLOSET

For larger closets, wire, wood or melamine shelving systems are excellent organization solutions. Although they are more expensive, wood or melamine systems are the sturdiest options. Since many of the wood-type shelving systems are installed for you by professionals, and therefore would not constitute a "Weekend Project," we used the wire shelving option in this closet. These systems are available at many department and storage specialty stores. Matching basket and drawer systems expand storage capacity, and accessories like the wire shoe organizer and the wire shelf/scarf rack take advantage of unused spaces like the back of a door. Be sure to assess your needs and measure your closet carefully before purchasing a system. The wire systems come with their own instructions and are easy to install. Have someone help you during installation.

SINGLE-DOOR CLOSET

With this single-door closet, we decided to keep the existing single rod and two shelves, and simply add a few accessories. To create extra hanging space in the closet, we suspended a second rod from the main rod. Although rods of this type (called "double-hung" rods) can be purchased at many specialty storage stores for about $25, we decided to make our own. This gave us the flexibility of deciding how far below the main rod it would hang, and how wide it would be. From this second rod we hung canvas organizers, which are half the height of regular organizers (12" high) and specifically designed for double-hung rods. This solution makes excellent use of the lower half of the closet. We also added hooks to the inside walls and the door for keeping belts, scarves and hats organized. The shelves above the main rod hold boxes of out-of-season and seldom-worn clothes. This keeps the shelves tidy and the clothes dust-free. If boxes are not see-through, label them well so that you don't have to pull them down to see what's inside.

The solution for this single-door closet is both stylish and space-savvy. We freshened up the look of the closet by painting it a cool lavender and painting the floor white. We moved the existing single rod and two shelves up just a few inches. To boost function, we hung a second-tier rod (shown top left, made of 1"-diam. dowelling and twist chain link) to accommodate 27"-high canvas organizers (for sweaters and shoes) and to make use of the "wasted" space under the shorter hanging clothing. Bags, purses and belts find a home on a new rack on the inside of the door and on new hooks on a side wall inside (shown top right), and less-used shoes, winter sweaters and other "storables" are stashed up on the shelves in boxes that coordinate with the closet's new colour scheme. Label storage boxes so retrieving items is easier.

MATERIALS & TOOLS

	Measuring tape
	Saw
4'	1"-diam. dowelling
2	$1\frac{9}{16}$" eye screws
2	43"-long pieces of twist-link chain
2	2" loose-leaf rings
2	1" S-hooks

Step 1. Determine height of double-hung rod

Determine the height requirements for the existing rod and the new double-hung rod. Be sure that the distance between the two rods is enough to hang shirts and other shorter items. Depending on the height of your closet, if you're adding a lower rod, be sure the existing rod is between 70" and 80" from the floor. We moved ours from 63" to 70" (this gave us just enough vertical space to work with, but if you can go higher we recommend it). We hung our lower rod 28" from the floor — giving us enough room for the canvas organizers (which are $26\frac{1}{2}$" long). Hanging the second rod 28" from the floor also leaves 42" between the existing rod and the lower rod, allowing space to hang blouses, blazers, short skirts and double-hung pants in between. We purchased two 45"-long pieces of chain link. If we hang the second rod 42" from the main rod (which is 70" from the floor), it means the second rod is 28" from the floor. This leaves $1\frac{1}{2}$" between the canvas space organizers and the floor. The chain link allows you to adjust the rod's height easily — simply move the S-hook to a higher link. Don't allow hanging items to

touch the floor — they will wrinkle, get dirty, and make it difficult to clean the floor.

Step 2. Determine width of double-hung rod

Decide how wide you want the rod to be. Allow enough space for long hanging items (dresses, long skirts and pants that can't be double-hung). A good rule to remember is that at least 25 per cent of the closet should be left as long hanging space. Therefore, the widest your double-hung rod should be is 75 per cent of the closet's full width. So once you determine the width you'll need for long hanging items, you will know the maximum width your double-hung rod can be. Our closet was 45" wide. We decided to leave 15" for long hanging space (about 33 per cent of the closet's width), so our double-hung rod is 30" wide.

Step 3. Make the double-hung rod

When you've determined all your measurements, purchase dowelling, chain, eye screws, S-hooks and loose-leaf rings. Use a saw to trim the dowel to the width you've chosen. With a drill bit slightly smaller than the eye screw, drill a hole about 1" in from each end of the dowel. Insert an eye screw into each of these holes. Attach one end of an S-hook to each eye screw. Attach the other end of the S-hook to one end of the chain. Attach the top ends of the chain to the main rod using the loose-leaf rings. Open up each loose-leaf ring, pass through a link and then close the ring around the main rod. To adjust the height of the lower rod, simply move the S-hook up or down to another link.

BUDGET

Budget is a major consideration in re-outfitting the closet. If your budget is small, fill the space with canvas hanging accessories with shelves for storing shoes or folded clothes like sweaters. They're inexpensive, and easy to install on your existing rod – a quick fix. If you decide to spend more money on an entire closet system, there are two alternatives: wire or wood. These are especially good in larger closets, and are sturdier than canvas. Less expensive than wood, the wire systems (which are usually coated with white plastic) are relatively easy to install and are well-ventilated. Look for a system that provides uninterrupted hanger movement. Wood or wood-type shelving is generally the most expensive option, but it provides a sturdy, long-lasting solution. We've included lists of the pros and cons of each system:

advantages	disadvantages
canvas • most inexpensive option • easiest to install • can buy pieces on an individual basis • easy to move • provides a "quick fix"	• not as sturdy as other options • may sag over time
wire • well ventilated: clothes can "breathe," low dust buildup • easy to install (can do it yourself) • many are adjustable • many are removable (can take it with you when moving) • less expensive than wood systems	• sliding wire hangers back and forth over time can wear down the plastic coating • wire shelves can leave non-permanent indentations on clothing
wood • these thicker materials (melamine, particleboard, MDF, wood veneer, solid wood) are less likely to bend or sag • often available in a wide variety of colours and finishes • provides you with a "furniture" feel • may be adjustable • may be removable (when moving)	• highest price range • more prone to dust buildup • may require professional installation

Essential measurements

Before you start planning your closet overhaul, here are a few numbers to keep in mind:

12"	minimum distance needed between closet back wall and hanging rod
35"	minimum height needed for hanging blazers, shirts, short skirts, folded-over pants
65"	minimum height needed for hanging long dresses, long skirts, pants hung at full length
25%	minimum portion of closet width that should be designated to full-length hanging
70" TO 80"	required height of upper rod if planning to add a lower rod
42"	minimum distance required between upper and lower rod to allow room for hanging shorter items from upper rod

Clutter control hints

- Start from scratch when reorganizing the closet. Take everything out and decide what gets worn and what doesn't. Banish what doesn't to less-frequently used storage space or give it away to charity.
- When possible, move out-of-season clothes to the guest room or basement closet or another storage area.
- Store shoes that are worn infrequently in boxes on the higher shelves.
- Group clothing items together in a way that makes sense to you. Most commonly, similar items are grouped together – blouses, short skirts, pants – so that individual items are easy to find.
- When storing items on higher shelves, use clearly written labels or see-through boxes so that you'll know what's stored up there.
- Use plastic or wood hangers; wire hangers can damage the shape of clothes over time.
- A single rod usually results in a lot of unused hanging space in the lower half of the closet. To add more hanging space to your closet, install a double-hung rod.
- If your budget and closet size permit, call in a closet specialist to install an intricate, personalized closet system.
- Steel rods are the strongest choice.

Project

Building Character

TRADITIONAL WALL PANELLING COMES OUT OF THE WOODWORK TO TAKE ON THREE CONTEMPORARY INCARNATIONS.

Editor's note:
Wavering over our wainscotting because you're not an ace woodworker? Cheat a little with prefab MDF panelling. And don't pass these projects up because your space is small — this type of "detailing" will give it presence.

Difficulty level:
Difficult

Projects:
Panelled wainscotting
Floor-to-ceiling raised panelling
Fabric panelling

Wood panelling can dramatically alter the look of a room. It adds texture in a clean, graphic way, bringing character to bland spaces. It can make new houses look older or lend age and atmosphere to an apartment or rental unit. Historically, panelling can be traced back to the 15th century and was popular in 18th-century houses, especially in entryways and major rooms like parlours and dining rooms. In those times, the lines of the panelling were quite simple, and the wood was often left unpainted. Here, we present three easy and contemporary ways of constructing and installing panelling. Because our panelling is painted, we were able to use inexpensive medium-density fibreboard (MDF) and still achieve the look of elegant panelling. In the dining room, the panelling rises just partway up the wall to a high chair-rail height. In the bathroom, the panelling runs from floor to ceiling. And in the bedroom, we "filled in" the wooden-trim-edged panels with bright fabric — a great variation on the upholstered-wall look that we show on page 126. Panelling really complements any style of room, from traditional to modern. You may choose to go neutral, as we show in the dining room; it's the classic choice for panelling. But for a fresh new take on this graphic wall finish, add colour: our bathroom panelling is finished in a cool, clean lilac. Or, to really jazz up a room as we've done in the bedroom with a soft cranberry-red floral, add swaths of warm-toned fabric — it's a softer take on the traditionally hard-edged look of wood panelling.

The panelling in this dining room resembles elegant original woodwork. This panelling has the most complicated construction of the three shown: the lower portions of the walls were layered with 4' x 8' panels of Masonite and then MDF strips were installed on top to create raised sections. Decorative moulding finishes the top and creates a baseboard.

PHOTOGRAPHY BY DONNA GRIFFITH

The cost of each panelling project will depend on the size of the room being panelled as well as the costs of the materials you choose. To keep costs low, run panelling only to chair-rail height as opposed to full ceiling height, select less intricate mouldings or choose inexpensive fabric.

PANELLED WAINSCOTTING

A raised panelling effect is created by applying sheets of Masonite directly onto the wall as a base layer, and affixing horizontal and vertical strips of medium-density fibreboard (MDF) on top of the Masonite.

MATERIALS & TOOLS

- Tape measure
- 4' x 8' x 1/4"-thick Masonite sheets
- 1/2"-thick MDF
- Sandpaper
- Level
- T-square
- Wood glue
- Hammer and nail punch
- 1 1/2" finishing nails
- Saw and mitre box
- Baseboard and chair-rail mouldings
- Quarter-round
- Primer and paint

Step 1. Determine height and spacing of panelling

Before purchasing materials, decide on the dimensions you'd like your panelling to be, including the height of the panelling, the width of each panel, and the distance between each vertical strip. Keep in mind that the MDF strips forming the raised part of the panelling should cover the seams between the Masonite sheets. The panelling we show is 49 1/2" h. (including moulding at top), the top horizontal strip is 5" h., the bottom horizontal strip is 12" h., and the vertical strips are 4" w. x 31" h. The vertical strips are spaced 20" apart. At the lumberyard, have MDF sheets cut to the size you want for your top horizontal strip, bottom horizontal strip and vertical strips.

Step 2. Build out the wall

Remove any existing baseboard mouldings. Build out the wall by affixing 4' x 8' x 1/4" Masonite sheets to it. The long side of each sheet should rest on the floor. Apply wood glue to the rough side of the Masonite sheets and nail them into place using 1 1/2" finishing nails. Continue to attach Masonite sheets end-to-end, until the walls are covered.

Step 3. Attach MDF strips to Masonite sheets

Lightly sand the MDF strips with sandpaper. Attach the bottom horizontal strips over the Masonite, using wood glue and a nail punch to countersink 1 1/2" finishing nails. These strips should rest on the floor. Next, attach the vertical strips over the Masonite, using the same glue and nail procedure. When attaching the vertical strips, cover the seams between the Masonite sheets. The vertical strips should fit firmly against the bottom horizontal strips. Space the vertical strips evenly along the wall. Finally, attach the top horizontal strips over the Masonite using the same glue and nail procedure. The tops of these strips should line up with the tops of the Masonite sheets.

Step 4. Finish panelling with trim

To give the panelling a finished look, add decorative moulding above the top horizontal strip. Before installing moulding, prime and paint it, allowing to dry and sanding between coats. With wood glue and countersunk 1 1/2" finishing nails, install the moulding above the top horizontal panel. The panelling we show layered two pine trims above each other, one slightly deeper than the other. The bottom part of the trim is 1" x 3/4", and the top part is 1 1/2" x 3/4". Mitre moulding to 45° angles in the corners of the room.

Step 5. Finish with baseboards

Prime and paint 1" x 6" baseboard mouldings. Install baseboard over the bottom horizontal panel, using wood glue and countersunk 1 1/2" finishing nails. The baseboard should rest on the floor. Mitre corners as necessary. Because the baseboard is only 6" high, part of the bottom horizontal strip will still be visible. Finally, paint, let dry and install quarter-round at floor level using wood glue and nails. Wipe away any excess glue.

Step 6. Prime and paint

Use wood filler to fill nail holes. Allow to dry. Prime and paint the panelling, allowing to dry in between each coat. The panelling we show is painted with Pratt & Lambert's Free Spirit (1670) latex paint.

FLOOR-TO-CEILING RAISED PANELLING

This project is similar to Panelled Wainscotting in that MDF strips are used to build out the wall. Here, the vertical strips are taken from the floor right up to the ceiling. Depending on the width of the panels you choose, the look of this project will vary.

MATERIALS & TOOLS

- Tape measure
- MDF strips
- Hammer and nail punch
- 1 1/2" finishing nails
- Panelling adhesive (sold in tubes that fit into a caulking gun)
- Level
- T-square
- Caulking and caulking gun
- Primer and paint

Step 1. Determine panel size

Determine the size of the panel strips. Also decide how much space you want between each vertical panel (so you know how many vertical strips you'll need). Go to a building-supply store and have them "rip" (or cut) 4' x 8' x 1/2" sheets of MDF to the desired

Left: In the bathroom, the projecting part of the "panelling" is made of pieces of MDF cut to size and glued (with special panelling adhesive) and nailed to the wall. The "recessed" part is the wall itself. Panelling like this can be used in any room where you wish to add graphic interest: a living or dining room, an unfitted kitchen, a hallway or bathroom.

Right: This pretty panelling style is most appropriate in an intimate room like a bedroom or sitting room, since it adds a wonderful cosiness. The wall is painted, cut-to-size fabric pieces are attached to the wall with spray adhesive (available at craft-supply stores), and cream-painted wood trim is nailed in place to frame the fabric.

widths. To determine the height of the vertical boards, measure the distance between the top board and the baseboard, then cut the vertical boards to this length so they fit snugly between the top board and baseboard. We were working with a 9' ceiling, and our base and top boards were each 6" h., so our vertical boards were 8' long. We made them 3 1/2" wide and placed them 7" apart.

Step 2. Attach horizontal boards

Using panelling adhesive and 1 1/2" finishing nails, attach the base and top boards to the wall. Countersink the heads of the nails with a nail punch.

Step 3. Attach vertical boards to wall

Apply a 1/8" bead of panelling adhesive from the top to the bottom of the back of the first vertical board and place on wall. Use a level and T-square to ensure that everything is straight before nailing board to the wall using 1 1/2" finishing nails at 1' intervals. Countersink the heads of the nails with a nail punch. Continue this process, measuring the distance between the boards each time another vertical board is added to ensure even spacing. Make pencil marks at the top and bottom of the wall where each board is to be attached to make this easier.

Step 4. Paint wall and panelling

Use caulking to fill any space between boards and wall or between vertical and horizontal boards. Prime and paint the wall and panelling, allowing to dry in between coats. We chose a lavender latex paint (Benjamin Moore 1396) to really liven up the bathroom.

FABRIC PANELLING

For this project, fabric is "framed" with painted moulding to create a panelled effect. By painting the frames cream and the wall a lighter shade of the red in the fabric, the fabric panels really stand out. Variations on this look include painting the frames a darker shade of the colour used on the wall, or, with white walls, painting the frame a shade similar to the fabric.

MATERIALS & TOOLS

- Tape measure and pencil
- Level
- T-square
- Fabric
- Spray fabric adhesive
- Moulding
- Paint
- Mitre box and saw
- Hammer and nail punch
- 1 1/2" finishing nails
- Panelling adhesive
- Caulking and caulking gun

Step 1. Determine panel size and placement

Determine the dimensions and placement of your panels, with your room size and ceiling height in mind. Ours were 6' x 2 1/2' on an 8' h. wall. We spaced the panels 1' apart. Adjust these dimensions to suit your room.

Step 2. Choose fabric and moulding

Choose fabric (we chose a pretty floral pattern) to coordinate with your room's decor. If you want to repaint your walls, do this now. Ours were painted with Benjamin Moore 1342 latex paint. For the frames, select decorative wooden mouldings.

Step 3. Mark wall with frame outline

With a pencil, mark the inner and outer edges of the moulding frame on your wall. Use a level and T-square to ensure right angles and even horizontal and vertical placement.

Step 4. Cut and attach fabric to wall

Cut fabric pieces larger than the inside dimensions of the frame but smaller than the outside edge. Spray adhesive onto the back of each piece of fabric and attach it to the wall within marked lines. Smooth out any air pockets from the centre of the fabric, moving outward (much like you would with wallpaper).

Step 5. Paint and cut moulding

For each frame, use a saw and mitre box to cut four pieces of moulding to the appropriate lengths with ends cut at 45° angles. Paint each piece and allow to dry. We painted the frame with Benjamin Moore 925 latex paint to coordinate with the cream in the fabric print, and so that the frames really stand out against the red wall.

Step 6. Attach moulding to wall

To attach the moulding to the wall, apply daubs of panelling adhesive 1' apart along the back of each strip. Position them on the wall, staying within pencilled reference marks. Once each frame is attached to the wall with adhesive, reinforce with 1 1/2" finishing nails, countersunk at 1' intervals all around.

Step 7. Touch up frames

Touch up any gaps at mitred corners, and fill nail holes with caulking. Once caulking is dry, use paint to touch up frames where you have used caulking.

Project

Open & Shut

OUR VERSATILE MODULAR DESIGN TAKES THE COFFEE TABLE TWO STEPS FORWARD.

Editor's note:
This table is a real find for a collector, especially one living in cramped quarters. It's already funky, but you can up the cool quotient further by using frosted plastic for the cubes.

Difficulty Level:
Difficult

This design for a smart new coffee table takes the classic piece not one, but two, steps forward. To boost its function, we added roomy storage "drawers" on casters underneath. And with both function and style in mind, we built in a glass-topped display case for storing and playfully showing off favourite collectibles. Finally, we gave it a contemporary look with a clean dark-chocolate frame and sleek panels of corrugated plastic. Our inspiration came from a similar table created by Gluckstein Design Planning for their room at Toronto's Graydon Hall Designer Showcase in spring 2000. The style of our table is modern with an Asian aesthetic — its geometric lines and sleek materials are reminiscent of a classic Japanese shoji screen. The construction is not as tough as you might expect. The main table is composed of wooden legs and rails, the glass top and a plywood tabletop base. The display dividers are made of three slotted pieces of maple board. And the cubes have simple wooden frames filled in with panels of translucent corrugated plastic. All in all, it's a thoughtful marriage of clever function, unexpected whimsy and clean, contemporary style.

Top: Though it would also look at home in a modern space, the coffee table is paired here with colourful urban traditional furnishings. The 38" x 24" x 20" table offers a lot for its size: it will fit comfortably into a small living room, but accommodates plenty of knickknacks and stored accessories. Bottom left: We filled the slots in our coffee table with an eclectic assortment of trinkets; each has a graphic or distinctly interesting shape. We topped the table with a sheet of tempered glass. Bottom right: Two deep storage cubes are set on casters for mobility. They slide tidily under the table where their contents are hidden from sight. Use them to store magazines, throws and pillows.

PHOTOGRAPHY BY JAMES TSE

MODULAR COFFEE TABLE

This coffee table is made up of a table "frame," and two "cubes" that slide under it on casters. During construction, remember that the "cubes" are not perfectly square.

MATERIALS & TOOLS

7	pieces of 1 1/4" x 1 1/4" x 8' maple
2	pieces of 1" x 6" x 8" maple
1	piece of 1/2" x 6" x 8" maple
2	sheets of 1/8" x 4" x 8' translucent corrugated plastic
80	1"- long 3/8"- diam. wood dowels
1	piece 1/4"- thick tempered glass (with polished edges) cut to 36 3/8" x 22 3/8"
	8" x 2" casters
	Tape measure
	T-square
	Mitre saw
	Sharp utility knife
	Router with 1/2" and 1/8" router bits
	Drill and 3/8" bit
	Chisel and mallet
	Handsaw
	100- and 150-grit sandpaper
	Wood glue
4	clamps minimum
	Stain, seal and lacquer (2 pints each)
	Paintbrushes

Step 1. Cut materials

Use a tape measure, square and saw or utility knife to mark and cut wood and corrugated plastic panelling to specified lengths:

For table legs, cube posts and rails:
From 1 1/4" x 1 1/4" maple, cut:
4 pieces @ 20" (4 table legs)
8 pieces @ 13" (8 cube corner posts)
8 pieces @ 16 1/2" (8 cube side rails)
8 pieces @ 18 1/2" (8 cube side rails)

For table rails:
From 1" x 6" maple, cut:
2 pieces @ 5" x 35 1/2" (2 side rails)
2 pieces @ 5" x 21 1/2" (2 end rails)

For table dividers:
From 1/2" x 6" maple, cut:
2 pieces @ 3 3/4" x 22 3/8" (short dividers)
1 piece @ 3 3/4" x 36 3/8" (long divider)

For bottoms of table and cubes:
From 1/2"-thick maple-veneered plywood, cut:
1 piece @ 23 3/8" x 37 3/8" (table bottom)
2 pieces @ 17 1/2" x 19 1/2" (2 cube bottoms)

For sides of cubes:
From 1/8" x 4' x 8' corrugated plastic, and using sharp utility knife, cut:
4 pieces @ 11" x 16 1/2"
4 pieces @ 11" x 18 1/2"

Step 2. Make router grooves

With a router, make a 1/2" x 1/2" groove in table rails (approximately 1/2" from bottom of 5" rail) for bottom of table to slide into (see Diagram 1).

Step 3. Drill dowel holes

With a drill and a 3/8" bit, drill two 1/2"-deep holes (for dowels) in the ends of the table rails and the insides of the table legs (see Diagram 1). First hole should be approximately 1" from the top, and second hole should be 2 1/2" below first.

Step 4. Make notches for glass top

Use saw to cut a 1" x 1" notch out of the corners of the table bottom (to fit around table legs once table is put together). Next, using a chisel and mallet, notch out a 1/4" x 1/4" x 1/4" section from the top inside corner of each of the table legs (see Detail, Diagram 1). This creates a ledge for the glass to rest on once the table is assembled.

Step 5. Cut finger slot in side rail

In order to be able to lift the glass and access the display cubbyholes, a finger slot must be created in one of the side rails. Measure and mark halfway along one of the 35 1/2" rails. Using a router, cut a semi-circular notch 1" wide x 3/4" deep out of the top of the rail (see Diagram 1).

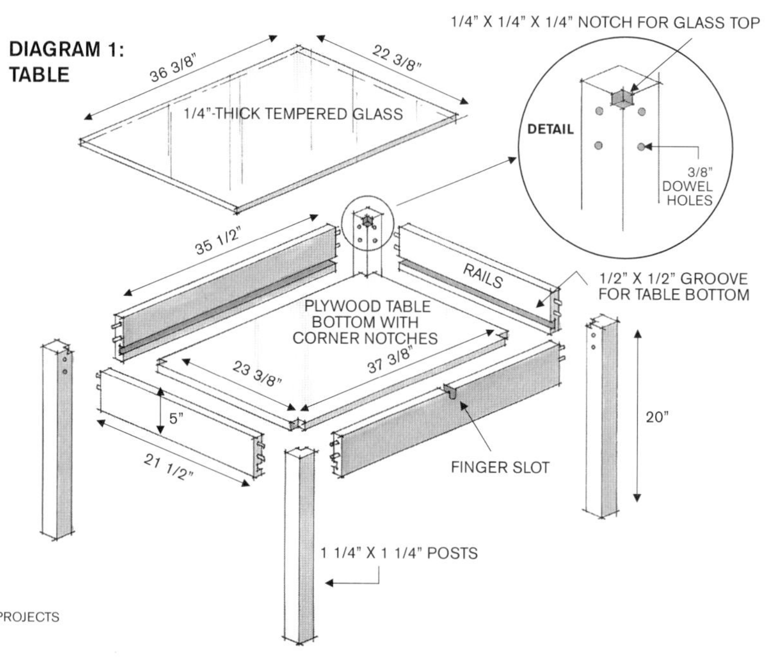

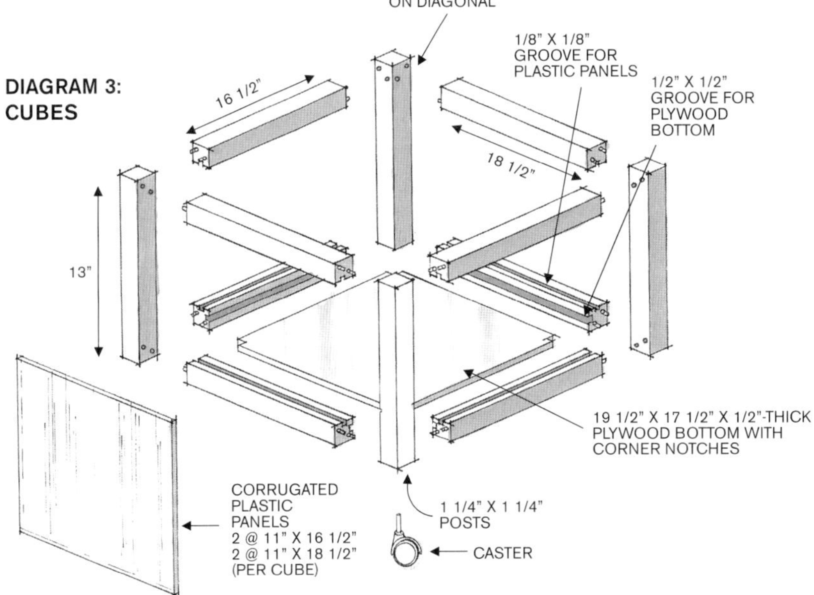

Step 6. Prepare table for assembly

Sand down all wood table parts using 100-grit sandpaper. Apply a small amount of wood glue into the dowel holes and around each dowel. Insert dowels into pre-drilled holes on the ends of the rails, leaving the holes on the legs open. Assemble the pieces in two halves, each consisting of two legs, a long side rail and a short side rail (as shown in Diagram 1). Clamp all joints and allow to dry 30 minutes.

Step 7. Assemble table

Slide the table bottom piece into the rail grooves on one half of the table. Slide the other half of the table into place, glueing and clamping the remaining joints, and wiping away any excess glue. Allow to dry for several hours.

Step 8. Finish table

Remove clamps and stain, seal and lacquer the assembled table, allowing to dry and sanding in between each coat with 150-grit sandpaper. Set aside and allow to dry completely.

Step 9. Assemble dividers for tabletop

To make the tabletop dividers, use a handsaw to cut a notch measuring 1¾" wide x 2" deep, out of the centre of the two shorter pieces of wood. Cut out two notches of the same dimensions on the long piece, 11⅝" apart and 11⅝" in from each end (see Diagram 2). These notches will allow the pieces to fit together, creating six display cubbyholes inside the tabletop.

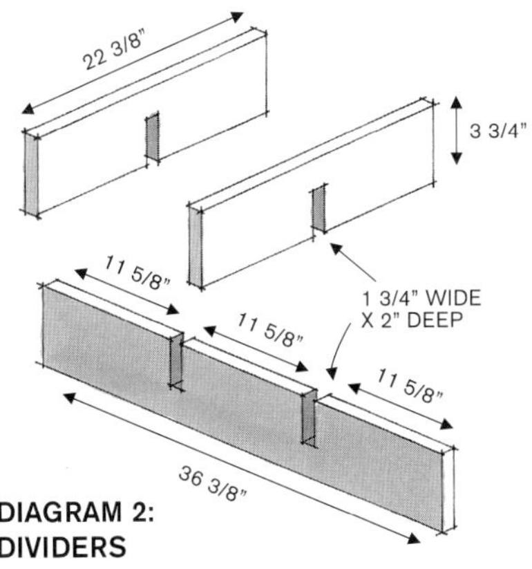

Step 10. Finish dividers

Stain, seal and lacquer divider pieces, allowing to dry and sanding in between each coat with 150-grit sandpaper. Allow to dry completely.

Step 11. Assemble tabletop

Fit the three divider sections together (see Diagram 2) and place inside the top of the table. Place glass on top. Glass will rest on the dividers and on the ledges created on the legs.

Step 12. Make router grooves in cube rails

Router out a ½" x ½" groove on the inside of each bottom rail of the cubes (down the centre of the rail) for the bottoms of each cube to slide into. For the plastic side inserts, router a ⅛" x ⅛" groove into the tops of the lower rails and bottoms of the upper rails (see Diagram 3). These grooves should also run down the centre of the rails.

Step 13. Drill dowel holes in cube rails

As you did for the table, drill two holes for dowels in each end of the upper and lower rails and the inside of each corner post. However, these two holes should be placed on the diagonal (see Diagram 3) to create a stronger joint. Be aware of the groove placements when drilling the holes.

Step 14. Make notches in bottoms of cubes

As with the bottom piece of the table, a notch must be cut out of the corners of each cube bottom to fit around the corner rails once the cubes are put together. Cut a ½" x ½" notch in each corner of both cube bottoms. Set bottom pieces aside.

Step 15. Prepare cubes for assembly

Sand down all cube pieces using 100-grit sandpaper. Place a small amount of wood glue into the open holes and around each dowel. Insert dowels into the ends of the top and bottom rails. Assemble each cube in two halves — each half with two vertical corner posts, a 16½" top and bottom rail and an 18½" top and bottom rail. Clamp all joints firmly, and wipe away any excess glue. Allow to dry for at least 30 minutes.

Step 16. Assemble cubes

Once dry, slide the bottom piece into the grooves on the insides of the bottom rails on one half of each cube. Slide the other half of the cube into place, gluing and firmly clamping these joints. Allow cubes to dry for several hours.

Step 17. Finish cubes

Remove clamps and stain, seal and lacquer the assembled cubes, allowing to dry and sanding in between each coat with 150-grit sandpaper. Let dry completely.

Step 18. Insert plastic panels

The plastic side inserts can be gently bent (but do not crease) and popped into place in the ⅛" x ⅛" grooves on both the top and bottom rails (see Diagram 3).

Step 19. Attach casters

Once the two storage cubes are fully assembled, turn them upside down and screw a caster into the bottom end of each corner post. This will allow the cubes to easily slide under the coffee table.

Project

FloorShow

CLASSIC '40S LINOLEUM RESURFACES IN THREE COLOURFUL DIY FLOOR MATS.

Editor's note:
These mats might look retro but with a classic pattern like blue-and-white ticking they'd go country. To keep the lino from lifting at the corners, be generous with the adhesive and rent a proper roller.

Difficulty level:
Easy

Projects:
Interlocking-rectangles living room mat
Garden-maze mudroom mat
Bar-code-striped kitchen mat

Think of linoleum flooring and you may naturally picture a make-do kitchen in a fixer-upper home. Well, think again. Linoleum has made a comeback, and not as much for its inexpensive price tag as for its aesthetic potential. It's a new favourite among designers, who are attracted to the colours available — a wide-ranging palette that makes creating bright, patterned flooring a snap. And it's an eternal favourite among nostalgia buffs influenced by subtle, simple '40s kitchen design. But today there's no need to keep lino in the kitchen. We've used sheets of Marmoleum, a thin, flexible, durable brand of linoleum, to create three floor mats that are stylish enough to be used anywhere in the house. They're especially practical for protecting wood floors, covering unsightly floor finishes or adding a quick jolt of colour in an otherwise neutral space.

Top: Easy underfoot because it feels like soft leather, a Marmoleum floor mat is a smart way to add colour. A '60s-inspired design of intersecting rectangles in a hot combination of blue, red and orange, this simple 4' x 6' mat is a striking counterpoint to the room's creamy walls and crisp white furniture.

Bottom left: Marmoleum is well suited to entryways or porches because it's durable and easily cleaned. The painted floor of this mudroom is protected by a mat with a retro garden-maze design.

Bottom right: Our small Marmoleum rugs have water-resistant vinyl backing to protect hardwood floors from water and wear in high-traffic areas. We designed this rug in a trendy bar-code motif, using scraps left over from the other projects.

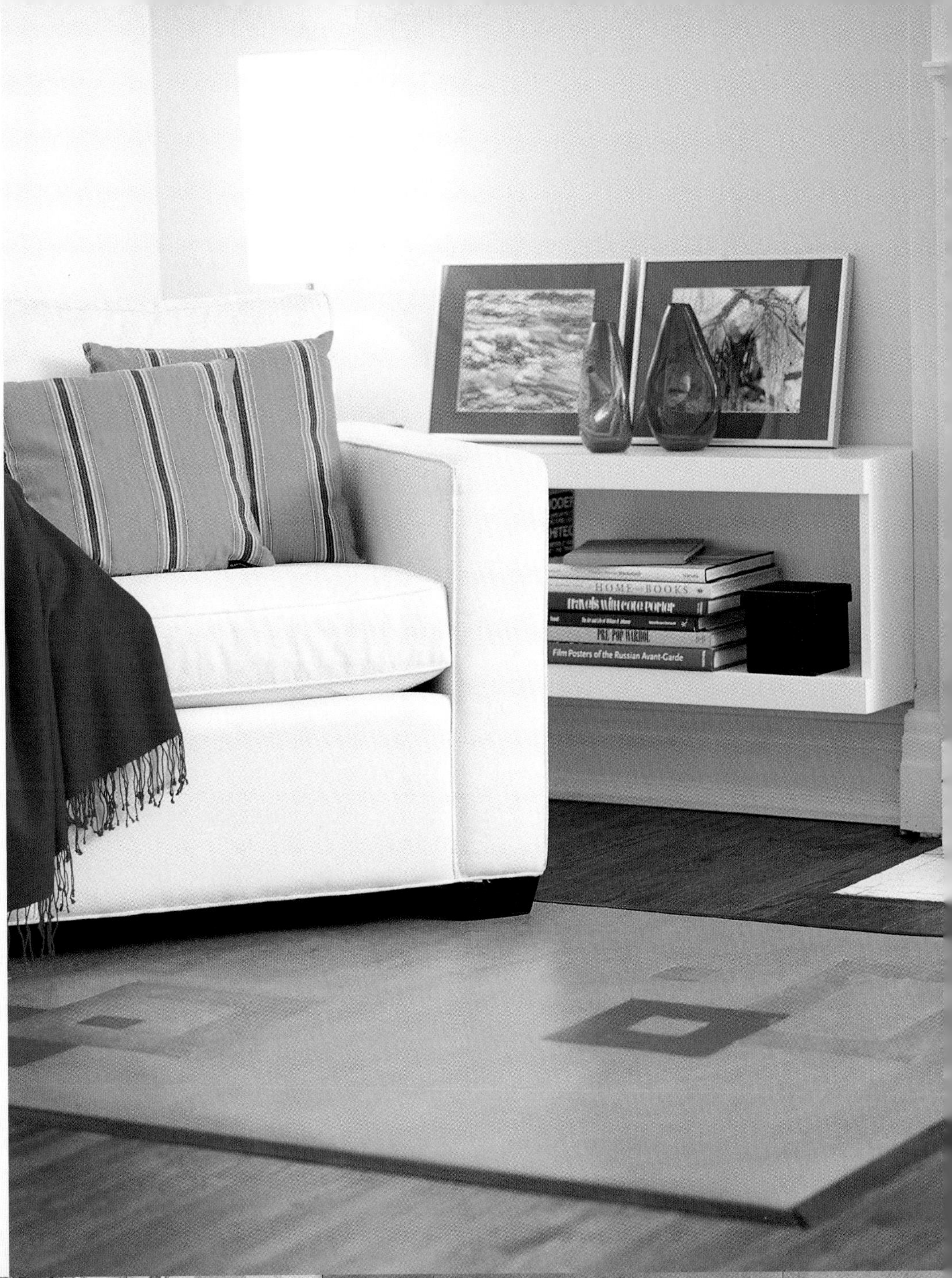

BuyingMarmoleum

- Marmoleum, a thin, flexible brand of linoleum, is sold at many flooring stores.
- Sheet Marmoleum is usually sold by the yard, in 78" widths. The five coloured sheets used for the living room and mudroom floor mats provided enough leftovers to make our five-colour bar-code-striped kitchen mat.
- Although we used new pieces of sheet Marmoleum, you may be able to find remnants at flooring stores that would work equally well.
- Marmoleum is also available in tile form. Tiles could be used for the mudroom and kitchen mats, butting the squares together to create the larger solid-coloured areas in the patterns, and cutting the tiles as required for smaller pieces.

PHOTOGRAPHY BY DONNA GRIFFITH

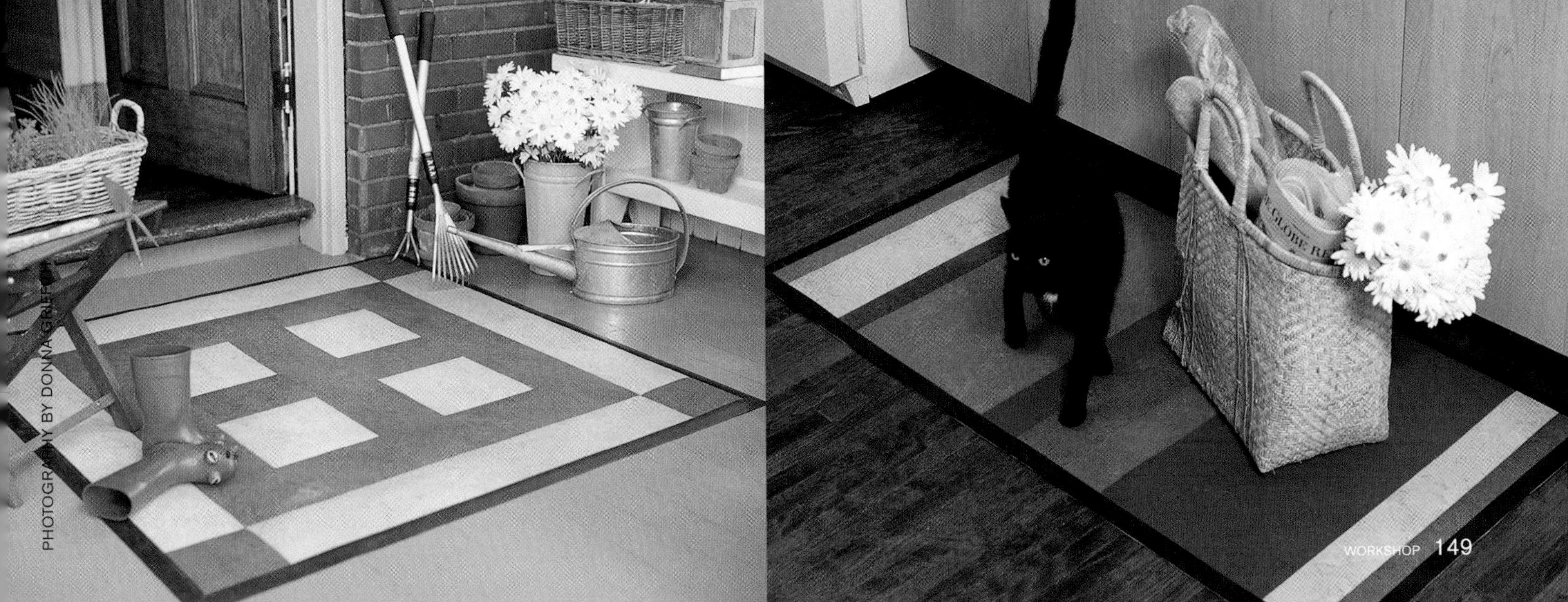

DIAGRAM 1

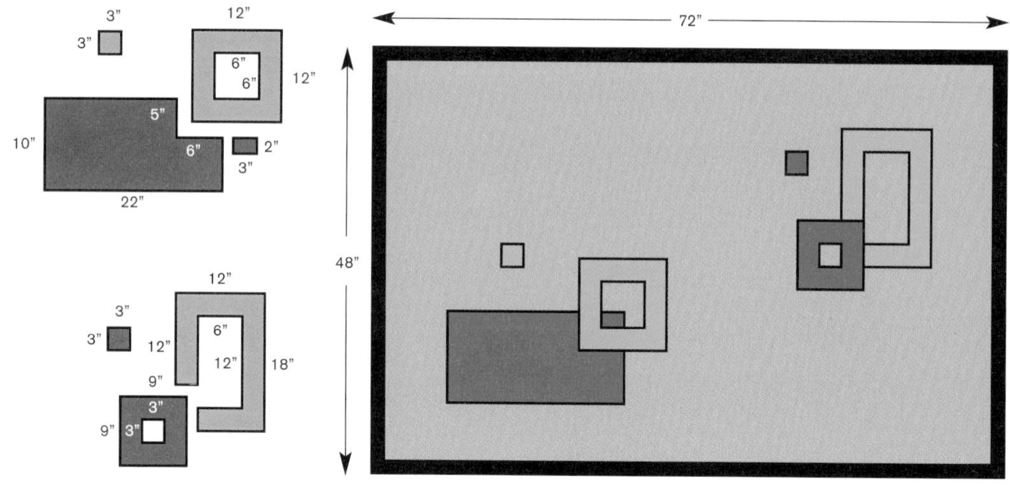

INTERLOCKING-RECTANGLES LIVING ROOM MAT

This mat measures 4' by 6'. For a heavy roller, we used a small lawn roller from a rent-all store. For the rubber edging, we used black reducer strip FV2202BK12 from The Home Depot.

MATERIALS & TOOLS

1 1/2 yds. blue Marmoleum
1/2 yd. red Marmoleum
1/2 yd. orange Marmoleum
Pencil and carpenter's square
Utility knife and 36"-long metal ruler
100-grit sandpaper
72" x 54" lightweight sheet vinyl
Linoleum adhesive and trowel
Heavy roller
22' 1/8"-thick, 1 1/2"-wide black rubber edging
Caulking gun and clear silicone adhesive

Step 1. Cut Marmoleum

Mark desired shape and size with pencil and carpenter's square (see Photo 1). Lightly score top of material with a utility knife, using metal ruler as a guide (see Photo 2). Fold wrong sides together and cut through to back (see Photo 3).

From blue Marmoleum, cut:

1 piece @ 48" x 72" *

From red Marmoleum, cut:

1 piece @ 10" x 22", with a 5" x 6" piece cut from one corner, and a 2" x 3" piece cut from the 5" x 6" piece, to be used within orange square (see Diagram 1)
1 piece @ 9" x 9", with a 3" x 3" square cut from centre
1 piece @ 3" x 3" for "floating" square (can cut from centre of 9" x 9" square)

From orange Marmoleum, cut:

1 piece @ 12" x 18", with a 6" x 12" rectangle cut from centre, and a corner cutout of 3" x 6" (see Diagram 1)
1 piece @ 12" x 12", with a 6" x 6" square cut from centre
1 piece @ 3" x 3" for "floating" square

* Four cutouts from this blue piece will be required to inlay blocks of other colours. These cutouts can be made by tracing around all other pieces after they've been cut and arranged. Blue cutout pieces can be used to fill spaces within orange and red cutouts (see Diagram 1).

Step 2. Sand edges

Sand all edges with 100-grit sandpaper to ensure a better fit when pieces are butted up against each other.

Step 3. Glue pieces to vinyl backing

Cut sheet of vinyl to 48" x 72". In a well-ventilated area, arrange pieces (as shown on Diagram 1) on vinyl. Sand edges again if a better fit is necessary. Remove pieces from vinyl. Apply linoleum adhesive to vinyl using a small trowel. Arrange pieces again and roll over entire surface with a heavy roller. Once adhesive is dry and mat is flat, use utility knife to trim any excess vinyl from perimeter.

Step 4. Add rubber border

Measure edges of mat and add 2" to each measurement. Cut 4 pieces of rubber edging to these measurements. Place strips around perimeter of mat, measure exact length, and mitre all ends of edging to 45° with a utility knife and metal ruler as a guide. Use a caulking gun to apply a bead of silicone adhesive inside the groove of the edging, and slide edges of mat inside groove. Allow to dry overnight.

GARDEN-MAZE MUDROOM MAT

This mat measures 4' by 4'. For a heavy roller, we used a small lawn roller from a rent-all store. For edging, we used reducer strip FV2202BK12 from The Home Depot.

MATERIALS & TOOLS

1 yd. yellow Marmoleum
1 1/2 yds. green Marmoleum
Pencil and carpenter's square
Utility knife and 36"-long metal ruler
100-grit sandpaper
54" x 54" lightweight sheet vinyl
Linoleum adhesive and trowel
Heavy roller
19' 1/8"-thick, 1 1/2" wide black rubber edging
Caulking gun and clear silicone adhesive

Step 1. Cut Marmoleum

Mark shape and size with pencil and carpenter's square (see Photo 1). Lightly score top of material with utility knife, using ruler as a guide (see Photo 2). Fold wrong sides together and cut through to back (see Photo 3).

DIAGRAM 2

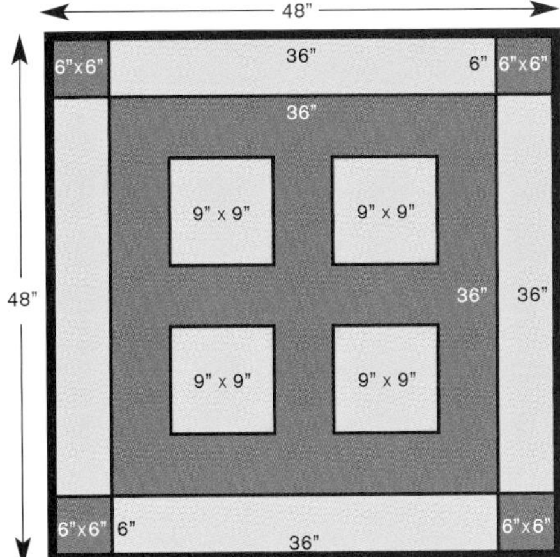

From yellow Marmoleum, cut:

4 pieces @ 6" x 36"
4 pieces @ 9" x 9"

From green Marmoleum, cut:

4 pieces @ 6" x 6"
1 piece @ 36" x 36", then cut four 9" x 9" cutouts from this piece, with a 6" border all around (these cutouts will be filled with yellow) (see Diagram 2)

Step 2. Sand edges

Sand all edges with 100-grit sandpaper to ensure a better fit when pieces are butted up against each other.

Step 3. Glue pieces to vinyl backing

In a well-ventilated area, arrange pieces (as shown on Diagram 2), on vinyl. Sand edges again if a better fit is necessary. Remove pieces from vinyl. Apply linoleum adhesive to vinyl using a small trowel. Arrange pieces on vinyl backing and roll over entire surface with a heavy roller. Once adhesive is dry and mat is very flat, use a utility knife to trim any excess vinyl from the perimeter.

Step 4. Add rubber border

Measure edges of mat and add 2" to each measurement. Cut 4 pieces of rubber edging to these measurements. Place strips around perimeter of mat, measure exact lengths, and mitre each end of edging to 45° with a utility knife and metal ruler as a guide. Use a caulking gun to apply a bead of silicone adhesive inside the groove of the edging, and slide edges of mat inside groove. Allow to dry overnight.

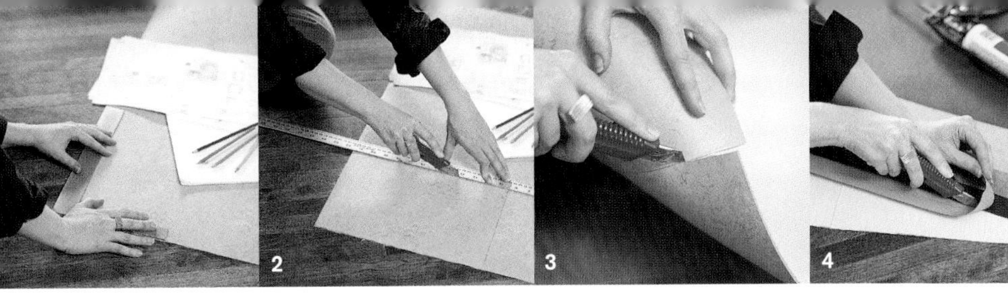

BAR-CODE-STRIPED KITCHEN MAT

This mat measures 2' by 4'. For a heavy roller, we used a small lawn roller from a rent-all store. For black edging, we used 1"-wide black carpet edging, to better suit the smaller size of this mat. This edging was simply glued in place around the top of the perimeter of the mat.

MATERIALS & TOOLS

1	yd. Marmoleum in total (from blue, yellow, orange, red and green Marmoleum scraps)
	Pencil and carpenter's square
	Utility knife
	Metal ruler (at least 36" long)
	100-grit sandpaper
	26" x 51" lightweight sheet vinyl
	Linoleum adhesive and trowel
	Heavy roller
13'	1"-wide black rubber carpet edging
	Caulking gun and clear silicone adhesive

Step 1. Cut Marmoleum

Mark desired shape and size with pencil and carpenter's square (see Photo 1). Lightly score top of material with a utility knife, guiding knife with a metal ruler (see Photo 2). Fold wrong sides together and cut through from front to back (see Photo 3).

From blue Marmoleum, cut:

1 piece @ 4" x 24"
1 piece @ 2" x 24"

From yellow Marmoleum, cut:

1 piece @ 5" x 24"
1 piece @ 3" x 24"

From orange Marmoleum, cut:

1 piece @ 12" x 24"
1 piece @ 3" x 24"
1 piece @ 2" x 24"

From red Marmoleum, cut:

1 piece @ 12" x 24"
1 piece @ 3" x 24"

From green Marmoleum, cut:

1 piece @ 2" x 24"

Step 2. Sand edges

Sand all edges with 100-grit sandpaper to ensure a better fit when pieces are butted up against each other.

Step 3. Glue pieces to vinyl backing

In a well-ventilated area, arrange Marmoleum pieces (see Diagram 3), on the sheet of vinyl. Remove pieces and apply linoleum adhesive to vinyl using a small trowel. Arrange pieces again and roll over entire surface with a heavy roller to flatten.

Step 4. Add rubber border

Measure edges of mat and add 2" to each measurement. Cut 4 strips of rubber edging to these measurements. Place strips around perimeter of mat, measure exact length, and mitre ends of each rubber strip to 45° with a utility knife and metal ruler as a guide. Use a caulking gun to apply a bead of silicone adhesive around the edge of the mat, and attach rubber edging. Allow to dry overnight. Trim around edges to cut off any excess vinyl backing (see Photo 4).

DIAGRAM 3

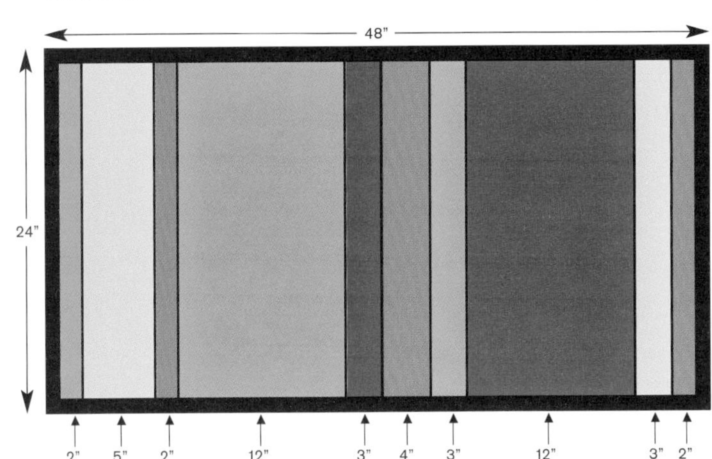

Project

Head of the Class

CRAFT A HANDSOME PANELLED HEADBOARD FROM AN OLD WOODEN DOOR.

Editor's note:
Simple and charming, this headboard was a huge hit with readers when we featured the project.

Difficulty level:
Average

If you've been coming up empty in search of that perfect headboard, stop pounding the pavement. We think you'd be hard-pressed to find a headboard — new or antique — as attractive as this one, crafted from a recycled five-panel door. Inspired by a design from reader Gail E. Matheson-Godreau, this is an ingenious and widely applicable project that can be made at a very low cost. To make the headboard, an old door is simply modified (by widening it with 2 x 4 posts on either side) to fit a queen-sized bed. If your bed is smaller you can cut it down; if it's a king-sized, the posts can be made wider. Supports are added to raise the door off the floor to the necessary height, then it's capped with simple decorative moulding to give it more presence. We finished our headboard with a coat of crisp white paint for a look that's fresh and country casual. If you prefer to see the wood grain and your door is in good condition, a dark stain would look elegant. You can still pound the pavement, but this time, start scanning local junk stores and neighbourhood sidewalks for a timeworn door that's ready for a new lease on life.

Our panelled headboard is country casual in crisp white. Give it a dark stain for a more traditional look.

PHOTOGRAPHY BY DONNA GRIFFITH

If you don't have an old, panelled wooden door on hand, check out a used-building-supply store. That's where building parts are salvaged, and sold to renovators and builders.

To fit a standard queen-sized bed, our finished headboard measured 65 3/4" wide (at its widest) by 54" high. Our instructions reflect that finished size. Measurements will vary depending on the size of your bed, the size of the door you use, and how high you want the headboard to be. Ours is 5 3/4" wider than a queen-sized mattress to accommodate the added fullness of bedding.

MATERIALS & TOOLS

	Panelled door
2	pieces 2" x 4" pine @ 7' long
1	piece 2" x 2" pine @ 6' long
1	piece 1" x 4" pine @ 6' long
	8' decorative moulding
	Dowelling
	#8 4" screws
	2" finishing nails
	2 1/2" nails
	1 1/2" finishing nails
	#10 1" screws
	Screwdriver
	Hammer
	Handsaw
	Wood filler
	Sandpaper
	Circular saw
	Measuring tape
	Electric drill
	Countersink bit
	Wood glue
	Mitre box or mitre saw
	Primer, paint and brush

Step 1. Remove door hardware

Place door on a large work surface or on two sawhorses. With a screwdriver, remove all door hardware, such as screws, hinges, handles and lock. Check the door thoroughly for nails, and remove with a hammer.

Step 2. Fill hardware holes

Using a handsaw, cut a block of scrap wood to fill the empty lock space, and a piece of dowel to fill the empty door handle space. Fill any remaining cracks or holes with wood filler, allow to dry, and sand smooth.

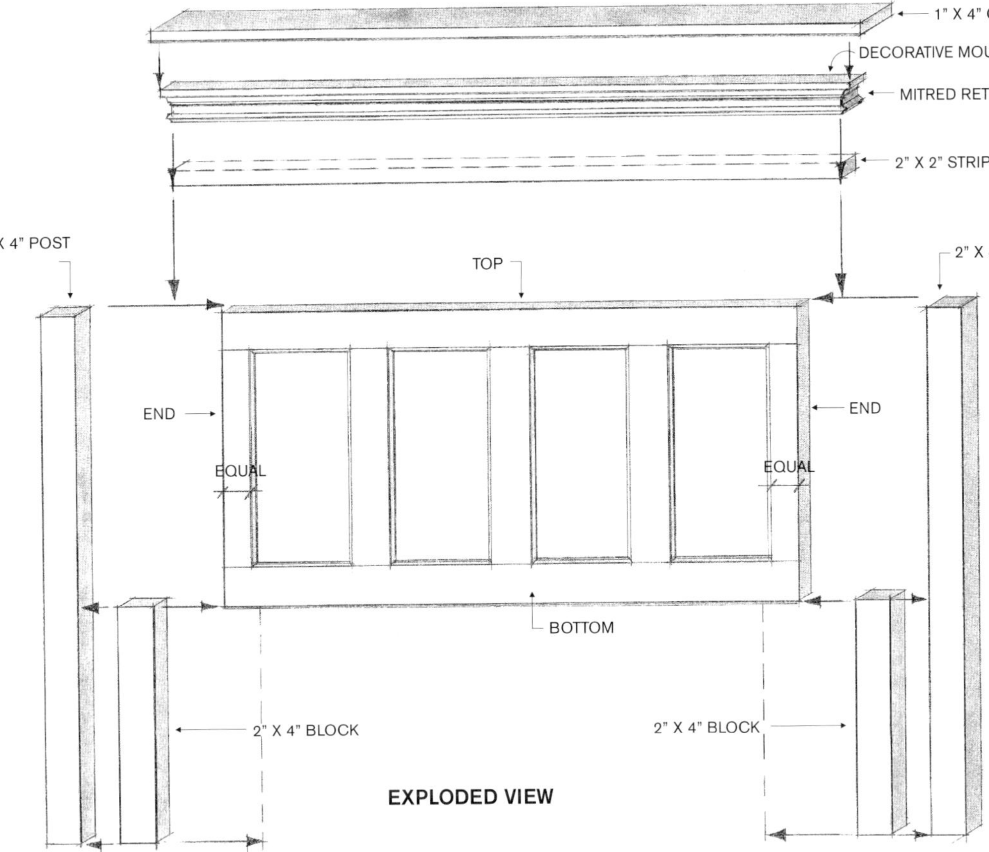

Step 3. Cut door to size

Using a circular saw, cut the door down to desired size (see Photo 2). Measure and mark so that the door's ends are of equal width, and so that its top and bottom edges are of equal width (see Exploded View). To maintain the four centre door panels while cutting the door down, trim at one or both ends (ours was originally a five-panelled door). We cut off one panel and trimmed the ends so that they were of equal width beyond the panel. After it was cut, our door measured 57 1/4" wide by 29 1/2" high, but your measurements may vary.

Step 4. Cut bedposts

Using a circular saw or a mitre saw, cut two pieces of 2" x 4" pine to 52" in length. These will be the posts that are attached to the ends of the door, and will extend from the floor to the top of the headboard (see Exploded View). These full-length bedposts (as opposed to the posts attached only at the bottom of the headboard) will make the headboard more stable and rigid. They will also widen the headboard to accommodate the bed width.

Step 5. Attach bedposts

Drill countersink pilot holes (four at each end) through the post and into the edge of the door. Remove the post, and run a bead of wood glue along the edge of the door. Using an electric drill and #8 3" screws, attach the posts to the ends of the door (see Photo 3). Have someone hold the posts in place as you screw them to be sure that they will be perfectly lined up with the door.

Step 6. Cut blocks and attach to posts

Using a circular saw or a mitre saw, cut two pieces of 2" x 4" pine to 22 1/2". These 22 1/2" blocks will be attached to the bottom half of the posts to widen them (see Photo 4 and Exploded View), making it easier to attach the posts to the metal bed frame brackets. Drill countersink pilot holes, remove blocks and apply wood glue, then screw blocks to posts using an electric drill and #8 3" screws.

Step 7. Build up top edge

Build up the top edge of the headboard with a strip of 2" x 2" pine cut to 57 1/4" long. Attach the pine strip to the door edge with wood glue and 2 1/2" nails.

Step 8. Cut and attach mouldings

Measure the width of the headboard. Cut decorative moulding to fit, with 45-degree mitres on each end. Measure the thickness of the door and cut two return (end) pieces of moulding with 45-degree mitres on one end of each (see Photo 5). Attach the pieces of moulding to the 2" x 2" pine strip with wood glue and 2" finishing nails.

Step 9. Cap top edge of door

To give the headboard added visual weight, cap the decorative moulding with a piece of 1" x 4" pine cut to the total width of the headboard (ours was 64 3/4"), including the posts and moulding returns plus 1/2" overhang at both ends and 1/2" overhang at the front and back. Use wood glue and 1 1/2" nails to attach. Construction is now complete and the headboard is ready for finishing (see Photo 6).

Step 10. Fill, sand and paint headboard

Fill any small nicks or holes in the door with wood filler. Allow wood filler to dry. Completely sand headboard. Apply primer, let dry. Sand. Apply 1 to 2 coats paint. (We used Para Paints' Ivory P1820-4 in a semigloss oil.)

Step 11. Attach headboard to bed frame

With an electric drill and #10 1" screws, attach the headboard posts to the metal bed frame.

Project

Build a Garden Shed

OUR CHARMINGLY RUSTIC CEDAR SHED PROVIDES A STORAGE SPOT FOR ALL OF SUMMER'S YARD ESSENTIALS.

Editor's note:
Use recycled lumber to keep the cost of this shed down, or substitute new 2-x-4s and paint the structure to give it rustic charm. Have fun adding unique hardware and cutouts to make it truly stand out.

Difficulty level:
Average

When Calgarians Liz Cooper and Brian Turnock were among the winners of our Style Search 1997 — for their striking transformation of a '50s bungalow into a Victorian-style two-storey using architectural salvage — we knew they were a pair to watch. Now the couple have put more salvage to good use, reclaiming a neighbour's old cedar decking to build this rustic garden shed. With its gone-to-seed design "inspired" by old-time outhouses, the shed makes the couple's backyard seem well removed from its city setting. And the informal style means this is an easy project for a novice woodworker — mistakes, cracks, crevices and other imperfections only add to the shed's rustic charm.

Opposite: Tucked into a corner of the backyard thick with greenery and flowers, the cedar garden shed – made from recycled decking and other demolition materials – looks like a remnant from Calgary's pioneer days.

Next page: There's plenty of storage space in this 3' x 3' x 7' h. garden shed. Shelving offers places to stack pots, hoses and tools. Seed packets hang on twine strung from old nails. Bags of fertilizer and peat moss can be neatly tucked away in the storage space located under the hinged bench.

PHOTOGRAPHY BY ROBERT LEMERMEYER

Project 35: Garden shed

This is a simple design, with six separately assembled pieces making up a whole shed. The six pieces consist of two sides, a back, a door, a roof and a floor. There is also an interior storage space with a hinged storage shelf. We used salvaged decking in our project, so the shed took on a rustic look, but new decking could be used. If you're using new materials, do not apply any wood sealer, and the shed will develop an aged look.

MATERIALS & TOOLS

	Tape measure
	Circular saw or handsaw
300'	2" x 6" cedar decking
1	4" x 4" post (at least 48" in length) for the base support
2	pieces 25" x 33" plywood (any thickness) to make roof sheathing
	36"-wide rolled mineral roofing (or any other roofing material, including shingles or galvanized-steel sheeting)
	Electric drill
200	2 1/2" deck screws
	Screwdriver
	Level
	Carpenter's square
	Jigsaw
2	large (3" w. x 6" l.) gate hinges for door
50	1 1/2" nails for roofing
	Hammer
2	small door hinges for storage shelf
	Rake head for door pull
	Leftover stain or paint

Step 1: Cut lumber

Use a tape measure and circular saw to cut wood to specified lengths.

For sides, back, door, floor:
From 2" x 6" cedar decking, cut:

- 18 pieces to 84" each (6 pieces for each side, 6 pieces for back)
- 6 pieces to 78" each (for door; one piece will be cut in half for doorjambs)
- 9 pieces to 30" each (3 crossbars each for both sides and back)
- 2 pieces to 27 1/8" each (top and bottom horizontal crossbars on door)
- 1 piece to 52" (diagonal crossbar on the door front)
- 2 pieces to 10" each (hinge-mount pieces)

For floor, hinged storage shelf:
From 2" x 6" cedar decking, cut:

- 6 pieces to 33" each (for floor)
- 2 pieces to 33" each (for floor crossbars)
- 4 pieces to 32" each (for hinged shelf)
- 6 pieces to 14" each (for vertical shelf support)
- 2 pieces to 24" each (for crosspieces for vertical shelf support)

For roof:
From 2" x 6" cedar decking, cut:

- 4 pieces to 24" each (for front and back roof rafters; these pieces are square cut, and joined with a diamond-shaped piece)
- 3 pieces to 33" each (for three perpendicular-crosspieces)

For gable ends of roof:
From 2" x 6" cedar decking, cut:

- 2 pieces to 33" each
- 2 pieces to 33" in length, but angle ends so pieces measure 16" in length along one side
- 2 pieces to 16" in length, but angle ends to measure 6" in length along one side

For support posts:
Cut 4 pieces of 4" x 4" post to approximately 12" each. Shape one end of each post into a point to be driven into the ground for supports.

Step 2: Assemble side, back and floor

To make one side wall, butt six pieces of the 2" x 6" together (planing isn't necessary, since cracks and spaces between pieces will add to the rustic look) so you have one assembled piece that measures 33" w. x 84" h. x 2" d. Lay one 30" crosspiece across the top, flush with the tops of the six pieces. Drill 12 evenly spaced holes through the crossbar (should work out to 2 holes in each 2" x 6" piece). Using the deck screws, screw the crossbar in place from the inner side of the wall. When crossbars are mounted, there will be a 1 1/2" space at each end for sides and back to overlap. Measure 1 1/2" up from bottom edge of six pieces, and draw a straight line across. Place bottom crosspiece so that it sits along this line; the 1 1/2" space is where floor will fit into sides and back. Screw crosspiece to bottom of side wall, following directions as above. Next, measure distance between top and bottom crossbars, determine centre, mark with a line, and affix third crossbar in centre, following steps above. Assemble the second side and back in the same way. To assemble floor, follow directions as above, but make your crossbars sit flush with both ends of your floor pieces.

Step 3: Make door and doorjambs

Cut one 2" x 6" door piece in half lengthwise so that you have two pieces that measure 2" x 3" x 78". These will be your doorjambs. To make door, lay out the five remaining 78" x 2" x 6" pieces, butting them against each other lengthwise. Measure down 6" from the top and measure 6" up from the bottom and mark with pencil. These will be the positions for the horizontal crossbars. Affix crossbars with screws as in Step 2. To affix the diagonal crossbar, hold 52" length of 2" x 6" diagonally across the door, with top at left and bottom at right. Mark a line with pencil across top and at bottom where diagonal crosspiece will need to be cut in order to fit neatly within your two horizontal crossbars. Cut the diagonal crosspiece on these lines. Using two screws in each plank, similar to technique in Step 2, screw into place from inside of door to outside.

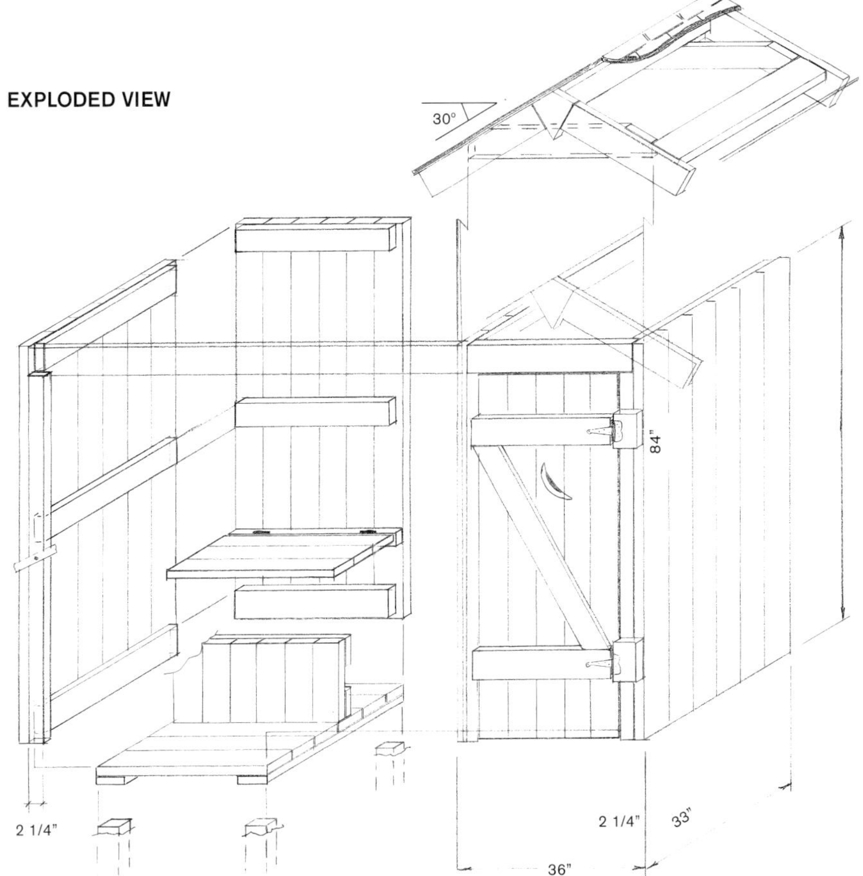

Step 4: Anchor posts in ground

Measure the square area where shed will sit, and mark each corner on the ground. Dig four 11"-deep holes to bury each post (this will make sinking the posts easier). Drive a 4" x 4" post into each hole, leaving approximately 1" left above ground, with outside corner of each post sitting flush with outside corner of where shed will sit. Use a level to determine that the four posts sit flush with each other. This will provide four level corner supports so that the shed won't sag or tip over time.

Step 5: Assemble body of shed

Using two screws, one each at right side top and bottom crosspieces, join your right side and back. Use a carpenter's square to ensure right angles. Repeat with left side, again using only two screws, one each at left side top and bottom. Place the floor so that it sits on the four corner supports, with floor crosspieces running from front to back. Move the 3-sided structure onto the floor. With bottom crossbars of structure sitting on floor, drill diagonally downward through crossbars and into floor. Screw sides and back structure to floor, using two screws for each piece of 2" x 6" (a total of 36 screws).

Step 6: Make design in door

Before mounting door, hand-draw a moon-shaped design (or other shape, as desired) on the front. Using the drill, make a hole large enough in which to fit a jigsaw blade. Using the jigsaw, cut the design into the door. There's no need for precision; flaws will add character and rusticity.

Step 7: Attach doorjambs and door

Stand doorjamb pieces against front edge of side walls. Drill two holes at top and two holes at bottom, running from side walls through into doorjambs. Screw both doorjambs into place. With door sitting in place, mark where you will attach hinge-mount pieces (they will be flush with door crosspieces). Drill holes, and using four screws each, screw in place. Attach hinges to door, then attach hinges to hinge-mount pieces.

Step 8: Make roof and gables

Cut two identical angular diamond shapes out of cedar scraps. These sit at front and back where roof rafters meet, so that rafters need not be mitred, but instead sit square against each "diamond." This also provides some detail at the front and back peaks of the roof. Each piece should measure 6" on the longest two sides where the rafters will attach. With two front rafter pieces sitting at desired angle, place decorative diamond piece on top and screw all three pieces together to make front rafters. Repeat process to make back rafters. Attach front and back rafters together using three 33" perpendicular pieces, screwing through rafters into ends of side perpendicular pieces, and through diamonds for centre perpendicular piece. Nail plywood sheathing in place and cover with two pieces of rolled roofing material cut to size of roof. Nail into place, with nails evenly spaced every 5" along edges. Cut another piece of rolled roofing to approximately 8" wide, and fit over peak with 4" each side. Nail in place every 5". Attach front and back gable pieces (they should form a triangular shape) by fitting up inside the front and back of roof structure. Screw into place from back to front through gables into rafters. Place roof on structure and screw to main body of shed.

Step 9: Make hinged storage shelf

Using three pieces of 2" x 6", and following instructions in Step 2, make shelf. Use scrap cedar as crosspieces on underside of shelf. At 14" up from floor, attach a crosspiece to back wall, on which to hinge shelf. This can be made with scrap cedar. Hinge shelf to back crosspiece. With shelf lifted, make vertical shelf support, following instructions in Step 2. Mark where it needs to sit in order that it meets the shelf at a right angle. Screw vertical shelf support in place from outer sides of shed, into ends of crosspieces.

Step 10: Add details

The head of an old rake missing its handle is simply bolted into the door from behind. A piece of scrap cedar was used for the latch. Drill a hole into the middle of a rectangular piece of wood using a drill bit one size larger than the size of nail you are going to use. This will allow the latch to rotate when nailed in place. If desired, shelving can be added by cutting pieces of 2" x 6" to 33" in length, five pieces per shelf, and setting them in the shed, side by side, supported on the crossbars. If desired, use stain or paint to darken any visible ends of freshly cut wood.

Project

Remaking the Bed

BUILD A SLEEK MODERN PLATFORM BED THAT TEMPERS SPARE MINIMALIST DESIGN WITH THE WARMTH OF NATURAL WOOD.

Editor's note:
Beds are by nature cosy, but with its sleek aesthetic, this one works best in an airy, open space. The platform and side tables make it wide, so measure your room carefully before you build.

Difficulty level:
Difficult

Long considered just the homely pedestal of the decidedly downscale futon, the platform bed now takes centre stage as a most fashionable furnishing. Inspired by the simplicity of the Japanese tatami mat, our queen-sized design features a deep-set base that gives the illusion the frame is floating. The edges of the extra-wide platform keep nighttime reading within reach, and for practicality we added a no-fuss side table and a simple headboard. The sophisticated look of our bed is deceiving, however. The materials — maple-veneer plywood and three standard Masonite slab doors — are easy to find and affordable, and the project is suitable for an amateur woodworker, making this an easy way to bring sleek modern style to the bedroom.

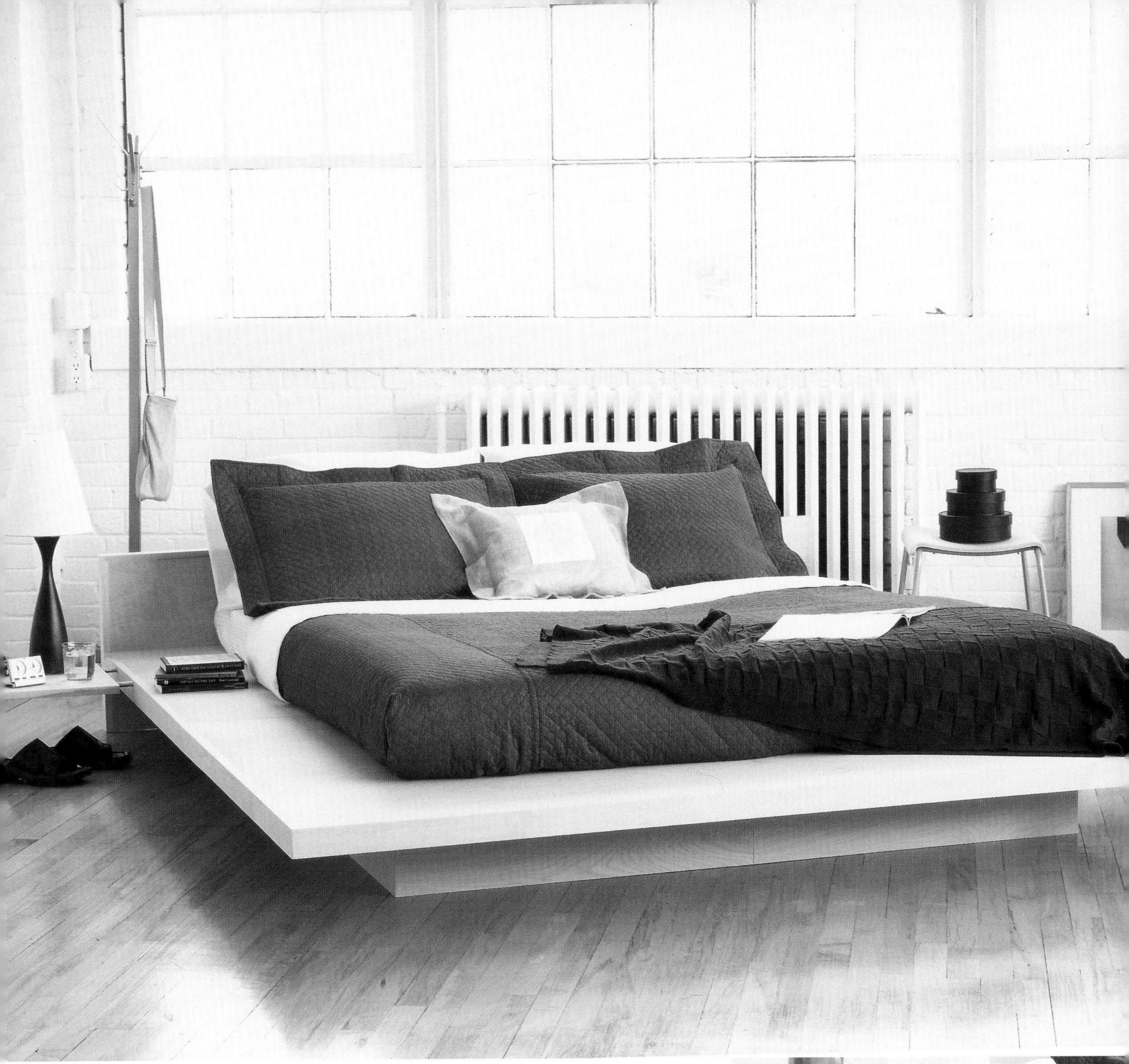

Shown here in a loft setting, dressed in charcoal linens, the low-riding platform bed looks stylish and inviting. A deep-set base gives the substantial queen-sized bed a feeling of lightness, and the unadorned rectangular headboard keeps pillows propped for bedtime reading.

A slab of trimmed maple veneer, secured by a pair of metal dowels that slip into holes in both the table and bed frame, becomes a handy side table. Its weightless look makes it the perfect mate for the Eastern-inspired bed.

PHOTOGRAPHY BY VIRGINIA MACDONALD

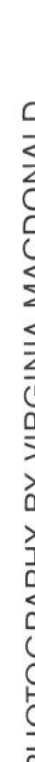

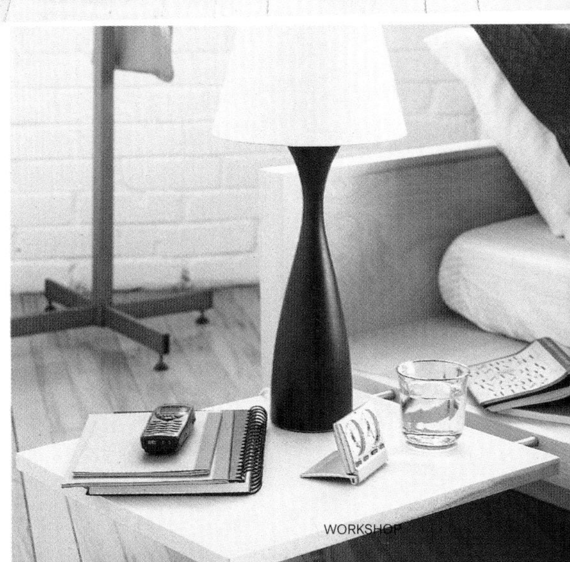

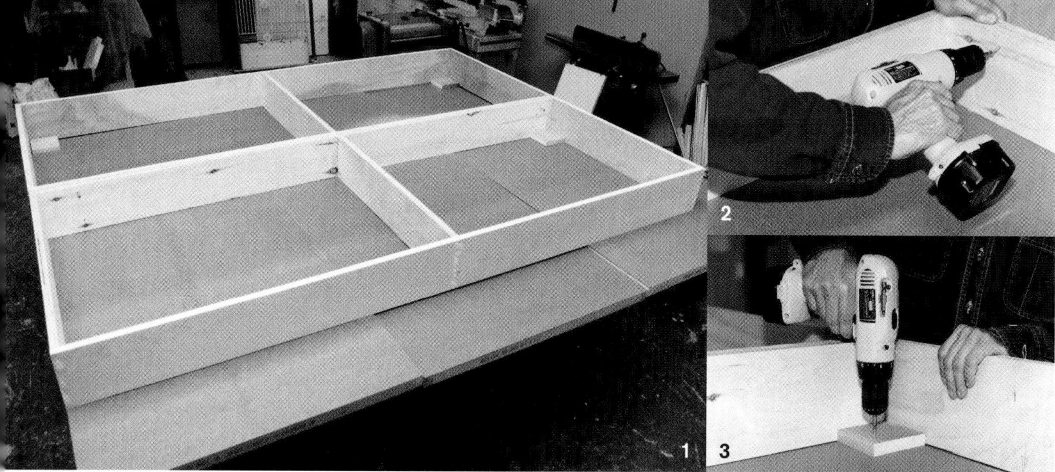

Our queen-sized platform bed measures 80" w. x 90" l. It has a 10"-wide overhang at the foot of the bed and on both sides. At the head, we skipped the overhang in favour of a handsome headboard. The base, or kick, of the bed measures 60" w. x 80" l. to support a standard queen-sized mattress.

MATERIALS & TOOLS

4	48" x 96" sheets 3/4"-thick maple-veneer plywood*
	Table saw
	White glue
100	finishing nails
	Latex wood filler
	Sanding block
	120-grit sandpaper
3	30" x 80" x 1 3/8" Masonite slab doors
	Pencil
	Drill with #8 through drill bit, 1/2" bit or Forstner bit, and Pilot bit
	1 1/2" #8 wood screws
6	pieces 4" x 4" x 3/4" scrap wood
40	feet 1" x 2 1/8" solid maple
	Mitre box
	Handsaw
	Clamps
	Cloth
	Stubby screwdriver with a Robertson bit
	2" #8 wood screws
	Masking tape
	Hammer
2	5" x 1/2"-diam. stainless steel rods
	Clear urethane, Danish oil or stain

* If maple veneer is unavailable, birch veneer is a good substitute.

Step 1. Build base

The base of the bed is made in two sections that can be disassembled to make the bed easy to transport. Each section consists of an open maple-veneer-plywood box, measuring 80" l. x 30" w. x 6" h. To make this structure, start with one 48" x 96" sheet of 3/4"-thick maple-veneer plywood and use a table saw to cut four pieces measuring 80" x 6". (Keep all finished surfaces of plywood facing up during cutting so you don't damage the veneer.) Set aside the rest of this sheet; it will be cut into pieces for the headboard and side table. From a second sheet of maple-veneer plywood, cut six pieces measuring 30" x 6".

Assemble each box so that it consists of two 80"-long side pieces supported by a 30" piece at each end and an additional 30" piece in the middle for support. Make sure the grain runs in the same direction all the way around each box.

Spread ample amounts of white glue evenly at each end of each piece of plywood, and attach the pieces together. For additional strength, reinforce each corner with approximately seven finishing nails. Reinforce the cross piece as well. Install some of these nails along the outside corner and some from the inside of the base, hammering them diagonally so they run securely through both pieces of wood. Let base dry 8 hours.

Fill all of the outside nail holes with latex wood filler and, using a sanding block and 120-grit sandpaper, sand the surfaces smooth.

Step 2. Build platform base

Set the three Masonite doors side by side, long sides together, onto a clean flat surface. Make sure that the edges are pressed tightly together. Place the two box frames upside down across the three doors so that the frames are flush with each other on their long sides and the length of the frames is perpendicular to the length of the doors (see Photo 1). Make sure that the top end of the frames is flush with the long edge of one of the doors to accommodate the headboard. There will be a 10" overhang at the sides and foot. Check to make sure that the base is square on the doors by measuring for equal distance around the perimeter of the base. Adjust the placement accordingly and use a pencil to trace the outside edge of the frame onto the doors to use as a permanent guide.

Step 3. Join base pieces and prepare doors

With the two frames still lying on top of the doors, use a drill and eight 1 1/2" screws to join the two frames together along their abutting long sides to form one large frame. Space the screws evenly along the 80" length of wood (see Photo 2).

Make sure the frames are within the pencil marks, then place 4" x 4" x 3/4" scrap blocks of wood tightly in several corners of the frame at the head and foot, so that there are three blocks at the head and three at the foot. Using white glue and two 1 1/2" diagonally positioned screws, fasten each scrap block to the underside of the doors. The blocks will act as guides, so that the bed can be assembled the same way each time and so that the doors stay in place on the frames (see Photo 3).

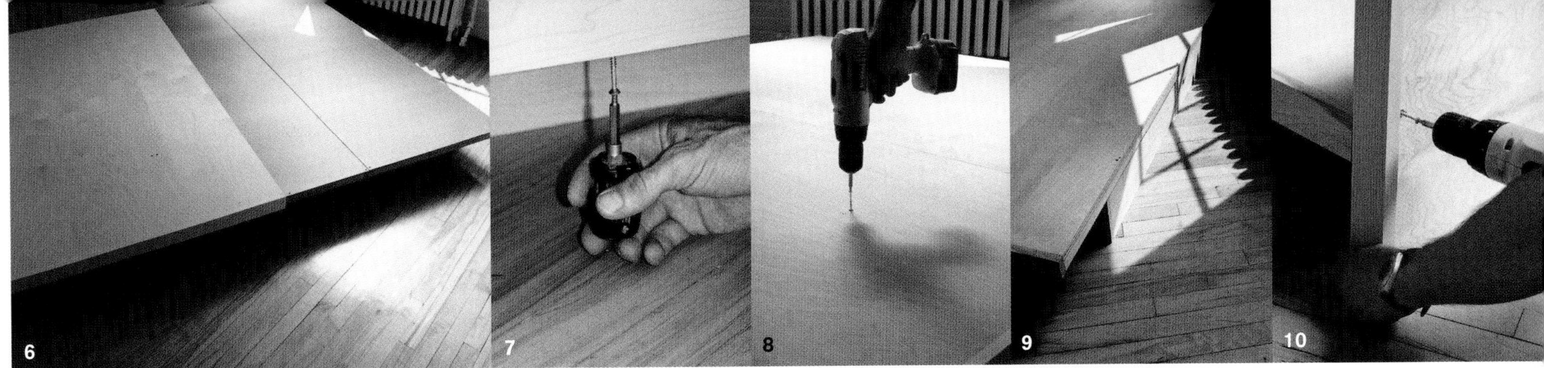
6 7 8 9 10

About 8" in from the edges of the platform, on the long sides of the bed, use a Pilot bit to drill holes every 16" along the doors. (These holes will later be used to properly secure a piece of maple-veneer plywood to the top of the doors.) Turn bed right side up.

Step 4. Assemble platform top

From each of the remaining two pieces of 48" x 96" plywood, cut one 45" x 80" slab. Placed horizontally on top of the three doors, with a seam in the middle, these pieces will form the finished platform top.

Once the platform top pieces are cut, band their edges with solid maple for a finished look. The solid maple banding will be 2 1/8" wide. Using a handsaw, cut two pieces of maple to 45" in length and two pieces to 45 3/4" for the side edges of the platform top. Using the saw and mitre box, cut a 45° mitre on one end of each of the 45 3/4" pieces. For the foot end of the platform top, cut one piece of solid maple to 81 1/2" on the long side with a 45° mitre cut in each end. The top edge of the platform does not need banding as the headboard will cover it.

Using white glue, attach the banding to the sides and foot of the platform slabs (when the top is on the bed this banding will hang down by 1 3/8" as is visible in Photo 4 on the headboard piece, which gets trimmed with banding later in the project). Wipe away any excess glue with a damp cloth. Clamp and let dry overnight. Smooth any rough areas using a sanding block and 120-grit sandpaper (see Photo 4).

Step 5. Assemble bed

Place the base on the floor. Top with the doors, which should pop easily into place because of the guide blocks (see Photo 5). Place the two finished platform slabs on top of the doors (see Photo 6). Using a stubby screwdriver with Robertson bit and 2" screws, screw doors to finished slabs from underneath using pilot holes made in Step 3 (see Photo 7).

Next, look underneath the bed to locate the seams between the doors. Using a pencil, draw a line continuing the seam around the banding to the top of the slab and mark a point at 16" in from the edge of the finished slab. Repeat at each door seam on both sides of the bed. Countersink two pilot holes and screw in 2" screws on either side of each of the four points marked (see Photo 8). Lightly sand out pencil marks.

For additional security, along the top end of the bed screw in four extra screws through the slab and into the base, making sure that they are no less than 16" from the side edges of the platform (see Photo 9).

Step 6. Finish bed

Finish bed with either a clear urethane, Danish oil or a combination of both. If you want a different colour, select the stain of your choice. Test out your options on scrap wood before committing to a stain colour. Whichever you choose, be sure to apply at least one coat of clear urethane on top to protect the wood.

Step 7. Make headboard

The headboard and the side table can both be made with "off-cuts" (extra pieces) of the maple-veneer plywood. Use a 90" x 18" piece for the headboard and attach banding in the same fashion as Step 4, allowing for mitred corners. Banding should extend 1 3/8" off the back of the headboard (the side that will face the wall) (see Photo 4). Finish headboard with clear urethane, Danish oil, a combination of these, or a stain of your choice. Let dry thoroughly.

Set the finished side of the headboard against the assembled bed and, using a pencil, draw a guide line along the top of the platform onto the finished side of the headboard. Remove the headboard and measure 3/8" down from the guide line and lightly mark a second line. Countersink five evenly spaced pilot holes through the headboard along the second line. Put the headboard in place and using 1 1/2" screws, attach the headboard to the frame through the back of the headboard (see Photo 10).

Step 8. Make side table

The side table is made from a 16" x 19" x 3/4" slab of maple-veneer plywood that is banded with solid maple. Cut the solid maple to 1/4" x 3/4" and band the table in the same fashion as in Step 4, using mitred corners. Finish table with clear urethane, Danish oil, a combination of both, or a stain of your choice. Let dry completely.

Measure 3" in from both corners of one edge of the now-finished table and mark these two points with a pencil. Using a 1/2" bit, or Forsner bit, drill a hole in each of the marked spots, being careful to make both of them exactly 1 3/4" deep. To ensure that each hole is the same depth, mark a 1 3/4" depth on the drill bit with a piece of masking tape. Hammer a 5" stainless steel rod into each hole until it stops. Hold up the table alongside the edge of the platform bed in the spot where you would like to install it. Mark points for the location of the rods. Using the same bit, drill two 1 3/4"-deep holes at these marks making sure that they lie in the centre of the platform slab, not the centre of the banding. Fit the table and the rods into place using a hammer. Use a block of wood for cushioning (see Photo 11).

11

Project 37

Vanity Fair

CREATE AN ELEGANT BATHROOM FURNISHING FROM AN OLD DRESSER FITTED WITH A SINK AND FAUCET.

Editor's note:
Think beyond the standards: there's such a variety of potential sink bowls available, in materials from steel to porcelain to copper. A great way to add character to a boring builder bathroom.

Difficulty level:
Difficult

Chic and handsome, this mid-century modern bathroom vanity looks like something you might come across in a trendy furniture boutique or a hip New York hotel bathroom. But its provenance is much more humble, its pricetag quite affordable: it's simply a recycled dresser that's been refinished and fitted with a new sink and faucet. Inspired by a design by reader Jacqueline Lutz, our vanity is easy to recreate — you'll need some carpentry skills to cut a hole for the basin and modify the interior of the dresser, and some basic plumbing knowledge to hook up the taps and drain. Beyond that, you're just refinishing a piece of furniture. Cleverness aside, our vanity is versatile, too. The small stainless steel sink makes a tidy addition to a powder room, or, with its high gooseneck faucet, works equally well as a wet bar for entertaining. If you prefer a more classic look, choose a traditional, dark wood dresser; if cottage casual is your style, a weathered pine or distressed, painted piece could be inset with a white porcelain sink. Perhaps best of all, this project lets you incorporate the current unfitted look without the cost of a bathroom renovation.

We were inspired by Jacqueline Lutz's conversion of a standard dresser to create this mid-century modern bathroom vanity.

PHOTOGRAPHY BY TED YARWOOD

The small stainless steel sink looks sleek and tidy in the powder room.

Our materials list includes plumbing parts required for our basic stainless-steel bar sink. When shopping for plumbing parts at your local hardware store, be sure to ask a sales assistant for help in pulling together all necessary parts for your sink.

There are two types of basins (sinks): bathroom basins, which fit 1 1/4" drains; and bar basins, which fit 1 1/2" drains. Most bathroom faucets incorporate a 1 1/4" pop-up drain assembly. Depending on the sink you choose, you may have to purchase a separate drain assembly. Be sure your sink and faucet set are compatible.

When looking for a wooden cabinet or dresser to convert into a vanity, pay close attention to the dimensions of the cabinet. Ideally, purchase your sink first so that you can choose a cabinet with the right dimensions — something that is wide and deep enough to accommodate the sink, leaving space at the back of the cabinet to fit a faucet set as well as space at the front of the cabinet so that the sink doesn't run up to the front edge. The cabinet should also be approximately 32" high — standard vanity height.

If you're converting a cabinet with shelves or a dresser, you'll probably have to cut through the back and bottom of shelves or drawers to accommodate plumbing parts and pipe. This will make the drawers somewhat unstable, so you may need to fix the top drawer permanently in place by screwing it to the frame of the cabinet from beneath and filling the screw holes and touching them up with paint or stain. If you really want to use the

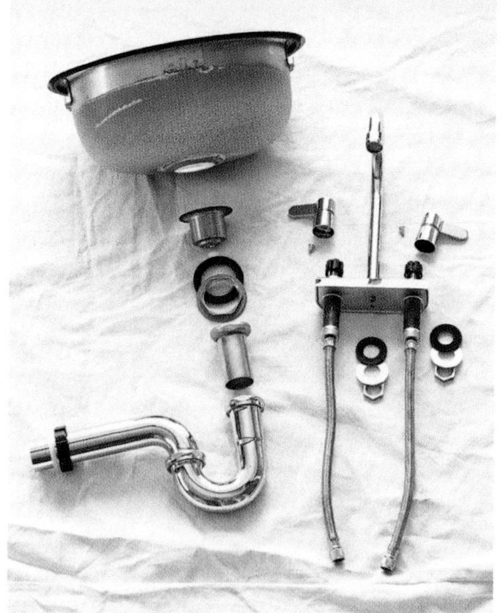

drawers that had parts cut out of them, consider lining them with plastic baskets so smaller items do not fall out the back or bottom.

MATERIALS & TOOLS

- Cardboard
- Sink
- Pencil and ruler
- Sharp utility knife
- Masking tape
- Electric drill with 1" drill bit
- Jigsaw
- Faucet set
- Wrench
- Paintbrush, or roller and tray
- Varathane
- Water supply lines
- Drain assembly
- Chrome P trap (may be supplied with the sink)
- 2 1/2" hole saw*

* Available at tool rental companies

Step 1. Make sink hole template

Many sinks come with templates to help guide you in cutting the hole in the vanity top. If your sink does not come with a template, make one yourself from cardboard. Set the sink upside down on a piece of cardboard and trace around the lip of the sink onto the cardboard with a pencil (see Photo 1). Remove the sink. Measure and mark all the way around the first outline at points 5/8" in from the line you've just drawn. Join the marks together; you will have made a second, smaller outline, 5/8" in from the first outline. With a sharp utility knife cut a hole in the cardboard along this second, smaller sink outline (see Photo 2). This will be the template for cutting the sink hole in the top of the cabinet.

Step 2. Cut sink hole

With masking tape, securely tape the cardboard template to the top of the cabinet in the spot where you'd like the sink to be situated. With a 1" drill bit, drill a hole into the cabinet, just inside the cardboard template. This hole will enable you to get the jigsaw started. With a jigsaw, cut the sink hole, following the hole in the cardboard template as you go (see Photo 3).

Step 3. Drill faucet holes

To determine the faucet placement, drop in the sink — you can gauge by eye the best location for the faucet. Remove the sink. Centre the faucet set on the cabinet just behind where the sink will sit. Mark the spot with masking tape. With a pencil, mark the tape with the location of the faucet spout and the 4" centre-to-centre tap measurement (i.e., 2" to either side of the faucet spout). Drill the holes for the faucets at those points 4" apart using a 1" drill bit (see Photo 4).

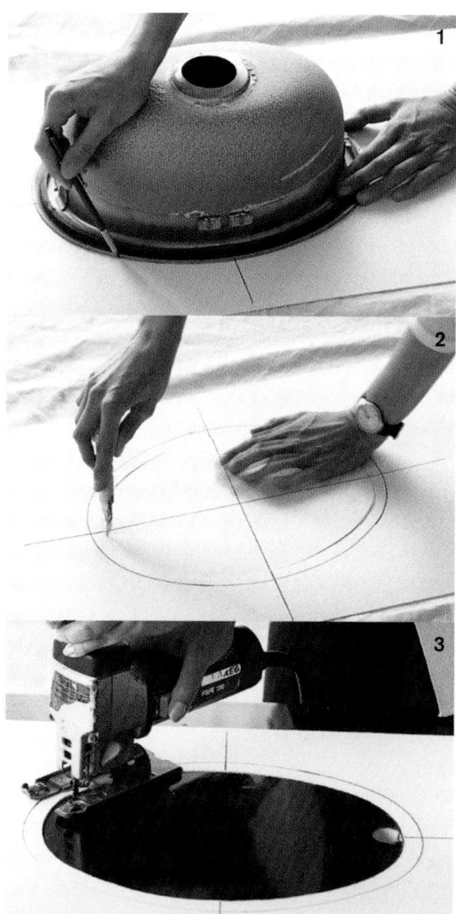

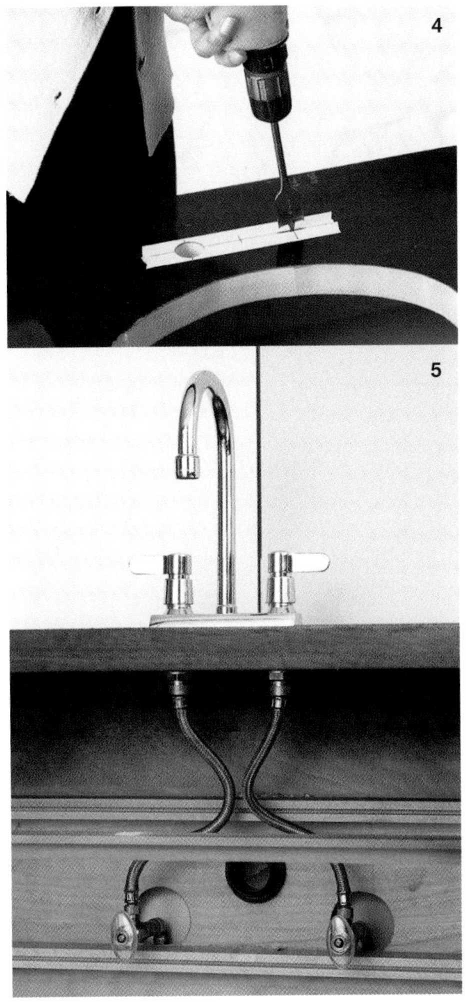

Step 4. Varathane vanity top

With a paintbrush, or roller and tray, apply several protective coats of clear varathane to the top of the vanity. Be sure to varathane the cut edge of the sink hole as well; this will seal the wood and protect it from water seepage and wetness. Allow varathane to dry completely before proceeding.

Step 5. Cut holes in cabinet back

To determine the position of the drain pipe and water supply shut-offs on the back of the cabinet, measure their locations on the wall and transfer these locations to the back of the cabinet. Using a 2 1/2" hole saw, cut holes in the back of the cabinet to accommodate the drain pipe and the water supply shut-offs. (The holes must be big enough to clear the handles of the shut-offs.) Install cabinet against wall (see Photo 5).

Step 6. Attach faucet

Turn off the water supply shut-offs. Drop in the faucet set and tighten it into place from underneath. The faucet set will come with all the necessary parts (i.e., washers, rubber rings, etc.; see our "Materials" picture for assembly parts). With faucet set firmly in place, attach the water supply lines. Connect these to the water supply shut-offs coming out of the wall, and tighten.

Step 7. Install drain assembly and sink

Depending on the sink you use, the drain assembly parts will be 1 1/4" or 1 1/2". We used a bar sink, which required a 1 1/2" drain assembly. (Bathroom sinks will need a 1 1/4" pop-up assembly, which should come with a bathroom faucet set.) Set the drain into the sink, and the rubber washer and nut onto the drain beneath the sink, and tighten. Screw on the tail piece. Drop the sink into the sink hole (see Photo 6). Our sink had clips to hold it into place.

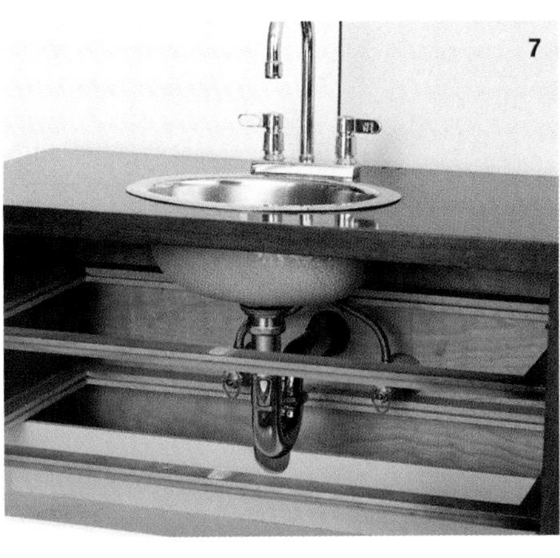

Step 8. Attach P trap

Attach the P trap onto the tail piece and to the trap adaptor coming out of the wall (see Photo 7). The drain assembly will determine the size of the P trap (i.e., either 1 1/2" or 1 1/4"). Turn on the water supply shut-offs.

Step 9. Modify dresser drawers

Measure and mark on the drawers the distance from the back of the cabinet to the front point of the P trap. As well, mark the locations and the widths of the water shut-offs; the drawer will need to clear these too. With a jigsaw, cut out of the back and bottom of the drawers according to these measurements so that the drawers can now adequately clear all plumbing parts, water shut-offs and adaptor (see Photo 8). Slide the drawers back into place (see Photo 9).

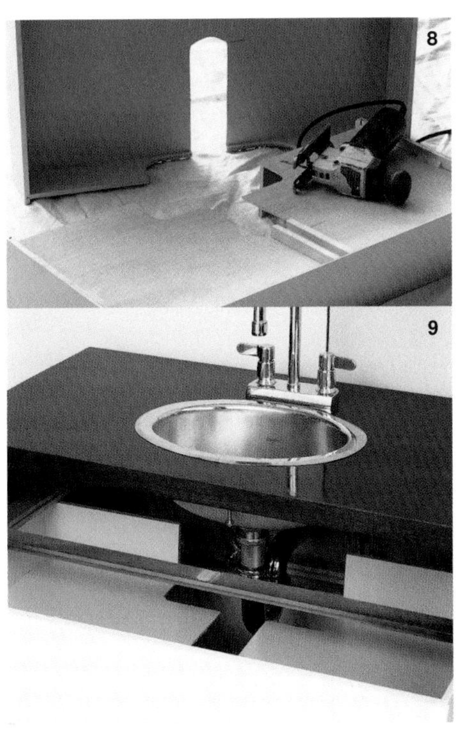

Project

The New Sheers

BRING HOME TODAY'S COOL FROSTED PLASTICS WITH TWO FRESH TAKES ON HOUSEHOLD FIXTURES.

Editor's note:
These pieces give your rooms a sleek, modern look, but serve a more practical purpose too: hiding clutter or disguising unappealing views. And they're great for renters — affordable and removable.

Difficulty level:
Average

Projects:
Shutters
Cabinetry panels

Rendered cleanly in translucent materials — milky Plexiglas and textural ribbed board — two standard design elements take on sculptural beauty. Our creations marry a contemporary, almost industrial, aesthetic with sleek avant-garde frosted plastics, which softly diffuse light and emphasize only silhouettes. Give kitchen cabinets a facelift with new corrugated-plastic cupboard panels. For more of a challenge, cover a window with white Plexiglas shutters that gently soften the natural light. The materials are affordable and easy to find. Whichever project you choose, be sure to warm up your streamlined installation with softly coloured accessories for a look that reads cool yet friendly.

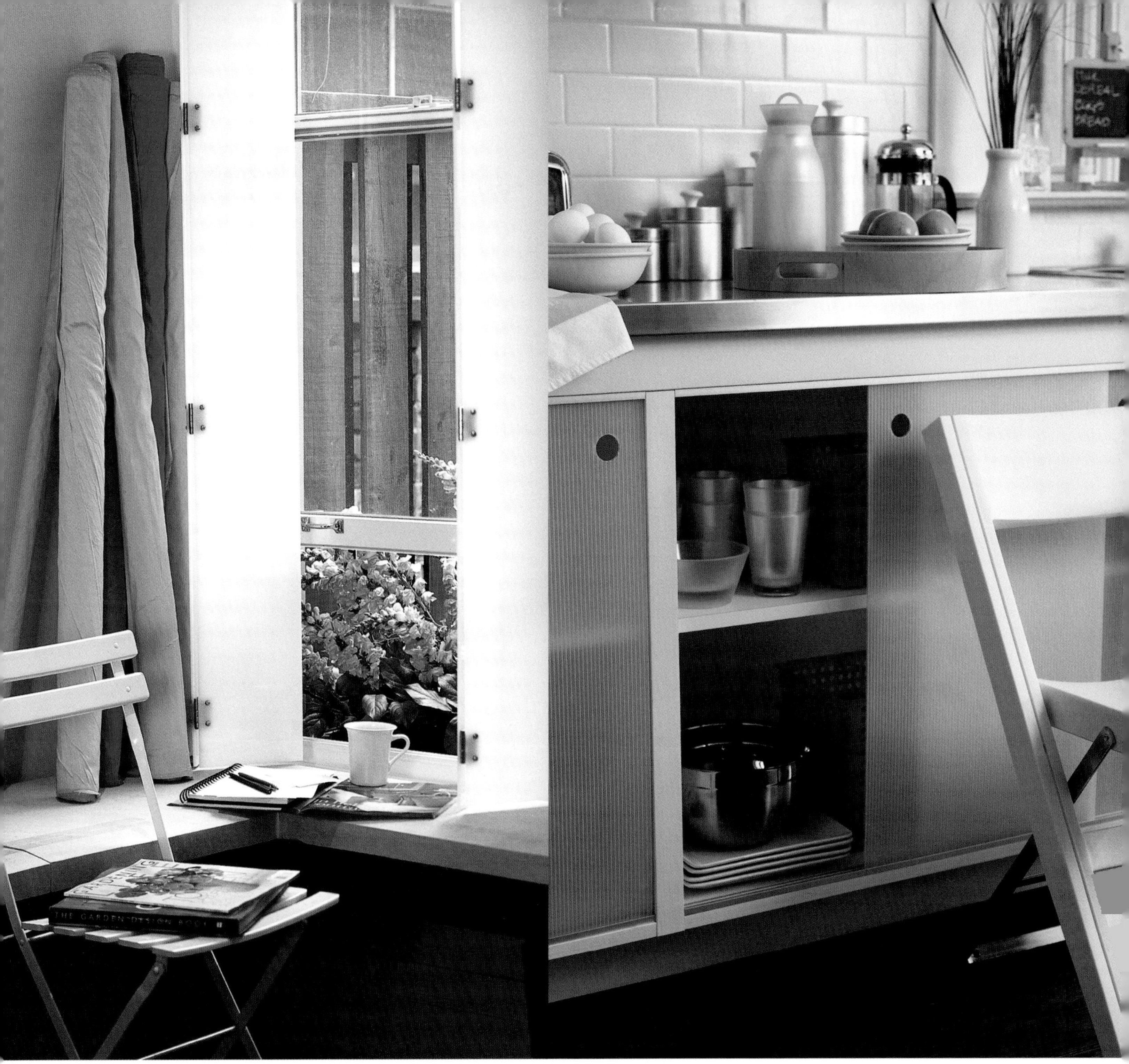

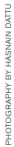

Sleek, unadorned panels of white Plexiglas replace traditional louvred shutters on this tall, narrow window, offering privacy but allowing in soft, filtered light.

Slide ribbed plastic panels into metal door tracks to lend modern flair to standard kitchen cabinets. A simple cutout acts as a finger pull for easy access.

PHOTOGRAPHY BY HASNAIN DATTU

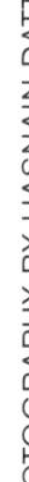

Project 38: Frosted Plexi projects

CABINETRY PANELS

MATERIALS & TOOLS

- Measuring tape
- Pencil
- 4' x 8' sheet of 3/16" corrugated plastic
- Mitre box and hacksaw
- Satin U-track for 1/4" door (we used 24'}
- Fine file
- Marker
- Drill
- 1 1/4" spade bit for drill
- #4 screws
- Screwdriver
- Scrap wood for jig (we used 1" x 4")
- Clamp
- Fine-grit sandpaper
- Masking tape

Before you buy the corrugated plastic, measure for the door panels as explained in Step 1, then have corrugated plastic cut to size at a plastic retailer.

Step 1. Measure for door panels

For the width of each door panel, measure the width of the cupboard opening, divide that in half and add 5/8" to the measurement to account for the cupboard doors overlapping. For the height, measure the height of the opening. From that, subtract the measurement of two thicknesses of U-track base and another 1/8" for clearance space. Have two panels of the corrugated plastic cut to those measurements.

Step 2. Measure, cut and drill U-track

Using a mitre box and a hacksaw, cut four pieces of U-track that fit the width of the cupboard exactly. Smooth the rough ends with a fine file. Next, mark the locations of the screws along the U-track with a marker. Mark them at least 2" in from the ends of each piece of track and about 12" apart along each piece of track, making sure that when one door is in place, half the screws will be accessible on the other side of the track.

Using a drill bit that fits into the trough in the U-track, and that will make a hole that will accept the head of a #4 screw, drill part way through into the bottom of the U-track. Do not go all the way through. Switch to a smaller bit (one that will fit the body of a #4 screw), and continue drilling through the track (see Photo 1). File the bottom side of the U-track smooth.

Step 3. Install top U-tracks

With a screwdriver, attach two of the tracks to the top of the cupboard opening — one directly in front of the other, and flush with the edge of the cabinet (see Photo 2). The heads of the screws must be slightly recessed from the trough of the track to allow the doors to ride smoothly.

Step 4. Make jig for cutting finger holes

To measure and cut the finger holes, you will need to make a jig. Clamp together two pieces of scrap wood (ours were 1" x 4" cut to 6" long each) so that they are flush. Now, determine the centre point of the finger hole on the top piece of wood. First, measure 2" in from the side of the wood and mark. Then measure 2" plus the thickness of the track (ours was 3/8") from the top of the wood and mark this point. Mark where the two points meet; this will be the centre of the finger hole.
Using a 1 1/4" drill bit, drill a hole through the top block only using the mark you have just made as your centre point (see Photo 3). Remove the clamp, leaving 3/16" of space between the two pieces of wood for a piece of corrugated plastic. Place a third block up against the top edge of the two blocks and screw in place (see Photo 4).

Step 5. Cut finger holes

Slide one corrugated plastic door panel into your jig, making sure that it is properly aligned with the top and side of the door panel. Clamp the jig in place very gently so you do not bend the plastic. Using the same drill bit you used to make the hole in the jig, drill through the plastic (see Photo 5). Repeat for second door. With fine-grit sand-paper, sand edges of holes.

Step 6. Sand door edges

With masking tape, mask off the face of each door at the edges. Sand the edges of the doors until they are smooth.

Step 7. Install doors

Hold one of the bottom tracks firmly against the bottom of one door so that the top of the door sits in its place within the upper track (see Photo 6). Then swing the bottom into place. Repeat with the other door and the last piece of track. Push the tracks to their correct locations. They should be flush at the edge of the frame. Screw both tracks in place, sliding both doors to one side, then the other, along the tracks to access the screw holes (see Photo 7).

SHUTTERS

MATERIALS & TOOLS

- Measuring tape
- 49" x 97" sheet of 6-mm #020-4 white acrylic Plexiglas*
- Table saw with a 10" triple chip blade
- Oscillating sander
- Sanding block and various grits of sandpaper
- 1" x 2" wood (for template)
- Black marker
- 16 zinc round butt hinges with 3/4" reach and about 2" high (height can vary)
- 10/24 zinc Robertson head screws
- 10/24 hexagonal nuts
- Combination square
- Pencil
- Awl
- Thick cardboard
- Clamps
- Drill
- Socket wrench
- #8 flat washers and neoprene pads (to fit screws)
- Electric screwdriver

* Ask the plastic retailer you buy your plastic from to cut it to your measurements, or cut it yourself at home with a table saw.

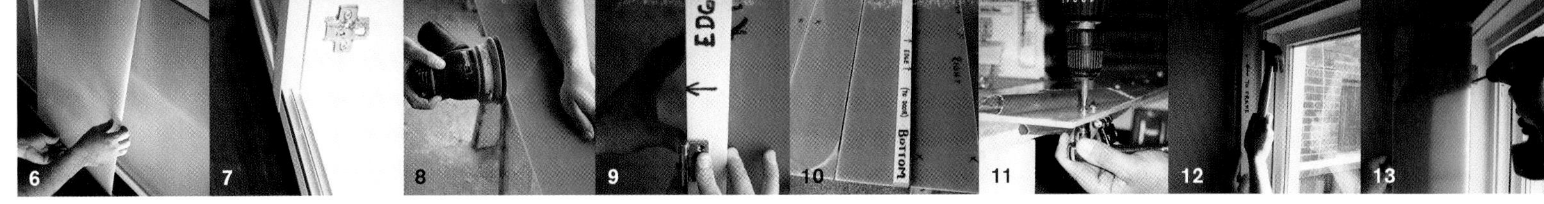

Step 1. Measure for shutters

Measure the width of the window opening at the top, middle and bottom (to account for an uneven window frame) and use the narrowest width measurement. Subtract 1/8" for each edge that will be hinged and 1/8" for centre crack between the two shutters. (We made four shutters, so allowed for space for 5/8".) Divide the width by the desired number of panels.

Measure for the height at three different spots, and take the smallest height measurement. Subtract 1/4" from the measurement to allow for 1/8" at the top and bottom so the shutter fits right into the window frame.

Step 2. Cut shutter panels

Do not remove the blue plastic protective coating from the Plexiglas. Cut each panel to size using a table saw with a 10" triple chip blade (or have it cut to size at the plastic retailer). Finish the edges with an oscillating sander (see Photo 8). Start with a coarse-grit sandpaper and work up to a fine-grit sandpaper, running it flat along the edges of the Plexiglas. Follow with a hand-held sanding block and bevel the edges of the Plexiglas.

Set up a padded work surface and lay out the Plexiglas so that you have the approximate spacing between the panels that you will have when they are mounted in the window. This will be the layout for the shutters, and from this you will determine the edges that the hinges will be located on. We had hinges along the outer edges, and the next edges in from those. There are no hinges along the centre edges.

Step 3. Measure for hinges

To determine the location of the hinges you will need to make and use a wood template (see Photo 10). To make the template, cut a piece of 1" x 2" wood to the height of the plexiglass panels plus 1/8" (the extra 1/8" at the top of the template will later allow for a 1/8" clearance of the panels within the window frame). Using a black marker, label one end of the template as the "Top." Measure 1/8" down from the top of the piece of wood and mark with a black marker. Then measure 4" down from this point and mark this point as the location of the top hinge. Then measure 4" up from the bottom end of the wood, and mark this point as the location of the bottom hinge. Using the marker, label this end of the wood template as the "Bottom." Divide the remaining space equally to allow for two more sets of hinges.

Step 4. Mark hinge holes on template

Place a hinge on the edge of the template, centring it on one of the points marked in Step 3. Use a combination square to mark and set the measurement from the centre point of the screw hole to the inside edge of the hinge. Use this combination square setting to mark the locations of the other hinges. Draw a straight line through each of these points down the template to create the cross marks for the location of each hinge.

Centre the holes of one of the hinges over the cross marks and trace the holes with a pencil (see Photo 9). Repeat for each hinge location, then punch the centre points of the circles onto the template using an awl.

Place the template on one of the Plexiglas panels on the hinge side making sure that the bottom and side edges are flush (see Photo 10). You will have 1/8" of the template sticking out beyond the top edge of the Plexiglas. Placing a piece of protective card between the clamp and the Plexiglas to avoid denting, gently clamp the Plexiglas and template together. Using a power drill, pre-drill all of the holes through the template and through the Plexiglas. Repeat for all edges of Plexiglas that will have hinges attached, being sure that the bottom of the template is flush with the bottom of the Plexiglas.

Step 5. Attach hinges

Remove the template and peel back the blue vinyl protective coating from the Plexiglas only enough to have room to install the hinges. Using a socket wrench and a power drill on a low torque setting, screw the hinges to the Plexiglas at the pre-drilled locations, placing a washer and a thin neoprene pad under the head of each screw to keep the Plexiglas from cracking, and backing each screw with a hexagonal nut (see Photo 11). You will end up with two sets of bifold panels.

Step 6. Mark hinge locations on window

So that the shutters are fitted tightly into the window frame, you will need to set the hinges slightly inside the window frame. With someone helping you, pick up one set of shutters and hold it in the window frame. Adjust it to determine a placement where the shutters fit snugly in the window frame, but are still able to rotate 90 degrees. You should have 1/8" clearance at the top and bottom of the shutter. Mark the locations of all the holes in the hinges onto the window frame. (These marks are made to pinpoint the setback that your shutters need; the final hinge locations will be located at this setback, but should be plotted out with the template, as directed below, for the most accurate measurements.) Draw a straight line vertically through each mark so that it will be visible when you line up the template on the window frame.

Using the wooden template that you created before, double-check the hinge locations on the window frame. Hold the template up to the window frame and align the holes you just marked with the holes on the template. Make sure that the top of the template lines up with the top of the window frame. Nail the template in place if desired (see Photo 12). Then, using an awl, mark all the holes through the template onto the window frame.

Step 7. Attach shutters to window frame

Drill pilot holes in the marked places using a drill bit that's slightly smaller than the screw. Screw panels in place with electric screwdriver and zinc Robertson head screws (see Photo 13). Repeat on other side, check alignment and shim as needed with small pieces of cardboard placed behind the hinges. Peel off blue coating.

Project

Four Inspirational Makeovers

TRANSFORM OLD JUNK INTO NEW TREASURES.

Editor's note:
If vintage flea-market pieces aren't your thing, don't pass on these projects: our directions provide good, basic information on refinishing, refitting and reupholstering that'll work for pieces of any style.

Difficulty level:
Average

Projects:
Console table
Slipper chair
Lamp base
Fire screen

With decorating taking an eclectic turn, unique furnishings bring a current look to rooms. Although you can pick up eclectic pieces at decorating shops, it's more rewarding to "create" them yourself, tailoring old junk to suit your style. Flea markets are filled with undiscovered treasures just waiting to be transformed. With that in mind, we hit the stores for makeover fodder: affordable finds, aesthetically challenged, but with good bones and structural soundness, and the potential to become signature pieces. Then we got to work stripping, painting, upholstering and refitting. Whether you try our projects, or get creative with your own, don't forget our formula: bring plain old good junk to life with a little hard work and a lot of imagination.

Top left: Topped with a 3/8"-thick piece of sandblasted glass, a weathered tub rack is reborn as a funky console table. The sandblasted underside of the glass has been treated with a special protective coating to prevent fingerprints and smudges, and the edges have been polished to a smooth finish for safety. Top right: Suited in new wool-flannel upholstery, a shabby junk-store chair is transformed into sophisticated seating. We went to Silva Custom Furniture to get the straightforward how-to for this project. To finish the chair, we spray-painted the legs a glossy "lacquer" black and removed the arms, turning a tatty '50s lounge chair into a sleek, low slipper chair. Bottom left: This one's as quick as "quick fixes" get! Antique shutters are oiled up and hinged together to make an instant fire screen, a decorative cover-up for an unusable fireplace. Salvaged architectural fragments, from old doors and windows to antique corbels and columns, are excellent candidates for conversion — keep an eye out on garbage day for rejects. Bottom right: A once-dated spool lamp base boasts a modern monochromatic profile when painted white and topped with a shade in the same colour. (We splurged on a custom shade; a ready-made one would work equally well.)

PHOTOGRAPHY BY CURTIS TRENT

CONSOLE TABLE

The vintage washtub stand we found at a junk store was topped with a piece of 3/8"-thick sandblasted glass to create a console table. If you find a structure that would make a good table base, consider topping it with glass. At a glass store, have a piece of sandblasted glass cut 1/4" larger than the top of the table base. (Check the Yellow Pages under glass suppliers and cutters.) Have sandblasted underside of glass treated with a protective coating to prevent smudges and fingerprints, and have edges of glass polished for safety. Where glass sits on rough wood, we installed small round rubber tabs from a hardware store to prevent the underside of glass from scratching. Before converting anything into a glass-topped table always be sure the supporting structure is stable. If needed, tighten screws or bolts, dismantle and reglue parts, or rebuild structure.

SLIPPER CHAIR

We went to Silva Custom Furniture to get straightforward upholstery instructions for this project. We chose to cover our slipper chair in new wool-flannel fabric. We removed the existing arms to give the chair a sleeker profile.

MATERIALS & TOOLS

- Adjustable wrench
- Hammer
- Screwdriver with assorted heads
- Wood filler
- 120-grit sandpaper
- Spray-paint
- Pry bar (or any thin, flat tool that will remove staples)
- Needle-nosed pliers
- Dacron pillow wrapping
- Sharp scissors
- Heavy-duty staple gun and staples
- Measuring tape and yardstick
- Fabric
- Tailor's chalk
- Needle and thread (in same colour as fabric)

Step 1. Dismantle chair

Using necessary tools (we used an adjustable wrench, hammer and screwdriver), dismantle chair, unscrewing legs and arms. Set aside nuts, bolts and screws; you'll need these to reassemble chair later.

Step 2. Fill, sand and paint chair

Fill any small holes and nicks in wooden parts of chair with wood filler. Let dry. Lightly sand all exposed wood with 120-grit sandpaper to get a smooth finish and allow for proper paint adhesion. Wipe off all dust. We chose black lacquer spray-paint for ease of application. Hold spray-paint can 4" to 5" from surface and spray evenly in sweeping motions. This technique will prevent drips and result in a smooth paint finish. Follow directions on paint can for drying time between coats. Apply several coats for an even finish.

Step 3. Remove fabric

Use a small pry bar to pry up staples and remove existing fabric from chair frame. Be sure to work away from your body, so tools do not slip and injure you; wear safety goggles to protect your eyes. Use needle-nosed pliers to grab staples and twist them slightly to pull out. If staples cannot be removed, or if they break in half, bang them into frame with a hammer so that they don't catch on new padding and upholstery fabric.

Step 4. Attach Dacron padding

To give chair an extra layer of padding, we covered the existing foam, still in reasonable condition, with Dacron (found at upholstery-supply stores). Lay out an uncut piece of Dacron (it should be larger than the front face of the chair back). Set the chair back face-down on top and pull up edges of Dacron to cover front and sides of back. Leave an excess edge of approximately 1" all the way around; this will be trimmed later. Pull Dacron around to back of chair back in small sections and staple it to back edge of frame about 1/4" from outside edge. Once trimmed, this will be a neat edge. At corners, pull Dacron straight up and over the point, and staple into place. Then grab the sections to the left and right and staple into place. This will prevent bunching, allowing Dacron to lie flat in the corners. Where necessary, snip Dacron to fit around extruding chair parts. Our chair back had supports that connect it to the seat so we had to cut a straight line toward the chair back on either side of the wood. Staple Dacron that lies between the supports to the frame and fold the piece that lies on top of the support along the width of the wood. When the entire piece is stapled in place, trim edges of Dacron, getting as close to staples as possible. Repeat procedure for seat.

Step 5. Measure and cut fabric

To determine the length of fabric needed to cover the seat, place the tip of a tape measure at the bottom of the front face of the chair seat and measure upwards along the front face, across the surface of the seat and down the back face of the seat to the bottom of the back face. To find the width of fabric needed to cover the seat, repeat this method starting at the bottom of one of the side faces of the seat and measuring up over the seat and to the bottom of the other side face. Add 2" to each measurement to allow a 1" excess of fabric around each edge. Lay fabric out on flat surface. To make sure fabric measurements are totally accurate, with a yardstick and tailor's chalk, put a number of markings down the length of the fabric at the desired width. Join these marks, and you'll have a straight line. Repeat for length. Cut fabric. Repeat for chair back.

Step 6. Upholster seat and back

Lay out seat fabric, right side down. Set seat face-down on fabric. Pull up all sides of fabric to ensure the length and width of the fabric are matched with the length and width of the seat. Begin with the side of the fabric that is on the far side of the seat, and gently pull the fabric up and around the seat. Staple the centre of the edge of the fabric to the underside of the seat. Repeat for the side nearest you and then the two other sides so there is one staple on each underside of the seat. These staples keep the fabric in place, preventing it from shifting as you work. Begin with the side opposite you when stapling the fabric in place, then move to the side nearest you, then to the left side and finally the right side. Staple each side out from the centre staple toward corners, but don't staple all the way to corners yet; you'll need fabric at corners to make pleats.

At each corner, smooth the fabric out and over toward the outside edge. Continue the line of staples to about 1 1/2 from the corner along the same line you have been following. Fold the fabric into sections, ensuring that you leave enough fabric for the pleat. Smooth the fabric down along the side and staple into place. Trim excess fabric to prevent bunching. There will be one pleat per corner of the seat. To achieve a clean, smooth front, our chair's pleats are located on the front and back of the seat and face out toward the sides of the seat. Fold the finishing piece over and staple along the edge, making a neat tailored pleat at each corner. Staple remainder of fabric in place on underside of chair along pleat fold. Repeat for front face of chair back.

Step 7. Upholster back of chair back
Because the back of the chair back is exposed, it needs to be covered so no staples or seams are visible. The final effect should be of a smooth, seamless panel. Lay chair back on its front face. Measure back of chair back and add 2" to length and width. Cut fabric to this size. Place fabric on top of chair back, right side up. Fold top edge of fabric under. Flip the fabric up and staple the top edge of fabric you just folded under, along fold line; you will be stapling through the wrong side of the fabric. When you flip the fabric back down, the staples will be hidden underneath. Handstitch other three edges in place. To do this, fold under the remaining three sides of the backing so that you have a neat folded edge along each. Pin in place. Using a needle and thread, closely stitch along the seam of each side of the back panel. Try to keep back panel as tight as possible. Finally, stitch bottom edge in place, smoothing as you sew.

Step 8. Reassemble chair
Reassemble chair, reversing the order in which you dismantled it. Replace any screws, bolts or nails that are no longer usable.

LAMP BASE

MATERIALS & TOOLS

- Lamp base
- 120-grit sandpaper
- Wood filler (optional)
- Masking tape
- Primer and paintbrush
- Semi-gloss oil paint
- Paint thinner
- Aerosol spray-paint unit or oil paintbrush

Step 1. Lightly sand lamp base using 120-grit sandpaper and, if necessary, fill any small nicks and chips with wood filler. Allow to dry and sand again. Wrap lamp cord with masking tape to protect from paint.

Step 2. Apply a light coat of primer to lamp base with paintbrush. Allow to dry. Apply a second light coat of primer. Allow to dry. Sand lightly.

Step 3. If you are using a paintbrush with the oil paint, use an oil brush and brush on paint sparingly to avoid runs and drips. Apply as many coats (probably two or three) of semi-gloss as are needed to give a uniform finish. Allow each coat to dry thoroughly before applying the next. We used an aerosol sprayer to apply the semi-gloss oil paint; this tool, available at many paint stores, gives a smooth, professional-looking finish, and allows you to spray on any colour you choose rather than being restricted to standard spray-paint colours. The sprayer kit contains an aerosol sprayer and a screw-on paint jar. Thin a small amount of paint by adding 1 to 2 parts paint thinner per 10 parts paint. Pour thinned paint into jar and screw onto aerosol sprayer. Spray on paint in sweeping motions from top to bottom. With this method, paint will go on evenly and won't drip. Allow to dry overnight. Spray on second and third coats as needed. Between coats, thoroughly clean aerosol can and sprayer by rinsing them with paint thinner. Precise instructions are provided with unit.

FIRE SCREEN

Old shutters offer myriad possibilities. Hinge tall shutters together to create a room divider. Affix smaller shutters to open kitchen cabinetry in lieu of doors. A mix of aged shutters makes an interesting interior window covering. Our shutters measured 38 1/2" high and each panel was 7" wide, a perfect size for covering an unusable fireplace (because they are wood, do not use shutters with a fireplace that is in use).

MATERIALS & TOOLS

- Wood glue
- Hawes Scratch Cover with lemon oil (or paint or stain)
- Masking tape
- Hinges and screws
- Screwdriver

Step 1. Our shutters were in excellent condition save for a few broken louvres. To fix split louvres, put dabs of wood glue along one piece and press pieces together; clamp with masking tape. Wipe away glue that squeezes out; allow to dry about one half-hour. If shutter side pieces have loosened and allowed louvres to fall out of their grooves, refit louvres into slots and glue top and bottom pieces back into side pieces.

Step 2. If your shutters, like ours, are made of unfinished or stained wood, a good oiling is all that's needed to revitalize them. We used Hawes Scratch Cover with lemon oil, which restores lustre to natural wood. (Hawes is not appropriate for varathaned or lacquered wood, but you won't likely find shutters finished in this way. If varathaned shutters need a touch-up, brush on a new coat of varathane.) If you choose to paint your shutters, use a brush and apply light coats to prevent dripping. Note: Hawes is toxic.

Step 3. Select hinges that are appropriate for the size of your shutters. We used small brass hinges near top and bottom of each panel.

Project

All in a Day's Work

OUTFIT AN UNUSED NOOK WITH FOUR SMART OFFICE PROJECTS.

Editor's note:
The cube storage featured here may look rigid but practically speaking, it's very flexible. Built in different configurations, it would work in a bathroom, kid's room, even at the bedside.

Difficulty level:
Average

Projects:
Wall unit
Desk blotter
Steno chair
Slipcover
Banker's chair

Some people would give anything for a home office. Well, how about one wall? Our office nook can easily fit into your spare bedroom, and it looks so warm and inviting, you'll actually want to work. (See the dreary Before shot to compare!) We started with an easy-to-build wall unit that provides display space, a cork board and a spot for storage; our office accessory projects add a hint of desktop style. We transformed a secondhand desk chair with fabric slipcovers, and revamped a side chair with a coat of fresh paint. To pull it all together, we installed breezy plaid curtains and a fresh sisal carpet, and coated the walls in creamy yellow. Best of all, we didn't devote all our savings, or all our time, to putting this home office in working order. Neither will you.

A fresh colour palette, wall-mounted storage unit and organized desk transform this dreary spare room into a welcoming home office.

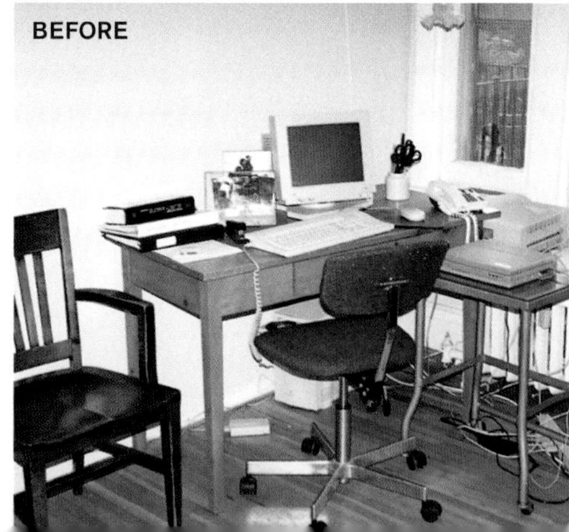

PHOTOGRAPHY BY VIRGINIA MACDONALD

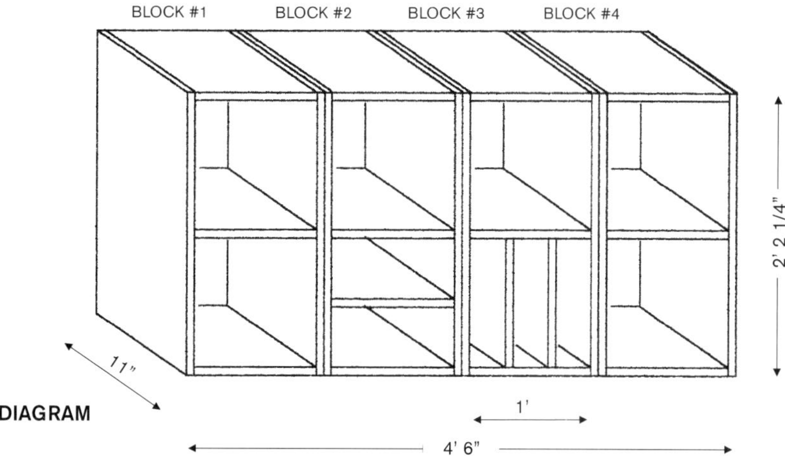

DIAGRAM

Project 40: Office makeover

WALL UNIT

This project uses a biscuit joiner, a power tool used for cutting slots in wood, into which are inserted wooden "biscuits." The thin, flat biscuits allow two pieces of wood to be joined without screws or nails, providing a neat, smooth appearance. Adjust your biscuit joiner to accommodate #20 biscuits. Biscuit joiners are available at most hardware stores.

MATERIALS & TOOLS

1	4' x 8' piece 1/2" MDF
	1 3/4" #8 screws
2	4' x 8' pieces 3/4" MDF
	1 1/4" #8 screws
	Primer and paint or stain
	Wood filler
	Wood glue
1	1' x 5' piece 3/8" cork
1	package #20 biscuits
	Contact cement
	Circular saw
	Biscuit joiner
	Sand block
	Masking tape
	20-grit sandpaper
	Drill and countersink bit
	Clamps

Step 1. Ask the lumberyard to cut 1/2" MDF to 36 1/4" x 54". Ask them to cut 3/4" MDF into five 8' x 11" pieces. From those five pieces, using a circular saw, cut eight 26 1/4" x 11" vertical pieces (gables); cut twelve 12" x 11" shelves; and cut three 11" x 12" dividers. Cut one 12 3/4" x 11" spacer block. Sand all cut edges.

Step 2. Put gables together in pairs. Decide which end of each gable will be at top of unit. Mark all top edges with pencil. Determine which face of each gable will face the inside of each portion of unit (all slots will be cut on inward-facing sides). Mark all inward-facing sides. Place first gable on work surface, marked side up, with one 11" end against a vertical block. Clamp in place. Hold biscuit joiner vertically, so base is up against vertical block and nose is sitting on gable. Make sure outer edge of biscuit joiner is flush with outer side of gable. Hold biscuit joiner firmly as it can kick. Pressing trigger, cut slot in gable. Slide biscuit joiner to other side of gable and cut another slot. Spin gable around so other 11" end is set against vertical block. Cut two more slots, as above. To make centre slots for shelves, place gable on work surface with bottom end against vertical block. Place spacer block on top of gable, with 11" end against vertical block. Push base of biscuit joiner up against edge of spacer block, with nose down on gable so outer edge of biscuit joiner is flush with outer side of gable. Make a slot. Slide biscuit joiner to other side of gable and cut another slot. Repeat above steps for remaining gables.

Step 3. Choose which side of each shelf will face down and make a mark on that side. On the edge, draw an arrow pointing to that side. Set first shelf on work surface with one 11" end against vertical block. Clamp in place. Hold biscuit joiner down on work surface, so nose is up against opposite 11" end of shelf, and, making sure outer edge of biscuit joiner is flush with outer edge of shelf, cut a slot. Slide biscuit joiner to other side and cut another slot. Spin shelf around so other 11" end is up against vertical block and make two more slots, as above. Repeat for remaining shelves and dividers.

Step 4. Select one pair of gables for Block #3 (see Diagram). Measure in 6 3/8" from the bottom end of each and mark with a pencil in two places across the gable. This will mark placement of divider. Line spacer block up to the 6 3/8" pencil marks on one gable and clamp into place. Set biscuit joiner nose down on gable, with base up against end of spacer block, so outer edge of biscuit joiner is flush with outer side of gable. Cut slot. Slide biscuit joiner to other side of gable and repeat. Repeat above steps for facing gable.

Step 5. Select middle and bottom shelf for Block #2 (see Diagram). On bottom side of middle shelf, measure in 3 1/2" from both 11" ends and mark with a pencil in two places across shelf. These will mark placement of dividers. Line up spacer block with marks and clamp into place. Set biscuit joiner nose down on shelf with base up against end of spacer block, so outer edge of biscuit joiner is flush with outer side of shelf. Cut slot. Slide biscuit joiner to other side of shelf and repeat. From other end, line up spacer block with marks and clamp into place. Make two more slots as above. Repeat these steps to cut slots on top side of bottom shelf.

Step 6. With masking tape, cover all slots in gables and shelves. Prime and paint, or stain, all pieces. Let dry.

Step 7. Remove masking tape. For Block #1 and Block #4, put a dab of wood glue into slots of first pair of gables. Insert #20 biscuits into slots. Put a little glue on the slotted ends of three shelves and set into place between gables. For Block #2 and Block #3, put a little glue on slotted sides of shelves where necessary, insert biscuits into slots and set into place with dividers. Attach shelves to gables as with Block #1 and Block #4. Clamp each block together until glue is dry. If you don't have large enough clamps, screw blocks together:Using a #8 countersink bit, drill three pilot holes into outer sides of gables, along level of each shelf. Attach gables to shelves using 1 3/4" #8 wood screws.

Step 8. Screw together all four blocks with 1 1/4" wood screws. Screws should be placed into the gables, close to the edges, where the gables meet the shelves. Fill holes in outer gables with wood filler and touch up with paint. To attach back piece, drill three pilot holes into back piece, where the back will meet the gables, with a #8 countersink bit. Attach back piece using 1 3/4" #8 wood screws. Back piece will hang 10" past bottom edge of unit. Cut cork to 54" x 10". With contact cement, glue cork to unit overhang.

DESK BLOTTER

Use scraps left over from the blotter to cover a holder for pens and pencils.

MATERIALS & TOOLS

3 yds. plain fabric
Thick matte board cut 1" larger on all sides than the calendar pages
Hot-glue gun or glue stick
Large desk calendar refill pages

Step 1. Cut one panel of fabric 2" larger than board on all sides. Cut two panels, each 1" larger than board on all sides. Cut two 10" x 10" squares of fabric. Cut one piece fabric 9" wide, at a length 1" wider than board.

Step 2. To cover board, place first panel of fabric, wrong side up, on work surface. Place board in centre of fabric. Fold up edges and glue onto board with hot-glue gun or glue stick.

Step 3. Lay next two fabric layers for back panel, right sides together, on work surface. Fold each 10" x 10" square diagonally to make a triangle. Place each triangle between two back panel pieces at bottom two corners, so folded edge faces towards centre and two raw edges line up with raw edges of back panels. Fold 9"-wide top piece in half lengthwise. Place it along top edge, between the two back panels, so folded edge is lined up with top edges of back panels. Pin all pieces into place.

Step 4. Begin sewing at centre of bottom edge, leaving a 1/2" seam allowance. Continue along bottom edge, up one side, along top, down other side and along bottom, leaving a 4" opening before starting point. Clip all corners below seam to reduce fabric bulk. Turn slipcover inside out and poke corners into place. Topstitch gap. Insert fabric-wrapped board into slipcover. Lay calendar inserts on top of board.

STENO CHAIR SLIPCOVER

This seat cover stretches over the seat like a shower cap. The backrest cover is made of three panels, cut and sewn together to fit around the joint where the spine meets the backrest. It is secured behind the spine with Velcro.

MATERIALS & TOOLS

1 1/2 yds. muslin
1 package 1/4"-thick elastic
Pencil or tailor's chalk
Stick pins
1 1/2 yds. fabric
1 piece Velcro (about 2" x 6")

Step 1. Drape a piece of muslin over seat and trace perimeter with pencil or tailor's chalk. Add a 2" seam allowance all around. Cut out pattern and lay it on top of fabric. Cut fabric to pattern. Serge outside edges to prevent fraying.

Step 2. Sew elastic to edge of fabric, pulling elastic taut as you sew — this will create tension required to hold slipcover on seat.

Step 3. Drape a piece of muslin over front of backrest and chalk perimeter onto the muslin. Add a 1/2" seam allowance all around. Cut out pattern and lay it on top of fabric. Cut fabric to pattern.

Step 4. Stick a line of straight pins into your existing upholstery at the rear of the backrest, starting at the top in the centre of the backrest and stopping at the point where the spine is joined to the backrest. Continue pinning below that point until you reach bottom edge of backrest. Drape muslin over rear of backrest. Chalk downward along line of pins, around the point where spine meets backrest, and down centre to bottom edge. Also chalk around perimeter of the left half of backrest. Outline should resemble a fat "C." Add a 1/2" seam allowance all around. Add an additional 2" to the edge that runs to the bottom edge of backrest, from the point where spine meets backrest, to create a flap onto which Velcro will be stitched. Cut pattern and lay it on top of fabric. Cut fabric to pattern. Cut a mirror image of the pattern from fabric for other side of backrest. Sew two pieces together down the centre using a 1/2" seam allowance. Stop sewing when you reach the centre cutout.

Step 5. Sew back panel to front piece, right sides together, using a 1/2" seam allowance. Hem all raw edges. Topstitch Velcro pieces to the strips that will overlap behind the spine.

BANKER'S CHAIR

MATERIALS & TOOLS

120-grit sandpaper
Wood filler
Primer (we used Fresh Start by Benjamin Moore)
Paint (we used HC148 Jameston Blue oil eggshell paint by Benjamin Moore)

Step 1. Lightly sand chair. Fill nicks and holes with wood filler. Let dry and sand over.

Step 2. Prime and let dry. Paint with two coats of oil eggshell paint, allowing each coat to dry fully between coats.

Project

Mirror Image

FOUR DIY PROJECTS THAT ELEVATE THE MODEST LOOKING-GLASS TO STARRING ROLE STATUS.

Editor's note:
To give rooms a light, airy look, substitute sandblasted glass (one of today's hottest materials) for mirror on some of these projects. This would be particularly effective on a kitchen backsplash or bathroom door.

Difficulty level:
Difficult

Projects:
Ceramic-tiled mirror
Mirrored tile
Mirror-blocked door
Mirrored backsplash

What could be more elegant than an oversized mirror perched on a classic mantel, or more fittingly understated than a frameless circle of reflective glass floating over a contemporary vanity? A mirror not only enlarges a small room but, when designed to suit its surroundings, can become the very focal point of the space. We've developed four striking designs, one for each room in the house. Our projects use various shapes of mirror, and unique framing and support systems. The materials are affordable and easy to find, and the directions relatively simple (we suggest having the mirror cut to size by a glass retailer, as we did), making any of these projects ideal for the amateur woodworker.

Top left: Backed with MDF and framed with 1" x 1" white ceramic tiles, an inexpensive metal-edged mirror becomes the main attraction in a traditional, wainscotted bathroom. Top right: An understated mantel simply sparkles when paired with a mirror of timeless distinction. Made from 12" x 12" mirrored tiles, mounted on MDF and framed with classic moulding, the result could pass for an antique. We played it up with bright flowers and black accents. Bottom right: In this update on the mirrored closet, an ordinary bedroom closet door is blocked with four equal sections of mirror, framed with 1" x 4" wood, for a modern look that's both architectural and decorative. Bottom left: Dressed in a coat of glossy red paint, a narrow mirror with a simple wood frame becomes a funky backsplash in a spare, modern kitchen. The cleverly placed mirror creates the illusion of more space. The frame, made from 1" x 4" pine, and mirror are simply glued to an MDF backing.

PHOTOGRAPHY BY VIRGINIA MACDONALD

CERAMIC-TILED MIRROR

The metal-framed mirror that we used in this project measured 17" x 30". Our finished ceramic-tiled mirror measured 25 3/4" x 36 3/4".

MATERIALS & TOOLS

- Tape measure and pencil
- 1" x 1" ceramic tile on backing
- 4' x 8' sheet of 3/4"-thick MDF
- Circular saw (with mitre mechanism), jigsaw or handsaw and mitre box
- Metal-framed mirror
- Caulking gun and silicone adhesive
- Scissors
- Regular trowel
- Ceramic tile adhesive
- 1/4" notched trowel
- 1/4" x 1/4" burl
- Primer, paint and paintbrush
- Finishing nails and hammer
- Pre-mixed siliconized white tile grout
- Large sponge
- Bucket and water
- Wood filler or spackling compound
- Low-tack masking tape

Step 1. Determine how wide and high the frame of the mirror should be, based on where the mirror will hang and the size of the metal-framed mirror you buy. We found our mirror at a Home Depot; most hardware stores carry similar mirrors. We determined that three rows of tiles would not only be aesthetically appealing as a frame, but also create a final product that would be a good size above the vanity.

Step 2. Using a tape measure, measure the width of the tiles on their backing (this will include the grouting spaces between them). Add to that measurement an amount that will take into account the extra grout space around the outside edge of the tiles (about 1/8"). The measurement will determine the overall width of the mirror's border. Multiply this dimension by two and add it to the length and width of the mirror to determine the size of the MDF backing. Using a circular saw, cut a piece of MDF to this size. The "off-cut," or extra, MDF can be used for another project.

Step 3. Measuring in from each edge of the MDF, mark with a pencil the width of the tile border determined in Step 2. Centre the metal-framed mirror within the outline. Glue the mirror to the MDF backing using a caulking gun and silicone adhesive, covering about 60 per cent of the surface with glue. Allow to dry for 24 hours.

Step 4. Using scissors, cut the pieces of backed tile to fit around the top, bottom and side edges of the mirror. Position all the tiles to ensure a proper fit. You may find that the longer side of the mirror will require two or more strips of tile fitted together, depending on the overall length of the tile you buy; the grouting will camouflage any dividing lines.

Step 5. Remove one section of tiles from its position on MDF and, with a regular trowel, apply ceramic tile adhesive to MDF. Run a 1/4" notched trowel over adhesive to spread it evenly and lay tiles on top (see Photo 1). Repeat on the remaining sides. Allow to dry for 24 hours.

Step 6. To cover rough edges of MDF, cut 1/4" x 3/4" burl into four pieces equal to the length of the sides of the MDF frame. Mitre the corners where they will meet. Apply a coat of primer to each piece and let dry. Paint all pieces with one coat of paint in colour of your choice and allow to dry. Mount the burl pieces on the edges of the MDF with finishing nails. This will create a more finished edge.

Step 7. Using a regular trowel, apply pre-mixed, siliconized white tile grout to the tiles. Apply it evenly, on the diagonal, and press hard so the grout fills all spaces between the tiles (see Photo 2). Allow to set for 20 minutes. Wipe off excess grout with a damp sponge and water until clean. Allow to dry for 24 hours.

Step 8. Once everything has dried, fill the nail holes with wood filler. Allow to dry. Mask the edges of the tile with tape and apply a final coat of paint to the burl trim.

MIRRORED TILE

MATERIALS & TOOLS

- 4' x 8' sheet of 3/8"-thick MDF
- Pencil and ruler
- 12" x 12" mirrored tiles
- Circular saw (with mitre mechanism), jigsaw or handsaw and mitre box
- 2"- to 4"-wide moulding
- Primer, paint and paintbrush
- Finishing nails
- Hammer
- Caulking gun, silicone adhesive and construction adhesive
- Wood filler or spackling compound
- Low-tack masking tape

Step 1. Select the moulding with which you'd like to frame your mirror. Starting in one corner of the 4' x 8' sheet of MDF, measure in the width of the moulding you've chosen (ours was 2 1/2" wide) and trace a border along those two sides with a pencil. Lay out the mirrored tiles on the MDF, lining the first one up with the pencil-marked corner (see Photo 3). Once all tiles are in place, trace a pencil line along the two unmarked edges of the mirrored tiles, then measure and mark a second set of lines beyond these that are as far away from the mirrored tiles as the width of the moulding. Using a circular saw or jigsaw, cut the MDF sheet down to this size. The "off-cut," or extra, MDF can be used for another project. Our final square of MDF was 41" x 41".

Step 2. For the frame, cut four lengths of moulding, each measuring the length of the outer edge of the MDF. (You could also use trim, dado or picture frame for edging.) We cut each piece to 41" long. Using a circular saw with a mitre mechanism (or a handsaw and mitre box), mitre both ends of each piece to a 45° angle, making sure the edge of the moulding that you want on the outside of the frame is the longer edge on all four pieces (see Photo 4).

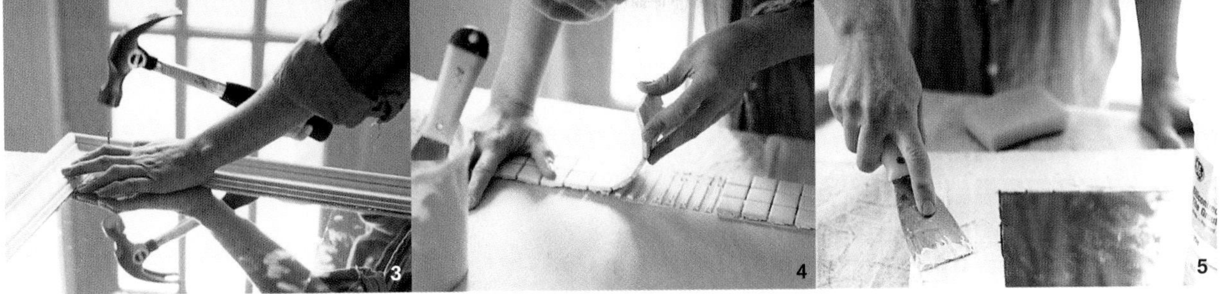

Step 3. Paint all pieces of moulding with primer. Let dry completely. Paint all pieces with one coat of paint in colour of your choice. We used white latex paint that matched the mantel trim.

Step 4. At one corner of the MDF, position two of the pieces of trim perpendicular to one another. Glue (with construction adhesive) and nail the pieces in place (see Photo 5).

Step 5. Apply a quarter-sized dab of silicone adhesive to each corner, and to about 60 per cent of the back of each piece of mirror, and press the mirrored tiles into place. Be sure to place the first row right up against the moulding. When all of the mirrored tiles are glued in place, glue (with construction adhesive) and nail the remaining pieces of moulding to the MDF. Allow to dry for 24 hours.

Step 6. Fill all nail holes with wood filler or spackling compound and allow to dry. Using low-tack masking tape, tape off the edges of the mirror that meet the moulding. Apply a second coat of paint to the moulding and to the side edges of the MDF backing.

MIRROR-BLOCKED DOOR

MATERIALS & TOOLS

- Screwdriver
- Pencil and ruler
- 4 pieces of mirror (cut to size at a mirror or glass retailer)
- 1" x 4" pine
- Circular saw or jigsaw
- Primer, paint and paintbrush
- Caulking gun, silicone adhesive and construction adhesive
- 4 metal clamps
- File
- Low-tack masking tape
- "C" pull handle (optional)

Step 1. Remove the door from its hinges and lay on a flat surface. Measure and mark a 3½" border (a 1" x 4" is really only 3½" on its wide side) around the perimeter of the door, and from the distance between the top and bottom pencil lines, subtract 10½" to allow for three pieces of 1" x 4" between the mirrors. Divide this number by four to get the height of each piece of mirror. The width of each piece of mirror will be the width of the door minus 7" (for the side border pieces).

Step 2. Have a mirror store cut four pieces of mirror to the specified size.

Step 3. Measure the height of the door and cut two pieces of 1" x 4" pine to this length. These will be the side borders. To allow room for the hinges, line up one of the boards with the door opening and mark the location of the hinges with a pencil. Using a circular saw or jigsaw, cut notches in the board. Measure the distance between the location of the side borders, and cut five pieces of 1" x 4" pine to this length. These will be the horizontal crossbars. Apply a coat of primer to all pieces. Let dry completely, then paint all pieces with one coat of paint in the colour of your choice (we used a white alkyd wall and trim enamel from Para Paints, #3000, that matched the trim in the room).

Step 4. Attach the top horizontal crossbar, and the side board that is on the opposite side from the hinges, to the door using a caulking gun and construction adhesive. About 60 per cent of the back of each board should be covered with the adhesive to ensure proper adhesion. Once these are attached, apply several blobs of silicone adhesive to the back of one mirror and place tightly in the corner of the new wood frame. Attach one of the horizontal crossbars to the door using the construction adhesive. Work your way down the door attaching crossbar and mirror pieces. Do not attach the hinge side border yet. Attach clamps to the 1" x 4" on the edges of the door to hold everything in place. Allow to dry for 24 hours.

Step 5. Make any adjustments to second side border by filing down edges or cutting hinge notches deeper using circular saw. Glue (with construction adhesive) and clamp the side board in place. Allow to dry for 24 hours.

Step 6. Using low-tack masking tape, tape the edges of the mirror. Apply a final coat of paint to wood. Allow to dry completely. For greater decoration, attach a "C" pull handle in place of a doorknob. Reinstall door.

MIRRORED BACKSPLASH

MATERIALS & TOOLS

- 4' x 8' sheet of ¾"-thick MDF
- Pencil and ruler
- Rectangular mirror
- Circular saw (with mitre mechanism), jigsaw or handsaw and mitre box
- 1" x 4" pine
- Primer, paint and paintbrush
- Caulking gun, silicone adhesive and construction adhesive
- Finishing nails
- Hammer
- Wood filler or spackling compound
- Low-tack masking tape

This is based on the same principle as framing a piece of mirror with wood and mounting it on an MDF backboard. Follow the directions for Mirror-Blocked Door, with the following changes: this project uses 1" x 4" wood as a frame instead of a dado moulding. The width of the frame will therefore be 3½" (a 1" x 4" is only 3½" wide). Our finished mirror, with frame, measured 58½" x 18". (The "off-cut," or extra, MDF can be used for another project.) The frame will consist of two pieces of 1" x 4" that are, on their longer sides, as long as the length of the MDF backing and two pieces that are, on their longer sides, as long as the width of the MDF backing. Our backsplash is finished with glossy red paint (Para Paints Stop EX114). Glue mirror in place using construction adhesive, covering 60 per cent of the back of the mirror unit with adhesive. Support the mirror with anything heavy, and allow to dry for 24 hours.

Project 42

Kitchen Hangups

TWO KITCHEN PROJECTS DESIGNED TO MAKE SHORT WORK OF STORAGE DILEMMAS.

Editor's note:
Update these wooden racks to suit today's sleeker, more modern kitchens with dark-brown stain and a coat of matte varathane.

Difficulty level:
Very easy

Projects:
Hanging pot rack
In-line rack

Try forcing, stacking or jiggling another pot into that overcrowded kitchen cupboard and you may consider giving up cooking for good. Few things are as frustrating as lack of practical storage in the kitchen. The solution lies in hanging storage, one of the smartest ways to organize culinary paraphernalia and maximize the space you have. And while there are plenty of hanging racks on the market, making your own is easy. Here are two clean-lined hanging pot rack designs — a traditional rectangular wooden frame fitted with dowels and S-hooks, and an "in-line" rack, a length of lumber fitted with eye hooks and S-hooks. Each project requires only a few materials and a little time, so don't get hung up over the lack of storage space in your kitchen — get building!

Suspended from the ceiling by hooks and chains, this 16" x 24" rack made of 1" x 2" pine and dowelling holds plenty of pots despite its small size. The unit is fitted with stainless steel hardware for a pared-down look.

PHOTOGRAPHY BY TED YARWOOD

Project 42: Hanging pot racks

HANGING POT RACK

The finished size of this rack is 16" x 24".

MATERIALS & TOOLS

- 2 pieces 1" x 2" clear pine @ 4' long
- 2 pieces $\frac{7}{8}$" dowel @ 4' long
- 8 $\frac{3}{8}$" dowel plugs
- 8 $1\frac{1}{4}$" #8 wood screws
- Wood glue
- 11 3" open S-hooks
- 100- and 150-grit sandpaper
- 4 $2\frac{1}{16}$" screw-in eye hooks
- 8 S-hooks approx. 2" x $\frac{3}{16}$"
- 4 2' pieces of chain (exact lengths depend on room height)
- Clear sealer
- 4 $2\frac{1}{16}$" screw-in eye hooks or drywall ceiling hooks
- Drywall toggles or butterfly bolts (if installing rack in drywall)
- Handsaw (back saw) and mitre box
- Tape measure, ruler, pencil
- Electric drill
- $\frac{7}{8}$" Forstner (flat bottom) drill bit
- $\frac{3}{8}$" wood drill bit for countersinking screw heads (to accept plugs)
- $\frac{1}{16}$" wood drill bit to pre-drill screws
- $\frac{7}{64}$" wood drill bit to pre-drill for eye hooks
- Paintbrush
- Robertson screwdriver and/or drill bit

Step 1. Cut lumber

Use a mitre box and a handsaw to cut the following pieces (see Photo 1):

For sides, cut two pieces 1" x 2" pine @ $22\frac{1}{2}$"
For ends, cut two pieces 1" x 2" pine @ 16"
For dowel crosspieces, cut four pieces $\frac{7}{8}$" dowel @ $23\frac{1}{4}$"
For dowel plugs, cut eight pieces $\frac{3}{8}$" dowel @ $\frac{1}{8}$" long (or to depth drilled)

Step 2. Drill crosspiece holes

Measure and mark location of dowel holes on two end pieces. Two outside holes are located 3" in from the outermost edges, and two centre holes are spaced 3 $\frac{5}{16}$" apart. Using electric drill and $\frac{7}{8}$" bit, drill four dowel holes in 2"-wide side of the 1" x 2". Do not drill right through the 1" x 2"; stop about $\frac{3}{8}$" — the depth of the drill bit head — into the wood (see Photo 2).

Step 3. Drill dowel plug holes

To neatly cover the screws that hold the frame together, we used small dowel plugs. Pre-drill the holes for these plugs now. Using a $\frac{3}{8}$" wood drill bit, drill two holes in each end of the end pieces — approximately $\frac{3}{8}$" in from the edges, and evenly spaced across the width of the 2" side of the wood to a depth of about $\frac{1}{4}$". (These plug holes are visible in Photo 3.)

Step 4. Assemble frame

Apply wood glue to the edges of the 1" x 2" frame that will abut. Using $1\frac{1}{4}$" #8 wood screws, screw one end piece to the two side pieces to make a U-shaped configuration.

Step 5. Install crosspieces and hooks

Insert the four lengths of dowel into the dowel holes in the end piece of the U (see Photo 3). Run the 3" S-hooks along the four dowels — you will not be able to fit them over the dowels later. (We used 11 S-hooks; you may want to use more or less, depending on the size and number of items you wish to hang.) Fit the remaining end piece onto the dowel crosspieces. Attach this final end piece to the side pieces as you did with the first one, with wood glue and screws (see Photo 4).

Step 6. Install dowel plugs

Apply dabs of wood glue to ends of plugs and insert into screw holes. Lightly sand all sides and edges of rack.

Step 7. Attach eye hooks and chain

Using a $\frac{7}{64}$" bit, pre-drill eye-hook holes approximately 1" deep into the tops of the end pieces. These holes should be approximately $\frac{3}{4}$" in from the ends to steer clear of the wood screws. Screw in eye hooks. Attach S-hooks to eye hooks, and attach chain to S-hooks (see Photo 5).

Step 8. Seal rack

Once assembled, finish rack with two to three coats of clear sealer, allowing it to dry completely between coats.

Step 9. Attach rack to ceiling

If the ceiling joists run in the direction and location required for the pot rack, then screw four eye hooks directly into the joists; measure and mark a 16" x 24" rectangle on the ceiling and screw a hook in at each corner. For installation into drywall, use a drywall toggle or butterfly bolt, and screw four holes into the drywall ceiling. Hook a 2" x $\frac{3}{16}$" S-hook into each eye hook, then link a suspension chain to each S-hook.

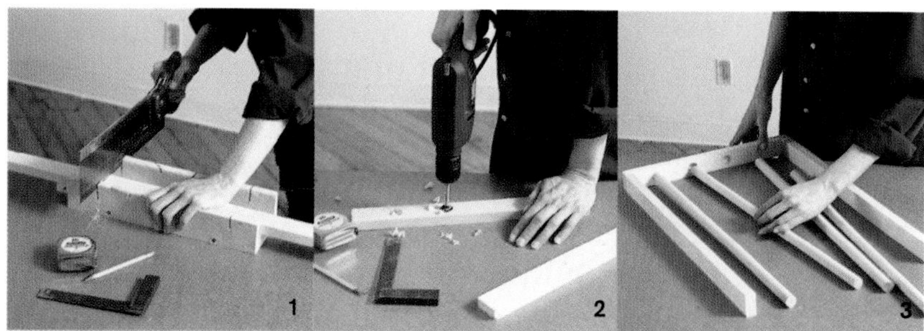

No project could be simpler than this streamlined pot rack, which can be built in under an hour. Chunky eye hooks, S-hooks and chains give both our racks the industrial aesthetic that's popular in today's kitchens. Suspend the in-line rack almost flush with the wall if you plan to use it for utensils and small pots; for larger pots, install it 6" to 8" from the wall.

IN-LINE RACK

The finished size of this rack is 3" x 32".

MATERIALS & TOOLS

1	1" x 3" clear pine @ 3'
	Clear sealer
6	1/4" x 2" eye hooks with nuts
8	1/4" washers
2	5/16" x 3" eye hooks with nuts
10	S-hooks (at least 3/16" in size)
2	2' pieces of chain (exact lengths will depend on height of room)
2	drywall ceiling hooks
	Drywall toggles or butterfly bolts (if installing rack in drywall)
	Handsaw and mitre box
	Ruler, pencil and measuring tape
	Electric drill
	1/4" wood drill bit
	5/16" wood drill bit
	100- and 150-grit sandpaper
	Paintbrush

Step 1. Cut lumber

Using mitre box and handsaw, cut the 1" x 3" down to 32" in length.

Step 2. Prepare pot hook holes

Our pot hooks are small 1/4" x 2" eye hooks fitted with S-hooks. With ruler and pencil, lightly draw a line along centre of underside (one of the 3"-wide sides) of board. Next, using measuring tape and pencil, mark location of pot hook holes. We spaced our holes 2" in from either end and 5 5/8" apart, allowing for six hooks. Using electric drill and a 1/4" bit, drill pot hook holes through board. Lay a piece of scrap wood beneath board to prevent the final layer of wood from "breaking out" as you drill through the wood. The hooks will be attached to the wood after it is sealed.

Step 3. Prepare suspension hook holes

The pot rack is suspended by two lengths of chain linked to 5/16" x 3" eye hooks, located at either end of the board. Use a pencil and ruler to mark the location of eye hooks, approximately 5" in from either end and centred in the middle of the board. Using an electric drill and a 5/16" drill bit, drill eye-hook holes right through the board. As before, to prevent the other side of the board from breaking out around the holes, lay a scrap piece of wood beneath it. The eye hooks will be attached to the wood after it is sealed.

Step 4. Sand and seal

Using 100- or 150-grit sandpaper, lightly sand all faces and edges of the board. Seal the board with two to three coats of clear sealer, allowing each coat to dry thoroughly before applying the next.

Step 5. Attach hooks

Screw the larger "suspension" eye hooks through top side of the board, at either end, and secure below with nuts and washers. Screw the smaller eye hooks through underside of the board and secure with nuts and washers at the top. Link S-hooks into eye hook on underside to form pot hooks.

Step 6. Install rack

Attach the rack to the ceiling as directed in Hanging Pot Rack, Step 9.

Project

Closet Aspirations

KICK-START YOUR SPRING CLEANING WITH A LINEN CLOSET MAKEOVER.

Editor's note:
These days, custom-designed closets are all the rage, but if you don't have the budget for one or don't want to refit a rental, these clever ideas provide a host of alternative solutions.

Difficulty level:
Average

Projects:
Installing shelves
Hanging storage bag

Open the door to your linen closet and look inside. Do sheets and towels tumble out? Are laundry and bath supplies crammed into corners? Is valuable space wasted because of poor organization? If so, here is the answer to your problems. We've pulled together the information you'll need to organize your closet efficiently. We've included shelving options, installation information, and some suggestions for what to store, where to store it and how to deal with clutter. There's no time like the present to overhaul the old and start fresh — we hope these quick closet makeovers will inspire.

Above: Knot-free and non-aromatic clear cedar shelves replaced dingy painted shelving in this conversion. We subdivided one of the shelves to create diminutive compartments for baby linens. Wicker baskets house sheets, towels and toiletries. Aromatic cedar strips were nailed to the back wall to repel moths; scented shelf paper adds freshness.

Right: Fitted with inexpensive, easy-to-clean melamine shelves, this oversized closet offers plenty of space for table linens and guest bedding. A wicker trunk, antique suitcase and hatbox provide closed storage. Lavender sachets scent the closet, and brass labels make finding everything a snap!

Next page: Wire shelving, basket storage and a shoebag-style organizer make the most of this narrow, all-purpose apartment closet. We installed the third and fourth shelves closer together so linens can be easily organized into small, neat piles. Pretty soaps are stored unwrapped to add fragrance.

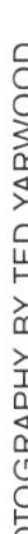

PHOTOGRAPHY BY TED YARWOOD

Freshenup

Playing up scent is our favourite way to add a note of luxury to the linen closet. The heady perfume of lavender is perhaps the most classic closet fragrance. (Don't allow lavender to touch linens directly, as its oils can damage textile fibres; instead, use the tiny blossoms in sachets.) Aromatic cedar does double-duty, scenting the air and repelling moths. Line walls and shelves with fresh-smelling cedar slats, or tuck aromatic cedar blocks among woollen blankets and linens. If you prefer fruit and floral scents, raid your bathroom or kitchen cupboards for perfumed guest soaps and scented candles; remove any plastic wrapping and store in an attractive basket in the linen closet. You'll freshen up even the stuffiest space. Scented shelf paper, often available in pretty florals, stripes or checks, is both decorative and aromatic.

Keepingclosetsshipshape

- Clear out your closet and sort out unused towels and linens.
- Store only frequently used linens and towels in the closet. Use older ones as spare sets at the cottage, painting dropcloths, rags or for pet bedding and bathing.
- Label shelves so finding linens is easy, for you or for guests. We used paper labels that slide into brass holders and can be quickly updated.
- Consider ways to stack sheets and towels that will be the most practical for the way you live: by size, colour or in sets.
- Put most-used items at eye level.
- Tie guest linen sets with ribbon for quick identification.
- Store children's linens on lower shelves so they're easy for little ones to access.
- Keep linens dry and clean, with "breathing" room around each stack.
- Protect blankets with clear plastic cases. Store them overhead or on the floor.
- For long-term storage, wrap laundered, unstarched linens in clean cotton cloth, not plastic; trapped moisture can cause mildew.
- Roll fragile or rarely used linens around cardboard tubes to stop creasing. Secure with ribbon.
- Line shelves on which antique linens are to be stored with acid-free tissue paper (available at specialty art stores).
- Consider coordinating the closet with your bedroom, bathroom or linens by painting it a complementary colour.

PLANNING THE SPACE

Before installing new shelves, assess the type and number of linens you have as well as any other items to be stored. Configure the closet to suit your needs, dividing shelves in half vertically and horizontally to store smaller items like children's or table linens. Reserve overhead and floor storage for bulky items like blankets, duvets, and even cleaning supplies or sporting equipment if you lack space elsewhere. In between, space shelves 15" apart where towels will be stored and 10" to 12" apart where sheets will be stored. (Too much space between shelves encourages high stacking, which can become messy.) Most linen closets will accommodate five to six shelves. If you plan to store cleaning or bathroom supplies in the closet, or incorporate pull-out baskets, measure bottle and basket heights, and plan shelf heights accordingly. If children will be using the closet, consider storing towels at lower levels within their reach.

STORAGE OPTIONS

Along with varying shelving configurations, basket storage is an efficient way to customize a closet. Wicker and wire baskets are useful for storing cleaning supplies and toiletries, or housing smaller linens like napkins, tea towels and baby bedding. (Be sure baskets will fit closet before purchasing.) To prevent snagging fragile linens, outfit wicker baskets with cotton

liners. Hatboxes are equally useful; line them with acid-free tissue paper when storing antique fabrics. Label baskets and boxes with tie-on tags. Where space is at a premium, a pocket storage bag like the one shown here is an ideal addition. (We've included sewing directions.) Fill pockets with cleaning supplies, toiletries, facecloths and hand towels.

SHELVING TYPES

- **Melamine shelving** is durable and easy to clean. It is sold in 4' x 8' sheets, or in 8'-long strips with 12" or 16" widths; the 8'-long strips are best suited to shelving. Order these at a hardware store, home-supply store or lumberyard, and, if possible, have lengths cut to fit the closet at the store. If cutting melamine yourself, use a circular saw and finish exposed edges with iron-on laminate tape. Install on wooden rails screwed into the closet walls.
- **Wire shelving** is especially useful because it permits air flow, keeping linens well ventilated and dry. Always use plastic- or epoxy-coated wire to avoid rusting. Wire shelving is available at home-supply and hardware stores in standard shelf depths of 16" or 20". It can be cut to fit your closet while you wait. Take exact closet measurements, and bring these with you to the store. Matching baskets are often available with wire shelving systems. Remember that wire surfaces can be harder to store small items on, and can leave indented lines on linens.
- There are two types of cedar that can be used in the linen closet. **Aromatic cedar** is attractive, freshly scented and pest repellent. It is sold in bundles of tongue-and-groove strips at many lumberyards. The thin strips are nailed directly onto the walls and shelves to completely line the closet. This cedar is pre-dried so it won't "leak" sap, but if you're concerned, line shelves with paper. A quick and less expensive alternative, with the appearance of cedar panelling but not the moth-repelling scent, is **clear cedar** shelving, which we used in our cedar closet. This type of cedar, which has no sap-releasing knots, is unlikely to leak; if concerned, line shelves with paper.

DIAGRAM 1

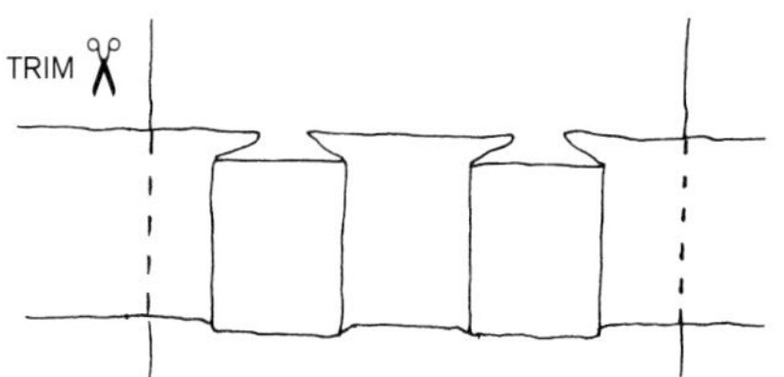

DIAGRAM 2

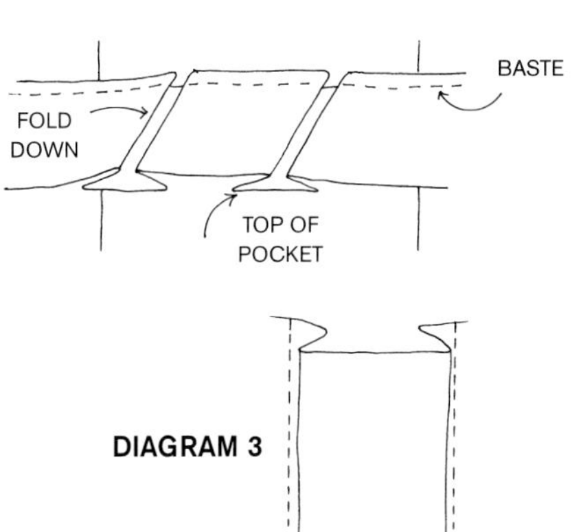

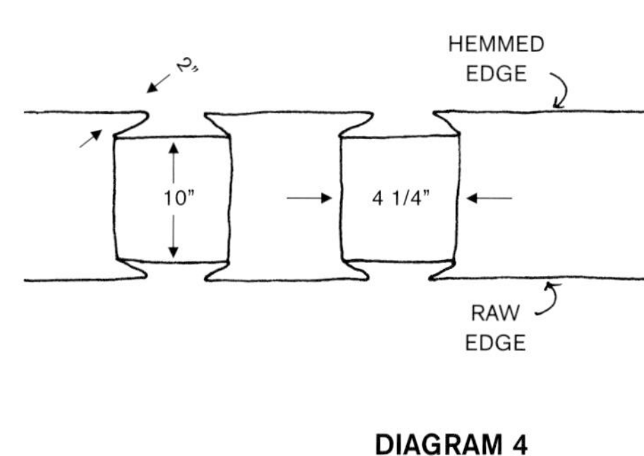

DIAGRAM 4

The 1"-thick wood is sold in 6", 8",10" and 12" widths in a variety of lengths. (Don't use any wood shelves that have a stained finish or knotty character; these can stain linens.) The shelves will need to be sanded to achieve a smooth finish, and rested on rails nailed to the closet wall. If your closet is deep, you may have to use two pieces of cedar to create one shelf. To create the 16"-deep shelves in our cedar closet, we used two pieces of 1" x 8" cedar cut to fit the width of the closet and installed on the existing supports. For fragrance, and to repel moths, place small blocks of aromatic cedar throughout the closet, or purchase a bundle of aromatic tongue-and-groove cedar slats and nail to the back wall of the closet beneath each shelf, as we did.

• Simple painted wood shelves are the standard for most linen closets. If you are making new shelves, use an inexpensive wood like pine, available in a variety of widths at the lumberyard. Cut shelves to size, sand, prime, then paint with an eggshell or gloss latex, or an oil-based paint. Line with scented shelf paper for a fresh and decorative accent.

INSTALLING SHELVES

• Wood, melamine or MDF shelving
Remove existing shelves and rails with a hammer or crowbar. (You may choose to leave existing rails in place, but consider adding a new shelf between two existing ones for smaller items.) Patch nail holes with spackling compound or wood filler. Allow to dry, then sand. Measure and mark new shelf locations. Screw or nail support rails — one long rail running along the back of the closet and two shorter rails on either side — into place. Prime, then paint, closet interior with a washable eggshell or gloss latex, or an oil-based paint.

• Coated wire shelving
Wire shelving systems are sold with specific installation instructions — read these carefully before leaving the store to ensure that you have purchased all of the necessary parts. The 16"-deep, epoxy-coated wire shelving we used was cut to length at the home-supply store, then modified at home with a hacksaw to fit around a 4"-square column in the back corner of the closet. In our case, supports and clips were screwed to the wall, and the shelves were clipped securely to these.

HANGING STORAGE BAG

Measure the closet door, and plan the length and width of your hanging bag accordingly. Remember that the bag has to fit in the closed closet. Take the door frame and the amount of space between the door and shelves into account; we had about 5" of space between the door and the shelves in which to fit the hanging bag we made. The final measurements of our bag are 30" l. x 13" w.

Step 1. Cut one large piece of fabric for the body of the bag, adding 1 1/2" to each side for seam allowance. (Our fabric was 16" w. x 33" l.) Hem the top and bottom edges of the body; turn the raw edge under 1/2" and press, then turn the edge under 1", press and stitch.

Step 2. Cut long pieces of fabric for pockets. (We wanted two rows of pockets so we cut two pieces of fabric 11" l. by 33" w.) Turn under and hem the top edge (one of the 33"-long sides) of pocket pieces, as described in Step 1.

Step 3. Form the pockets by making large pleats (see Diagram 1). (The final measurements of our pockets were 4 1/2" wide, 9" high, with a 2"-deep pleat on each side.) Pin them at the top and bottom and press the pleats with an iron. Using a basting stitch, baste along the bottom to secure the pleat. Keep the top of the pocket pinned. Press again.

Step 4. Place the top pocket piece on the body so the pockets are centred, and trim off any fabric that extends beyond the raw edge of the body sides (see Diagram 2). Make sure that the edges of the pocket piece extend to the side edges of the body piece; these edges will be folded under together and hemmed later on.

Step 5. Fold the pocket piece down on the body so the right sides are together, and stitch along the bottom to attach it to the body, leaving a 1" hem (see Diagram 3).

Step 6. Fold the pocket back up. Pin the side edges of the pocket to the side edges of the body. Baste the sides together.

Step 7. Repeat steps 3 to 6 for each row of pockets.

Step 8. Fold the side edges in 1/2" onto the front side of the bag and press, then fold the side edges over another 1" and hem. Folded forward, instead of under, this hem forms an attractive border around the bag. (This edging only works if your fabric does not have a "wrong" side. If your fabric only has a pattern on one side, fold the hem under instead of over, then press and stitch as described.)

Step 9. To divide the pockets and give them shape, stitch horizontally for the length of the pocket just beneath the pleat of each pocket on both sides (see Diagram 4).

Step 10. Grommet the top of the bag and install it on nails or hooks in the closet. We had our bag grommeted at a marine-supply company; you can do it yourself with a grommeting tool and grommets, available at home-supply and hardware stores. If your bag is longer than ours you may want to secure the bottom corners to the door as well so that the bag doesn't fly around when the door is opened and closed.

Project 44

Display's the Thing

EASY INSTRUCTIONS FOR BUILDING THE LATEST LOOK IN SHELVING.

Editor's note:
Not just for the living room anymore, narrow open shelving has become popular in kitchens too. Install shelves to run the length of the countertop, then load them up with everyday glassware or bowls.

Difficulty level:
Difficult

Projects:
Display rail
Shelving unit

When a blank wall is staring you in the face, simple, streamlined display shelving is the solution of the moment. Showing up in interiors everywhere, these narrow shelves, or "picture rails," span the width of the wall and are just deep enough to prop a picture or set a small objet on. The effect is appealingly modern and art-gallery minimalist, particularly when the rails are painted the same colour as the wall, letting pictures and photographs take centre stage. This project also incorporates a low shelf, installed just above the baseboard to serve as a side table, convenient for resting a drink or stacking books. Made simply with wood, glue and nails, the rails and shelf can be built in a day, then quickly painted and installed — leaving you enough time to pull out your pictures, books and favourite treasures and practise the art of display.

Display rails are the perfect solution if you're hesitant to make the picture-hanging commitment! Ours fit snugly between the wall and chimney; just 3 1/2" deep, they are built almost flush with the face of the chimney piece for a clean, customized look. The shelving unit below displays books and treasures.

PHOTOGRAPHY BY TED YARWOOD

DISPLAY SHELVES
What to Consider

1. Virtually any room is a good candidate for display shelves, but principal rooms are especially suited to this kind of architectural element. An uninterrupted span of picture rail lined with black-and-white photographs turns a plain living- or dining-room wall into an elegant feature wall.

2. Display rails look best when they are built in to fit the surrounding architecture – installed wall to wall or wall to moulding, rather than "floating" in the middle of the wall without any architectural starting and finishing points.

3. Depending on the size and number of pictures and collectibles you intend to display, you can install either a single rail, or several, one on top of another, as we did.

4. Adapt the scale of your display shelves to the size of the room you install them in, so that they relate to their surroundings. A large room can carry quite substantial, even chunky, rails while a smaller room should have finer shelves. Rails should also work with other architectural details in the room, like door and window mouldings, baseboards and mantelpieces.

5. Before building picture rails, take into account the size of your pictures, including their frames. The larger the pictures, the deeper the rails will have to be so you can safely lean them against the wall. If you have small artifacts to display, measure their bases and design and build rails accordingly. For average-sized framed photographs and pictures, as well as decorative objects, we recommend a minimum depth of 3 1/2".

DIAGRAM 1

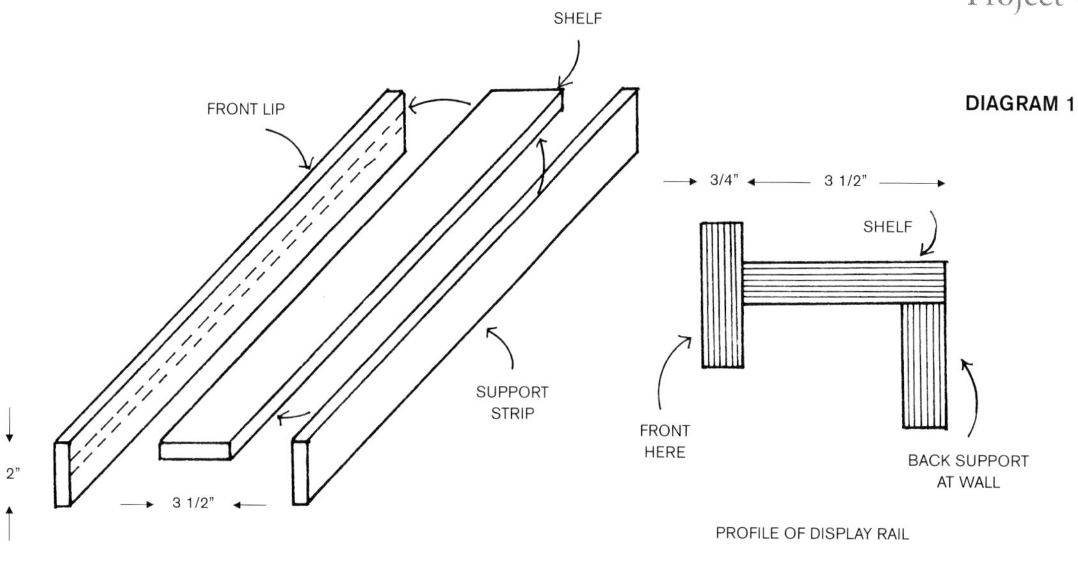

DISPLAY RAIL

Each display rail is made of a shelf, a back support and a front lip to hold pictures in place and prevent slipping. When determining the height of your shelves, and how many you want to install, consider the ceiling height, the height of any furniture sitting below the shelf, and, of course, the size of your artwork for display.

MATERIALS & TOOLS

- 4' x 8' sheet 3/4" MDF or pine
- 1 1/2" nails or 1 1/2" screws
- 2" nails or 2" screws
- Wood glue
- Wood filler
- Hand, jig or circular saw
- Hammer or electric drill with countersink bit and #8 driver bit
- Putty knife
- Level
- Fine-grit sandpaper
- Primer
- Latex or oil paint

Step 1. Cut lumber

Note: If you make the display rail from pine, you can buy it in pre-cut, 2 1/2" and 3 1/2" widths x 3/4" thickness at various lengths. The front lip and back support strip can be made from the 2 1/2" width, and the shelf can be made from the 3 1/2" width. This will save you having to cut the lumber. If you're making the rail from MDF, as we did, ask your lumberyard to make the cuts for you, or use a circular saw to cut it yourself.

Make the following cuts: For the shelf, cut one piece MDF @ 3 1/2" deep x desired length. For the front edge, or lip, cut one piece MDF @ 2" deep x desired length. For the back support strip, cut one piece MDF @ 2" deep x desired length.

Step 2. Attach shelf to back support strip

We assembled our parts using 1 1/2" screws. In order not to split the material when you drive in the screws you must first drill countersunk pilot holes in the pieces. If you wish you can assemble the parts using 1 1/2" finishing nails instead. If nailing together you don't need to drill the pilot holes, but in either case you must glue the parts together. If using screws, position the support strip under the shelf flush with the back edge and clamp or hold together. Drill pilot holes through the shelf into the back support strip with a #8 countersink bit, approximately 8" to 12" apart. Run a bead of wood glue along the edge of the strip. Reposition the shelf on the support and screw or nail the shelf to it. Clean away excess glue with a putty knife.

Step 3. Attach front edge (lip) to shelf

Position the front strip against the front edge of the shelf so its top sits about 3/8" above the shelf. Holding it in this position, drill pilot holes through the front and into the edge of the shelf, 8" to 12" apart, using a #8 countersink bit. Run a bead of wood glue along the front edge of the shelf and attach the edge strip to the shelf using 1 1/2" screws and a #8 driver bit. Clean away excess glue with a putty knife.

Step 4. Sand, prime and paint

Using a putty knife, fill the screw holes with wood filler. Allow to dry, and then sand with a fine-grit sandpaper. Prime and paint the display shelf, allowing to dry between coats.

Step 5. Install shelf

Measuring from the ground up, mark the desired rail location on the wall with a pencil. Use a level to ensure the rail is straight. Gently tap on the wall to locate the vertical wood studs — this is where you'll attach your rail to the wall. (Studs are usually spaced out across a wall at intervals of approximately 16".) Once you've found a solid area, drive a 2" finishing nail into the wall until it hits the wall stud. Measure 16" across the wall and repeat on the next stud. Drill pilot holes into the back of the rail at the same locations as the studs. Attach the rail to the wall using 2" screws. Fill the holes with wood filler. Sand when dry and touch up with paint.

SHELVING UNIT

The low shelf consists of a top and a bottom shelf, two end panels, a centre support panel and two back support strips (to screw the shelf to the wall), and front edges (to "finish" the front of the unit and match the display rails). We installed our low shelving unit 19" from the floor and 20" below the bottom rail.

MATERIALS & TOOLS

- 4' x 8' sheet 3/4" MDF or pine
- 1 1/2" nails and 1 1/2" screws
- 2" screws
- Wood glue
- Wood filler
- Hammer or electric drill with countersink bit and #8 driver bit
- Hand, jig or circular saw
- Fine-grit sandpaper
- Primer
- Latex or oil paint

Step 1. Cut lumber

With an electric saw or handsaw, or at the lumberyard, make the following cuts: For top and bottom shelves, cut two pieces MDF @ 9 1/4" deep x desired length. For the front edges, cut two pieces MDF @ 2" deep x desired length. For back support strips, cut two pieces MDF @ 2" deep x desired length. For vertical panels (ends and centre), cut three pieces MDF @ 9 1/4" deep x 12" long. The panels will join, and help support, the top and bottom shelves.

Step 2. Attach support strip to bottom shelf

Position one of the back support strips under the top shelf, flush with the back edge of the shelf. Drill pilot holes through the shelf, into the support strip, 8" to 12" apart, using a #8 countersink bit. Run a bead of wood glue along the edge of the back support strip. Attach the shelf to the back support using 1 1/2" screws, an electric drill and a #8 driver bit. Clean away any excess glue with a putty knife.

Step 3. Attach front faces to shelves

Position the front face against the front edge of one of the shelves flush with the top of the shelf. Drill pilot holes through the front face and into the edge of the shelf, 8" to 12" apart, using a #8 countersink bit. Run a bead of wood glue along the edge of the shelf. With 1 1/2" screws and a #8 driver bit, attach the front face to the shelf. Clean away excess glue with a putty knife. Repeat for front edge of bottom shelf piece.

Step 4. Attach end and centre panels

Position a vertical panel at either end of the bottom shelf, flush with the back edge of the shelf and, using a #8 countersink bit, drill pilot holes through the bottom of the shelf, into the edge of the vertical panel. Run wood glue along the edges of both pieces. Screw the panels into place from the underside of the shelf using 1 1/2" screws. Measure and mark the centre of the shelf. Attach the third panel to the centre, flush with the back edge of the shelf. (As before, run beads of wood glue along those edges of the panels that meet with the shelf and drill pilot holes prior to screwing together.)

Step 5. Attach top shelf to vertical panels

Place the top shelf on top of the vertical panels that have been attached to the lower shelf. Drill pilot holes through the shelf, into the top edge of each panel. Run a bead of wood glue along the same edge of each panel. Set shelf on top and screw into place.

Step 6. Attach back support strips to top shelf

Cut the second support piece in two so it fits between the centre and end panels. Flip the shelf onto its face. Run a bead of glue along the edges and ends of the back support strips and attach them to the top shelf with screws.

Step 7. Sand, prime and paint shelf

Using a putty knife, fill the nail or screw holes with wood filler. Allow to dry, then sand with fine-grit sandpaper. Prime and paint the shelf.

Step 8. Install shelf

Install like the display rails, screwing through top and bottom support pieces and into the wall where the studs are. See Display Rail, Step 5. Use a level to ensure shelf is straight, and attach to the wall with 2" screws. Fill screw holes with wood filler, sand and touch-up paint.

DIAGRAM 2

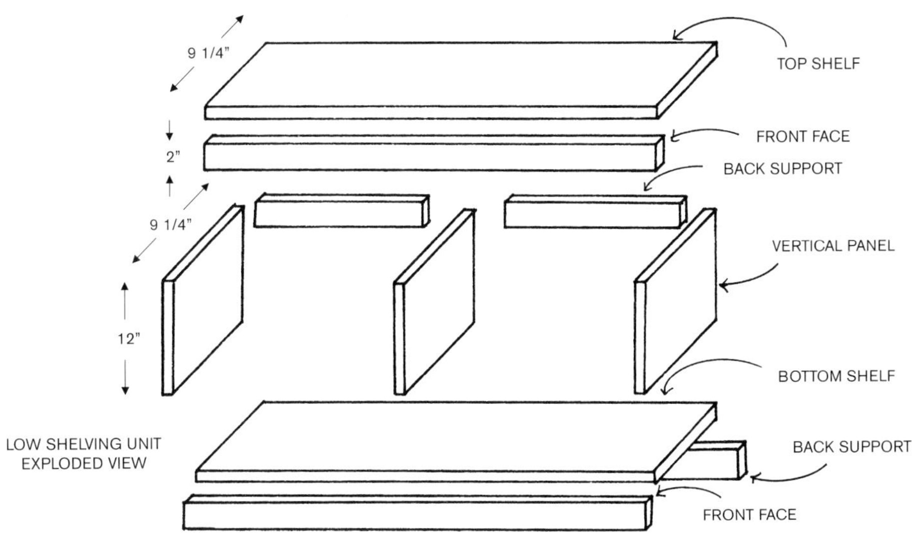

45 Project

Space Savers

TWO STYLISH SOLUTIONS COMBINE THE WARMTH OF WOOD AND SIMPLE MODERN DESIGN.

Editor's note:
Don't just store CDs in this rack – get creative with bright paint colours and use it in a child's room. Installed vertically or horizontally, it's just the right size for small books and toys.

Difficulty level:
Average

Projects:
Cubbyhole storage unit
CD unit

With a nod to the small space and an eye on modern design, we're featuring two woodworking projects you can always make room for — a CD tower and a movable cubbyhole storage centre. Designed as a grid of open shelves, the cubby unit is a natural for the front hall, organizing the everyday pileup of mail and magazines, shoes and sports equipment. Echoing this minimalist design, our CD tower is only nine inches wide and can be wall mounted, the ultimate in space-saving storage. For a clean, sleek look, we've made both projects from maple veneer on particleboard, which requires a circular saw to cut; similar units can be made, however, using a solid wood such as pine and a regular handsaw. The result will be the same: a place for everything and everything in its place.

Top: A perfect size for a narrow front hall, the cubbyhole storage unit also acts as a visual divider in a room. It's open at the front and back for access from both sides. Mounted on industrial casters, it can even serve as a trolley in a pinch. Bottom: Slim and streamlined, our modern CD tower holds about 160 CDs. Artfully placed accessories add graphic appeal.

PHOTOGRAPHY BY MARK MAINGUY

CUBBYHOLE STORAGE UNIT

Finished size: 35⅞" w. x 11" d. x 26½" h.

MATERIALS & TOOLS

- 4' x 8' sheet maple-veneered particleboard
- Maple-veneer edge tape
- ¾" #8 screws
- 5-mm shelf pins
- 4" industrial casters
- Clear varathane
- Circular saw (or handsaw if using solid wood)
- Cordless drill
- Iron
- #8 countersink drill bit
- 5-mm drill bit
- 150-grit sandpaper
- Measuring tape
- X-Acto knife
- Straight edge
- Square
- Clamps

Step 1. Cut veneered particleboard

If you are making this project from a wood veneer on particleboard, as we did, ask your local lumberyard to "rip" the sheets before you cut them into pieces. Veneer splits and chips easily and, in large sizes, is best cut with an industrial saw. Have the lumberyard make the following large cuts:

One @ 11" x 8'
Two @ 10" x 8'

At home, using a circular saw, cut the following smaller pieces (for consistent cuts use the cutting jig described at the end of the directions) from the pieces the lumberyard cut:

For the top and bottom:
2 pieces @ 10" x 34⅞"

For the end gables:
2 pieces @ 11" x 26½"

For the vertical dividers:
2 pieces @ 10" x 23"

For the shelves:
3 pieces @ 10" x 11"

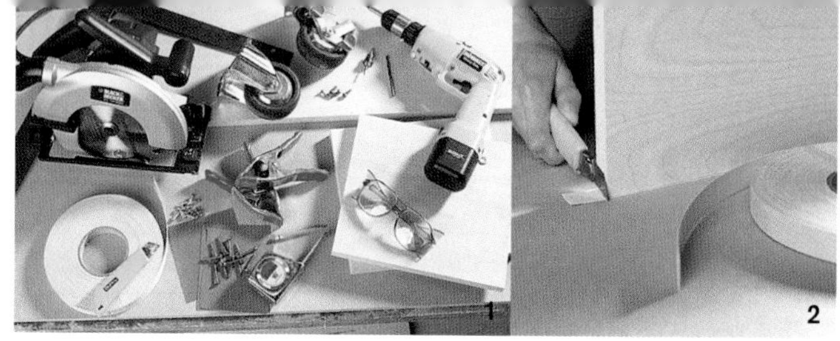

Note: Wood-veneer edge tape is sold at building-supply and lumber stores in a variety of lengths. Edge tape is applied with a hot iron that melts the adhesive on the back of it.

Step 2. Tape edges of veneered pieces

On both of the 10" x 34 7/8" pieces, choose one of the long edges as the front. On both of the 11" x 26 1/2" pieces, choose one of the long edges as the front. On both of the 10" x 23" pieces, choose one of the long edges as the front. On all the 10" x 11" pieces, choose one of the long edges as the front.

Cut pieces of tape approximately 1" longer than needed and iron them onto the front edges with a hot iron. Trim off excess with an X-Acto knife by standing the piece you are working on upright with the taped end down against a cutting board. Slowly draw the knife over the tape until it cuts through (see Photo 2). You should also tape the top and bottom edges of the end gables. If you are setting the unit up against a wall, don't worry about the back edges; if the unit will be sitting in the middle of a room, you will want to tape all visible edges. Once edges have been taped, sand them lightly.

Step 3. Mark locations of top and bottom shelves

On the insides of the end gables, mark the location of the top and bottom shelves. Lay one end gable flat on your work surface and, at what will be the top, measure in 1/2" from the front edge and mark. Then measure and mark 1" and 1 3/4" down from the top edge. These marks will indicate the location of the top shelf. Using a straight edge or ruler, draw parallel lines at these marks (see Photo 3). Repeat at the other end of the gable to indicate the location of the bottom shelf. Repeat for the second end gable.

Next, measure and mark the location of the screws, which will attach the end gables to the top and bottom shelves. On your work surface, lay both end gables with the marked sides face down and, from each end, measure in 1 3/8". Mark this point and with a square and pencil, draw a faint line across the gables. From the edges of the gable, measure 2" along the line you have just drawn and make a mark. This is where you will drill the screw holes.

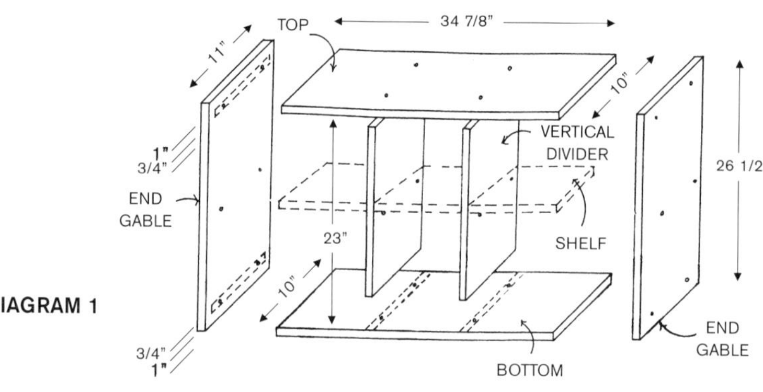

DIAGRAM 1

Step 4. Measure and mark locations of vertical dividers and screw holes

Lay the top and bottom shelves flat on your work surface and from each end, measure in and mark at 11 1/8" and 11 7/8". With a square, draw lines across the shelves at each of these marks (see Photo 4). Next, measure and mark the location of the screws that will attach the vertical dividers to the top and bottom pieces. Flip over the two shelves and from each end, measure and mark at 11 1/2". With a square, draw faint lines across each shelf at these marks. From the edges, measure in along these lines and mark at 1 1/2". This is where you will drill the pilot holes.

Step 5. Pre-drill screw holes

Using a #8 countersink bit, pre-drill screw holes into end gables and top and bottom shelves where you've marked (see Photo 5). There will be a total of 16 holes. To prevent chipping or splitting of veneer when drilling, lay the veneer pieces on scrap wood while drilling and drill through the veneer into the scrap.

Step 6. Measure and mark locations of shelf pins

The shelves are supported by 5-mm steel shelf pins, inserted into both end gables and the vertical dividers. Begin by marking one end of each vertical divider and end gable as the top. Make sure that the taped edge of the divider will face outwards. On the inside of the end gables, measure and mark down 13 3/4" from the top end and 2" in from the front and back edges. These will be the locations of the two shelf pins. Repeat on the other gable. On the vertical divider, measure and mark 12" down from the top end and 1 1/2" in from the front and back edges.

Step 7. Drill shelf pin holes

Use a 5-mm drill bit. On the end gables, drill holes just deep enough to accommodate pins. On the vertical dividers, drill the holes right through the wood to accommodate shelf pins in each side. Remember to drill into a scrap piece of wood.

Step 8. Sand and finish

Lightly sand all of the surfaces. Sand with the grain and lightly sand or "break" the corners to eliminate sharp edges. Finish all of the pieces of the storage unit with paint, stain or varathane.

Step 9. Attach end gables to top and bottom shelves

Because the top shelf is set in 1" from the top of the end gables and the bottom shelf 1" from the bottom of the end gables, it is a good idea to use a 1" "spacer" block to position these shelves. Clamp the spacer block to the end of the end gables. Because the top and bottom shelves are 1" narrower than the two end gables and must be centred on the end gables, prop the top and bottom pieces up on scraps of 1/2" plywood (see Photo 9). Screw the end gables into the top and bottom shelves.

Step 10. Attach vertical dividers

Set vertical dividers in 11 1/8" from the inside of the end gables by using an 11 1/8" spacer block. Insert vertical divider and screw through top and bottom pieces at pre-drilled points (see Photo 10). Repeat for the second vertical divider.

Step 11. Attach casters and shelves

Use 3/4" #8 screws to attach casters to bottom of unit. Insert shelf pins and shelves (see Photo 11).

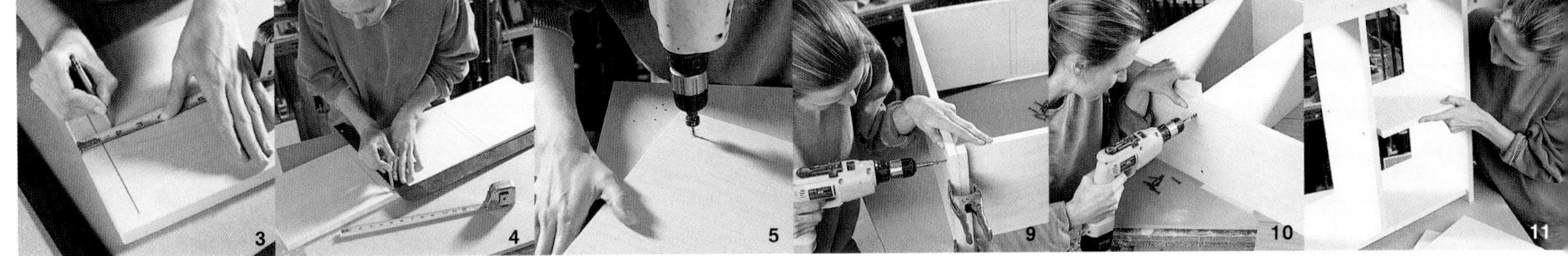

CD UNIT

Finished size: 9" w. x 7" d. x 59-1/2" h.

MATERIALS & TOOLS

- 4' x 8' sheet maple-veneered particleboard
- Maple-veneer edge tape
- 1 1/4" #6 screws
- Clear varathane
- Circular saw (or handsaw if using solid wood)
- Cordless drill
- Iron
- #6 countersink drill bit
- 5-mm drill bit
- 150-grit sandpaper
- Measuring tape
- X-Acto knife
- Straight edge
- Square
- Clamps

Step 1. Cut veneered particleboard

If you are making this project from a wood veneer on particleboard, as we did, ask your local lumberyard to "rip" the sheet before you cut it into pieces. Veneer can split and chip easily, and, in large sizes, is best cut with an industrial saw. Have the lumberyard make the following cuts:

Two pieces @ 7" x 8'
One piece @ 8" x 8'
One piece @ 61/2" x 8'

At home, with a circular saw, cut the following smaller pieces from the pieces the lumberyard cut:

For the sides, from the two 7" x 8' lengths: two pieces @ 59-1/2" long

For the back, from the 8" x 8' length: one piece @ 59" long

For the top, bottom and eight shelves, from the 6-1/2" x 8' piece: 10 pieces @ 8" long.

Step 2. Tape edges

Wood-veneer edge tape is sold at building-supply and lumber stores in a variety of lengths. Edge tape is applied with a hot iron that melts the adhesive on the back of it.

You will need to tape the top, bottom and one edge of the side pieces, the top and bottom of the back piece, and one long edge of each shelf. Cut pieces of tape approximately 1" longer than needed and iron them onto the front edges with a hot iron. Trim off excess with a very sharp X-Acto knife by standing the shelf taped-end down against a cutting board. Slowly draw the knife over the tape until it cuts through. Sand edges lightly.

Step 3. Mark screw hole locations

From the top edge of each side piece, measure 1/2" down and 1 1/2" in from the front and back edges. From this first measurement, measure and mark 1 1/2" in from the front and back edges and every 6 1/2" down the side, until you reach the bottom. These marks indicate where you will drill the pilot holes for the shelves. Use a #6 countersink bit and drill each hole, placing the wood on top of a scrap piece of board to keep the veneer from chipping.

Step 4. Sand and finish

Using 150-grit sandpaper, lightly sand all the surfaces. Sand with the grain and lightly sand or "break" the corners to eliminate sharp edges. Before assembling, paint, stain or varathane all pieces of the CD unit.

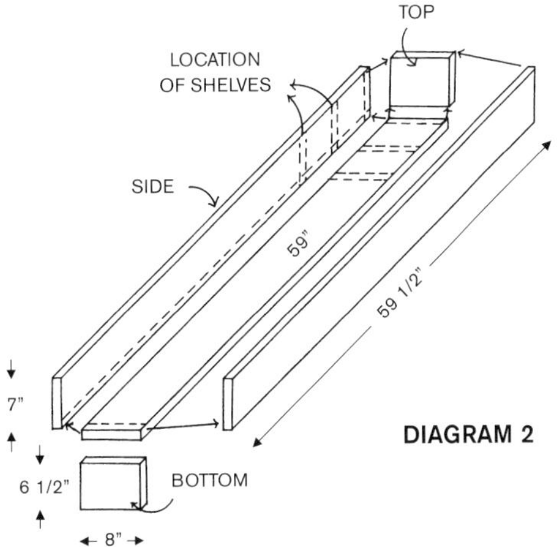

Step 5. Attach shelves

Measure and mark 1/4" down from the top of one side panel. At this mark, clamp the top shelf into position between the two side panels, flush with the front edges of the side pieces. (This will leave a 1/2" space at the back of the shelves, which will later be filled by the back.) Because the shelves are only 1/2" thick, there is a risk of splitting the wood. Once you have clamped the shelf into position, finish drilling the pilot holes that already run through the unit's sides into the edges of the shelves. Attach the side panels to the shelves using 1 1/4" #6 screws. Make two 6" spacer blocks to space out the next shelf as you work your way down. Accuracy is important for this project. Because you will repeat this step to attach all the other shelves, it is worth the extra time to make accurate spacer blocks.

Step 6. Fit and attach back

With the CD unit lying face-down on your bench, set the back panel into place on the back edge of the shelves, flush with the top of the top shelf and the bottom of the bottom shelf. Turn the unit over, keeping the back shelf flush with the top and bottom shelves. With a pencil, carefully mark on the back panel the locations of the top and bottom and every second shelf. Remove back panel. Draw lines across the back panel locating the centre of each of these shelves. Fit the back panel in place and flush with the top and bottom shelves. Drill two pilot holes at 1 1/2" in from the edges of the back panel, along the shelf centre lines and into the back edges of the shelves. Screw into place with #6 1 1/4" screws.

Project 46

Bamboozled

GIVE FURNISHINGS A TROPICAL TWIST WITH THESE SIX EASY PROJECTS.

Editor's note:
A sturdy, timeless material that works with almost any decor, bamboo looks casual without being unrefined, traditional without being stuffy. Today's trend is to dark bamboo: stain it ebony for an up-to-the-minute look.

Difficulty level:
Average

Projects:
Bamboo-wrapped vase, wastebasket and lampshades
Tripod table
Lamp base
Curtain rods

Lately, bamboo is shooting up everywhere with a casual flavour that makes it a natural source of inspiration for simple summer projects. Popular both for its environment-friendly status and because it speaks to today's trend for things Asian, this versatile material comes in many different sizes and tones. It's also affordable and easy to find — look for it at gardening stores and nurseries, in your local Chinatown, or at specialty bamboo and rattan stores. We've come up with six decorative projects ranging from easy-to-make bamboo-wrapped votives to a handy tripod table. Every project is straightforward — perfect for the budding craftsperson.

Top: Exotic flowers look at home in a vase wrapped in bamboo poles, and a tired wastebasket gets a new lease on life covered with a tortoiseshell-look bamboo blind. Quirky bamboo blinds create a soft light when used over lampshades.

Bottom centre: Paired with a traditional linen lampshade, an oversized bamboo pole makes a handsome lamp base. Because the poles are hollow, they are a natural housing for wiring.

Bottom left: An inexpensive wicker tray becomes a table with Eastern appeal when paired with large bamboo poles crisscrossed and tied into a tripod. Votives wrapped in brown matchstick blinds create an ambience of serenity.

Bottom right: A simple and creative solution for hanging drapery, bamboo poles make curtain rods with character.

PHOTOGRAPHY BY ROB FIO

BAMBOO-WRAPPED VASE, WASTEBASKET & LAMPSHADES

We wrapped a paper lamp, lampshade and wastebasket with bamboo blinds and a vase with bamboo poles. Once the strings on a blind have been cut, they will unravel and the poles will come loose. Handle them carefully and retie the strings as soon as possible.

MATERIALS & TOOLS

- Tortoiseshell-look or matchstick bamboo blinds, 2' to 2'-6" wide
- 1/8"-diam. bamboo poles, shortest length available
- Scissors
- Garden pruners
- Ruler or measuring tape
- Glue gun and glue sticks
- Handsaw
- Coarse-grit sandpaper

For the paper lamp, lampshade, wastebasket:

Step 1. Unwind and mark blind

Work with only a section of blind, because it is difficult to manoeuvre a full roll of blind. Start by lining up one edge of the blind with one edge of the object to be wrapped. Carefully unwind the blind so that it covers the object entirely, but with no overlap, and mark this point. This will give you the measurement for the circumference of the object. Allow another four inches of excess and mark this point as well.

Step 2. Cut strings

Place the blind on a flat surface. Find the excess point, then use scissors to cut the strings that hold the bamboo sticks in place at that point. Carefully pull out the extra poles to the first marked point and re-knot the strings.

Step 3. Cut blind

Realign this shorter section of blind with the object and mark the desired height. Lay the blind flat again. With a ruler and felt-tip marker, draw a straight line across the slats of the blind, using the marked height as the guide line. Cut the blind along this marked line with a pair of pruners. Bamboo slats can be thick and hard to cut and each slat must be cut individually. Matchstick blinds are easy to cut with a good pair of scissors.

Step 4. Glue slats in place

Hold the blind in position around the object and with a glue gun, glue the first few slats. Hold them in place until they're secure. Alternate between applying the glue in strips along the object and unwinding the blind and holding it in place. Continue until the object is covered.

For the vase:

Step 1. Mark and cut poles

Line up one of the poles along the side of the glass vase and, with a felt-tip pen, mark the desired height on the pole. For a cleaner look, mark a point that is at least 1" higher than the top edge of the vase. Measure this height and mark it along several 4'-long poles. Then cut along these marks with a handsaw to create several shorter "sticks" until you have enough (when placed side by side) to cover the vase. You should get several sticks from one pole. (We needed 25 sticks, 12" high, to cover a vase with a 3" diameter, so we bought seven poles.)

Step 2. Glue sticks to vase

Apply glue along the length of one of the sticks, stopping at the point that lines up with the top edge of the vase. Hold it in place against the glass until it stays put. Choose each pole carefully before glueing — because of their knuckles, certain poles will align better with others. For extra strength, turn the vase upside down and carefully fill the spaces between the glass and the poles with glue. You can do this at the vase opening as well. Sand any rough edges.

TRIPOD TABLE

In this project, three large bamboo poles are screwed together in a teepee formation and tied with cane to form a table base. A piece of medium-density fibreboard (MDF) screwed onto the legs supports a tray.

MATERIALS & TOOLS

3	40" bamboo poles, 2" diam.
1	piece MDF, approx. 1'-10" square
1	yd. cane strip
3	#8 screws 1 1/2" long
3	#8 screws 2" long
	Wood stain
	Finishing nails
	Circular wicker or rattan tray, approx. 2' in diam.
	Handsaw
	Compass
	Jigsaw
	Paintbrush
	String

Step 1. Cut poles

Using a handsaw, cut the bamboo poles into three sections approximately 40" long. Saw both ends of each pole off on a 30° angle. Make sure that the angles are cut in opposite directions at each end so that the pole has a long side and a short side. (The angle at which the poles are cut will differ according to the desired height of the table and the size of the tray. The lower the table and the larger the tray, the bigger the angle has to be.)

Step 2. Cut MDF

On the MDF, use a compass to draw a circle that is slightly smaller than the diameter of the tray. Cut out with a jigsaw (you may also be able to find pre-cut circles at craft centres or fabric stores.)

Step 3. Secure and wrap legs

Divide the circle evenly into three, and mark three points around its edge. Hold one of the legs with the hollow opening centred on that point and drill an angled pilot hole through the leg and into the MDF tabletop. Don't allow the drill to come through the other side of the tabletop. Do this for the other two legs, then insert 1 1/2" #8 screws into the holes to attach the legs. All three legs should meet in the centre. Holding the three legs together where they meet, drill pilot holes through one leg and into the next. Screw together gently with 2" #8 screws. To make the cane malleable, soak it in a tub of warm water for 30 minutes. Dry it off and wrap it around the legs at the point where they join, covering the screws. Tuck the end in on itself and let it dry.

Step 4. Stain MDF and attach tray

Apply a coat of stain to the edge of the MDF in a colour that complements the tray. We used Minwax Wood Finish in Ebony. Allow to dry. Attach the tray to the MDF top with finishing nails or a glue gun.

LAMP BASE

In this project, a bamboo pole is wired into a lamp by inserting a steel pipe into its centre and running wire through the channel. A bamboo pole is perfect because of its hollow cavity. The lamp parts are available in the electrical department of most hardware stores.

MATERIALS & TOOLS

- Bamboo pole, 5" x 18"
- 3/8" threaded steel pipe
- Flat steel washer
- Serrated lock washers
- Hexagonal lock nuts
- Lamp parts: brass canopy plate to fit over top of pole (5" diam.), 1" brass neck, harp, socket cap, light socket sleeve, light socket with switch, lamp cord with moulded or polarized attachment plug, lampshade
- Drill
- Ruler
- Wrench
- Screwdriver
- Wire strippers

Step 1. Drill hole for pipe

Some bamboo poles are completely hollowed out, while others will have thin fibrous membranes running horizontally across the inside. Intact membranes are preferable, as they will help hold the pipe in place. Penetrate the membranes by drilling a 1/2" hole at both ends of the 5" x 18" pole. The membranes are fairly thin and the steel pipe should push through any other membranes farther inside the pole.

Step 2. Drill notch for lamp cord

Drill a 1/8" notch on the side of the bottom of the pole to allow the lamp cord to run out.

Step 3. Determine height of pipe channel

The steel pipe channel houses the lamp cord within the base. Your local hardware store should be able to cut pipe to your specifications. The pipe channel is the "spine" of the lamp, to which the socket cap, light socket and the harp are attached, so it must be long enough to run from the bottom of the base up to the bottom of the socket cap. Determine the length of pipe channel you require by adding the height of the bamboo pole and the height of the "neck" you are using. (The neck conceals the portion of pipe that protrudes from the lamp base. We used a 1" brass neck.) Add an additional 1/2" to this overall height, to allow for an extra 1/2" of pipe exposed at the top of the neck, which the socket cap is screwed onto.

Step 4. Secure pipe in lamp base

Insert the pipe into the bamboo lamp base and secure it very gently against the membrane at the bottom of the base with a flat steel washer and a hexagonal nut, screwed onto the pipe.

Step 5. Attach canopy plate and neck

Slip the round brass canopy plate and neck over the length of pipe that protrudes from the top of your bamboo pole, then slip on a serrated lock washer, screw on a hexagonal nut and tighten. The pipe channel should now be stabilized and centred through the middle of the lamp base.

Step 6. Attach harp and socket cap

Slip the harp and a serrated lock washer over the remaining exposed pipe (1/2"). Screw on the socket cap. Tighten the set screw at the side.

Step 7. Thread lamp cord through pole

Thread the lamp cord through the bottom of the lamp so that it travels up the pipe channel and comes out through the socket cap. Make sure that 4" of cord emerges from the top of the cap. Using wire strippers, gently grasp the cords, one at a time, and pull to strip the insulation, exposing 1/2" to 5/8" of wire. Twist the wire strands so there are no loose ends.

Step 8. Tie underwriter's knot

Separate the 4" of lamp cord by gently pulling it apart. Following the diagram carefully, tie an underwriter's knot to provide a strain relief for the cords. Pull the underwriter's knot down so that it sits snugly in the socket cap.

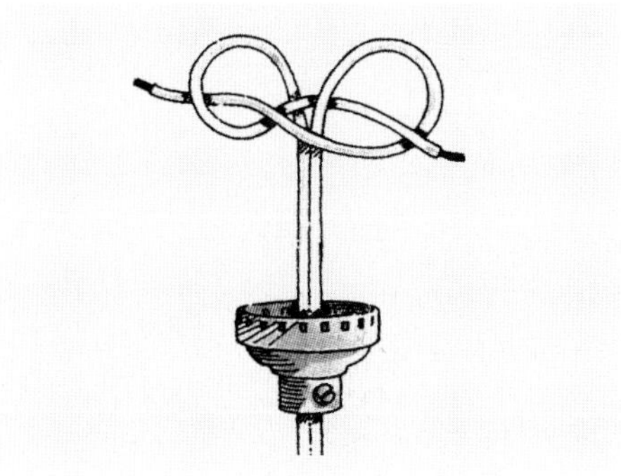

Step 9. Attach wires to socket

Wrap one wire around the silver screw on the socket and tighten. Wrap the other wire around the brass screw and tighten. If the wires are coloured, attach the black wire to the brass screw and the white wire to the silver screw.

Step 10. Attach socket, sleeve and shell

Sit the light socket in the socket cap. Slide the socket sleeve and shell down over the socket cap and snap the assembly into place. Screw in the bulb and attach the lampshade to the harp.

CURTAIN RODS

For this project, simply choose finials you like and buy bamboo poles large enough that the finials will fit snugly on their ends. Cut bamboo poles to desired length, allowing enough room, if possible, after a knuckle for the finial to fit on. Push or twist finials onto ends of pole.

47 Project

Easy to Build Kitchen Island

THIS MOBILE UNIT OFFERS EXTRA STORAGE AND PREP SPACE FOR THE SMALL KITCHEN.

Editor's note:
This classic piece is a natural at the cottage, but, with the materials available today, there are endless options for adapting its style. Consider a stone or stainless top, funky industrial casters, a different paint colour.

Difficulty level:
Difficult

There isn't a cook around who wouldn't trade his or her favourite recipe for extra storage space and another work surface in the kitchen. Just one more spot to chop, mix or open out a cookbook and one extra shelf to store jars, baskets and the ever-cumulative *batterie de cuisine* can make all the difference. If the kitchen of your dreams isn't in the works, then this mobile island is a must. Our design is simple: a melamine box that's screwed together and stabilized by a centre panel, then clad with tongue-and-groove boards. A maple chopping block and open shelves for storage make the unit both practical and great-looking — well worth a weekend's work.

PHOTOGRAPHY BY MICHAEL MAHOVLICH

Project 47: Portable kitchen island

Finished size: 36" high x 23" deep x 23" wide; chopping block top, 25" x 25"

MATERIALS & TOOLS

1	sheet 4' x 8' x 3/4" white melamine
	Iron-on melamine tape (used here, Bennett Iron On)
48'	3"-wide tongue-and-groove wainscotting, cut into approx. 36" lengths
16'	outside corner mould
	1 1/2" #8 screws or particleboard screws
	25" x 25" maple butcher block
	1" finishing nails
4	3" casters
	3/4" #8 screws
4	plastic shelf supports
	Wood filler
	Sandpaper
	White oil-based paint

Step 1. Assemble materials for base

Have a lumber store cut the following pieces from a sheet of 4' x 8' x 3/4" white melamine.

For sides:
2 pieces @ 31 1/4" high x 23" wide

For top, bottom, fixed shelf:
3 pieces @ 22 1/2" wide x 23" deep

For centre support panel:
1 piece @ 22 1/2" wide x 21" high

For removable shelf:
1 piece @ 11" x 22 1/4" (optional)

Step 2. Tape edges of melamine

Finish the exposed edges of the melamine pieces with white iron-on melamine tape. Cut pieces of tape to cover the 31 1/4" edges of the side panels and the 22 1/2" edges of the top, bottom and shelf panels. Cut the pieces of tape a little longer than the actual measurement to allow for neat trimming. You do not have to cover the edges of the centre support panel, as they will not be exposed.

With a medium-hot iron, iron the tape onto the exposed edges, pressing it down as you go with a block of wood. Trim the overlap with an X-Acto knife.

Step 3. Assemble base

The base of this island is actually just a box, held together with screws. Starting with the side pieces of the box, pre-drill holes (called pilot holes) for the screws, approximately 3/8 from the top and bottom of each piece. These pilot holes will enable you to "countersink" the screws rather than leaving them flush with the surface. When countersunk, screws will create a tighter and sturdier join. Drill four or five holes, evenly spaced, approximately 4" to 5" apart. Use a #8 countersink drill bit which is sized for #8 screws and slightly smaller. Fit the top and bottom panels between the side panels and screw the box together, using 1 1/2" #8 screws. If you have clamps, use these to hold the box together and keep the panels aligned while you tighten the screws.

Step 4. Measure shelf and centre panel locations, drill pilot holes

In order to give the base extra stability, a centre support panel is inserted vertically and attached to the bottom and sides of the box. A shelf rests on top of this and is attached to either side of the box.

Measure first for placement of the shelf, approximately 8" down from the top of the box. Pencil a horizontal line across the outside of either side panel to indicate this location and serve as a guideline for the screws. Next, draw a vertical line down the middle of each side panel to indicate the location of the centre support panel (imagine the letter T sketched on the outside of both side pieces). Drill pilot holes, evenly spaced along these lines. Turn the box upside down and draw a line down the centre of the box from front to back.

Step 5. Attach centre support panel

Set the box on its side and insert the centre support panel so that it lines up with the pilot holes you have just drilled. Attach the panel to the bottom of the box first. Screw the first screw in, then check that the panel is centred by measuring for equal distances on either side of it. Next, screw the panel to either side of the box, checking that it is centred.

Step 6. Screw in shelf

Insert the shelf and ensure it is level; adjust it if necessary. Screw it into the pilot holes on either side of the box.

Step 7. Wainscot side panels

We used 3" tongue-and-groove boards to clad the side panels of the box. If you are using 3" tongue-and-groove, you will need 8 pieces @ 31 1/4" long for each side. Set the box on its side and, using 1" finishing nails, nail on the boards one at a time. Hammer nails on an angle into the tongue of each board (i.e., the piece of wood that fits into the groove of the next board). Make sure that the tongue-and-groove is flush with both the side and top edges of the panels. Fill the nail holes with wood filler and sand when dry.

Step 8. Attach corner mould and paint sides

Corner mould is applied to finish the rough edges where the wainscotting and melamine meet. It is L-shaped moulding that fits over the outside corners of the box. Cut four pieces of corner mould @ 31 1/4" long to fit the sides and two @ 22 1/2" long to fit the bottom edges. Mitre the corners for a neat finish and attach with 1" finishing nails. Fill the nail holes and sand when dry. Prime and finish-coat the wainscotting with white oil-based paint.

Step 9. Attach casters

Screw the casters into the bottom of the box at each corner, approximately 2" in from the corner, using 3/4" #8 screws.

Step 10. Attach butcher-block top

Maple butcher block can be ordered in custom sizes through kitchen manufacturers and retailers; expect delivery in two to four weeks. Some specialty kitchen-supply stores stock butcher block in standard sizes so you can pick it up on the spot. We used a 25" x 25" x 1 1/2" piece of butcher block for our island to allow for a little overhang over the base, but you can also use a piece cut to fit the box exactly. Attach the butcher block by screwing it on from underneath, using 1 1/2" #8 screws.

"Season" the surface by rubbing in a good-quality olive oil or mineral oil. Thin the oil by warming it in a pan on the stove — this way it will sink in better. All sides and edges of the butcher block should be oiled twice. Allow one full day between coats.

Step 11. Install removable shelf and accessorize

Measure for the extra shelf location and drill four holes on the inside of the box, approximately 1" in from the front and back of the box. Rest the shelf on shelf supports inserted in the holes. To ensure a level shelf, make sure the holes are all the same distance from the bottom. Accessorize with any hooks or towel racks you want to add to the trolley. Screw onto the side panels.

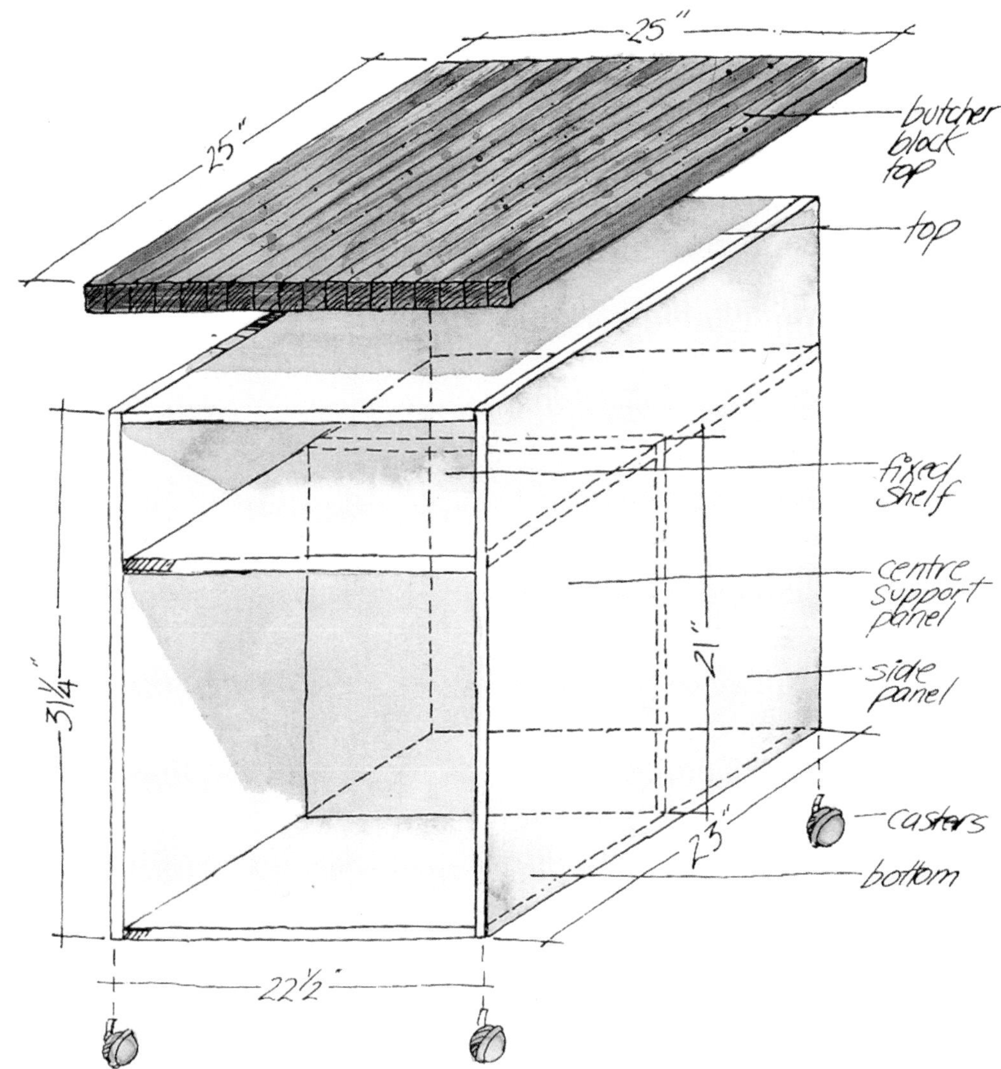

ILLUSTRATION BY BARBARA GRIFFIN

Project

HallOrganizer

END FRONT DOOR CLUTTER WITH A TRELLIS-STYLE HALL ORGANIZER.

Editor's note:
Give this simple rack a sleeker, less country-casual look with a coat of dark brown stain. Instead of wooden pegs, install cool brushed-nickel knobs and replace the brass hooks with stainless steel.

Difficulty level:
Easy

A spacious front hall or all-purpose mudroom is a luxury many of us live without. Narrow entranceways and closet-sized vestibules mean that the proverbial place to hang your hat is often nonexistent, and the classic catch-all console table is relegated to another room altogether. Our solution? A space-saving "trellis" hall organizer that's outfitted with hooks and pegs and mounted flush to the wall. Made entirely from 1" x 2" pine pieces, a few dabs of glue and a handful of nails, this is truly an afternoon project, and the result is as pretty as it is practical. Use it to hang up hats and scarves, umbrellas and walking sticks, keys and shopping bags. Dress it up with a bunch of dried flowers and a miniature mirror for style. Or, if space isn't at a premium in your house, adapt it to hold pots and pans in the kitchen, or gardening tools in the back shed.

PHOTOGRAPHY BY MICHAEL MAHOVLICH

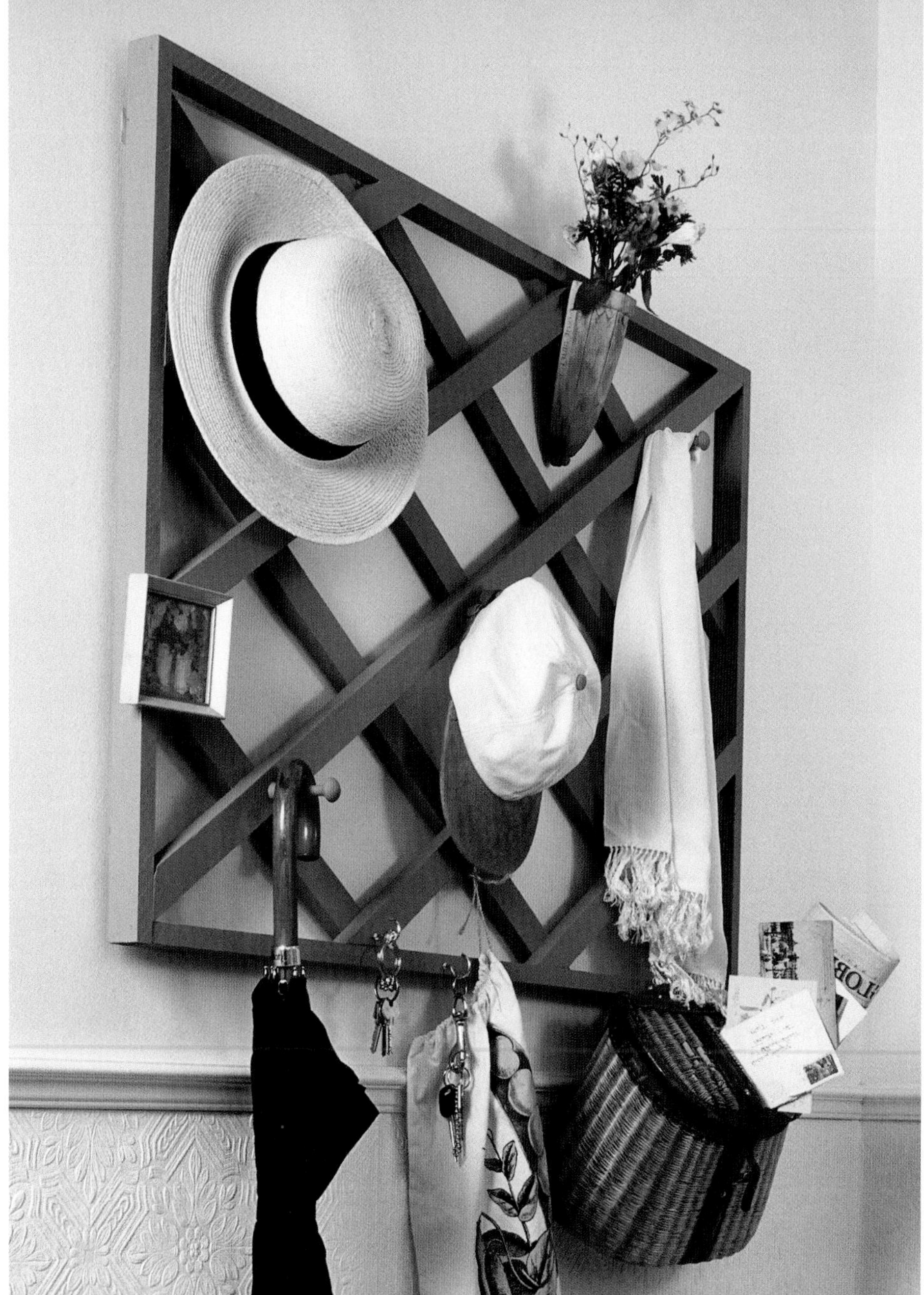

Project 48: Trellis hall organizer

Because this project uses only 1" x 2" pine for the frame and the lattice, the end result is a flush surface, only 1 1/2" deep. The lattice is made of five pairs of slats so you only need to measure a slat length once and then transfer the measurement to another piece of pine for the second slat of the pair. The slat lengths are determined by laying the 1" x 2" diagonally across the frame at 6" increments from the first centre pair. The following instructions are for a 30" h. x 42" w. horizontal trellis. Depending on the size of your hallway and available wall space, make it larger or smaller to suit, and change the spacing between slats accordingly. If you like, you can mount it vertically rather than horizontally.

MATERIALS & TOOLS

2 10' pieces of 1" x 2" clear pine
2 12' pieces of 1" x 2" clear pine
2" finishing nails
1 1/4" finishing nails
Wood glue
Shaker pegs and brass cup hooks
Brass screw eyes for hanging
Screws
Saw
Hammer
Electric drill
Measuring tape

MAKING THE FRAME

Step 1. Cut 2 pieces of 1" x 2" pine @ 30" each.

Step 2. Cut 2 pieces of 1" x 2" pine @ 40 1/2" each.

Step 3. Lay the pieces out on the floor on their narrow edges (1" side up), and using 2" finishing nails, nail the frame together at each corner. For extra strength, apply a dab of wood glue to the end of each frame piece before nailing together. Note: For a horizontal frame, place the long pieces on the inside of the short pieces. For a vertical frame, place the short pieces on the inside of the long ones. This will give a more finished appearance to the frame.

MAKING THE FRAME "SQUARE"

Step 4. Make the frame "square" by shifting it until the diagonal measurement on either side is the same, i.e., by measuring from corner to corner on the diagonal (our measurement was 51 1/2"). It is important that the frame maintain a perfectly square or even shape when you measure for the slat length — measurements taken from an uneven frame will result in slats that are either too big or too small for the frame. Even pairs of slats, positioned at the right angle, are key to a successful lattice or trellis. When you have achieved a perfectly square shape, trace around the frame onto a piece of cardboard or paper taped to the floor. This will give you a record of the square frame so that if it loses its shape, you can easily adjust it.

MAKING THE LATTICE

Lattice is made by overlapping pairs of slats of wood diagonally, in opposite directions, and nailing them together, one on top of the other. This lattice is designed to sit inside the frame. Once you have made the frame, you are ready to measure and cut the slats.

1

2

3

Step 5. Measure and cut the first pair of slats (see Photo 1). These will be the longest slats, running across the centre of the frame on the diagonal, from corner to corner. With your frame square, lay a 10-foot piece of 1" x 2" pine across the frame on the diagonal and, with a pencil, mark at either end where it meets the inside of the frame. To ensure an accurate measurement, place a scrap of wood, a level or a ruler on top of the 1" x 2" and parallel to the frame and draw a line. These marks indicate where you will "mitre" (angle) the ends of the first slat.

Step 6. With your saw positioned on an angle, or using a mitre-box, saw off both ends of the slat (see Photo 2).

Step 7. Use this first slat to make a second slat of the same size by tracing the angled ends onto another piece of 1" x 2" or onto the remainder of the first piece. Saw off the ends. This first pair of slats makes up the two centre slats. Fit them inside the frame on the diagonal, one on top of the other, in opposite directions. Once the first pair of slats are fit tightly, they will keep the frame square. Note: If the slats are too big, sand or carefully chisel them down just enough so that they sit snugly within the frame. (Ours were 49 3/8" at the longest point.) It is better to cut the slats longer than shorter — a slat that is too big can always be cut down to fit, but one that is too small cannot be changed! Reserve the remainder of this wood to make another, smaller slat.

Step 8. Measure and cut the second pair of slats. The length of the second pair of slats and all those remaining is based on the spacing between slats, which is 6" (see Photo 3). With a measuring tape, measure 6" perpendicular from the middle slat out to the frame edge and mark this point on the frame with a pencil. Note: Place a small X just beyond the mark to indicate on which side the slat is to be nailed. Lay a piece of 1" x 2" pine diagonally across the frame. Line it up with the mark you have just made, and with your level on top of the 1" x 2" and parallel to the edge of the frame, draw a measurement line at either end of the 1" x 2" pine (see Photo 4). Cut the slat and, as before, transfer the length to another piece of 1" x 2" for the next slat. Lay this second pair of slats on the diagonal in the frame, in opposite directions, one on top of the other. Continue to measure and cut the next three pairs of slats in this manner, so that they are spaced 6" apart (that is, from the second pair of slats, measure for the third pair, and continue in the same manner for the fourth and fifth pairs). In total you will have five pairs of slats that graduate in size — from the longest centre slats to the smallest corner slats — all spaced 6" apart.

Step 9. With all the slats laid one on top of the other inside the frame, check that they are spaced 6" apart and have a snug fit.

Step 10. Using 1 1/4" finishing nails, nail the top slat to the bottom one where they intersect, 1/4" in from the outside edge of the slat at either edge (i.e., two nails per slat). Start in the middle and work your way out along the centre slats, to the corners. Be sure to continually check that the slats are lined up with the marks you have made on the frame.

4

ATTACHING THE FRAME TO THE LATTICE

Step 11. Nail the frame to the lattice where they intersect, with 1 1/4" nails. Keep the front face flush with the frame (see Photo 5).

Step 12. With an electric drill, drill peg holes where the slats intersect. Apply a dab of glue to the peg and insert it into the hole. Allow to dry.

Step 13. Lightly sand and paint or stain the trellis. Screw in hooks where required. Attach screw eyes to the top of the frame.

5

Project 49

Easy to Build Plate Rack

BRING ENGLISH COUNTRY CHARM TO YOUR KITCHEN WITH THIS EASY-TO-BUILD PLATE RACK.

Editor's note:
To update this rack, give it the appearance of a built-in – like the cabinetry found in traditional "fitted" English kitchens. A quick coat of paint the same colour as the other cabinetry does the trick.

Difficulty level:
Average

Every kitchen can use extra storage space, and this easy-to-make plate rack is one of the prettiest ways to get it. Designed to accommodate full-sized dinner plates and hook-hung teacups or coffee mugs, a plate rack is perfect for displaying your favourite antique china or keeping on hand those pieces you use the most. Our simple design is made from standard-sized pine pieces, tongue-and-groove panelling and wooden dowels; most lumberyards will even cut these materials to length for a small fee. With basic hand and power tools, a cabinet like this can easily be assembled over the weekend. Start by picking up supplies Friday night, then hammer them together Saturday morning. Once it's built, take Sunday afternoon and have fun finishing it with an "antique"-type milk paint or coloured wood stain for a weathered, washed look. A stencilled-on folk-art design or a fruit or floral motif turns a unit like this into a one-of-a-kind piece that's worthy of handing down.

PHOTOGRAPHY BY MICHAEL MAHOVLICH

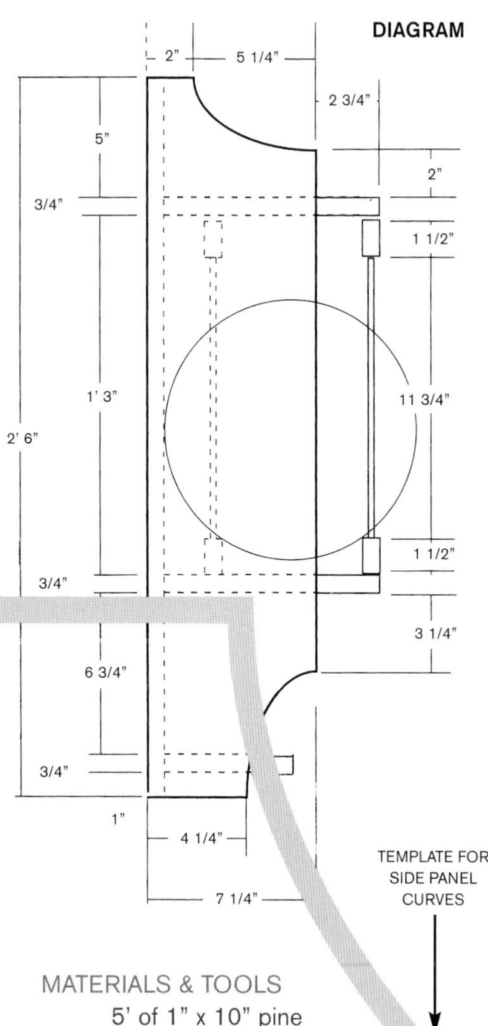

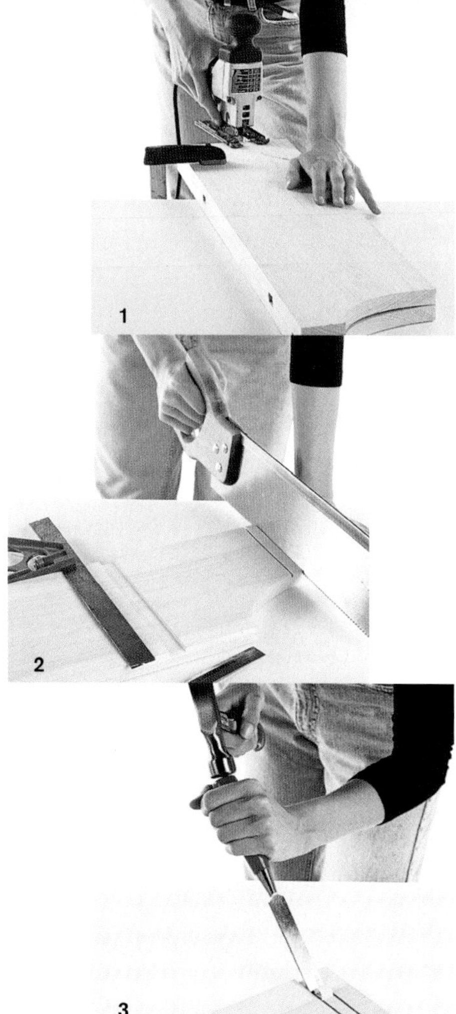

Project 49: Wall-hung plate rack

MATERIALS & TOOLS

	5' of 1" x 10" pine cut into two pieces
8	pieces 1/4" x 4' dowel cut into twenty-four pieces
10'	of 1" x 2" pine cut into four pieces
6'	of 1" x 8" pine cut into two pieces
1	2'-8" piece 1" x 6" pine and 2' of 1/2" x 1/2" pine
24	feet 1" x 4" tongue-and-groove pine (V grooved or beaded) cut into eight pieces
	2" finishing nails
2	pairs 1 1/2" hinges
	1 1/2" finishing nails
	Wood glue
	Jigsaw or coping saw
	Handsaw
	Drill and 1/4" drill bit
	Hammer
	Nail set
	3/4" chisel
	Screwdriver
	Square
	Tape measure
	Utility knife
	Clamps

Step 1. Side panels

A. Cut two side panels (about 2' 6") from the 1" x 8" pine. Clamp pieces together, then mark a square line near one end. Measure 2' 6" from this line and mark a square line at the other end. Cut pieces to length.

B. With pieces still clamped together, mark out the curves on the top and bottom of the panels, using the template provided. Draw a knife along the mark to avoid chipping when you cut. With a jigsaw or coping saw, cut out the curves. While the pieces are still clamped, sand the curves smooth.

C. Lay out and cut dados for shelves.

Note: A dado is a groove cut into the face of a board, into which the edge of another board is inserted. The dado helps support the shelf and makes the joint much stronger. Remove the clamps, but hold the pieces together, stand the panels on the back edge and open them out flat like a book, so that the two back edges are together, and what will be the inside faces are facing up. From the drawing, measure out the locations of the shelves and mark on both pieces at the same time. With a square and knife, score the two edges of the dados.

D. To indicate the depth of the cuts, on the front and back edges of the side panels, place marks 1/4" down at the locations of the dados. With your hand saw, carefully cut along the inside of the knife cuts (see Photo 2) to the 1/4" depth. Now with a 3/4" chisel (see Photo 3), gently tap out the wood between the saw cuts to form your dados. Note: It's better to have the dados too small than too big. If the shelf is too big, the ends can be sanded a little so they fit into the dados.

Step 2. Back

Cut the tongue-and-groove into eight 2' 6" lengths. Remove the tongue from one strip. This will allow the back to fit tightly against the side panel.

Step 3.

Fit together the tongue and groove strips to make up the back panel. With the pieces held firmly together, measure the width of the panel and use this measurement to determine the length of the shelves.

Step 4. Shelves

Cut the shelves to length. Their length must be 1/2" longer than the width of the back panel so they may be inserted into the dados cut into the side panels.

Step 5. Rails

From the 10' piece of 1" x 2" pine, cut rails for rack to length. They should be 1/4" shorter than the width of the back panel that you measured in Step 3.

Step 6.

Sand all pieces. It is easier to sand the pieces before assembly. Also, at this point, you should test-fit all the pieces. If necessary, a little trim or extra sanding will make the final assembly much easier.

Step 7. Assembly

A. Set out the two side panels on their back edges, at approximately the proper "back panel" distance apart, and then lay them down on their outside faces, and fit together the tongue-and-groove strips for the back panel and place between the side panels. Place shelves in their proper location on top of the back panel. Spread glue in the first of the dados of the side panels and along the ends of the corresponding shelf, being careful not to apply glue to the portion of the shelf that extends beyond the side panels.

B. Holding the two pieces firmly together, drive three nails through the side panel into the end of the shelf. Repeat this for the remaining two shelves. Now apply glue to the three dados in the other side panel and the other end of the three shelves, and carefully fit them together. Holding firmly, nail together.

Step 8. Back

Carefully flip over the assembled unit so that it is now resting on the front edge of the shelves. With a square, adjust the frame so that it is square, then line up the top edge of the strips that make up the back. Now, being careful not to move the frame out of square, and using the dados as a guide, drive one 1 1/2" nail through each strip of tongue-and-groove into the back edge of the shelves. Set aside and allow glue to dry (approximately 1 hour) while completing remaining steps.

Step 9. Racks

A. With the rails already cut to length (Step 5), which should be 23 3/4" for a 24"-wide back panel, you can now lay out the locations of the holes to be drilled for the dowels. Place an "X" on one end of each of the four rails and start the holes from this end. The first hole is 7/8" from the end of the rail to the centre of the hole (see Photo 7), and the remaining holes are 2" from centre to centre along the length of the rail, leaving 7/8" at the end. Now align the other three rails with the one marked out and with a small square transfer the marks to the other rails.

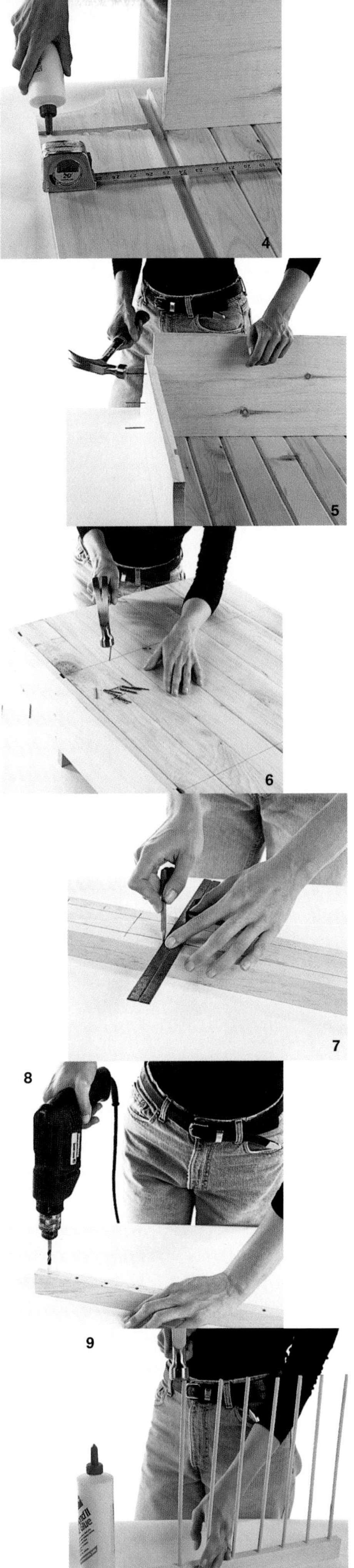

B. Using a 1/4" drill bit, drill the holes 1/2" deep. To make it easy to gauge the depth, wrap a piece of masking tape around the bit, 1/2" back from the tip, and drill the hole until the tape touches the rail (see Photo 8).

Step 10. Dowels

Cut the dowels to length. The height of the racks should be approximately 1/4" smaller than the distance between the two large shelves, which should be 15". Therefore, the completed rack should be 14 3/4" high, not including the two rails which are 1 1/2" high. Cut 24 pieces of dowel to 12 1/2". This will allow for a small clearance in the depth of the holes. When the dowels are cut, sand a slight taper on each end of the dowels. This will make room for the glue as well as making the assembly easier.

Step 11. Assemble racks

The rack is made up of 2 rails and 12 dowels. Make sure the 2 rails of each rack have the marked X's at the same end. Place a small amount of glue in each hole of one rail and spread around with a nail. Then gently tap each dowel into the rail. Apply glue to holes in second rail and carefully slide the rail over the end of dowels, tapping down until the height of the rack is 14 3/4" (see Photo 9).

Step 12. Mount racks

A. Attach the hinges to each completed rack, 3" in from each end. One rack is attached to the back of the top shelf, the other is attached to the front of the bottom shelf. With the unit lying down, mark a line on the underside of the top shelf 2 1/2" out from the back panel, then stand one of the racks on the underside of the top shelf with the open leaf of the hinges touching the line. Centre the rack and attach. Centre the other rack along the front edge of the lower shelf and attach.

B. Place two 2 1/2" blocks behind the inside rack on the bottom shelf to stop it from swinging. Attach a small turn button to the front edge of the top shelf to hold the front rack closed. This hinged construction allows for easy cleaning.

Project

Lighten Up

EASY INSTRUCTIONS FOR WIRING A FAVOURITE OBJECT INTO A LAMP.

Editor's note:
Lamp styles have changed since we first presented these ideas, but the basic wiring methods we show work just as well with more modern-shaped objects: cylindrical glass vases, tall woven baskets, or vintage '50s pottery.

Difficulty level:
Average

Projects:
METHOD 1: Wiring a lamp through the bottom of the base
METHOD 2: Wiring a lamp through the side of the base

Everybody has a favourite object around the house that would make a great lamp base — a colourful china vase, ginger jar, woven basket, candlestick, or even an antique tin! We'll show you how to wire your own table lamp — it's not difficult but it is important to follow the directions carefully. Be sure that all electrical components and wiring kits you purchase are certified by the Canadian Standards Association. When choosing a lamp base you will want an object that is hollow inside and wide enough from top to bottom to accommodate a piece of 3/8" diameter steel pipe. The ideal object to use is one that is hollow right through, such as our terra-cotta candlestick or antique wooden spools. If your object is not hollow straight through, as was the case with our ginger jar, basket and tin lamps, you will have to bore holes at the top and bottom of the lamp to accommodate wiring. If you are wiring a basket or metal tin as we did, weight it with steel weights or gravel.

PHOTOGRAPHY BY DAN HERINGA

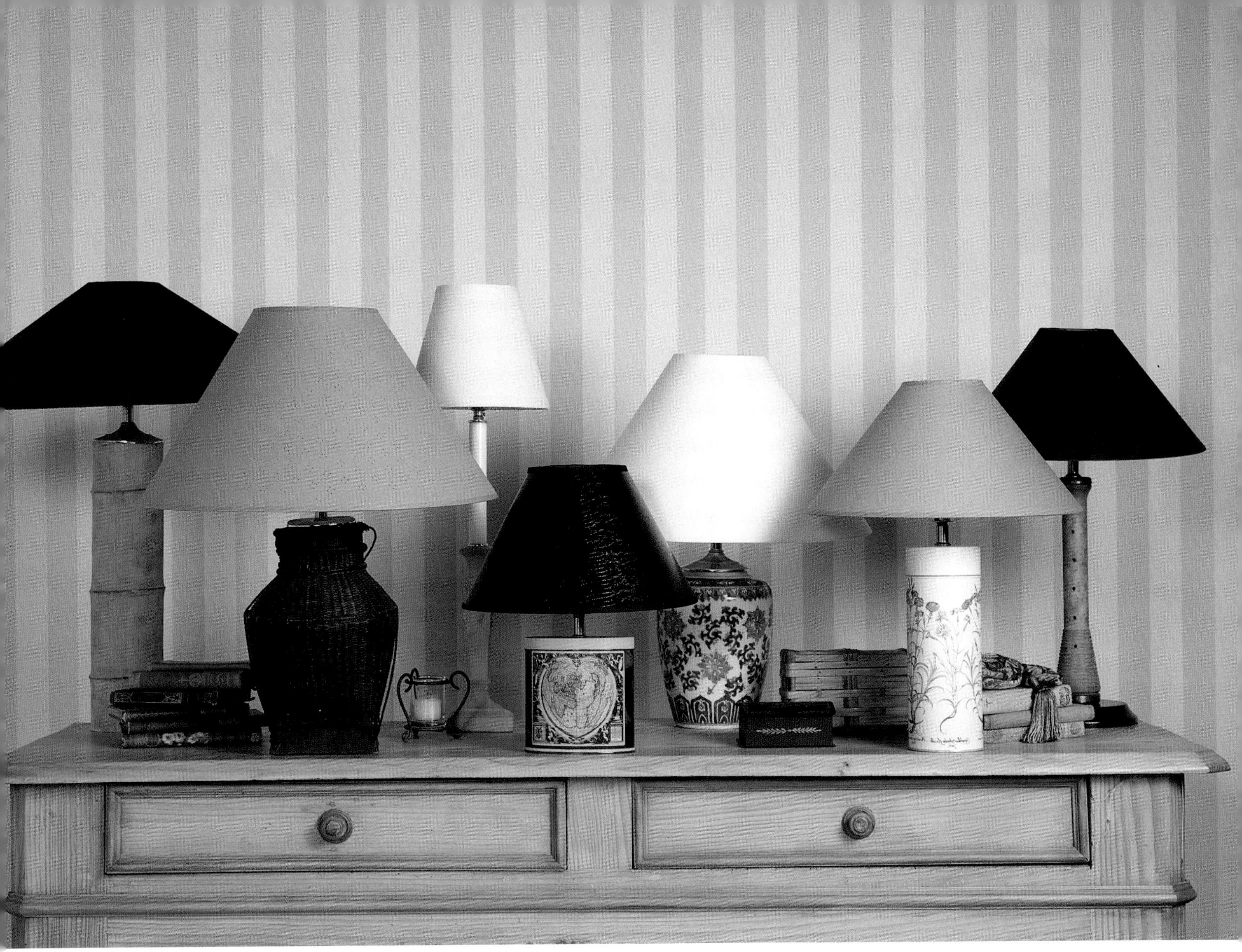

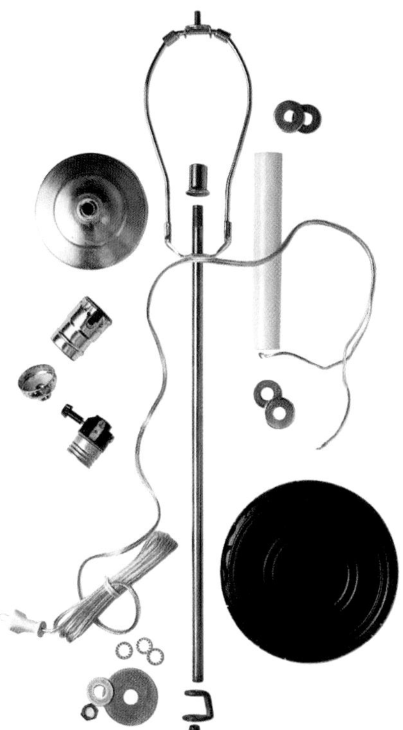

The majority of parts required for this project are available in the electrical departments of most large hardware stores. For specialty parts, such as necks, canopy plates and pedestal bases, as well as all other electrical components, consult your local lighting store.

MATERIALS & TOOLS

- Check ring and flat steel washer
- Candlestick plastic tubing neck
- Harp (for shade)
- Brass canopy plate
- Brass neck
- Light socket sleeve and shell
- Socket cap
- Light socket with switch – CSA certified trilight/high-low/one-way
- Lamp cord with a moulded or polarized attachment plug: type SPT-1 or SPT-2 and minimum size No. 18 AWG (American Wire Gauge)
- Serrated or fine-tooth lock washers
- Hexagonal lock nuts
- Round flat steel washer
- $^{3}/_{8}$"-diam. steel bushing (fully threaded)
- Steel hickey
- Pedestal base
- Multipurpose pliers and wire strippers
- Electric drill with ceramic, wood, and glass bits
- Measuring tape
- Screwdriver
- Adjustable wrench

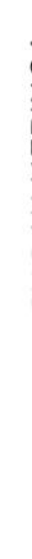

We are showing two sets of basic instructions for wiring a table lamp. The first set refers to:

Method 1: Wiring a table lamp through the bottom of the base.
The lamp cord is run out of the bottom of the base and pulled to the side through a notch (see Diagram 1). Use these instructions if your base has a sufficient cavity at the bottom to allow the cord to run out (i.e., the bottom of the base is not flush with the surface you are setting it on) or, if you are intending to set the base on a pedestal (which gives the cord room to come out through the bottom).

The second set of instructions refers to:

Method 2: Wiring a table lamp through the side of the base.
See Diagram 2. A cord hole must be drilled through the side of the base (as opposed to the bottom). Use these instructions if your base does not have a cavity at the bottom (i.e., the bottom of the base is flush with the surface you are setting it on) or if you are not setting the base on a pedestal.

Thanks to Lampshades Unlimited for instructional assistance.

METHOD 1: WIRING A LAMP THROUGH THE BOTTOM OF THE BASE

Step 1. Make hole at bottom of lamp

If you have chosen a ceramic base, like the blue-and-white ginger jar on the preceding page, turn the base upside down and pour a small amount of water into the concave underside of the base. Use an electric drill with a ceramic or glass bit and drill a hole approximately 1/2" in diameter. The water will facilitate drilling and result in a smoother hole. If you are using a basket or tin, perforate a hole through the bottom with a sharp tool .

Step 2. Determine length of pipe channel required

The steel pipe channel will house the lamp cord within the base (carrying the electrical current from the plug to the light socket). Pipe channel should be of standard gauge, 3/8" diameter, and threaded 1" at either end or fully threaded. Your local hardware store should be able to cut and thread pipe to your specifications. (Or, with a hacksaw and tap and die set, you can cut and thread pipe at home.)

Think of the pipe channel as the "spine" of the lamp to which all components are attached — the socket cap, light socket and, if you are using one, the harp to which the shade is attached. Therefore, the pipe channel must be long enough to run from the bottom of the base or the underside of the pedestal, up to the bottom of the socket cap.

The pipe channel is used in conjunction with a protective and decorative "neck" that conceals the length of pipe that protrudes from the lamp base. This neck sits between the top of the base and the bottom of the socket cap. Depending on the style of your lamp base and the overall height you want the lamp to be, the size of neck will vary. (For our ginger jar lamp, we used a squat 1" brass neck; for our terra-cotta candlestick lamp we used a piece of 5" white plastic tubing.) You will have to decide which type and size of neck best suits your base.

Determine the length of pipe channel you require by measuring the height of the lamp base, and adding to that the height of the neck you are using. Add an additional 1/2" to this overall height. This extra 1/2" of pipe is left exposed at the top of the neck and the socket cap is eventually screwed onto it.

Step 3. Insert pipe channel

Insert the pipe into the lamp base and secure it at the underside of the base with, first, a flat steel washer, second, a serrated lock washer and finally, a hexagonal lock nut, screwed on to the threading until it is flush with the end of the pipe.

Step 4. Attach neck

Depending on your style of base, slip either the plastic "candlestick" tube neck or a round brass canopy plate and neck over the length of pipe channel that protrudes from the top of your lamp base. The neck raises the socket to hide it under the shade and provides an attractive link between the lamp top and shade bottom. For our ginger jar, basket and bamboo lamps, we used a brass canopy plate and neck to protectively and aesthetically conceal the lamp interior. For our terra-cotta candlestick lamp, we used 5" of white plastic tubing to conceal the steel pipe channel and lengthen the look of the lamp.

The candlestick tube is used in conjunction with check rings and flat steel washers. Slip a check ring and one flat washer over the pipe channel, then the candlestick tube, then another flat washer and the second check ring. The candlestick tube neck conceals all but 1/2" of the remaining threaded steel pipe channel. Slip on a serrated lock washer, screw on a hexagonal lock nut and slip a second serrated lock washer over the pipe, then tighten with a wrench. The pipe channel should now be stabilized and centred through the middle of the lamp base.

If making a ginger jar or basket lamp, slip canopy and neck over pipe channel. The neck conceals all but 1/2" of the remaining steel pipe. Secure as above with lock washer, lock nut and a second lock washer. Tighten with a wrench carefully — too much pressure could cause the china base to crack or break. The pipe channel should now be stabilized and centered through the middle of the lamp base.

Step 5. Attach harp (optional)

If you are using a shade that screws onto a harp (as opposed to a shade that clips over a light bulb), attach the harp now. Slip the harp and a serrated lock washer over the remaining 1/2" exposed pipe.

Step 6. Screw on socket cap

Screw on the socket cap. Tighten set screw at side with a screwdriver.

Step 7. Run lamp cord through channel and strip insulation

Thread the lamp cord through the pedestal base and/or the bottom of the lamp so that it travels up the pipe channel and comes out through the socket cap. Examine the lamp cord to ensure that the plastic insulation is not damaged after it has been threaded through the pipe channel. Leave 4" of lamp cord coming out at the top of the cap.

Using a pair of wire strippers, gently grasp the cords, one at a time, and pull to strip them free of plastic insulation. Expose 1/2" to 5/8" bare wire strands. Twist the wire strands to make sure that there are no loose strands.

Step 8. Tie underwriter's knot

Separate the 4" of lamp cord by gently pulling it apart — it will separate easily into two cords. With the cords, tie an underwriter's knot (see Diagram 3) to provide a strain relief for the cords. Pull the underwriter's knot down so that it sits snugly in the socket cap. If necessary, cut excess cord and strip additional insulation. Note: The provision for a strain relief for the lamp cord is a requirement of the CSA standard for table lamps. Follow the diagram carefully.

Step 9. Connect wires to socket

Now you are ready to connect the wires to the socket. Wrap one wire clockwise around the silver-coloured screw on the socket and tighten it with a screwdriver. Wrap the other wire clockwise around the brass-coloured screw and tighten. If the wires are coloured, attach, as above, the black wire to the brass screw and the white wire to the silver-coloured screw. Tighten both screws.

Step 10. Snap on light socket

Sit the light socket in the socket cap. Slide socket sleeve and shell down over socket cap and snap the assembly into place.

Step 11. Attach lampshade

Either clip the shade over the lightbulb or screw it onto the harp with a decorative finial.

METHOD 2: WIRING A LAMP THROUGH THE SIDE OF THE BASE

For this set of instructions you will require additional parts. These are: a 1" piece of fully threaded steel bushing (pipe) and a steel hickey.

Instead of using a single piece of steel pipe inside the lamp, you will be using two pieces.

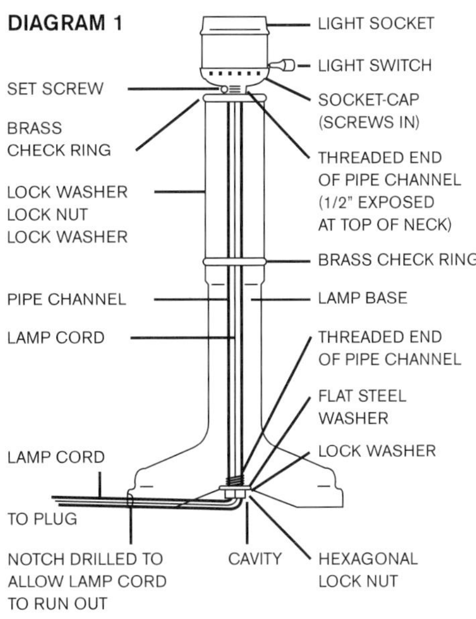

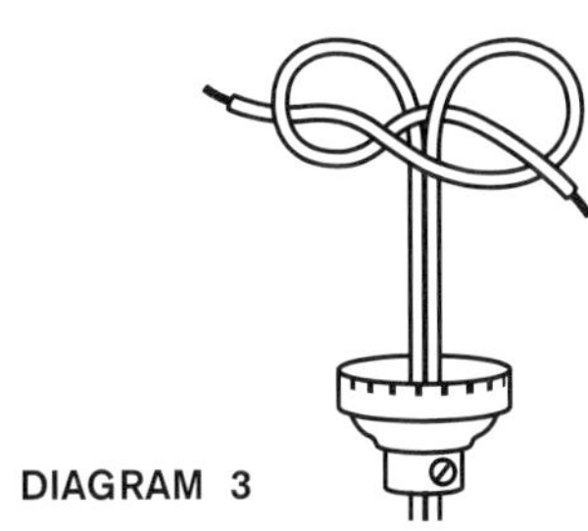

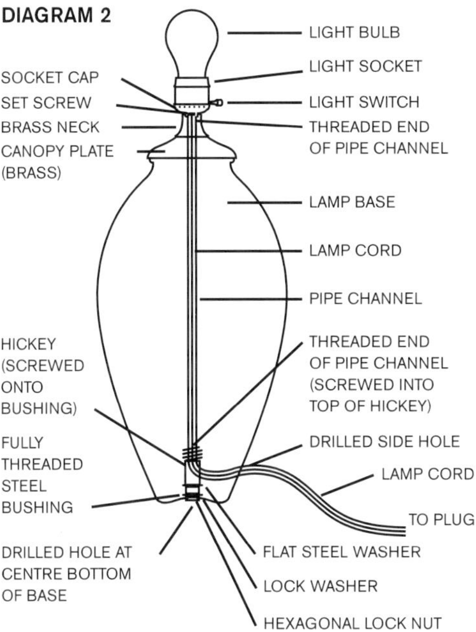

The smaller, fully threaded piece is called the bushing. This is attached to the bottom of the lamp and an "open connector," called a hickey, links the bushing to the pipe channel. The lamp cord is run through the side of the base, threaded through the hickey, and up into the pipe channel until it comes out at the top.

Step 1. Make centre and side holes

Follow Step 1, Method 1 for making a hole at bottom of base. Now, make a 1/4"-diameter hole at the side (near the bottom) of the base. Drill slowly if you are using a ceramic base — you will not be able to drill with water.

Step 2. Determine length of pipe required

This length of pipe will be shorter than that required for Method 1 as you will be using additional parts — a piece of threaded steel bushing and a hickey. Measure for length of pipe channel as per instructions in Method 1. Deduct from this the height of the bushing and the hickey. As per Method 1, add an additional 1/2" to this total. This extra 1/2" of pipe is left exposed at the top of the neck and the socket cap is eventually screwed on.

Step 3. Insert steel bushing

Insert a small piece of steel bushing into the bottom centre hole of the lamp base and secure it at the underside: first, with a flat steel washer; second, with a serrated lock washer; and third, with a hexagonal lock nut screwed on until it is flush with the end of the bushing.

Step 4. Screw on hickey

Screw the hickey onto the top of the bushing and down snug to the bottom of the base.

Step 5. Insert pipe channel

Screw the pipe channel to the top of the hickey. Note how the hickey serves as an open "connector" between the two pieces of pipe.

Refer to Method 1 for the remainder of the instructions, starting at Step 4. When running the lamp cord through the base (Step 7), thread it through the side hole, into the hickey and then up the pipe channel until it comes up through the socket cap.

Credits

COVER

Table and location courtesy of UpCountry, Vancouver (604) 875-9004, Toronto (416) 777-1700 or www.upcountry.ca; fabrics, Designer Fabrics, Toronto (416) 531-2810; ribbon, Mokuba, Toronto (416) 504-5358; paintbrushes, Woolfitt's, Toronto (416) 536-7878.

CRAFT

Wreathed in Glory: Wreaths

All ribbon, Masterstroke Canada, (416) 751-4193 or www.masterstrokecanada.com for retailers; all ornaments, Midwest of Cannon Falls, at Bowring stores, 1-800-939-GIFT (4438) or www.bowring.com; boxwood, reindeer moss, Teatro Verde, Toronto (416) 966-2227; artificial fruit, artificial quail eggs, large greenery wreath form, Royal Green, at craft stores; lichen wreath, Canatrade, (905) 670-0436 for retailers; partridge, Floridus, www.floridus.com.

Cameo Roles: Decorative appliqués

Frames, bed tray and washstand refurbishing by John Crossley; trumeau mirror made by Peter Fallico; white paint (Light Sugar 4150-1 1), taupe paint (Sandcastle 4149-42), chocolate brown melamine paint (Sicilian Umbre 4147-83), pink paint (Rich Rose 4139-31), all Sico, 1-800-463-7426 or www.sico.com; Anaglypta wallpaper, Steptoe & Wife Antiques, Toronto (416) 780-1707 or 1-800-461-0060 or www.steptoewife.com; handles, knobs, Lee Valley Tools, 1-800-267-8761 or www.leevalley.com; bevelled mirror, Adanac Glass, Toronto (416) 785-6309; MDF trim, wood appliqués, The Building Box, 1-877-277-3651 or www.thebuildingbox.com; ribbon, Mokuba, Toronto (416) 504-5358.

Works of Heart: Personalized gifts

Sewing by Brian Addis, Toronto (416) 538-9530; tealight holders, Candym Enterprises, 1-800-263-3551 for retailers; wire, beads, Soo Ling Beads & Beading, Toronto (416) 588-1994; champagne flutes, Caban, Vancouver (604) 742-1522, Toronto (416) 596-0386, (416) 366-4222, (416) 654-3316, Montreal (514) 844-9300; glass paint, decorative paper, claret paper, Loomis & Toles, Toronto (416) 703-4748; plain paper, stamp, stationery, ink, chartreuse paper, cards, The Papery, Toronto (416) 968-0706, (416) 962-3916 or www.thepackagingshop.com; ribbon, Mokuba, Toronto (416) 504-5358; wax, wax stamp, The Japanese Paper Place, Toronto (416) 703-0089; wool, gauze, magenta silk, Designer Fabrics, Toronto (416) 531-2810; plaid fabric, burgundy fabric, Primavera Interior Furnishings, Toronto (416) 921-3334; yarn, Romni Wools, Toronto (416) 703-0202; embroidery, Compu Tech Embroidery, Brantford, Ont. (519) 449-2282; hand towels, Lino, Toronto (416) 340-9853 or 1-877-402-LINO (5466) or www.linoliving.com for retailers.

Praising Cane: Caning

All pre-woven caning, W.H. Kilby, Toronto (416) 656-1065; journals, Roots Home, Toronto (416) 927-8585, Montreal (514) 845-7995 or 1-877-92-ROOTS; trim, cording, Mokuba, Toronto (416) 504-5358; cabinet, frames, tray and stand set, Ikea, 1-800-661-9807 or www.ikea.ca.

Beauty Treatment: Bath embellishments

Sewing, Wesley Seto, Toronto (416) 534-1226; beading, Robert Pehlke, Toronto (416) 588-2293; paint effect, Janis Zroback, Toronto (416) 484-9247; silks, Designer Fabrics, Toronto (416) 531-2810; ribbon, Mokuba, Toronto (416) 504-5358.

Good Things in Small Packages: Gift wrap ideas

Sizzle paper, vellum bags, The Creative Bag Co., Toronto (416) 631-6444; hair clip, Le Chateau stores; cardboard, Aboveground Art Supplies, Toronto (416) 591-1601; filing cabinet label, The Source, Vancouver (604) 684-9914; ribbon, Mokuba, Toronto (416) 504-5358; wrapping paper, The Japanese Paper Place, Toronto (416) 703-0089; fabric, Designer Fabrics, Toronto (416) 531-2810; tubes, watchmaker's tins, Lee Valley Tools, 1-800-267-8761 or www.leevalley.com; adhesive letters, Loomis & Toles, Toronto (416) 703-4748.

Tortoiseshell Buttons: Ideas using buttons

Handmade paper, The Japanese Paper Place, Toronto (416) 703-0089; price tags, Grand & Toy, 1-877-860-2910 or www.grandandtoy.com; linen napkins, hurricane lantern, Harvest At Home, Oakville, Ont. (905) 337-0398, Toronto (416) 466-0205 and (416) 485-2644; candlesticks, Absolutely Inc., Toronto (416) 324-8351; roman blind, waffle tea towel, Ikea, 1-800-661-9807 or www.ikea.ca; ribbon, Masterstroke Canada, (416) 751-4193 or www.masterstrokecanada.com for retailers; magnets, Home Depot, 1-800-668-2266 or www.homedepot.com.

SEWING

Sheer Bliss: Sheer fabric cover-ups

Sewing by Brian Addis, Toronto (416) 538-9530; white sheer fabric, white linen, Designer Fabrics, Toronto (416) 531-2810; pink sheer fabric, tan linen, King Textiles, Toronto (416) 504-0600; all ribbon, Mokuba, Toronto (416) 504-5358; floral duvet cover, floral fabric on bolster, Euro sham, waffle-weave sham, Au Lit Fine Linens, Toronto (416) 488-9662 or 1-800-363-6080.

It's in the Bag: Beanbag chairs

Sewing by Brian Addis, Toronto (416) 538-9530; all fabrics, Robert Allen, Toronto (416) 934-1330, Montreal (514) 938-2677.

Winter Wear: Wool melton accessories

Projects by Bev Hisey, Toronto (416) 703-6635; wool melton, Designer Fabrics, Toronto (416) 531-2810.

Floor Play: Floor cushions

Sewing by Brian Addis, Toronto (416) 538-9530; all fabrics, Designer Fabrics, Toronto (416) 531-2810.

Window Dressing: Sheer curtains

Sewing by Wesley Seto, Toronto (416) 534-1226; all fabrics, Designer Fabrics, Toronto (416) 531-2810.

Summer Dress: Garden furniture cover-ups

Sewing by Wesley Seto, Toronto (416) 534-1226; red linen, white fabric, red-and-white striped fabric, square cushion forms, Designer Fabrics, Toronto (416) 531-2810; striped and solid green fabrics, Sunbrella, through Gibson Textile Dyers, (416) 533-8565 or 1-800-387-0317 for retailers.

Under Cover: Throws

Creative consultant, Paul Keogh, Harvest Gifts, 1-888-722-8122; sewing by Lorinda Thomas; all fabrics, Designer Fabrics, Toronto (416) 531-2810.

Tailored Bedroom: Easy bed-dressing

Sewing by Mary Dobson; fabrics: Classic Ticking, Arabesque (on duvet), Parisol (on blind), Royale Damask (on pillowcases), all Waverly, www.waverly.com for retailers; grosgrain ribbon, Offray Ribbon, at Michaels, Lewiscraft and Wal-Mart stores across Canada, or visit www.offray.com.

PAINT

Get on Board: Blackboard paint projects

Interior design (kitchen blackboard) by Suzanne Dimma; table built by Ted Conrod; painting (drawers, placecards) by Janis Zroback, Toronto (416) 484-9247; blackboard paint (Blackboard Coating 287), red paint (1314), primer (Fresh Start 023 and Alkyd Enamel Underbody 217), all Benjamin Moore, 1-800-304-0304 or www.benjaminmoore.com; frames, chest of drawers, Ikea, 1-800-661-9807 or www.ikea.ca; Masonite, Home Depot, 1-800-668-2266 or www.homedepot.com.

Colour Blocking: Colour-blocked walls

Painting by Janis Zroback, Toronto (416) 484-9247; paints: Patchwork: green (428), yellow (924), pink (1374), Benjamin Moore, 1-800-304-0304 or www.benjaminmoore.com; blue, Tracery (30BG 72/051), lilac, Whistle Stop (50BB 72/032), Color Your World, 1-800-299-9940. Panels: lilac, Whistle Stop (50BB 72/032), wall colour, Impressionism (50BB 83/009), Color Your World, as above. Ceiling treatment: ceiling, Tracery (30BG 72/051), wall colour, Icy Pond (50GG 83/023) Color Your World, as above.

GARDEN

Sun Showers: Outdoor shower

Showerhead, arm, Barton Discount, Hamilton (905) 561-3521; shower elbow, faucet handle, Ontario Home Hardware, Toronto (416) 536-3809; lattice, hook, towel bar, faucet, deck tiles, copper pipe, The Building Box, 1-877-277-3651 or www.thebuildingbox.com; stain, Seaport Gray, Benjamin Moore, 1-800-304-0304 or www.benjaminmoore.com.

Mirror, Mirror: Mirror in the garden

Carpentry by Peter Fallico; mirrors, Adanac Glass, Toronto (416) 785-6309; arbour, lattice, cedar, Revy Home & Garden, www.revy.ca; wine barrel, Macedo Wine Grape Juice, Toronto (416) 652-0416; floor grates, The Door Store, Toronto (416) 863-1590.

Hangin' Out: Hammocks
Sewing by Brian Addis, Toronto (416) 538-9530; hammock construction by John Crossley; Sunbrella and Gottschalk awning fabrics, Gibson Textile Dyers, (416) 533-8565 or 1-800-387-0317 for retailers; grommeting, Genco, Toronto (416) 504-2891.

WORKSHOP

Brand New Life: Flea-market fix-ups
Console restoration, coffee table construction by Peter Fallico; chair, stool frame restoration by John Crossley; ribbon, Mokuba, Toronto (416) 504-5358; doorknobs, The Door Store, Toronto (416) 863-1590; mini-toile upholstery fabric, Titley & Marr's Esa (colour 004), ticking fabric, Malabar Ticka (colour 01), floral (on pillows), Titley & Marr's Kew (colour 003), W.H. Bilbrough, Toronto (416) 960-1611; black paint (on armchair, chair, stool), Black (P1912-5), paint (on piano stool), Ivory (P1829-4), stain (on sofa), Dark Walnut (ST35), white paint (on coffee table), Roman White (P1836-4), stain (on frames), Crabtree (ST9), all Para Paints, 1-800-461-7272 or www.para.com; chair re-caned by W.H. Kilby, Toronto (416) 656-1065; lamp replated by Mayfair Plating, Toronto (416) 461-4435; chair reupholstery, sofa reupholstery, Plush n' Plump, Toronto (416) 535-9774; rushing, through Canadian National Institute for the Blind, www.cnib.ca for locations; wood stripping, No Dip Furniture Stripping, Streetsville, Ont. (905) 826-2022; hinges, handle (for coffee table), Lee Valley Tools, 1-800-267-8767 or www.leevalley.com.

Found Storage: Recessed storage
Trim paint, Cloud White (CC-40), Benjamin Moore, 1-800-304-0304 or www.benjaminmoore.com; building supplies, Rona Home & Garden, 1-877-377-RONA or www.rona.ca.

Current Exhibition: Hanging systems
Rod, Umbra, 1-800-387-5122 or www.umbra.com; wire, connectors, plywood, stain, tacks, Home Depot, 1-800-668-2266 or www.homedepot.com; spring clips, Lee Valley Tools, 1-800-267-8767 or www.leevalley.com; glass (for frames), Adanac Glass, Toronto (416) 785-6309.

Fabric Softener: Upholstered walls
Panel construction, Peter Fallico; fabrics: Kerry linen-cotton blend in Alabaster, Novasuede in Bordeaux, Robert Allen, Toronto (416) 934-1330, Montreal (514) 938-2677; NuFoam sheet foam, Fairfield, at Home Depot, 1-800-668-2266 or www.homedepot.com.

Nuts & Bolts: Open shelving
Design inspiration, Pierre Hampshire, Hampshire Design, Toronto (416) 463-6129; Oak shelves, steel rods, nuts, washers, Home Depot, 1-800-668-2266 or www.homedepot.com.

Screen Play: Garden trellis
Trellis built by George Meagher at The Trellis Works, Toronto (416) 535-7353.

Behind Closed Doors: Sorting the closet
Schulte wire shelving system, wire drawer unit, shoe rack, belt and scarf rack, hangers, skirt hangers, Solutions, Toronto (416) 752-5559, Whitby, Ont. (905) 433-8746; white paint on closet wall and floor, Accolade Interior Flat Super One-Coat White, purple wall paint, Brandy Flame (1128), all Pratt & Lambert, 1-800-289-7728 or www.prattandlambert.com; yellow, white, flowered and clear boxes, four-hook racks, 4" hooks, wooden hangers, Ikea, 1-800-661-9807 or www.ikea.ca; canvas sweater organizer, shoe bag, Space Age Shelving, 1-877-727-2003 for locations.

Building Character: Panelled walls
Panelling built by Mike Hora, Toronto (416) 538-0621; purple wall paint, 1396, red wall paint, 1342, cream trim paint, 925, all Benjamin Moore, 1-800-304-0304 or www.benjaminmoore.com; cream wall paint, Antique White 2207, cream panelling paint, Free Spirit (1670), Pratt & Lambert, www.prattandlambert.com or 1-800-289-7728; red fabric, Designer Fabrics, Toronto (416) 531-2810.

Open & Shut: Cube coffee table
Table construction by Cesare Da Ponte.

Floor Show: Linoleum flooring
Mats made by Cameron MacNeil; Marmoleum, Forbo Resilients, Merit Decorating, Toronto (416) 534-6337, or Forbo Resilients, Toronto (416) 661-2351 or www.forbo-resilients.com; rubber edging, Home Depot, 1-800-668-2266 or www.homedepot.com.

Head of the Class: Panelled headboard
Door, ReStore, Toronto (416) 755-7353; headboard paint, Ivory (P1820-4), Para Paints, 1-800-461-7272 or www.para.com.

Remaking the Bed: Platform bed
Bed built by Daniel Bowden, Franklin Custom Carpentry & Cabinets, Toronto (416) 537-5048.

Vanity Fair: Bathroom vanity
Faucet, taps, American Standard, 1-800-387-0369 for retailers; cabinet, Eye Spy, Toronto (416) 461-4061; sink, Anstaline series by Kindred, Home Depot, 1-800-668-2266 or www.homedepot.com.

The New Sheers: Frosted Plexi projects
Cupboard doors, shutters built by Daniel Riccio; panel sewn by Brian Addis, Toronto (416) 538-9530; rolling rack, King's Display Racks & Mannequins, Toronto (416) 703-0231.

Four Inspirational Makeovers: Flea-market redos
Glass for table, Adanac Glass, Toronto (416) 785-6309; lamp paint, 967, Benjamin Moore, 1-800-304-0304 or www.benjaminmoore.com; lampshade, Eric's Designer Lampshades, Toronto (416) 482-0282; cabinet paint, Arctic Char (B838-1), Para Paints, 1-800-461-7272 or www.para.com; casters, Ikea, 1-800-661-9807 or www.ikea.ca; grey flannel, Designer Fabrics, Toronto (416) 531-2810.

All in a Day's Work: Office makeover
Slipcover fabric, Designer Fabrics, Toronto (416) 531-2810.

Mirror Image: DIY projects
Legged mirror designed by Scott Francisco; red paint, Stop (EX114), Para Paints, 1-800-461-7272 or www.para.com; mirrored tiles, Canadian Tire, 1-800-387-8803 or www.canadiantire.ca; 1" x 1" tiles, Country Floors, Vancouver (604) 739-5966, Toronto (416) 922-9214, Montreal (514) 733-7596; door pull, Summerhill Hardware, at Elte, Toronto (416) 785-1225 or 1-888-276-3583 or www.elte.com; aircraft cable, nicropresses, Genco, Toronto (416) 504-2891.

Kitchen Hangups: Hanging pot racks
All racks built by Randy Steffan; towels, Embros, Toronto (416) 923-1808.

Closet Aspirations: Closet makeovers
Storage bag sewn by Sheri Graham Delagran; brass labels, The Source, Vancouver (604) 684-9914; wire shelving, basket, Home Depot, 1-800-668-2266 or www.homedepot.ca; fabric for storage bag, Designer Fabrics, Toronto (416) 531-2810.

Display's the Thing: Picture rails
Shelf paint, 967, Benjamin Moore, 1-800-304-0304 or www.benjaminmoore.com.

Space Savers: Storage solutions
Storage units built by Andy Johnston.

Bamboozled: Ideas with bamboo
Tortoiseshell-look bamboo blinds, matchstick blinds, cane tie, split bamboo poles, W.H. Kilby, Toronto (416) 656-1065; armoire, bamboo blinds on armoire, finials, Ikea, 1-800-661-9807 or www.ikea.ca.

Easy to Build Kitchen Island:
Portable kitchen island
Island designed and built by Andy Johnston; butcher block is available at Country Furniture, Vancouver (604) 738-6411; Denca Cabinets, Calgary (403) 252-5552; Display Fixtures, Winnipeg (204) 987-7393; High Tech, Toronto (416) 861-1069; Sun Bakery Equipment, Moncton (506) 858-8990; Jessom Food Equipment, Dartmouth, N.S. (902) 468-8778; Sanitary Products, St. John's (709) 579-2151.

Hall Organizer: Trellis hall organizer
Paint, Spinach Green (B674-2), Para Paints, 1-800-461-7272 or www.para.com; Shaker pegs, Lee Valley Tools, 1-800-267-8761 or www.leevalley.com.

Easy to Build Plate Rack: Wall-hung plate rack
Rack designed and built by Andy Johnston.

Lighten Up: Wire a lamp
Tin lamp bases, Imprints, London, Ont. (519) 685-1112 for retailers; bamboo pole base, W.H. Kilby, Toronto (416) 656-1065; all lampshades (except on candlestick and blue-and-yellow tins), Ikea, 1-800-661-9807 or www.ikea.ca.

Index

Contributors

SINCERE THANKS TO ALL WHO MADE THIS BOOK POSSIBLE.

PHOTOGRAPHERS

Alan Kaplanas
Andreas Trauttmansdorff
Ashok Charles
Curtis Trent
Dan Heringa
Donna Griffith
Hasnain Dattu
James Tse
Joanne Tsakos
Luis Albuquerque
Mark Mainguy
Michael Alberstat
Michael Mahovlich
Rob Fiocca
Robert Lemermeyer
Ted Yarwood
Virginia Macdonald
Yvonne Duivenvoorden

EDITORS

Cameron MacNeil
Carolyn Kennedy
Delia Mamann
Erin Feasby
Hilary Smyth
Jennifer Hughes
Kate Quetton
Katie Hayden
Meg Crossley
Morgan Michener
Sally Armstrong
Suzanne Dimma

OTHERS

Amanda Greig
Barb Woolley and the team at Hambly & Woolley
Barbara Griffin
Bonnie Cook
Brian Turnock
Gail E. Matheson-Godreau
Heather Cosman
Jacqueline Lutz
Jason Rees
Liz Cooper
Maarten Sluyter
Priscilla Wikkerink
Rita Godlevskis
Sabrina Linn
Steve Cosman
Terry Iwaskiw
Kim McArthur and the team at McArthur & Company

PHOTO CREDITS

Michael Alberstat 118
Project: Found Storage

Luis Albuquerque Photography 114
Project: Flea-Market Fix-Ups

Ashok Charles 108
Project: Backyard Classic

Hasnain Dattu 168
Project: The New Sheers
70 Ward Street
Toronto, Ontario
M6H 4A6
Phone: 416-535-1955
Website: westsidestudio.com

Yvonne Duivenvoorden 10
Project: Wreathed in Glory
Email: yvonned@the-wire.com

Rob Fiocca 38, 200
Projects: Tortoiseshell Buttons, Bamboozled

Donna Griffith 20, 24, 28, 50, 96, 100, 122, 130, 136, 140, 148, 152
Projects: Works of Heart, Praising Cane, Beauty Treatment, It's in the Bag, Mirror, Mirror, Hangin' Out, Current Exhibition, Nuts & Bolts, Behind Closed Doors, Building Character, Floor Show, Head of the Class
Website: www.donnagriffith.com

Dan Heringa Photography 216
Project: Lighten Up

Alan Kaplanas 46
Project: Sheer Bliss
Website: www.alankaplanas.com

Robert Lemermeyer 156
Project: Build a Garden Shed
51-30th Ave S.W.
Calgary, AB, T2S 2Y4
Website: www.eye51.com

Virginia Macdonald 14, 32, 54, 58, 62, 92, 126, 160, 176, 180
Projects: Cameo Roles, Good Things in Small Packages, Winter Wear, Floor Play, Window Dressing, Sun Showers, Fabric Softener, Remaking the Bed, All in a Day's Work, Mirror Image
Website: www.virginiamacdonald.com

Michael Mahovlich Photography 42, 204, 208, 212
Projects: Words & Music, Easy to Build Kitchen Island, Hall Organizer, Easy to Build Plate Rack
Website: www.mmphotos.com

Mark Mainguy 72, 196
Projects: Under Cover, Space Savers

Andreas Trauttmansdorff 132
Project: Screen Play

Curtis Trent 66, 172
Project: Summer Dress, Four Inspirational Makeovers

Joanne Tsakos 82
Project: Get on Board

James Tse 144
Project: Open & Shut

Ted Yarwood 76, 86, 104, 164, 184, 188, 192
Projects: Tailored Bedroom, Colour Blocking, Build a Cedar Potting Bench, Vanity Fair, Kitchen Hangups, Closet Aspirations, Display's the Thing
Toronto
Phone: 416-367-4615
Email: ted.yarwood@sympatico.ca
Website: portfolios.com/tedyarwood